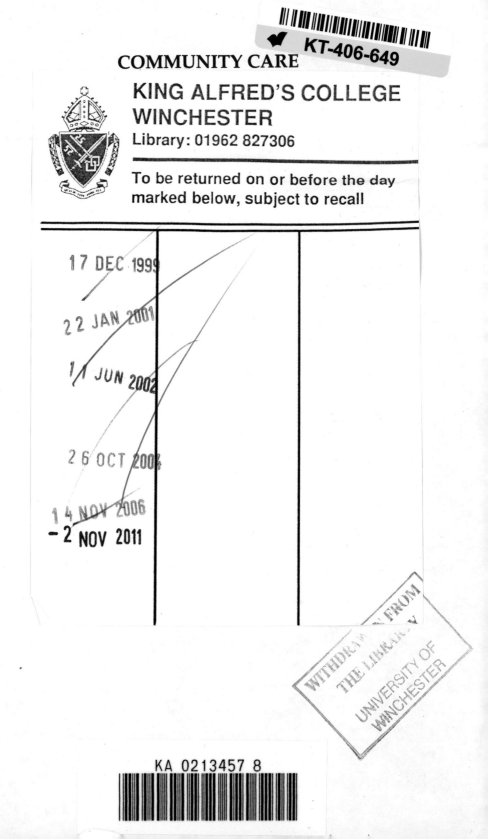

This Reader forms part of The Open University course *Community Care* (K259), a core course for the Diploma in Health and Social Welfare. The selection of items is therefore related to other material available to students. It is designed to evoke the critical understanding of students. Opinions expressed in it are not necessarily those of the Course Team or of The Open University. If you are interested in studying the course or working towards the Diploma, please write to the Information Officer, School of Health and Social Welfare, The Open University, Walton Hall, Milton Keynes MK7 6AA, UK.

Also published by Macmillan in association with The Open University

HEALTH AND WELLBEING
Edited by Alan Beattie, Marjorie Gott, Linda Jones and Moyra Sidell

MENTAL HEALTH MATTERS
Edited by Tom Heller, Jill Reynolds, Roger Gomm, Rosemary Muston and Stephen Pattison

SPEAKING OUR MINDS
Edited by Jim Read and Jill Reynolds

THE CHALLENGE OF PROMOTING HEALTH
Edited by Linda Jones and Moyra Sidell

PROMOTING HEALTH
Edited by Jeanne Katz and Alyson Peberdy

HEALTH PROMOTION
Edited by Angela Scriven and Judy Orme

DEBATES AND DILEMMAS IN PROMOTING HEALTH
Edited by Moyra Sidell, Linda Jones, Alyson Peberdy and Jeanne Katz

COMMUNITY CARE: A READER

Second Edition

Edited by

Joanna Bornat, Julia Johnson, Charmaine Pereira
David Pilgrim and Fiona Williams

at The Open University

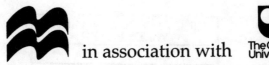 in association with

First edition 1993
Reprinted four times
Second edition 1997

Published by
MACMILLAN PRESS LTD
Houndmills, Basingstoke, Hampshire RG2 1 6XS
and London
Companies and representatives
throughout the world

ISBN 0–333 69846–0 hardcover
ISBN 0–333 69847–9 paperback

A catalogue record for this book is available
from the British Library.

This book is printed on paper suitable for recycling and
made from fully managed and sustained forest sources.

10 9 8 7 6 5 4 3
06 05 04 03 02 01 00 99 98

Printed and bound in Great Britain by
Creative Print & Design (Wales), Ebbw Vale

Contents

II   Care

III Policy

Acknowledgements

The authors and publishers wish to thank the following for permission to use copyright material:

Cambridge University Press for material from Janet Finch and Jennifer Mason, 'Filial obligations and kin support for elderly people', *Ageing and Society*, Vol. 10, 1990; and Peter Townsend, 'The structured dependency of the elderly: a creation of social policy in the twentieth century', *Ageing and Society*, Vol. 1, No. 1, 1981; Centre for Human Service Technology for material from Bryan Glastonbury, 'Risk, Information Technology and Social Care', New Technology in the Human Services, Vol. 8, No. 3; Community Care for material from Ann MacFarlane, 'The Right to Make Choices', *Community Care*, 1.11.90; Confederation of Health Service Employees for material from *Community Care: Which Way Forward?*, 1990; Critical Social Policy for material from Harriet Cain and Nira Yuval-Davis, 'The Equal Opportunities Community', *Critical Social Policy*, Vol. 10, No. 2, 1990; Disabled Peoples' International (European Region) Independent Living Group for a statement from the Strasbourg Independent Living Expert Seminar, April, 1989; Free Association Books for material from Joanna Ryan (with Frank Thomas), 'Concepts of Normalization' in *The Politics of Mental Handicap*, 2nd ed., 1987; Freedom to Care for 'Ten Principles of Accountability'; Guardian News Service Ltd for material from Kate Cooney, 'Carers may be angels but does that make their dependents devils?', *The Guardian*, 2.1.91; and John Palmer, 'Expanding Community may find itself tongue-tied', *The Guardian*, 19.3.91; The Controller of Her Majesty's Stationery Office for material from R. Snaith, ed. *Neighbourhood Care and Social Policy*, 1989, *Residential Care: A Positive Choice* and *Community Care: Agenda for Action*; Joint Unit for Social Services Research on behalf of Social Services Monograph for material from Jane Hubert, 'At Home and Alone: families and young adults with challenging behaviour' in *Better Lives: Changing Services for People with Learning Difficulties*, ed. Tim Booth, 1990, Social Services Monographs: Research in Practice, Sheffield; Joseph Rowntree Foundation for material from Judith Hudson, Lynn Watson and Graham Allan, 'Housing Choices and Community Care' in *Findings: Housing Research 168*; Kings Fund Centre for Health Services Development for 'A ten-point plan for carers'; and Andrea Whittaker, 'Involving people with learning difficulties in meetings' in *Power to the People*, ed. Liz Winn, 1990; Macmillan Press Ltd for material from Gillian Dalley, *Ideologies of Caring*, ed., 1996, pp. 121–8; Malcolm Payne, *Social Work and Community Care*, 1995; MIND for material from *Waiting for Community Care*, 1990; Jenny Morris for an edited version of material from *Pride Against Prejudice: Transforming Attitudes to Disability*, The Women's Press, 1991; National AIDS Trust for an extract from the Declaration of Rights for People with HIV and AIDS, UK Declaration Working Group; National Black Community Care Network at Sia for their Black Carers Charter; National Council for Voluntary Organisations for 'Rural Voluntary Action Needs: A Ten Point Plan'; and Margaret Simey, 'Reflections of a voluntary worker' in *Active Citizens: New Voices and Values*, eds. N. Fielding, G. Reeve and M. Simey, Bedford Square Press, 1991; National Council for Civil Liberties for material from '50,000 Outside the Law', 1951; The Observer Ltd for abridged material by Mukti Jain Campion, *The Observer*, 14.7.91; PSI Publishing for Clare Evans, 'Disability, Discrimination and Local Authority Social Services 2: Users' Perspectives' from Gerry Zarb (ed.), *Removing Disability Barriers*, 1995; Random Century UK for material from Margaret Forster, *Have the Men had Enough?*, Chatto & Windus, 1989; Jim Read and Jan Wallcroft for 'Checklist on how workers can empower service users' from *Guidelines for Empowering Users of Mental Health Services*, COHSE/MIND, 1992; Routledge for material from Eileen and Steven Yeo, 'Community as Services' in *New Views of Co-operation*, ed. Steven Yeo, 1988, Routledge; Joan Busfield, *Managing Madness: Changing Ideas and Practice*, Unwin Hyman, 1986; and Martin Bulmer, *The Social Basis of Community Care*, Unwin Hyman, 1987; Sheil Land Associates Ltd on behalf of the author for material from Cherril Hicks, *Who Cares? Looking After People at Home*, Virago, 1988; Southwark Council, Social Services Department, for their Charter of Rights; Survivors Speak Out for their Charter of Needs, 1987; Values into Action for an extract from their promotional material.

Every effort has been made to trace the copyright holders but if any have been inadvertently overlooked the publishers will be pleased to make the necessary arrangement at the first opportunity.

Introduction

'Community care' as a term can be approached from a multitude of directions. It has a long and shifting history. It has been shaped and determined by policy changes. At the same time as it is a distinctive range of professional practice, it is also some people's everyday experience of life, the inspiration of a movement away from institutional care and towards supported life in the community, a euphemism for women's labour in the home, and the focus for intense debate and controversy. It is in fact a slippery concept, used as a slogan by the political left and right. This collection of articles, accounts, statements and quotations brings together as many different perspectives on commmunity care as can be managed in one book.

Community Care: a Reader reflects these many differing meanings and conflicting perspectives. The book stands on its own as a collection of writings on key issues of contemporary debate. Readers who are interested in following up more of the issues with practical examples and debates may like to know that it links to the Open University course and pack K259 *Community Care*, for which it is the set text. For more information on the course and pack contact: The Information Officer, School of Health and Social Welfare, The Open University, Walton Hall, Milton Keynes, MK7 6AA. Students on the course are directed to read, make notes and analyse these articles and excerpts as part of their study.

The four parts of this Reader were originally each compiled by a different editor. For this second edition, some new chapters have been introduced and others have been updated. Each of the four parts, 'Community', 'Care', 'Policy' and 'Practice, are organised along similar lines, juxtaposing new thinking with some of the 'classics' of community care policy and thought. Each is introduced by an anthology illuminating its facets and furrows through literary quotations, personal accounts, commentaries, policy statements and charters and declarations. While some of the articles in each section may be familiar to readers with knowledge of the field, others have been written especially for this volume.

The five editors worked collectively but divided their responsibilities between the four sections. Charmaine Pereira's section on 'Community' highlights issues of place, control, representation, identity and agency. Fiona Williams's section on 'Care' links debates around gender, race, citizenship and provision. In 'Policy', David Pilgrim includes articles and excerpts that reflect the shifts and turns of policy development through the twentieth century as care moved from large institutions into the community. Joanna Bornat's 'Practice' section, with a selection of articles and charters written by experienced practitioners and users, draws on examples of care and support highlighting issues for carers, both paid and unpaid, and for users of services. Julia Johnson worked with all the original editors and authors to update and revise the second edition of the Reader, which has become something of a classic in the literature of community care.

The editors would like to thank Sonia Morgan for her meticulous checking and chasing up, and for resisting and indulging, in their proper places, editorial whims. Stella Allinson worked on this second edition, carefully attending to deadlines and smoothing the process for all concerned. We would also like to thank Gillian Parker for her help in editing articles in the 'Care' section, Naomi Connelly for her help in editing some parts of the 'Practice' section, and Serena Stewardson and Antonet Roberts for their careful work in word-processing the manuscript.

Part I

COMMUNITY

1

Introduction

What do we mean by 'community' and who, or what, is the 'community' in 'community care'? In this section of the Reader, we bring together a number of writings that focus in different ways on the diverse aspects of 'community'. Some of the texts are autobiographical or reflective in form, others are articles discussing issues of policy and of action. There are writings too that address the ways in which 'community' is 'presented' to us and its inherent complexities and contradictions.

The senses in which the word 'community' can be used are notably wide-ranging. The range of usage is reflected in the edited anthology: 'The breadth of community', a collection that highlights the elusive meanings of 'community'. Some of these meanings and their associated values – solidarity, interest and identity – are the focus of Joanna Bornat's chapter on 'Representations of community'. She discusses questions of representivity and exclusion, reflecting on the place of myth within this – which communities are we talking about and how are they remembered?

What is the significance of 'community' for women? Fiona Williams argues that community and women are interconnected in complex and contradictory ways: *which* women and *which* communities are of central importance. By understanding 'community' as women's *space* – the space that belongs to women and within which they can begin to determine some of its conditions – as well as women's *place* – the place to which they are relegated and over which they are denied control – we can begin to make sense of some of the contradictions. Martin Bulmer considers social networks as fabrics of resources sustaining community care. In a review of different approaches to understanding social networks he draws on theories that emphasise the actions people take to sustain and support each other within communities. However he leaves us with a question. If networks are such a common feature of everyday life, what is their specific relevance for care?

Social change has brought with it, among other things, changes in the social relationships of modern urban communities. The implications of

3

this for neighbouring form the focus of the extracts from 'Neighbour-hood care and social policy'. Philip Abrams and his colleagues (authors of the writings edited by Ray Snaith) are keen to emphasise the limita-tions of informal care among neighbours who may only know each other in passing. Neighbourliness, if it were to play any part in neighbourhood or community care, would have to be *organised*. The ways in which neighbours may get drawn into caring are the subject of the chapter by Suzy Croft and Peter Beresford, in which they describe their personal experience of caring for their next-door neighbour, an older person with senile dementia.

We conclude this section with two views of community service. The first extract is by Margaret Simey, reflecting on her past as a voluntary worker. The second, by Eileen and Stephen Yeo, places this piece in context by reflecting on the social forces behind such work. The writing touches on contradictory currents underlying community involvement: charitable work by middle-class women and working-class struggles to improve living conditions.

In focusing on the diverse and elusive senses of 'community', our aim is not solely to raise questions about what exactly we mean by the word but to deepen our understanding of any action based on the premise of 'community'.

2

Anthology: The Breadth of Community

Compiled by CHARMAINE PEREIRA

The word 'community' is, nowadays, a ubiquitous term. It crops up in all kinds of situations though its meaning remains elusive. 'Community' has been used in senses that include the personal, political, cultural, geographical, historical, national and international. This anthology brings together a number of writings on 'community', the aim being not so much to clarify the meaning as to illustrate the breadth of its usage. The choice of extracts is not intended to be comprehensive and has been, necessarily, selective. Diversity of style and presentation, not to mention content, have been the criteria for selection.

An extract from Jocelyn Cornwell's sociological text **Hard-Earned Lives: Accounts of Health and Illness from East London,** *Tavistock, London, 1984, pp. 40–50.*

Thirty years ago, Young and Willmott's (1957) description of social life in Bethnal Green established that place as the model of 'community' in modern urban settings. [. . .] By 'community' they meant two things: the existence of some kind of collective life that residents identify with, and a social life and social relationships based on reputation rather than status (i.e. on *who* people are to each other rather than *how much* they own or possess).

The definition of 'community' became stronger and more exaggerated in the course of their research careers. Originally Young defined 'community' simply as 'a sense of solidarity with other people sharing a common territory' (Young, 1955: 33). In *Family and Kinship*, Young, with Willmott, began to develop the idea that 'community' is collective life, lived on the streets and in public places, but at the same time they acknowledged the central importance of privacy and of 'your home being your own' to people surrounded at very close quarters by many others. [. . .] By the time they wrote *Family and Class in a London Suburb* (Willmott and Young 1971), they were making the straightforward assertion that collective life was more important than life in the home. [. . .]

The other aspect of community, of people knowing one another because of who they are to each other rather than how much they own, relies on them having lived together and known one another a long time, but there is also something more to it. Young and Willmott saw relationships in Bethnal Green as finer, more moral and essentially *more human* than relationships on the new housing estate they called Greenleigh, because they did not involve questions of money and status. [. . .]

Young and Willmott's romantic vision of harmony and friendliness in Bethnal Green is not supported by reports of social life in 'face-to-face' communities, either in our own society in the past, or in other societies. In these studies [. . .] attention is more commonly paid to what Bailey (1971) calls the 'small politics' of everyday life which encourage enmity as much as friendship, and in which gossip and flattery, one-upmanship and ostracization are all powerful weapons. [. . .]

It is not novel to criticise Young and Willmott for romanticising Bethnal Green. [. . .] However, it is especially intriguing in the context of the present study because the interviews for the study contain public accounts of community that present a similarly romanticised version of 'community' life in Bethnal Green. [. . .] They were statements addressed to 'the public' in the sense that they reiterated old themes that people knew were acceptable; in some instances they could be best described as extended cliches. [. . .]

Neighbourliness, friendliness and concern for others (in the past), in contrast with selfishness, competitiveness and snobbery (in the present) were the main themes of the public accounts of community. [. . .] The dominant elements [. . .] were the fact of *similarity* between people and the shared experience of poverty or near-poverty. Again and again people said that money had introduced a new materialism and had undermined the trust in others that provided the basis for the relationships they had with their neighbours:

> Ann Cullen: 'I knew when I lived in Golden Row that I could walk out my front door and leave it open and no one was going to rob me, because I was the same as them. But I couldn't do that here. Not for the people in here. [. . .]'

Having money, they said, not only makes people mistrust one another's motives, it also gives individuals the means *to purchase* their own necessities and allows them to become less dependent on communal life. Private washing machines replaced the public laundry; private cars replaced weekends spent in the market or working on the garden; private televisions and videos replaced football and the local pub. [. . .]

The portrait of community life – past and present – painted in private accounts were very different. As well as the willingness to help the invalid neighbour, it included the turning of the blind eye to other people's troubles; as well as the open doors and the familiarity with others, it included the arguments, fights and brawls, particularly over children, and the petty snobberies that kept people apart from each other. [. . .] In place of the active concern for the welfare of others, the impression the private accounts of community life gave was that of the over-riding importance of looking after oneself and one's own. [. . .]

Florrie Neagle: 'All rough people, years ago.'
Harold Neagle: 'All stick to one another.'
JC: 'Were you part of that?'
HN: 'Oh, yes. I came home one day from work and she's in the middle of the flats having a fight with two women. I went up to someone and said, "What's all the bother?" He said, "It's your old woman having a fight." '
JC: 'Doesn't sound like you were all sticking together.'
FN: 'No, well it's kids.'
HN: 'It's children. If you had children, and she's another tenant in the flats, and her kids are hitting your kids, you'll go down after them.'
FN: 'You're not going to just stand there, are you?'

[The interviews] demonstrate such radical differences in the way people experience community and in what they know about it that [. . .] the idea of 'a community life' existing at *any* time, in the past *or* in the present, seems something of a fiction. [. . .] It is particularly striking when the differences are between men and women living in the same household. [. . .]

Mick Chalmers: 'I think the world has changed since I was a kid 'cause, I mean, I remember I used to live down a turning just like this, and I can remember when I was a kid, like in the summer we used to [. . .] all the street doors would be open and there'd be chairs out in the streets, and you'd walk along and talk to them. I mean you can walk down here in the daytime and you don't even see a soul. I mean I don't know who lives two doors away from me. You'd come home and me Nan would say, "Your Mum ain't in, she's out somewhere", and I'd go along and I'd walk in all the houses looking for me Mum. And, you know, all the doors were open and you'd just walk in.'
Sarah Chalmers: 'See, what it is, with Mick it's different, but with me, I can walk outside the door, walk round the shops where it would take me five minutes to walk there and back, and I'll be out about half an hour, three-quarters of an hour. Because I bump into people that I know and talk and everything else. So I think it's more friendlier when you're in an area and you know people than when you don't know them.'

Mick and Sarah do not experience 'the community' in the same way as each other, so neither of them is capable of giving a fully rounded account of 'community'. The spaces they occupy – socially as well as geographically – are different. [. . .] Nowadays, the men rarely work locally, and most of their sense of community comes from the atmosphere of the local pub (if they are drinkers). Women, on the other hand, occupy a much wider range of communal spaces – the shops, the street, the school gates, their relatives' houses – and they have a much wider variety of contacts, not only with shopkeepers and other mothers, but also in the schools, pubs and blocks of flats where many of them are employed as cleaners.

---

*From **Paid Servant**, a novel by E. R. Braithwaite, New English Library, London, 1962, pp. 84–6.*

There were several other visitors there when I arrived. [. . .] It was a friendly, informal gathering, with topics of conversation varied and interesting while they lasted. [. . .]

Eventually conversation got round to current changes within the social structure in Britain, and this in turn led to discussion on the various immigrant groups in the country and their contributions to its social, cultural and economic development. [. . .] So it fluctuated, back and forth, coming now to the inevitable question of mixed marriages. [. . .]

I tried to stay on the outer edge of these discussions, hearing, feeling, remembering, recording it all in my mind, or as much as was possible; now and then a question would be put to me and I'd be compelled to say my piece. As when someone suggested that, in mixed marriages, the children were the chief sufferers as they could find no place in either camp, so to speak. To this I replied:

We seem to be ignoring one important factor. Irrespective of who his parents are, a child born into a family is part of that family, so he naturally belongs, and needs from them love, companionship, help, guidance, encouragement, advice and example in positive living. He needs these things irrespective of his parents' racial origins. If he is born into a community where tolerance prevails, then there is no special problem. However, a coloured child born in Britain, for instance, not only needs the things I have mentioned, but is severely handicapped without them, because the community considers his colour a handicap and therefore imposes special pressure and proscriptions upon him. He needs these things not as insulation against the pressures, but as sources from which to draw strength in order to meet and deal with them with wisdom, courage and resolution.

And supposing, for argument's sake, such a child didn't have parents to comfort and advise? Then he is a sitting duck for everything the community feels like throwing at him.

Community is a blanket word like 'nation' or 'club'; we can so easily wrap ourselves in it and become anonymous. It must be remembered that we contribute to those prejudices as much by not protesting against them as by deliberately acting in agreement.

––––––––––––

From **Behind the Frontlines**, *by Ferdinand Dennis, Victor Gollancz, London, 1988, p. 146.*

Tiger Bay: a rainbow estate

Tiger Bay is officially known as Butetown. It is a council estate of less than a square mile. Its boundaries are so well defined that once there, a visitor could quite easily forget where he [*sic*] is. On one side is a railway line and canal. On the entrance side is the main road I'd been driven along, and beyond that an old dock wall, a high barrier of crumbling gray and black stones. A small commercial area servicing Cardiff Docks stands at one end; and at the other is Cardiff city centre.

Tiger Bay has much in common with Liverpool 8. Together they represent Britain's oldest settlement of people of African descent. Tiger Bay is not so old, though. It developed along with Cardiff Docks. From the second half of the nineteenth century, Cardiff was the paramount coal-exporting city in the world. Black sailors began arriving then, but their numbers really grew after the First World War.

Along with African and West Indian sailors, Tiger Bay also became home to Asians, southern Europeans, Filipinos and Chinese. In its heyday Tiger Bay was an exciting cosmopolitan community.

––––––––––––

Extract from an article by the political correspondent of the **Guardian**, *John Palmer, 19 March 1991.*

Expanding community may find itself tongue-tied

More and more 'no-vacancy' notices are appearing on the windows of the European Community's 'Tower of Babel'. Given the lengthening queue of countries seeking to join the Community, it is not difficult to see why the EC bureaucracy believes there is no room for any more languages.

Language is an extremely complex and politically sensitive issue in the EC. The present 12 member states use nine official languages – Danish, Dutch, English, French, German, Greek, Italian, Portuguese and Spanish: plus Irish as far as the publication of constitutional and official documents is concerned.

From **The Crack**, *by journalist Sally Belfrage, Grafton, London, 1987, pp. 68, 71.*

On the night of Saturday, April 3rd, a gang of armed and masked men entered two houses in Ormeau Road, shooting and wounding a youth in each house before disappearing. No organization has claimed responsibility for this act. [. . .]

As the mothers in this district, we wish to make known to those responsible, that this community, Ormeau Road, has had too much death and destruction in its midst. [. . .] We want an end to death. We want to live in peace with one another and nearby communities. We want to try to provide a better life for our young people, so that they can feel wanted, so that they have self-respect, a place in the community [. . .]

[. . .] The way the politicians have them believing, the Catholic community in these hard-line areas thinks there's no poor Protestants, that all the Protestants are working. In the Protestant hard-line areas, they think the same of the Catholics. When you hit the Women's Information Group, you discover that we're all in poverty. Let me tell you, when I rise in the morning, my first thought's not what religion I am.

By sociologists Niva Yuval-Davis and Floye Anthias, in **Woman-Nation-State**, *Macmillan, Basingstoke, 1989, pp. 3–4.*

The boundaries of the state

One major issue in this context is the delineation of the boundary between 'the state' and 'the nation'. There is the further problem of delineating the state from the economy and the gamut of social institutions, social groups and relations that may be conceptualised as part of 'civil society'. [. . .] The tendency in much of the literature on the state to identify it with 'the nation' is linked to the historical fact that nationalism in the West has been a central force in the development of the nation-state. The ensuing conflation of the boundary of the state with that of the nation fails to recognise that state processes can be more delimited than national processes. There are often groups of subjects (minorities; and

sometimes as in South Africa, majorities) that are excluded from participation in the state or are a special focus of state concerns as well as
national liberation struggles by minorities who reside in more than one
state (like the Kurds or the Palestinians). Nor does it take account of the
opposite, that is that the state can extend beyond the boundary of the
nation, so that the nation-state form may be replaced by a supranational
structure as, for example, potentially lies in the European Community.

---

*From **Tales of Two Cities**, by D. Murphy, Penguin, Harmondsworth, 1987, p. 68*

I wondered then – how *territorial* is all this? Now many Bradfordians
object to the cooking smells of curry; a century ago they objected to the
cooking smells of bacon and cabbage, the traditional Irish dish. [. . .] The
sense of being invaded, especially if your own status in society provides
little sense of security, must stimulate very primitive feelings. Then, to
justify the hatred you find within, it becomes necessary to build up an
image of a cruel, dishonest, dirty, lazy, drug-pushing community – the
sort of people it is proper to despise, if you are 'decent English'.

---

*Extract from **Home is where the Heart is: Voices from Calderdale**, by
R. Rooney, B. Lewis and R. Shuhle, Yorkshire Art Circus/Continuum, Castleford,
West Yorkshire, 1989.*

Caring about the neighbours as much as you care for your own house is
what constitutes a good neighbourhood. You can be as friendly and as
nice as pie, but if you move into a nice area and paint your house black
and play music all night you won't get on. Likewise if you spend all your
time caring for your house and garden and you have little time for Mr
Jones next door, then you're ruining the neighbourhood. It's like everything else – you need balance.

Your closest friends were the women whose kitchens faced yours over
the other side of the backs. Most of our lives revolved around kitchens.
That is where the tub was and where a mess could be made without too
much trouble. It was the community who looked after the children. If
you were going upstairs to do a bit of vacuuming then you shouted to a
neighbour and she kept an eye on your child. Later in the day you would
do the same for her. If a child wanted a drink he or she didn't necessarily
go home but went to the nearest door. My husband reckons that a well
worn track goes from our door to the biscuits.

---

*From the text **The Family and Social Change**, by C.Rosser and C. Harris, Routledge and Kegan Paul, London, 1965, p. 12 .*

A different atmosphere altogether, I tell you. The children are all over the place now, and you never know where they are going next. The Mam holds them altogether somehow, but I don't know what it's going to be like when she's gone. You want to see them get on, of course – the Mam is always saying that she doesn't want to stand in their way – but we've lost something from the old days, I can tell you. They don't *cling* as we did. Once they're married, they're off. I sometimes wonder just what we've gained, taking things all round. Not that I want to put the clock back – I remember it all too well for that – the misery and the pinching and the poverty. And when I say 'poverty' I don't just mean poor, I mean *real* poverty – and no messing about. I don't want to go back to that, but I do think we've lost a lot too when I look at the way the children seem to live, hardly ever seeing one another except when they meet here at their Mam's and hardly knowing who their neighbour is. Tell you the truth I wouldn't like to live with any one of them. We lived all together in the old days in Morriston – now they all seem to live in worlds of their own.

---

*By B. Bryan, S. Dadzie and S. Scafe, **The Heart of the Race: Black Women's Lives in Britain**, Virago, London, 1985, pp. 159–60.*

It was as a result of (their) experiences of a racist police force that Black women began to organise against specific incidents of abuse and against legislation like the 'SUS' law which legitimised police brutality.

Because it was our children and community who were victims of this law, Black mothers were in the forefront of campaigns like the 'SCRAP SUS' initiative. This began in a Black woman's front room in Deptford and eventually swept throughout the Black community, uniting the generations in a call for the law to be scrapped.

[. . .] Over the next few months, we held a series of public meetings and demonstrations, wrote to the press, organised a petition, made badges – everything we could think of to publicise the SUS issue. It was important to us that the television and newspapers should acknowledge how the SUS law was being used by the police against Black kids. Eventually they began to take a very unusual interest in our grievances and they got reported quite widely in the media. That's how people outside the Black community got to know about SUS. Black mothers covered the groundwork which made SUS into a public issue. It was only after this that the local Community Relations Council decided to get off their backsides and get involved in it too. Before that, they didn't want to know.

Extract from **The Road to Wigan Pier**, *George Orwell, cited within B. Campbell's* **Wigan Pier Revisited**, *Virago, London, 1984, pp. 31, 3.*

As you walk through the industrial towns you lose yourself in labyrinths of little brick houses blackened by smoke, festering in planless chaos round miry alleys and little cindered yards where there are stinking dustbins and lines of grimy washing and half-ruinous w.c.s [. . .] at their very worst the Corporation houses are better than the slums they replace. The mere possession of a bathroom and a bit of garden would outweigh almost any disadvantage. [. . .] If people are going to live in large towns at all they must learn to live on top of one another. But the Northern working people do not take kindly to living in flats.

[. . .] If George Orwell were to return to Sheffield today he'd see the metamorphosis from spacious if spartan semi-detached suburbias to dense tower blocks. An epitaph to this era of modern housing stands on the crest of the city – where once there was a slope of slums, there now stands a barrage of flats for thousands. They were hailed in their day as 'bold' and one of the most 'uncompromising' developments of the fifties, which simply meant that they were deliberately ugly – the genre of 'brutalism'. The only concession to the consumers in this awful, artless building is an attempt to build community spirit into the structure, as if this, one of the few social assets of the working class, would otherwise be given no natural home. The architects built a system of simulated streets in the air and presumably the people are supposed to play their part in making it all a success by playing in those streets, which measure three metres wide. There is nothing in the 'street' other than front doors – no shops, pubs or laundries, cafes or telephone boxes, no places to gather. So the only point of being in the street is to come and go, which is precisely all that people do. The designers also wanted to provide privacy. They did this not by providing sheltered gardens or sound insulation, they just put no windows in the street. Blind alleys.

By Colin Ward, **The Child in the Country**, *Bedford Square Press, London, 1988, pp. 34–5.*

We all have, according to temperament, two contrasting perceptions of the village.

One is of the ancient, unchanging community, somehow insulated from time, meeting most of its needs from its internal economy, with its blacksmith and farrier, carpenter, builder and undertaker, general store and carrier (maintaining a few, if regrettable contacts with the outside world), and its life centred around the pub and the church, with its rectory whence the rector's wife and daughters dispensed charity to the deserving poor.

The other perception of the village is of the contemporary village, inhabited by commuters, weekenders and the retired, with the indigenous population confined to the estate on the fringe, where the smithy is now a petrol station, the pub is full of fake beams and pool tables, while of the two general stores one is an antique shop and the other a wine bar and restaurant.

A whole shelf of books describes the transition from one of these perceptions to the other, dating the change from the time when the authors ceased to be children. Thus, 'During the 1940s the scene was virtually as it had been for generations, apart from one or two mechanical innovations, with men working on the land, boys following in their fathers' footsteps, and women busying themselves with the home and family. Characters who had been moulded by the hardness of life, the machinations of moneymaking, or the infidelity of the elements, lived and worked together in the village to form a real community. [. . .]

[. . .] a whole series of important points needs to be made about the view of history this represents.

The first is that far more devastating changes occurred in rural life at the time when landowners pursued their policy of enclosure; the second is that the whole thrust of the agricultural industry for 150 years has been to dispense with labour, and that the days when it was possible for us to see 'boys following in their fathers' footsteps' ended long before the author I have quoted was born, while the days when girls wanted to follow in their mothers' footsteps, not into domesticity but into domestic service, ended when they realised that there were alternatives to the exploitation involved. A new generation of domestic employers brings into English rural life servants from the poor half of the world, sending their International Postal Orders back home from the village post office just to support their families. They are villages where the crucial decision about whether a sub-post office remains viable depends on such global accidents.

The third point to be made is that villages were never hermetic communities: there always were comings and goings; and the fourth is that rural settlements have always consisted of several different communities who happened to occupy the same territorial space. The gap between them in the past was infinitely greater than the gap between different rural residents today. The class gradations of English society (and to an even greater degree in the Anglo-ascendancy in Wales, Scotland and Ireland) ensured that village people and village children lived in a world entirely different from that of their betters [*sic*].

Extract from a paper by Harriet Cain and Nira Yuval-Davis in **Critical Social Policy**, *Vol. 10, No. 2, 1990, pp. 6–7.*

The 'equal opportunities' community

In early 'Race Relations' legislation the term 'community' was adopted from its common usage in British social policy of the time which tended to use it in relation to working class neighbourhoods, in a romantic and conservative fashion. However, during the 60s and 70s, the American meaning was imported, in which 'community' was used to describe ethnic minorities (Anthias and Yuval-Davis, forthcoming). This created inconsistencies and confusions which became highlighted during the 80s.

The confusion with relation to the boundaries of 'the community' is crucial in understanding some of the issues which have bogged down and have created obstructions, divisions and frustrations in anti-racist struggles. Is 'the community' everybody who lives in a certain area, is 'the community' a particular grouping conscious of itself as a grouping or is 'the community' paradoxically, all those who have been excluded from feeling part of 'the community'? We would argue that in the specific sphere of the 'race relations industry' and in the urban politics in Britain of the 80s, the hegemonic answer to 'who is "the community"' has made three conceptual jumps and the following conflations:

(a) From focusing the attention on disadvantaged sections of the population, motivated by populist and democratic aspirations, 'the community' in actuality has become to a large extent reduced to the categories of 'Equal Opportunities' – previously excluded to a large extent from definitions of 'the community'.
(b) From focusing on the 'Equal Opportunities' disadvantaged sections of the population, the politics of 'the community' have become reduced to the voluntary sector and local government sponsored organisations which aspire to represent and serve them.
(c) From focusing on the disadvantaged section of the population, 'community' has become reduced to a large extent to the 'professional community activists'.

We shall now turn to looking at some of the ways these conflations have occurred.

Social policy conceptions of 'the community' have often ignored marginal sections in the population. The intimate, close and rooted image of 'the community' implied a homogeneity composing family, neighbourhood and parish, all of whom conformed to an hegemonic culture, often English, and usually working class. It was against this mould that the 'popular planning' approach, heralded by the GLC and other radical local authorities has been developed in the late 70s and early 80s. They struggled to include in this vision of 'the community' all those previously excluded, and which, at least in some areas of the 'inner city', constitute a major part of the local population, be it single parents, gays, blacks, refugees, etc. However, in doing so, their assumption has been that all the various equal opportunities groupings, whether gay, black, refugee etc., share intrinsically common objectives. This, however, brought new contradictions in its wake, as the various groupings viewed themselves in very different and autonomous terms, often creating conflict and competition as a result of the ways the social planners had constructed them.

---

*Personal account in **Inventing Ourselves**, a collection of accounts from the Hall Carpenter Archives, Lesbian Oral History Group, Routledge, London, 1989, pp. 105–6.*

Gilli Salvat:
No-one had ever done youth work with young lesbians before, so it was all highly controversial. We were taking a hell of a risk with everything we did so we had to work very carefully and strictly, but it was a wonderful experience. For the first time as youth workers we could be entirely 'out' and feel that we were truly working for the development of 'our' young people. It's great to see them now, out and being proud and productive people.

My work is [. . .] threatened by Thatcher's government by its attack on lesbian and gay rights and local democracy. Not only has my job been at risk by the cuts in local government spending, but the introduction of Section 28 of the Local Government Act. This Section directly threatens the community that lesbians and gays have struggled so hard to build in the last twenty years.

Personal accounts from **Walking After Midnight,** *Hall Carpenter Archives, Gay Men's Oral History Group, Routledge, London, 1989, pp. 184, 211, 217.*

Zahid Dar:
In mid '82, I went to a weekend of gay workshops at South Bank Poly where people were saying what the gay community needed was a centre as a focus point for the community; a while after that there was talk that the GLC were willing to fund one. When I went to my first meeting, I couldn't believe my ears. You know, at County Hall in November '82, people talking about a gay centre.

Lesbians and gays support the miners

David Donovan of the Dulais mining community:
You have worn our badge, 'Coal not Dole', and you know what harassment means, as we do. Now we will pin your badge on us, we will support you. It won't change overnight, but now 140,000 miners know that there are other causes and other problems. We know about Blacks, and gays, and nuclear disarmament. And we will never be the same.

Mike Jackson:
We obviously had a lot of political fighting to do within our own community. One cry which was always a bit hurtful was, 'Why are you doing all this for the miners? There's people dying of AIDS and the lesbian and gay community needs support.' For a start, a lot of people in LGSM did lots of things for the community anyway. We didn't support the miners with regard to whether they supported us or not. We supported them because we were socialists, but we were attempting to be 'out' to them and we hoped there would be a dialogue.

Account from **Generations of Memories,** *by Jewish Women in London Group, The Women's Press, London, 1989, pp. 6–7.*

For those of us who grew up in Britain, the school history we learned was the one in which English kings and one or two queens led a triumphant march from the Stone Age to the present day. It was followed by a history of the Greeks and Romans which didn't mention their occupation of the Jews' land and the consequent oppression of the Jews, or the contribution the Jews made to resistance against their empires. The rest of school history was a cosy anglocentric celebration of a past in which the other peoples of the world were by and large either subject peoples or enemies. Usually, that history stopped at the First World War. And the ordinary people of Britain were presented as a monolithically white, English-speaking mass who either lined the streets to cheer the great or erupted dangerously as mobs.

Some of us encountered Jewish history at school in the shape of scripture lessons; some of us went to *cheder* as well, where we also learned to read Hebrew. This history was largely based on Bible stories of the tribes of Ancient Israel. Where women played any part at all, they were just as likely to have been temptresses and schemers, like Jezebel and Delilah, as heroines, like Esther and Deborah.

Our mothers' stories were very different. For most of us, 'our' history was one which included flight from persecution and sometimes the threat of death, and subsequent migration from country to country. There are few of us who have grown in the same countries as our mothers, and some of them in turn had come to live in different countries from their mothers or their grandmothers. The stories they had to tell us were often of the ways of their own families as part of the Jewish communities of Middle and Eastern Europe; of lives sometimes lived in poverty and fear, more rarely in an insecure prosperity. There were also stories of lives strong in resisting oppression, and others which told of becoming part of a middle-class establishment, which later only too readily turned its back on them.

Through these stories many of us learned that it was the women in our families who had so often been the ones responsible for taking on those movements across continents to safe homes. It was the women who kept the memory of who and what had been in the past. For those of us who came from religious backgrounds, it was often the women who found ways to give us a consciousness of Jewishness as more than a religion, a nationality, a personal identity. For them, it meant a way of life which shaped every aspect of their existence.

[. . .] The lives of those women born and brought up in Britain (let alone those born and brought up in Europe) in some respects resemble those of gentile women of the same generation, but they differ significantly in others. The terrain in which those lives have been mapped out is different. [. . .] The view from a little terraced house may be the same, but the interior view is different.

---

*From **The Jerusalem Bible**, edited by A. Jones, Popular Edition, Darton, Longman and Todd, London.*

Introduction to the Acts of the Apostles

Acts is in the form of a single continuous narrative. It begins with the birth and the growth of the primitive Christian community in Jerusalem and tells of the founding of the community in Antioch by Hellenist Jews and the conversion of St Paul; it goes on to show the spread of the

Church outside Palestine through the missionary travels of Paul and ends with his captivity in A.D. 61–63. [. . .]

32   The whole group of believers was united, heart and soul: no-one claimed for his own use anything that he had, as everything they owned was held in common.

34   None of their members was ever in want, as all those who owned land or houses would sell them, and bring the money from them

35   To present it to the apostles; it was then distributed to any members who might be in need.

Extract from **There Ain't No Black in the Union Jack**, *by Paul Gilroy, Hutchinson, London, 1987, pp. 233–5.*

For the social movement of blacks in Britain, the context in which [. . .] demands have been spontaneously articulated has been supplied by a political language premised on notions of community. Though it reflects the concentration of black people, the term refers to far more than mere place or population. It has a moral dimension and its use evokes a rich complex of symbols surrounded by a wider cluster of meanings. The historical memory of progress from slave to citizen, actively cultivated in the present from resources provided by the past, endows it with an aura of tradition. Community, therefore, signifies not just a distinctive political ideology but a particular set of values and norms in everyday life: mutuality, co-operation, identification and symbiosis. For black Britain, all these are centrally defined by the need to escape and transform the forms of subordination which bring 'races' into being. Yet they are not limited by that objective. The disabling effects of racial categorisation are themselves seen as symbols of the other unacceptable attributes of 'racial capitalism'. The evident autonomy of racism from production relations demands that the reappropriation of production is not pursued independently of the transformation of capitalist social relations as a whole. The social bond implied by use of the term 'community' is created in the practice of collective resistance to the encroachments of reification, 'racial' or otherwise. It prefigures that transformation in the name of a radical, democratic, anti-racist populism.

[. . .] Community is as much about difference as it is about similarity and identity. It is a relational idea which suggests, for British blacks at least, the idea of antagonism – domination and subordination between one community and another. The word directs analysis to the boundary between these groups. It is a boundary which is presented primarily by symbolic means and therefore a broad range of meanings can co-exist around it, reconciling individuality and communality and competing definitions of what the movement is about.

Entry for the word 'community' in Raymond Williams's **Keywords**, *Flamingo, 1983, pp. 75–6.*

Community has been in the language since C14. [. . .] It became established in English in a range of senses: (i) the commons or common people, as distinguished from those or rank (C14–C17); (ii) a state or organised society, in its later uses relatively small (C14–); (iii) the people of a district (C18–); (iv) the quality of holding something in common, as in **community of interests**, **community of goods** (C16–); (v) a sense of common identity and characteristics (C16–). It will be seen that senses (i) to (iii) indicate actual social groups; senses (iv) and (v) a particular quality of relationship. [. . .] From C17 there are signs of the distinction which became especially important from C19, in which **community** was felt to be more immediate than SOCIETY (q.v.), although it must be remembered that *society* itself had this more immediate sense until C18, and *civil society* [. . .] was, like society and *community* in these uses, originally an attempt to distinguish the body of direct relationships from the organised establishment of *realm* or *state*. From C19 the sense of immediacy or locality was strongly developed in the context of larger and more complex industrial societies. **Community** was the word normally chosen for experiments in an alternative kind of group-living. It is still so used and has been joined, in a more limited sense, by **commune** (the French *commune* – the smallest administrative division – and the German *Gemeinde* – a civil and ecclesiastical division – had interacted with each other) and with **community**, and also passed into socialist thought (especially *commune*) and into sociology (especially *Gemeinde*) to express particular kinds of social relations. The contrast, increasingly expressed in C19, between the more direct, more total and therefore more significant relationships of **community** and the more formal, more abstract and more instrumental relationships of *state*, or of *society* in its modern sense, was influentially formalised by Tonnies (1887) as a contrast between *Gemeinschaft* and *Gesellschaft*, and these terms are now sometimes used, untranslated, in other languages. A comparable distinction is evident in C20 uses of **community**. In some uses this has been given a polemical edge, as in **community politics**, which is distinct not only from *national politics* but from formal *local politics* and normally involves various kinds of direct action and direct local organization, 'working directly with people', as which it is distinct from 'service to the **community**', which has an older sense of voluntary work supplementary to official provision or paid service.

The complexity of **community** thus relates to the difficult interaction between the tendencies originally distinguished in the historical development: on the one hand the sense of direct common concern; on the other hand the materialization of various forms of common organization, which may or may not adequately express this. **Community** can be the warmly persuasive word to describe an existing set of relationships, or the warmly persuasive word to describe an alternative set of relationships. What is most important, perhaps, is that unlike all other terms of social organization (*state, nation, society,* etc.) it seems never to be used unfavourably, and never to be given any positive opposing or distinguishing term.

3

Representations of Community

JOANNA BORNAT

I am satisfied that the picture I have tried to draw was neither exceptional nor one-sided. Talking to middle-class people who did not live in working-class districts, I find that few realise how bad conditions were such a comparatively short time ago.

(Jasper, 1969, p. 127)

Everyone can write a book. We believe that by enabling people to speak for themselves we can make our own history.

(Noakes, 1975)

These two quotations come from early publications in what tends to be described loosely as 'community publishing'. Each is typical of ideas that have driven a popular literary movement since the late 1960s. Among A. S. Jasper's reasons for writing is the desire to inform, to reveal and to reach out to others distanced from him by time and class. The second quotation champions the cause of popular self-expression and the appropriation by working-class people of a discipline, history. Groups like Centerprise and QueenSpark are representative of the most self-conscious of local publishing ventures of the 1970s and 1980s.

Among the most radical of the community publishing groups, those with membership in the Federation of Worker Writers and Community Publishers, the language used to explain aims and practice is the language of representation, empowerment, self-determination, appropriation and creativity. Other agencies with less radical philosophies – libraries, archives, museums, schools, colleges, social services – have followed suit with locally produced accounts published in accessible formats.

This literature emerges through a variety of processes of production. Community publishers are frequently given finished manuscripts to be considered for publication. Some represent many hours of detailed, individual, solitary reconstruction of a personal past, or the need to commit feelings, emotions, experience into a literary form. Sometimes the final publication is the result of a lengthy and supportive collaboration between people with professional training in writing or teaching and others who at a relatively late stage in life are discovering their ability to express themselves in written words. Whatever the origin of the account, the process of production from manuscript to printed page is one of collaborative activity. In practice the process varies from co-operative groupwork for the majority of groups affiliated to the Federation, to a form of benign editorial decision-making by one person in most other cases.

The result is usually the small booklet, its narrative drawn from first hand experience, typically of working-class life usually located in urban areas during the early and middle decades of the twentieth century. This genre includes poetry and fiction, which is more subversive of myths of community, more critical of the individual's relations to different communities. What I want to look at here, through an examination of over 50 such narratives, is community history writing. I have excluded from consideration collections of reminiscence produced by the commercial book trade. The focus here is on booklets with origins in collective traditions of publishing or which have in the main emerged through local rather than national initiatives.

Implicitly and explicitly, the theme of community runs through these published narratives. If these accounts have such a powerful appeal then we should perhaps consider what their ideas of community comprise. I want to consider some issues which seem to me to be relevant. I want to look at solidarity, interest and identity.as the values and meanings of community in community publishing and to consider the question of representivity and exclusions. Finally I want to draw out some implications for the practice of community history writing in general and reflect on the question of myth.

3.1 The values and meanings of community

In those days, too, there was real neighbourliness. You see, you might be four or five families in that house, and perhaps the one at the bottom would make some tea and she'd shout up the stairs 'I've just made a cup of tea – coming down?' And they'd more or less take it in turn each day, and if there was anyone in real dire straits, and couldn't pay their way, I've known a neighbour take their own sheets off the bed, wash 'em and pawn 'em to help them out. That's how it was in those days – real good neighbours. I mean they'd never let anyone starve. We never used to lock our front doors – not a bit of string or nothing, the house was open day and night. The gas meters were on the stairs, and we never lost a ha'penny. There were real criminals of course – but never against their own.

(White, 1988, p. 26)

It is possible to find regional variants of this passage from the Euston Road area of north London in verbal and written accounts of urban working-class communities throughout Britain. The values are explicit: communality, 'never let anyone starve'; solidarity, 'never against their own'; honesty, 'we never lost a ha'penny'; interdependency, 'take it in turn each day'. They are pinned down physically in descriptions of community as place and in the detailed restoration of domestic life. The details of the physical and spatial fabric of community life come in descriptions of house interiors, streets of leisure, entertainment, education, welfare and employment experiences. Communities are rarely mapped out with street plans or in terms of systems of administration or local politics. The elements of community described in community publishing are rooted in domestic work, farms, mills, mines and the strategies developed for survival in country and town. The accounts describe domestic skills and the interdependency which adversity requires. Elizabeth Roberts, in her study of working-class women's lives in the north-west between 1890 and 1940, argues that these routines and skills operated on a neighbourhood basis and extended further than the blood ties of family to neighbours. Drawing on oral evidence she argues that remembered communities were not areas or neighbourhoods but often 'no more than three streets' (Roberts, 1984, p. 184)

Where privacy was physically and economically a luxury, then the reality of community life is not always positively recalled:

Everybody knew everybody. They'd peep out from behind the curtains and say, 'There goes May Sleeth, she's off . . . You could imagine it, could you? 'She's off again, up to no good'. If you spoke to a boyfriend or if you let the boy bring you to the corner of the street, it was really bad. Actually, my parents did not like me to take boyfriends home.

(Davey, 1980, p. 7)

Community could be an oppressive experience if remembered from the perspective of some of its more junior members, who were without the power that economic or parental status conferred.

Community as a system of shared values and as a spatial arrangement of supportive, if sometimes intrusive, structures is well delineated in the accounts. Community as shared interest is less well described. Class interests, depicted through personal accounts of resistance and action, do recur, most usually attached to workplace and industrial life in accounts from men. The Co-operative Movement appears as a functioning interest group which was akin to community in its inclusiveness (Salt *et al.*, 1983, p. 6).

Collective interest tends to be recalled through paid work experiences or through political action. The General Strike is most vividly recalled by those who were directly involved, miners and transport workers predominantly. It is the oral account which allows the detailed workings of the strike as a process of social interactions to emerge:

> With the strike of course it meant that as a youngster of 15 I was liberated from the pit. All my pals of fifteen and sixteen – all of us – we were really liberated. It was a magnificent glorious summer so that we spent the time more or less tramping and getting into Newcastle with collecting boxes and getting support in places like Gateshead from those people who were working.
>
> (Durham Strong Words Collective, 1979, p. 58)

Community history as the retrieved history of an interest group recurs in the many accounts of individual women's lives. Accounts from children of their own mother's struggles and triumphs, managing budgets, drunken partners, credit arrangements and family crises, together construct a picture of working-class women which is not one of passive domestic isolation. Community life is described through the dimensions of family life in these accounts, consequently it is the memory of women in the family and of survival and protection which predominates. Robert William Harvey grew up in Bristol in the 1930s with his mother and half-brother:

> Mother was better; so we could go home again. How lovely, we were free again to see one another. Mother could not go away for a rest. One came out of hospital in those days, worked, and got on with it. No sick pay and whatnots. We had become poor. The rent had to be paid. We had no money coming in. It was time to sell the things we had that could be sold, while Mother got better so that she could work longer hours.
>
> (Harvey, 1976, pp. 15–16)

Communities of interest do not appear with much frequency; possibly the revival of a declared interest depends on the reconstruction of a collective experience by those who had membership in certain events, campaigns or movements. But communities of identity are strongly represented. The choice of a title may be a selling point, but it also indicates a sense of belonging: 'The Island' (Centerprise, 1979), *Millfields Memories* (Knight, 1976), *Reminiscences of a Bradford Mill Girl* (Newbery, 1980), *Shipley Fowk Talking* (Shipley Community History Group, n.d.) A sense of identity expressed simply as belonging is used in more complex ways, however. Between older and younger members of the working class, communities of identity confirm pride in survival and resilience. They may also induce a unity that intervening decades may have shaken. The result may be the reconstruction of a white remembered past.

3.2   Community exclusions and individual invisibility

Community publishing broadens our understanding of the past by including the experience of those whose accounts play little part in a public history of nation and state. In terms of process and outcomes it challenges the norm in publishing. But how representative of community experience are the communities portrayed? I want to go on to look at the issue of exclusions and the extent to which some members may have become invisible through the process of recall.

Within community publishing there are a growing number of examples of accounts drawing on the experience of minority ethnic and racialised groups. Early accounts published drew on work produced in literacy and English centres (Bandali, 1977; Elbaja, 1978; Gordon, 1979). Later accounts from Jewish writers in London and Manchester (Spitalfields Books, 1979; Spector, 1988; Cohen, 1989) have been followed by accounts drawn from manuscripts and from interviews, some produced, in dual language text, from Polish, Greek Cypriot, Iranian, Chinese, Somali and Bangladeshi people (Kyriacou, 1990; Tse, 1994; MAMA, 1995; Ara and Chatterjee, 1995). These have contributed a multicultural perspective to community publishing.

Community publishing's growing multiculturalism counteracts its tendency otherwise to present a uniquely white working-class and Western urban image of community life. Taken as a whole the literature presents a more accurately representative perspective than the literature of commercial publishing. Taken separately the books draw on strongly delineated and separated social and cultural traditions of family and community life, even when traced through the dislocations of migration and rehousing. Nevertheless, the experience of exclusion and division tends to be unevenly described even amongst those accounts drawn from the minority communities. Most can testify to the existence of discrimination or racism. Teresa Burke recalls working in London between the wars:

> On my half day, my sister would come and meet me in Lewisham and we'd go and look round the shops. My sister had a habit of looking at the boards in Lewisham, and on the poster it would say 'NO IRISH NEED APPLY'.
>
> (Schweitzer, 1989)

What these accounts rarely reveal is how people felt about these exclusions within that community. An exception is a collection of dual-language accounts by Asian women. Mandira's story vividly describes the experience of lived exclusion:

> Though I was not fluent in my English and been home whole day with my son I tried to make friendship with my neighbour, as she was on her own, also as

same age as my aunt [who spent all her] life in our family when she became widow at age 13 years. I felt concern about her well being. We used the same corridor. If I had not seen her I knocked at her door and asked about her health and whether she needs any shopping. I was shocked when she thought I am being nosey and became rude. I started to go out more meet few neighbours on the street and came to know how horrible inconsiderate noisy people we are.

(Centerprise, 1984)

A Traveller from the Westway site in London turns round the idea of community, invoking it as a force for exclusion:

The first time when this site was opened the community here broke this site up for keeping the Travellers from getting in, to settled [*sic*] down. The council repaired that and they broke it down again.

(Kyriacou, 1990)

What frames the experience is the constraining force of an opposing community whose identity is delineated as other, by means of power and hence with the ability to determine inclusion. Division is described in separated accounts. In the memory of white working-class people, issues of race and ethnicity are in the main absent. For instance children might earn money lighting fires for Jewish households on Friday nights. An Irish woman has fond memories of working as a maid in a Jewish household, but the interface between the experience is described in terms of observed difference, not by familiarity or awareness of experience (Centerprise, 1979, p. 23; Schweitzer, 1989, p. 62).

The accounts I have looked at so far provide a key to identifying exclusions on the basis of race or ethnicity. What all the communities of community publishing still lack are accounts from those whose participation in community life has been determined and shaped by other dominant, socially determined divisions. I want to go on to look at the experience of physical and mental impairment.

My initial search through more than 50 booklets produced in the community publishing tradition revealed little to indicate that physically or mentally disabled people were members of these communities. Looking for references to disability, I found few accounts from people with either physical or mental impairment. Considering that the literature draws on a time when most disabled children either stayed at home or lived in the community (Hurt, 1988), it is surprising that neither they nor their family members appear to be included in the reconstruction of the experiences of community. There are accounts of life in children's homes and in the workhouse (Harvey, 1976, pp. 22–3; Crump, 1980; Peckham People's History, 1983, pp. 85–6; Schweitzer, 1989, pp. 51–6). There were many passing references to disabled siblings, relatives, and, occasionally,

neighbours. However, at the time of that first search through the literature, the perspective of someone with first-hand experience was relatively rare. Hugh Macdonald is one of the few people who writes as a
disabled person. He was born with spina bifida:

> I was in a pram till I was 8. Mother used to take me to Leith Links to
> watch the cricket. I was only at the pictures once in my life, and that was when
> I was 12 – in Shettleston to see 'Pinocchio' (1940). I remember saying, 'I'm too
> old to go to the pictures, so l never was back.
>
> (Griffiths and Vestri, 1985, pp. 10–11)

Since that first search there have been many additions to the literature of
community publishing, but still the 'voice' of disabled children and
adults seems to be missing from these collectively constructed accounts.
The situation may change as more disabled people begin to write their
own histories and life stories and find sympathetic local publishers.
More recent writing by disabled people includes David Barron's account
of being fostered in the 1930s and living in a mental handicap institution
until his release in 1955 with his 'Certificate of Sanity' (Barron, 1996),
Ernest 'Tom' Atkins' 'Personal Experience of Polio' (1994) and *Positive
Tales*, stories by learning disabled people in Milton Keynes (Bessant *et al.*,
1996).

As with the accounts of minority ethnic experience, the opportunity
for representation seems to emerge through separate reconstruction.
Working with groups of people with learning difficulties has enabled
stories of exclusion and personal history to emerge. Invisible people re-
emerge in the telling of their own stories. Margaret remembers:

> When I was a little girl I was put away. I was 14 and a half. I went to Cell
> Barnes to live because they said I was backward. My dad refused to sign the
> papers for me to go, but the police came and said he would have to go to
> prison if he didn't. I cried when I had to go with the Welfare Officer.
>
> (Atkinson, 1991, p. 45)

At the time of revising this chapter (1997) there was still only one
example of a community-published account of gay and lesbian life.
Published by QueenSpark, *Daring Hearts* is an account of gay and lesbian
life in Brighton after the Second World War. Once again, however, a separate approach to recall and writing has provided the basis for community history.

3.3   Community myth?

Without the separately generated accounts, the image of community that emerges from community publishing is one that is supportive, if at times stiflingly so. It is one in which problems are resolved through changes in economic or political fortune. Family finances improved as children grew up and brought in wages. War brought a degree of social change and opportunities for new employment and housing. The community changes its shape physically as people marry, go their separate ways or die. But in the recall and the writing it persists as a remembered and indivisible whole. Raphael Samuel argues that with its devotion to place, community history has steered itself clear of those issues that suggest the complexity of human relationships (Samuel, 1979). And it seems that it takes something more akin to a secondary analysis of interview data to bring out social class differences (Werbner, 1980). For some the whole idea of community history is better avoided as a species of persistent false consciousness (The Work Group, 1976, p. 18).

If community publishing has found the representation of difference and division difficult to include, surely we need to look for explanations as to why this may be, and whether this matters or invalidates the accounts given.

The urge to represent the past in the present is understandable, but by focusing on the remembered topography of community and family life what we may be ignoring are the parallel continuities of value and per-ception. If memories of community seem to exclude the non conforming experience of the person with disability or of the gay man or lesbian woman, this is because past inhibitions and prejudices are continuous, though differently expressed, with the present. Community publishing looks back to a past with an understanding that is continuous with that past. A mother in York who describes bringing up her disabled daughter may evoke strong resonances for similar mothers and children 50 years later:

> We had no idea she was handicapped for about three years . . . and it was rather hard then because . . . nobody seemed to know – they didn't do much in that way with spastics, I don't think they understood . . . right in the middle of the war. . . . If you'd anyone handicapped when Elizabeth was young there were a lot of people who feared you; they didn't mean to be but they avoided you because I think they were frightened they might get involved.
>
> (York Oral History Project, 1987, p. 56)

Monica Jules' account reminds us of the isolation of the parent of a child with learning difficulties in the 1980s:

Afterwards I was told my son is autistic which is a kind of mental handicap. It was a great shock to me. I could not believe it. They said he is not a normal child. There was nothing I could do to help my son except try my best to look after him until I can get more help and support from the social service.

(Jules, 1987, p. 41)

Her account, with others (Beaumont Writers' Group, n.d.), helps to bring out a more complete understanding, but they stand alone as separate experiences unless we are encouraged to incorporate them into a more complex community history.

To be unaware of our own prejudices and blinkered perceptions is not unusual; however, it may be that the processes of community publishing encourage such tendencies.

The generation of accounts and their assembly into either a single narrative or a collectively produced anthology may preclude reflection and individual introspection. Even when the account is not collectively produced, the author's words will, once published, be subjected to local collective scrutiny. While separately organised groups may willingly and freely discuss and disclose experiences of racism, or of discrimination on grounds of disability, it is unlikely that a mixed group could encourage similar openness (see Gray, 1984). What seems to be a quality of the membership of groups producing community publishing is their similarity of background and experience. Whether worked on alone or as a group, the result is an emphasis on particular sets of shared memories. I want to go on to look briefly at processes in collective reconstruction as a means to understanding why these patterns may be recurring.

Discourse analysis reveals the way in which collective memory is reconstructed through cues and strategies in conversation (Middleton and Edward, 1990). Those community publishing texts that have relied on the generation of accounts from discussion might find, from analysis, that there are observable patterns in the discussion, patterns that relate as much to the social interactions of the group members as they do to the content of what is being discussed (Boden and Bielby, 1983).

Another issue arises in relation to the process of interviewing or in the taking of oral accounts. Stories that are collected in a group or in one-off interviews may suffer from the lack of opportunity to improve or to amend (Jewish Women in London Group, 1989, pp. 16–17). Jocelyn Cornwell's work in Bethnal Green (Cornwell, 1984, pp. 16, 40–54) suggests that both the frequency of the interview and the way in which questions were framed determined whether or not a 'public' or a 'private' account was given to her. In public accounts, which tended to be given at an early stage, the description of community in the past was one that conformed well to that given of Somers Town, quoted earlier. Subsequently, and if people were invited to tell a story rather than to answer a direct question, they would give what she describes as a 'private' account. From this it became clear that community life also included rivalries, snobberies, fights and a willingness to ignore other people's troubles.

My final point relates to the issue of life stage and shared perspectives. In the main the contributors to community publishing are older people recalling experience from their younger lives. For family and community this has obvious implications. A child or a younger person's view of community relationships may well be limited to their knowledge, feelings and interest at the time. But when this is overlaid with a perspective from a stage in life when change and loss may be major preoccupations, the perspectives from the two periods may be difficult to relate. Dorothy Jerrome's work highlights the importance that friendships between peers have for older women (Jerrome, 1990). Using the sharing of experience to build friendships has become part of the repertoire of social-work skills in work with older people (Fielden, 1990). While the positive values of such consolidating approaches must be appreciated, it is also important to be aware of negative payoffs: the formation of closed groups, the construction of a comfortable shared perspective.

Do the underlying meanings of conversational strategies, the hazards of interviewing and the dilemmas of group management suggest that community publishing is involved in myth construction? The answer to this is almost certainly yes. At an earlier and more defensive stage in community publishing this might have been a difficult perspective to admit to. More recent work by oral historians suggests that by ignoring the creation of myth we impoverish our understanding of the past and of ourselves (Samuel and Thompson, 1990).

Constructions of community life necessarily include stories which may have the status of art or fable. At another level, the symbolism, shape and content reflects particular preoccupations of generation and opportunity, often the amalgam of perspectives from quite separate ends of the lifespan. To accept the role of mythic reconstruction is to widen the significance of the accounts. They become not only a substantive form in their own right, they are also indicators of feeling and of perspective. To understand the contribution of myth is to focus on what is neglected as much as what is included in published accounts. If community publishing neglects issues raised by the divisions and exclusions of community life, then this may tell us something about those recalled communities and about the processes of community history writing today. Perhaps, as Alessandro Portelli suggests, fabulation helps us to understand what the hopes and fears of the older generation are and to recognise continuities and discontinuities in human action (Portelli, 1988).

Acknowledgement

Thanks to Al Thomson of the Federation of Worker Writers and Community Publishers for his suggestions and supportive critical approach.

References

Ara, S. and Chatterjee, D. (1995) *Home to Home: Reminiscences of Bangladeshi Women in Sheffield*, Sheffield City Libraries, Sheffield.

Atkins, E. (1994) *One Door Closes Another Opens: A Personal Experience of Polio*, Waltham Forest Oral History Workshop, Waltham Forest.

Atkinson, D. (ed.) (1991) 'Past times' (unpublished).

Bandali, S. (1977) *Small Accidents: the Autobiography of a Ugandan Asian*, Tulse Hill School, London.

Barron, D. (1996) *A Price to be Born*, Mencap Northern Division, Harrogate.

Beaumont Writers' Group (n.d.) *The Beaumont Writers' Group*, Gatehouse, Manchester.

Bessant, P. *et al.* (1996) *Positive Tales: Nine Lives in a Book*, Living Archive Project, Milton Keynes.

Boden, D. and Bielby, D. del Vento (1983) 'The past as resource: a conversational analysis of Elderly Talk', *Human Development*, Vol. 26, No. 6, pp. 308–19.

Centerprise (1979) *'The Island': the Life and Death of an East London Community 1870–1970*, Centerprise, London.

Centerprise (1984) *Breaking the Silence: Writing by Asian Women*, Centerprise, London.

Cohen, H. (1989) *Bagels with Babushka*, Gatehouse, Manchester.

Cornwell, J. (1984) *Hard-Earned Lives: Accounts of Health and Illness from East London*, Tavistock, London.

Crump, J (1980) *The Ups and Downs of Being Born*, Vassall Neighbourhood Council, London.

Davey, D. (1980 *A Sense of Adventure*, SE1 People's History Project, London.

Durham Strong Words Collective (1979) *But the World Goes on the Same: Changing Times in Durham Pit Villages*, Erdesdun Publications, Whitley Bay.

Elbaja, M. (1978) *My Life*, Shoreditch School, London.

Fielden, M. A. (1990) 'Reminiscence as a therapeutic intervention with sheltered housing residents: a comprehensive study', *British Journal of Social Work*, Vol. 20, pp. 21–44.

Gordon, I. (1979) *Going where the Work is*, Hackney Reading Centre, London.

Gray, R. (1984) 'History is what you want to say: publishing people's history – the experience of Peckham People's History Group', *Oral History*, Vol. 12, No. 2, autumn, pp. 38–46.

Griffiths, S. and Vestri, P. (1985) *Changed Days: More Stories and Reminiscences from the Prestonfield Remembers Group*, Edinburgh University Settlement.

Harvey, R. W. (1976) *A Bristol Childhood*, WEA Western District.

Hurt, J. S. (1988) 'The inter-war years', in *Outside the Mainstream: A History of Special Education*, Batsford, London.

Jasper, A. S. (1969) *A Hoxton Childhood*, Centerprise, London.

Jerrome, D. (1990) 'Intimate relationships', in Bond, J. and Coleman, P. (eds), *Ageing in Society: an Introduction to Social Gerontology*, Sage, London.

Jewish Women in London Group (1989) *Generations of Memories: Voices of Jewish Women*, The Women's Press, London.

Jules, M. (1987) *Wesley My Only Son*, Hackney Reading Centre, London.

Knight, D. (1976) *Millfields Memories*, Centerprise, London.

Kyriacou, S. (ed.) (1989–10) *Travelling Light: Poles on Foreign Soil; The Irish in Exile: Stories of Emigration; In Exile: Iranian Recollections; The Forgotten Lives: Gypsies and Travellers on the Westway Site; The Motherland Calls: African–Caribbean Experiences; Xeni: Greek Cypriots in London*; Ethnic Communities Oral History Project.

MAMA EastAfrican Women's Group (1995) *Shells on a Woven Chord*, Yorkshire Arts Circus, Castleford.

Middleton, D. and Edward, D. (eds) (1990) 'Conversational remembering: a psychological approach', in *Collective Remembering*, Sage, London.

Newbery, M. (1980) *Reminiscence of a Bradford Mill Girl*, Bradford Metropolitan Council.

Noakes, D. (1975) From a foreword note in *'The Town Beehive' a Young Girl's Lot, Brighton 1910–1934*, QueenSpark, Brighton.

Peckham People's History (1983) *The Time of Our Lives*, Peckham People's Publishing Project, London.

Portelli, A. (1988) 'Uchronic dreams: working class memory and possible worlds', *Oral History*, Vol. 16, No. 2, pp. 46–56.

Roberts, E. (1984) *A Woman's Place an Oral History of Working Class Women, 1890–1940*, Blackwell, Oxford.

Salt, C., Schweitzer, P. and Wilson, M. (1983) *Of Whole Heart Cometh Hope*, Age Exchange, London.

Samuel, R. (1979) 'Urban history and local history', *History Workshop*, Vol. 8, Autumn, p. vi.

Samuel, R. and Thompson, P. (1990) *The Myths We Live By*, Routledge, London.

Schweitzer, P. (ed.) (1989) *Across the Irish Sea*, Age Exchange, London.

Shipley Community History Group (n.d.) *Shipley Fowk Talking*, Bradford.

Spector, C. (1988) *Volla Volla Jew Boy*, Centerprise, London.

Spitalfields Books (1979) *Where's Your Horns? People of Spitalfields Talk About the Evacuation*, Spitalfields Books, London.

The Work Group (1976) 'A critique of "community studies" and its role in social thought', University of Birmingham, Centre for Contemporary Cultural Studies.

Tse, Y. (1994) *Half the Sky: Stories and Photographs by Women of the Chinese Community*, Birmingham City Council, Birmingham.

Werbner, P. (1980) 'Rich man poor man – or a community of suffering: heroic motifs in Manchester Pakistani life histories', *Oral History*, Vol. 8, No. 1, pp. 43–8.

White, M. (1988) *And Grandmother's Bed Went Too: Poor but Happy in Somers Town*, St Pancras Housing Association in Camden, London.

York Oral History Project (1987) *York Memories at Home: Personal Accounts of Domestic Life in York*, York, Oral History Project.

4

Women and Community

FIONA WILLIAMS

It is now a common observation that the invisible threat in government reports and policy documents that ties the notion of 'community' to that of 'care' is, by and large, women (see, for example, Chapters 11, 14 and 18). It is mainly, though not entirely, women who form the focus for the dynamics of care and support. But what of 'community'? Are women principal actors here, too? And what does 'community' mean for women? In this chapter I suggest that community has different and con-tradictory meanings for women. Community may represent the space where women can begin to define and determine their own needs and conditions for existence. At the same time it may also represent the outer limits of women's restriction to domestic duties and limited access to an independent income and way of life – where women 'know their place'.

4.1   Space and place

Community has a particular significance for many women. It is the point of negotiation over public provision; it is a site of organisation and struggle over welfare issues; and it is the arena of paid, unpaid and low-paid work. As such, community represents an overlap of the public world of production and politics with the private world of home and care. It is the point at which women's private business becomes trans-lated into public issues – from dependant into claimant; from unpaid to paid worker; from personal into political.

The notion of community, though, is complex, and can mean different things to different women. When women organise collectively for better child-care provision, for safer roads and streets, or when they organise to provide some of these things themselves, then community becomes women's *space*. That is, community becomes the space, in terms of both territory and opportunity, in which women can begin to determine and redefine some of its conditions. On the other hand, community may be defined and constructed in a way that limits women's control and choice. State community care policies often represent this restricted sense of community in the way they assume the responsibility of women to provide unpaid care in the community. In this way, community becomes women's place, the *place* to which they are relegated and belong: a place that represents not so much a bridge from the private to the public, but an extension of the private.

This distinction between 'space' and 'place' has its roots in the different meanings ascribed to community in general. The first – space – is derived from the sense of community representing a collective striving for communal values based on principles of cooperation. Early examples of this were the Utopian thinkers of the late eighteenth and early nineteenth centuries who attempted to build communities on the basis of cooperation and equality, including equality between men and women (Taylor, 1983). The second idea of community – of women's place – is derived from the community ideal that imposes harmony upon a divided, conflictual and alienated world. Far from attempting to change things, this ideal seeks to promote integration based upon people's acceptance of their 'place' as subordinate or superior in the community. Victorian religious ideas of 'the rich man at his castle, the poor man at his gate', where the world was yet 'bright and beautiful', espoused this ideal. Within this ideal not only do rich and poor know their place, but men and women too, for the hierarchical relations within the community tend to be seen as based upon, and emanating from, the hierarchical relations within the family (Davidoff *et al.*, 1976). The sense of community as harmony in the face of division and inequality has been influential in state social policy programmes of social intervention from the Community Development Programme of the 1960s to the various community schemes in policing, health and social work in the 1970s and 1980s. And the notion that at the community's core are ordered families with a traditional sexual division of labour is implicit and explicit in government reports on community care and law and order (see Langan, 1992 and Williams, 1992b). Although this distinction between space and place is significant for women, it has also to be set against how community is experienced by people today. The ideals of community described above stress both locality and unity, and they imply rurality, whereas in reality communities (based on locality) have seldom realised the unified ideal, and today are increasingly marked by urbanism, cosmopolitanism and differences of identity, as Dick Hebdige explains:

> The values and meanings attached to place and homeland remain as charged as ever but the networks in which people are caught up extend far beyond the

neighbourhoods in which they're physically located or the alliances to which they are consciously committed.

The forcible immigration, enslavement or containment of populations from both Africa and Europe, for instance has created transnational identity networks. . . . Diasporic identities can link an unemployed youth in Johannesburg to a bank clerk in Brixton, or a secretary in Brooklyn to a complex web of sympathies and solidarities.

(Hebdige, 1990, p. 20)

4.2   Confined to community?

In Jocelyn's Cornwell's study of London East End working-class community (see Chapter 2) she observes gender differences in the experiences of community. For women, the social relationships of the community are more significant in their lives; they 'occupy a much wider range of communal spaces – the shops, the street, the school gates, their relatives' houses' (Cornwell, 1984, p. 50). But how far does the importance of community in this sense of immediate locality actually reflect an exclusion from the outside world? How far does it reflect limited access to money, job opportunities, independent transport and time? Are women locked into community? Factors such as poverty, (lack of) time and independent transport can restrict the sphere in which people develop social relationships, and these particularly affect women.

Women figure disproportionately amongst poor people. Of the major groups in society who experience poverty – old people, single parents, low-paid and unemployed people, disabled and long-term sick people – women are over-represented (Glendinning and Millar, 1987). In terms of their access to sources of income, whether this is through paid work in the labour market, through forms of income maintenance, or through household or family income, women are disadvantaged. In the first case women's average gross weekly wage is only around two-thirds that of men. They are concentrated increasingly in low-paid and part-time work. And there are added racial dimensions to these inequalities. Black women workers have, on average, lower rates of pay than white women workers, although Afro-Caribbean women in particular are more likely to work full-time and therefore earn, in total, more. However they do so in jobs with unsocial hours, poor rates of pay and worse conditions (Arnott, 1987). These disadvantages at work are reflected in the benefits and pensions that women receive – if they receive them, for in many cases married or cohabiting women have no eligibility to benefits in their own right, but only as a dependant of their male partner. Even so, more women than men survive on minimal state benefits and pensions. In 1984 2.3 million single women and 1.0 million married women were living on supplementary benefit (income support) compared with 1.2

million single men and 1.0 million married men (Department of Health and Social Security, 1987). Over the 1980s and 1990s social security policies have reinforced these forms of gender inequality (Glendinning, 1987; Land, 1994), though, historically, women have always been more likely to be poor (Lewis and Piachaud, 1987).

In terms of women's access to household income, there is evidence to suggest that men maintain greater control over the household resources than women, even though women usually carry greater responsibility for managing resources for the needs of the whole family, especially where those resources are scarce. Women may not only suffer poverty, they will probably have the responsibility for managing poverty too. In the process, it is also more likely that women put the needs of others in the family before their own (Graham, 1984; Pahl, 1988). Dependency on a male wage, therefore, may be as risky as dependency on paid work or on a state benefit or pension. However, dependency upon a male wage has never really been a viable option for the majority of black women or poor working-class women whose male partners have been marginalised from access to decently paid work (to a 'breadwinner' wage).

Women's lack of access to resources may, then, serve to lock them more securely to home, neighbourhood and locality. This constraint may be reinforced by other factors', many women do not own a car or have access to a family car, and are therefore dependent upon public transport. Women who work, especially those who work part-time, are likely to work within their locality in order to give them greater flexibility to do their shopping, caring and other domestic work. For many women with paid work and domestic responsibilities time becomes a premium, and this again restricts their mobility (Mackenzie, 1988, pp. 34–6). Resources in the community may also be inaccessible to disabled women, intensifying their restriction.

These restrictions are compounded by unequal opportunities for women within the community. Leisure facilities are often seen as men's space – pubs, clubs, playing-fields – unless they are designated specifically as women's – women's nights, women's groups. In political groups or neighbourhood and community organisations, men may hold the key positions of power while women raise funds and make tea. Streets may be seen as unsafe at night, and secluded areas unsafe by day for women and children. Fear of violence or sexual and racial harassment are particularly intense for vulnerable groups such as older women and disabled women. The threat of racial abuse or violence can also prevent black men and women from feeling comfortable outside their own immediate communities. Indeed a combination of racism and sexism, poverty and local housing resources and policies, can imprison black women in their neighbourhoods in very specific ways:

The accumulated effects of twenty-five years of racist housing policies have ensured that growing numbers of black women are imprisoned on the upper floors of dilapidated tower blocks in every inner-city with little hope of escape. If our white neighbours harass us, or if our men abuse us, we often have no choice but to leave, exposing ourselves and our children to the traumas of homelessness.

(Bryan *et al.*, 1985, p. 95)

The confinement of women –particularly women in poverty – to their neighbourhood has also to be set against trends in patterns of leisure and consumption. Over the 1980s consumption has become a major leisure-time activity for those who have managed to retain access to a decent and uninterrupted income. Increasingly facilities such as cinemas and shopping precincts (as well as other services such as post offices and hospitals) are not local but in city-centre or out-of-town complexes. The inaccessibility of these facilities to single parents, older or disabled women (and men) represents another dimension of exclusion from a way of life experienced by the majority.

At the same time, in this way of life there seems less room for community in its collective or communal sense. Some writers see the rise of materialism as heralding the decline of communal solidarity (Seabrook, 1982; Roberts, 1984). From this viewpoint, what links the private world of the family or household today to the public world of, in this case the market-place, or to welfare provision, is its ability to *consume*. The family represents an important consumption unit, choosing its household furnishings and food along with its health care, housing and the right schools for its children. Insofar as community is seen as meaningful, then it is as a vehicle for the defence of property against some outside threat, as in Neighbourhood Watch schemes. However, as we detail below, new lines of solidarity have emerged across and within the bonds of frugality.

Limited access to money or transport and fear of violence are not the only factors to confine women to their locality. Middle-class married women may often find themselves in suburbs or rural villages, their lives restricted by child-care responsibilities and effectively banished from the cities where their husbands work. On the other hand, for some women the very nature of unprotected city life provides the possibility for freedom and new solidarities, as Elizabeth Wilson explains:

While women have been shifted away from urban space and *equated* with anti urbanism, in an often subtle and indeed subliminal way, minority groups have twisted an advantage from being at the interface of urban freedom and ideological repression. Like the bohemian subcultures (to which some blacks and gays were always drawn), their emergence was in part the result of prejudice and labelling. It was also the reaction to stereotyping; urban cultures were part of a process of self-definition. Lesbians and gay men created communities or 'ghettoes' both for safety and for a sense of identity.

(Wilson, 1991, p. 120)

Confinement, marginalisation and exclusion can themselves create the bonds that turn place into space.

4.3   Women in action

Insofar as many women have, for a variety of reasons, found themselves confined in particular ways to their 'place' within the community, what have they made of it? Many women, as the quotation earlier from Jocelyn Cornwell noted, develop an organic relationship with their immediate community. For mothers in particular, it is where they shop, meet other mothers and work. The development of such relationships is not, however, inevitable. Mothers of young children may be severely limited in the access to anything other than superficial relationships or may face exclusions through difference – being new to an area, being black in a white community, having a disabled child. Some women may find that they have less support than others. In a study by Ann Oakley and Linda Rajan (1991) of the support and networks of pregnant women, they found that more working-class women than middle-class women experienced isolation and lack of social support. Nevertheless it is usually women who are at the front line of negotiations over nurseries, schools, housing, health and other welfare agencies. Not surprisingly, then, women have also been central in community-based actions to organise, defend or protest about such services.

In her journey through the north of England in 1984, Beatrix Campbell commented:

in all the towns I visited there was a plethora of women's groups fighting their local authority landlords, fighting for nurseries, for better health care for women, organising mothers' and toddlers groups, girls' rights in youth clubs and children's playschemes. They are often less insistent about expressing disappointment at men's non-cooperation because they barely expect it to be otherwise, though their criticisms are fortified by the existence of feminism in the culture at large. Women's community politics around housing, health and children – the same preoccupations as united their working class antecedents throughout the twentieth century – are a continuing indication of women's resilience.

(Campbell, 1984, p. 197)

This involvement of women in local struggles has a long tradition. For example women led 'corn riots' over the high prices and scarcity of corn in Dover in 1740, in Taunton in 1753 and in London in 1800. In 1831 women led mass demonstrations in Merthyr Tydfil against debt collection during a period of economic depression (Beddoe, 1983). During the First World War women in Glasgow, London and Leeds organised strikes against rent increases (just as during 1988–9 women in Leeds organised successfully against the takeover of their council housing estates by housing action trusts).

Such forms of action represent women's attempts to gain greater control over the conditions in which they collectively live – their space. At the same time, however, women's involvement in struggles in the community also reflects their relative exclusion from the major traditional forms of working-class political protest – the trade unions and the labour movement. It also reflects the resistance by the labour movement to take up those issues not directly concerned with wages and conditions. This is not to minimise the importance of struggles by women trade unionists nor the occasions when the labour movement has supported women's issues – for example trade union support in the 1970s for women's right to abortion. It means that politically the community has been both women's space and women's place – that is, one of the few areas open to women to organise over issues of direct importance to them.

This process of marginalisation from the main institutions of political struggle applies to many groups of resistance – black people and minority ethnic groups, disabled people, poor people, many of whom, of course, are also women. The organisation of claimants' unions, of self-advocacy groups for disabled people, of Afro-Caribbean women against racist educational assessment procedures or of Bangladeshi men and women against racist immigration controls which divide their families, are often based in the community. In most cases, too, these sorts of struggles have long histories (see, for example, Rowbotham, 1974; Sivanandan, 1982), which diverge from the history of the labour movement and are also quite separate and distinct from the history of community work (as told, for example, in Craig, 1989). Nevertheless it is significant that some of the major trade union struggles in the 1970s and 1980s gained strength from this sort of community organisation. In the 1970s the strikes by black men and women workers at Grunwick and Imperial Typewriters found support from the black community long before being recognised by the trade union movement. The 1984 miners' strike was a defence of long-established communities and the work upon which they depended using trade unionism combined with support and the collective organisation of the women in the mining communities. Interestingly, too, the very involvement of the women in such a central way challenged and to some extent transformed the traditional male–female relations that had been part of the culture of those communities. What had been women's place became their space to organise and to change.

In 1991, in the aftermath of a rash of riots by young men in different metropolitan suburbs, Beatrix Campbell revisited some of the places she described in her journey in 1984 and quoted above. In her book *Goliath: Britain's Dangerous Places* (Campbell, 1993), she contrasts the reactions of men and women to the increased unemployment that ravaged many working-class communities from the late 1980s. Women's response has been largely one of collective and individual strategies of survival and solidarity. For men, particularly young men, their responses – which in extreme forms are manifested in petty crime, brutal control over urban spaces and doing drugs – represent, to Campbell, an attempt to reassert in different ways the power and privileges attached to men and masculinity. The breakdown of 'traditional' working-class community life – of male breadwinner, male authority and dependent wife and children – has also meant different things for men and women. For women, it has enabled them to break out of the constraints of domestication and dependence and to cross the divide between the public and private spaces. For men, however, it has removed the political, personal, cultural and institutional rationales for their cooperating with women. This has left women with the responsibility of challenging men to work with them, collectively and constructively, rather than destructively and against them in these new conditions .

The way in which involvement in 'public' issues such as workplace strikes has impacted upon women's capacity to challenge 'private' issues within the family represents an important shift in the influence of the second wave of feminism from the 1960s. The impact of the women's movement had a considerable influence upon women's issues and women's organisations in the community (Williams, 1989; Dominelli, 1990). First, it strengthened the demand that higher priority be given for issues traditionally regarded as 'women's concerns' – care of children or older relatives, for example. Second, it succeeded in turning the 'personal' into the 'political' by putting on the agenda areas of women's lives previously hidden from general concern, such as rape, abuse, violence and sexuality. Third, women's organisations and campaigns have thrown new perspectives on old issues – such as the organisation of education, training and employment opportunities geared to women's needs, or issues of physical and mental well-being. They have also challenged the assumption that work is what men do and where they organise, and home is where women's unpaid work is rewarded through men's pay and their conditions improved by virtue of men's struggles. And it is also the case that many of these campaigns have been carried out in the localities or communities, for example the setting up of refuges for battered women, well-women clinics and rape crisis centres.

Feminist campaigns and struggles have also been influential by incorporating their own demands for change into ways of organising. So, for example, the refuge movement for women suffering from domestic violence has attempted to organise refuges along non-hierarchical and non-bureaucratic lines involving the users of the service in the running, decision-making and caring for and counselling others in the refuge. This attempt to challenge the unequal relationship between the providers of services (often professionals) and the users of the services has also been reflected in the women's health movement. Women have campaigned not only for recognition of their own health needs but also for greater control of and say in, for example, childbirth and reproductive rights. This has also involved attempts to demystify professional, in this case medical, knowledge so that women can gain greater knowledge of their own bodies.

From this highlighting and development of struggles over women's issues has emerged a further important understanding: that women's interests, needs and experiences are themselves different, mediated by differences of class, race, disability, age and sexuality. For example, white women's groups have drawn attention to the lack of seriousness with which the police handle victims of rape or domestic violence. However a black women's problems in this situation are compounded by the hostility of white police towards both black women and black men (Mama, 1989). Similarly, the issue of reproductive rights affects women in different ways. The right to abortion needs to take into account the right to *have children* for infertile women, women who have been subjected to unwanted sterilisation or women who have had their fertility limited – disabled women, black women, Third World women, poor working-class women. In addition, campaigns that focus on women's needs as wives and mothers can be in danger of ignoring the needs of women who may be neither – older women, lesbians, women without children (Williams, 1992a). The acknowledgement of the diversity of women's experiences has emerged through the development of groups that represent new lines of solidarity – Afro-Caribbean and Asian women, disabled women, lesbians, older women, single parents, carers. At the same time this development has been seen by some as undermining the possibility for women's *united* strength to push for general improvements in areas such as low pay and child-care provision (Adams, 1989). The challenge lies, perhaps, in the need for united action that also recognises different experiences and needs.

To conclude: in different ways community can be the space that women struggle to define as theirs, whether it be for health facilities that are responsive to their needs; for better housing and transport; for freedom from sexual and/or racial harassment; for non-racist and non-sexist child-care provision and space to play; for collective forms of saving, buying and distribution; for equal training and employment opportunities; or for the space to celebrate and not hide their sexuality or ethnicity. At the same time community can in different ways be the place to which women are confined. This is a crucial contradiction in the lives of women and their relation to community.

Acknowledgement

My thanks to Lyvinia Elleschild for her comments on an earlier draft of this chapter.

References

Adams, M. L. (1989) 'There's no place like home: on the place of identity in feminist politics', *Feminist Review*, No. 31, pp. 2–33.

Arnott, H. (1987) 'Second class citizens', in Walker, A. and Walker C. (eds), *The Growing Divide*, CPAG, London.

Beddoe, D. (1983) *Discovering Women's History: a Practical Manual*, Pandora Press, London.

Bryan B., Dadzie, S. and Scafe, S. (1985) *The Heart of the Race: Black Women's Lives in Britain*, Virago, London.

Campbell, B. (1984) *Wigan Pier Revisited*, Virago, London.

Campbell B., (1993) *Goliath: Britain's Dangerous Places*, Methuen, London.

Cornwell, J. (1984) *Hard-Earned Lives: Accounts of Health and Illness from East London*, Tavistock, London.

Craig, G. (1989) 'Community work and the state', *Community Development Journal*, Vol. 24, No. 1, pp. 3–18.

Davidoff, L., L'Esperance, J. and Newby, H. (1976) 'Landscape with figures: home and community in English society', in Mitchell, J. and Oakley, A. (eds), *The Rights and Wrongs of Women*, Penguin, Harmondsworth.

Department of Health and Social Security (1987) *Social Security Statistics, 1984*, HMSO, London.

Dominelli, L. (1990) *Women and Community Action*, Venture Press, Birmingham.

Glendinning, C. (1987) 'Impoverishing women', in Walker, A. and Walker, C. (eds) *The Growing Divide*, CPAG, London.

Glendinning, C. and Millar, J. (eds) (1987) *Women and Poverty in Britain*, Wheatsheaf, Brighton.

Graham, H. (1984) *Women, Health and the Family*, Wheatsheaf, Brighton.

Hebdige, D. (1990) 'Fax to the future', *Marxism Today*, January.

Land H., (1994) 'The demise of the male-breadwinner – in practice but not in theory: a challenge for social security systems', in S. Baldwin and J. Falkingham (eds), *Social Security and Social Change: New Challenges to the Beveridge Model*, Harvester Wheatsheaf, Hemel Hempstead.

Langan, M. (1992) 'Who cares? Women in the mixed economy of care', in

Langan, M. and Day, L. (eds), *Women, Oppression and Social Work*, Routledge, London.

Lewis, J. and Piachaud, D. (1987) 'Women and poverty in the twentieth century', in Glendinning, C. and Millar, J. (eds), *Women and Poverty in Britain*, Wheatsheaf, Brighton.

Mackenzie, S. (1988) 'Balancing our space and time: the impact of women's organisation on the British city, 1920-1980', in Little, S., Peake, L. and Richardson, P. (eds), *Women in Cities: Gender and the Urban Environment*, Macmillan, London.

Mama, A. (1989) 'Violence against black women: gender, race and state responses', *Feminist Review*, No. 32, pp. 30–48.

Oakley, A. and Rajan, L. (1991) 'Social class and social support: the same or different?', *Sociology*, Vol. 25, No. 1, pp. 31–60.

Pahl, J. (1988) 'Earning, sharing, spending: married couples and their money', in Walker, R. and Parker, G. (eds), *Money Matters: Income, Wealth and Financial Welfare*, Sage, London.

Roberts, E. (1984) *A Woman's Place: an Oral History of Working Class Women*, Blackwell, Oxford.

Rowbotham, S. (1974) *Hidden from History*, Pluto Press, London.

Seabrook, J. (1982) *Unemployment*, Granada, London.

Sivanandan, A. (1982) *A Different Hunger: Writings on Black Resistance*, Pluto Press, London.

Taylor, B. (1983) *Eve and the New Jerusalem*, Virago, London.

Williams, F. (1989) *Social Policy: a Critical Introduction, Issues of Race, Gender and Class*, Polity Press; Cambridge.

Williams, F. (1992a) 'The family: change, challenge and contradiction', in *Social Welfare and Social Work Yearbook 1992*, Open University Press, Milton Keynes.

Williams, F. (1992b) 'Somewhere over the rainbow: universality and diversity in social policy', in Manning, N. and Page, R. (eds) *Social Policy Review, 1992*, Social Policy Association, London.

Wilson, E. (1991) *The Sphinx in the City: Urban Life, the Control of Disorder, and Women*, Virago, London.

5

The Social Basis of Community Care*

MARTIN BULMER

'Community care' is concerned with the resources available outside formal institutional structures, particularly in the informal relationships of the family, friends and neighbours, as a means of providing care. Yet [. . .] 'community' is hardly a satisfactory term to convey the social basis of such care. No longer is its provision geographically confined to particular localities, however much this was so in the past. Some means is needed, all the same, to refer to the personal ties between those involved in informal relationships of one kind or another. The term 'social network' has come to be used extensively, as a means of relating abstract concepts such as institution or group to the activities and relations of actual people.

The concept of social network is particularly useful for the analysis and understanding of local level informal social ties, of what Clyde Mitchell in an early influential paper distinguished as personal relationships (1966, pp. 54–6). He contrasted these personal ties to institutionalised relationships at work, in a political party, a church, and so on, and to categorical relationships, as when members of different races (his examples were drawn from Southern Africa) met in the market-place and treated each other on the basis of perceived skin colour. Personal relationships are at the heart of informal care, but they are also a mainstay of local social relationships. The value of the term 'network' lies in avoiding the reification involved in talking about 'community', yet enabling one to talk about a wider set of informal relationships than just the family or the extended kin group. The set of relationships has broadened to include friends, neighbours and work associates. There has always been an analytical problem for the social scientist to find a means

---

*This is an abridged extract from *The Social Basis of Community Care*, Allen and Unwin, 1987, pp. 108–15.

of portraying such relationships. 'Social network' seems to be a useful way of doing so.

Community care', however, is a practical policy, not just a matter for detached academic debate. The pursuit of the policy has been hampered by confusing terminology, pre-eminently in the term 'community' itself. To what extent do 'social network' and associated terms such as 'social support' provide a way round these problems? This chapter examines some of these issues in the application of network analysis, and begins by looking at some instances of such use in the field of social welfare policy. This is a prelude to tracing the origins of the approach in social anthropology, and teasing out some of the analytic insights which it can provide. Examples of applications in social welfare show that ideas of 'social network' and 'social support' have been taken up with enthusiasm, particularly but not exclusively in North America, so much so as to constitute what one recent observer has called 'a kind of romantic ideology for social work practice' (Specht, 1986, p. 219).

5.1   Social networks in community care

In discussions of provision of care and service delivery, the concept of 'social network' has come to be widely used. In Britain, the key source has been the Barclay Report on social work, published in 1982. Barclay defines 'community' as made up of 'local networks of formal and informal relationships, together with their capacity to mobilise individual and collective responses to adversity' (p. xiii). The majority of people in trouble turn first to their own families for support. If this is lacking or insufficient, people turn to wider kin, friends or neighbours, because seeking help from such informal networks is socially acceptable and seen as less of a blow than approaching officialdom. Thus help from kin, friends and neighbours is referred to as provided by informal caring networks, usually locally based.

Such usage is an application of the terminology by now common in anthropology and sociology, but it then takes on a life of its own. The Barclay Report recognised that informal networks are complex and not always benign. If links are made between informal and formal care, formal carers need to develop detailed knowledge of informal networks and work in close understanding with them. Partnerships need to be developed between formal and informal carers. 'Caring networks in a community need to have ready access to statutory and voluntary services and to contribute their experience to decisions on how resources contributed by these services are used within their community' (Barclay Report, 1982, p. 202). The majority of social care in Britain is provided not by statutory or voluntary agencies but by individual citizens who are often linked into informal caring networks. These informal carers, Barclay argued, need to be brought within the ambit of professional care.

Applied to social work, this meant that, although individuals or families with problems remained the centre of attention, the focus should be upon individuals within the networks of which they formed a part. 'The circle of vision is extended to include those who form, or might form, a social network into which the client is meshed. Social workers have to be able to take account of a variety of different kinds of network. These will vary in size and in the bonds which hold them together' (Barclay Report, 1982, p. 205). The social worker could make use of the networks in three ways. The first is the most obvious, moving out from an individual to the kin, friends and neighbours who constitute that person's network, to identify and map the most significant personalities in a client's life. Secondly, social workers could identify and build on the ties between those in a neighbourhood, residential home, day, centre or hospital, to develop networks among people who live or spend time together. Thirdly, there was scope for developing networks among those sharing similar communities of interest or concern, for example, parents of mentally handicapped children.

The Barclay Report considered that a change was also needed in the orientation and role of social workers. What was pre-eminently required was an attitude of partnership.

> Clients, relations, neighbours and volunteers become partners with the social worker in developing and providing social care networks. We have already referred to the description of the relationship by one respondent as 'equal but different'; we might be prepared to go further and describe social workers as upholders of networks. This may make clear our view that the function of social workers is to enable, empower, support and encourage, but not usually to take over from, social networks.
>
> (Barclay Report, 1982, p. 209)

In its advocacy of community social work, Barclay was thus placing great reliance upon the notion of network and its potential for harnessing to community care. In doing so, it reflected earlier American enthusiasm for the potential of networks in promoting social care. An early paper was Collins and Pancoast's *Natural Helping Networks* (1976), which argued that natural helping networks had tremendous potential in social welfare.

> They exist as semi-permanent social structures in all cultures, in cities as well as villages, among people of every class. Their importance for social order and integration may increase rather than diminish as society becomes more complex. Networks are one of the most vital bridges between the individual and the environment. Helping networks are the informal counterpart to organ-

ised social services, and in many areas carry the largest part of the service load.

(Collins and Pancoast, 1976, pp. 28–9)

Collins and Pancoast's focus was upon mutual aid, particularly among neighbours, and they saw what they called 'natural networks' as one of the key means of social support, absorbing the load which formal services could not cope with. Various techniques were suggested for harnessing these networks, one of the most important of which was the identification of what Collins and Pancoast called 'central figures' or 'natural neighbours' in a locality. 'Central figures' possess sufficient psychic resources to be on top of their own life situations to be able to give to others and respond to the needs of others. Some may establish that role purely on the basis of informal personal ties – for example, the home-centred housewife who establishes links with other mothers and needy neighbours in the locality. Another way in which such nodal figures may emerge is through a particular occupational role – for example, local shopkeepers, meter readers for public utilities, local hairdressers and bar staff.

It is then suggested that social workers involved in neighbourhoods should seek to recruit such 'natural neighbours', through whom the social worker could work in the locality to draw on existing informal networks and extend them as a means of support. 'Central figures' would be encouraged to enlarge their social circle to increase the effectiveness of the social network used to provide informal care. This would bring in others previously unknown either to professionals working locally or to the 'central figure', both through personal efforts and referrals from other professionals, alongside whom the 'central figure' works. Social workers may refer other professionals to the 'central figure' to effect such introductions. Though the 'central figure' remains part of the informal system, the social worker recruiting such a person must be satisfied as to his or her competence and responsibility, for example in respecting the confidentiality of information acquired in the course of the work. In *Natural Helping Networks* both the notion of a network and the position of an individual at a key position in such a network assume central significance.

Such an approach to the analysis of informal care was taken further in work by Charles Froland and others at the Regional Research Institute for Human Services in Portland, Oregon. Their work uses the term 'helping network' more broadly

to describe a wide range of informal helping activities that staff in the agencies we studied have sought to identify, support and reinforce. . . . Emphasizing informal helping within the context of a *network* of relationships has distinct

conceptual advantages to more traditional ways of viewing social relationships. The concept of network in its most general form draws our attention
to the *structure* of relationships among a set of actors as well as the specific
exchanges which take place among them and the *roles* they play with each
other. Networks describe social relationships in fairly concrete terms. . . . Even
the most socially isolated individuals and the most anomic communities seem
to have a few relationships of this sort. We all use our networks when we need
information or special assistance. In turn, our networks influence us by chan-
neling and shaping the kinds of information we take in. They also require
certain forms of reciprocation as well as the ongoing effort of maintaining the
linkages. Networks are part of a sense of who we are.

(Froland et al., 1981, pp. 19-20).

In an analysis of the work of social welfare agencies in providing social
support through building upon networks, they identify five different
strategies which may be followed. (1) A *personal networks* strategy is used
by a professional worker to build upon the client's personal ties with kin,
friends and neighbours, involving these significant others in the client's
problems and their resolution. In some circumstances, attempts may be
made to expand the client's range of social ties and support. (2) A *volunteer linking* strategy, on the other hand, may be invoked in situations
where there is limited personal support. Here, an attempt is made to
match the client with volunteer supporters, not previously known to him
or her, who have had personal experience of the problem the client faces
or who are willing to provide help. For example, help for the physically
disabled was provided in one scheme by recruiting people who could
advise upon the problems of independent living in the community.

(3) *Mutual aid networks*, as a third type, aim to build peer support by
bringing together people who have experienced similar problems or
have common interests. Similar in aim to self-help organisations, they
are, however, informal without a charter or formal programme. Such
networks may sustain existing efforts, develop new sources of support,
or, in some circumstances, serve an advocacy role. Such networks can be
used to promote a sense of normalisation and social integration among
clients such as ex-mental patients, and in them members may give and
derive support without feelings of stigma or dependency.

The last two types of network build upon geographical propinquity.
(4) In *neighbourhood helping networks*, agencies seek to identify and form
relationships based upon existing local networks among neighbours, key
figures, and local influential people such as clergy. Their aim is to help
isolated individuals, promote local mutual aid, identify local issues and
promote informal social organisation, often with particular client groups
in mind such as the housebound elderly, the disabled or discharged
mental patients. Consultative relationships are established to work with
neighbours to identify problems, and to encourage local residents to

become involved in helping activities. It is in this type of network that the role of 'central figure' or 'natural neighbour' is most salient. It is claimed that 'staff may effectively reach an entire community through a manageable number of individuals who are central linking and referral agents within the informal social organisation of a community' (Froland *et al.*, 1981, p. 79).

Finally, (5) *community empowerment networks* aim to establish local action groups to meet local needs and provide community forums through which local opinion may be articulated and represented to policy-makers. Such an emphasis is more directly political, and involves working with neighbourhood leaders (who are not necessarily or even usually 'central figures' in informal networks), with local voluntary associations, and with opinion leaders in local business, trade unions and churches. An example is given of an agency who used such a strategy in an inner city Polish Catholic working-class neighbourhood to seek better mental health services. The aim is both to articulate the need for formal services and to show how they could, if provided, be integrated with the informal network existing in the locality.

In each of the five types of strategy, the concept of 'network' is central, as a means for understanding the informal ties that it is sought to tap or to create, and in characterising the way in which formal and informal provision can be combined. The term is central; without it the strategies could not be adequately described or contrasted with each other. The typology is useful because it broadens the reference covered by the term, and avoids equating social support with particular forms of helping such as 'natural helping networks'.

A different approach to the same set of issues, particularly salient in North American literature on mental health, is the use of networks in providing social support, with the emphasis upon support rather than network. A social *support* network may be defined as 'a set of interconnected relationships among a group of people that provides enduring patterns of nurturance in any or all forms, and provides contingent reinforcement for coping with life on a day-to-day basis' (Whittaker, 1983, p. 55).

The notion of social network has been pushed to its furthest extreme by American enthusiasts in the social work field who use the term 'networking' to refer to 'a purposeful process of linking three or more people together and of establishing connections and chain reactions among them' (Maguire, 1983, p. 13). It involves professionals working with informal helping networks in the manner described above, except that the process is conceived more actively and in more prescriptive terms.

People whose relationships or linkages with potentially helpful family and friends are tenuous can be tremendously helped by an informal networker. The social network analyses that allow us to define clearly who should be involved in the helping network, as well as what that person can provide and when it should be provided, are all available. By learning how to analyse a network, help make connections, and support constructive chain reactions, one need not leave to chance what must be done.

(Maguire, 1983, p. 23)

Maguire suggests that the active networker starts off with the insights and tools provided by social science to map existing networks and grasp the factual situation, before adding his or her own human judgement or clinical experience to develop a practical strategy which will work in the context of a fluid system of social ties. The technique of personal networking, for example, involves phases of identification, analysis and linking, by which networkers identify potential networks, analyse them and then link the person and the network into a more dense, caring and knowledgeable support system. The networker is the intermediary between the individual and his or her network.

These are some of the more direct applications in the field of community care. Yet an immediate difficulty is apparent: what does the term 'network' actually refer to? Does it not itself become a blanket term, equivalent to saying that all people have some personal ties and close relationships, but tending to tautology? If we are all members of such networks, what is the particular significance of such networks for care? Some of the uses of 'network' just discussed raise serious problems. These difficulties become apparent if one compares these applications to the original uses of this mode of analysis in the social sciences.

References

Barclay Report (1982) *Social Workers. Their Rule and Tasks*, National Institute for Social Work/Bedford Square Press, London.

Collins, A. H. and Pancoast, D. L. (1976) *Natural Helping Networks: a Strategy for Prevention*, NASW, Washington.

Froland, C., Pancoast, D. L., Chapman, N. J. and Kimboko, P. J. (1981) *Helping Networks and Human Services*, Sage, Beverly Hills.

Maguire, L. (1983) *Understanding Social Networks*, Sage, Beverly Hills.

Mitchell, C. (1966) 'Theoretical orientations in African urban studies', in Banton, M. (ed.), *The Social Anthropology of Complex Societies*, Tavistock, London.

Pilisuk, M. and Minkler, M. (1985) 'Social support: economic and political considerations', *Social Policy*, Vol. 16, No. 3, pp. 6–11.

Specht, H. (1986) 'Social support, social networks, social exchange and social work practice', *Social Service Review*, Vol. 60, No. 2, pp. 218–40.

Whittaker, J. K. (1988) 'Mutual helping in human service practice', in Whittaker, J. K. and Gabarino, J. (eds), *Social Support Networks: Informal Helping in the Human Services*, Aldine, New York.

6

Neighbourhood Care and Social Policy: Extracts*

PHILIP ABRAMS, SHEILA ABRAMS, ROBIN HUMPHREY
AND RAY SNAITH
Edited by RAY SNAITH

[*Neighbourhood Care and Social Policy*, published in 1989, is a major comparative study of organised neighbourhood care. The research was carried out some ten years earlier by Philip Abrams, Sheila Abrams, Robin Humphrey and Ray Snaith. Towards the end of the research, Professor Philip Abrams, the head of the Rowntree Research Unit in Durham University's Sociology and Social Policy Department, died unexpectedly. He left behind him a large body of work on neighbouring and local social care. The final text was edited by Ray Snaith.

Philip Abrams and his colleagues found, as many others have found, that most caring is undertaken by kin. The researchers ask how it might be possible to build the equivalent of close kin relations among people who are not related. Their analysis focuses on how organised schemes can mobilise resources within the community. Different kinds of neighbourhood care schemes are studied in the wider context of their social class milieu and official welfare environment.

Publication of *Neighbourhood Care and Social Policy* came at a time when official policy interest was increasingly focusing on the contribution of informal care to community care. Promotion of the role of the voluntary sector and the use of volunteers was becoming more widespread at the same time as statutory services were being reorganised on a localised basis. But although the research was government-funded, the recommendations of *Neighbourhood Care and Social Policy* have not been widely aired. Snaith's call for 'substantial financing of public and voluntary services', a 'strong but sensitive welfare state' and a vision of neighbourhood care, 'compatible with greater equality for women', came at a time of a Conservative government committed to restructuring the welfare state.]

---

*This is an abridged extract from *Neighbourhood Care and Social Policy*, DoH/HMSO, London, 1989, pp. 2–5 and 131–3.

6.1   Contexts and relationships

The activation of informal neighbourhood care [. . .] tells us little about the actual nature of the relationships between local people which generate the caring. Even in the traditional working-class community, most informal care was provided by kin *because* they were kin, rather than by neighbours as such, especially since a high proportion of relatives lived within walking distance of each other. Due to the disappearance or attenuation of the social context which produced mutual aid among non-related local people in working-class neighbourhoods, it is even more the case that, as Walker (1982) puts it, 'in practice, community care is overwhelmingly care by kin, and especially female kin, not the community'. [. . .]

The key to understanding the limitations of informal care specifically among nigh-dwellers is the realisation that the development of important reciprocity-based relationships has become increasingly problematic as a result of social change. The main factors which have affected the character of modern neighbouring are levels of disposable income for the majority, the increased entry of women into the labour market, the greater availability of state-provided care, increasingly privatised family living and increased geographical mobility. The combination of these social trends has transformed neighbouring today into being more a matter of choice than of constraint, and more influenced by the wish to define privacy than by need for help. Drawing on the exchange-theory formulations of Blau and Jackson, Abrams developed this argument as follows:

> Generally the old equation of problems, resources and closure which produced the diffuse trust and reciprocity of the traditional neighbourhood type networks, within which care in 'critical life situations' could effectively be provided for and by local residents, has plainly collapsed in the face of new social patterns. Most neighbours are not constrained and do not choose to make their friends among their neighbours. Those who do tend to be seeking highly specific solutions to highly specific problems which they cannot solve elsewhere and which make them 'expensive' people to befriend from the point of view of their neighbours.
>
> (Abrams in Bulmer, 1986)

Summing up the main arguments about neighbourhood care [. . .] informal neighbourly care is primarily a product of particular social contexts; such care is unlikely to develop spontaneously in local communities among non-related residents except in certain social contexts. A context such as a locale acts as a focus for relationships which themselves produce care, notably kinship, friendship, moral community, communities of interest and economic interdependence. Above all, a social

exchange relationship which is seen as valuable, necessary and potentially reciprocal is the carrier of care. Snaith (forthcoming) has argued
that felt closeness of informal relationships is what matters with regard
to the reliability, extent and intensity of care and support provided; that
such social closeness does not necessarily mean kinship, much less
nuclear family relationships; and that even family care is close (and a
genuine choice) where it is also of a mutual kind.

6.2   Organising neighbourliness

[. . .] [Significant efforts were made] by a number of voluntary and statutory agencies and, in particular, by local residents themselves to develop
systems of neighbourhood care. Within this broad spectrum of groups,
schemes and organisations, [. . .] [some] initiatives embodied the realisation that a process of formal organising to intervene and link with
informal care was necessary, in the face of the general withdrawal and
restrictiveness of modern neighbouring left to itself. The broad aim of
such initiatives was one of exploiting, mobilising, augmenting and
focusing the resources of informal neighbouring presumed to be latent in
different localities.

We see these efforts as responses, both grass-roots and official, to a
changed world, to a modern context of more impersonal and privatised
local life which leaves many people isolated, their neighbourhood care
needs unmet, despite the provision of certain statutory services. We also
see them as *crucial experiments* in identifying and testing the capacity for
neighbourliness (and, more generally, for voluntary neighbourhood
care) of current British society.

The local organisations resulting from these initiatives can be termed,
and were often called, Good Neighbour Schemes. [. . .] We defined a
Good Neighbour Scheme [...] as 'any organised attempt to mobilise local
residents to increase the amount or range of help and care they give to
one another' and further concluded that 'the aspect of neighbourhood
care that is emphasised in Good Neighbour Schemes is not so much that
of delivering services more efficiently or more cheaply, but quite simply
that of a more neighbourly society, a society in which the locality is a
setting for help and care among local residents'. Though they are formally organised, Good Neighbour Schemes seek to develop both helping
and everyday sociability, precisely those factors identified by Kuper
(1953), Shulman (1967) and McGahan (1972) as defining informal neighbouring.

Any soundly based analysis of neighbourhood care must take into
account the nature of, and the differences between, the underlying social
relationships within which that care is given. Although neighbourhood

care of the Good Neighbour Scheme type seeks to stimulate informal care by cultivating ordinary, everyday neighbourliness, it is very different from informal care provided by kin, friends or neighbours, relying as it does on a different social basis for generating help and friendliness. This informal sector of social care is made up kin, friends and neighbours, and care flows from these prior roles. By contrast, the formal sector of care is consciously organised, and caring roles are created by that process of organisation for people who are usually unknown to each other as well as to the recipients of their services. Abrams (1980) argued that 'much of the apparent consensus about the general desirability of more neighbourhood care that exists today exists only because those who think that neighbourhood care means more *localised formal services* and those who believe it means *stronger informal systems* have not yet appreciated the degree to which they are talking about different (and possibly incompatible) things'.

Responding to Abrams' article, Bayley (1981), while accepting the necessity for distinguishing between the two types of care, argued that to make a sharp separation in the way Abrams did was mistaken. He went on to advocate a policy of 'interweaving' informal with formal care. Analysis of this interweaving has to form a central part of any investigation of neighbourhood care; and in looking at the relative mix of different sources of neighbourhood care, and also at the relative power relationships embodied in the links between those sources, particular attention must be given to the main agent determining the overall pattern of neighbourhood care provision: the statutory sector with its overall welfare policy.

Discussion of goals aimed at by the informal sector of care raises the broader issue of the strategy adopted by the formal schemes for relating to their local catchment area or immediate service delivery needs, or also about preventive, long-term caring resources and networks. As a more radical question, what ought one to think of community development or of community politics, advocated by Abrams (1980) as a strategic option for neighbourhood care projects and the regeneration of informal networks?

6.3   The undesirability of reviving traditional neighbourliness

[One] issue concerning the informal sector which is relevant to policy-making centres on what are the realistic prospects for mobilising new community resources, i.e. for neighbours becoming volunteers on the frontiers of formal social service provision. Much of the political rhetoric which surrounds the idea of community or neighbourhood care still assumes, as the 1969 Good Neighbour Campaign did, that there are Good Neighbours waiting in the social undergrowth and simply needing an authoritative call to action. Such thinking lacks a proper understanding of how neighbours normally relate to one another in our kind of society. The myth of traditional community life as a 'densely woven world of informal strongly caring networks' serves to prop up a belief in the possibility and desirability of renewing or reinvigorating laudable, traditional ways of helping people on a local basis. Myths usually embody some truth, and the truth of the myth in this case lies in the nature of the historical context, which consisted of unpleasant conditions rendered less appalling by intense neighbouring.

Although traditional, informal social care was no doubt experienced as a matter of affective ties and cherished, trustworthy networks (as it was invariably remembered as such by the old people we interviewed, whether as clients, residents or helpers), it was in effect governed by an external setting that was essentially brutal and constraining. That context was one of poverty, insecurity, isolation and the lack of formal or welfare-state resources for satisfying needs. Under these circumstances, neighbourliness was impelled by the extreme social homogeneity of everyone being, so to speak, in the same boat. But it was also impelled by calculation. Patterns of neighbouring, then as now, were, to follow Anderson's (1971) argument, also *chosen* on the basis of available resources and in the face of particular costs and opportunities.

The modern realities of neighbourhood interaction demonstrate that in general, once the social context changes and conditions of social closure, insecurity and isolation and choicelessness cease to apply, neighbouring becomes a carefully restricted matter (Abrams in Bulmer, 1986). As involvement with neighbours increasingly becomes an option, the tendency to insure against being caught by the costs of doing so has also become increasingly evident. After all, the hallmark of being a neighbour is that it is potentially the 'cheapest' of all relationships, but it can also very easily be one of the most expensive in terms of time, commitment and foregone opportunities, precisely because of the proximity and face-to-face contact involved. It is not surprising, therefore, that modern neighbouring can be classified as implying a *managed relationship*, one which involves the maximising of certain rewards for minimal investments of time, energy or other resources. The result of this approach to neighbouring being taken is that people generally prefer and expect neighbourly tasks to be those involving emergencies and simple, localised predicaments (Litwak and Szelenyi, 1969). The modern mode of neighbouring is generally causal and guarded, whereby the Good Neighbour is almost universally defined as someone who is helpful, friendly *and* distant – there when you want him [sic] and very definitely not there when you don't. Informal relationships involving deeper commitment are made outside the locality, or with others not regarded as neighbours as such.

6.4 Where are the potential community resources?

Mobilising as sources of care people who live near each other is a policy matter, and those responsible for determining policy in this area must take into account both the true nature and the actual availability of resources that may be drawn upon as informal or voluntary bases for meeting social needs. Clearly, any formal intervention needs to be supportive of the small-scale or, exceptionally, intensive neighbourliness that is already spontaneously taking place. There do exist some survivals of the traditional mode of intense local neighbourly relationships. The major instance of this is provided by neighbours who are also, in fact, kin, especially mothers and daughters (or daughters-in law). It is family ties rather than bonds of proximity that are at work here to sustain local caring. There exist also, but in a more attenuated form than hitherto, the neighbourly resources of observation, gossip and concern. These can be used by formally provided services as linking, monitoring or preventive mechanisms, although there are inherent dangers of undesirable social control and intrusions of privacy which must be guarded against. In principle, mobilising local information systems as sources of 'referrals' represents a promising method of building bridges between the formal and informal worlds of social care, one which may serve as an alternative to more conventional visiting and helping schemes. [. . .]

Over and above the general impoverishment of informal relationships between local people, we observed a further limitation on non-kin-based informal care: the most neighbourly places were those where, objectively, neighbourly help was least needed, and vice versa. On our evidence, this was not only true of inner-city areas (Hayes and Knight, 1981), but of working-class areas generally, the main difference between these areas being only that there was more neighbourly friendliness, as opposed to neighbourly help, outside of the inner city: such as friendliness, however, was generally fairly superficial. We found that the family had much the same broad significance for all social classes, but that when it came to comparing the classes with regard to actual help given, working-class people, the unskilled working-class group in particular, felt that even the family was comparatively limited in what it was actually able to offer. Furthermore, while the middle- and upper-class groups felt to a considerable extent that they were readily able to turn to family, friends and neighbours for help, the working-class ones had much weaker links with friends and, particularly, with neighbours as sources of care. Indeed, both working-class residents *and* working-class helpers were markedly more likely to describe their locality as one where people kept themselves to themselves. The clients of neighbourhood care schemes were more isolated in working-class areas, again especially so in inner-city areas. It follows, on our evidence, that not only has the traditional model of working-class neighbouring largely vanished, but that to a considerable extent the world has been turned upside-down in that today it is more accurate to speak of middle-class than of working-class neighbourliness.

In addition to the above sources of informal care, there are the potential resources of people who can be termed possible exceptions to the modern mode of neighbouring, signified by residents having only a weak sense of attachment to a local area and weak affinities with the people who live in it. We are referring here to those categories of people who are 'compelled' to live locally. Such people, in principle at least, represent major potential sources of organised neighbourhood care, given an overall situation in which neighbours are characteristically by no means always available or willing to provide even limited kinds of informal or neighbourhood care. Powerful forces have brought it about that neighbours are unlikely to want close informal involvement with others (geographical and social mobility, class fragmentation, the sharp decline in the proportion of non-employed housewives [sic] and the increasing preference for a private, family-based mode of living are the major determinants). Nevertheless, a potential pool of neighbourly help exists among the 'exceptional' categories of residents: women confined to their home and children; elderly retired people, especially those without private transport or accessible kin or those who have lived most of their life in the neighbourhood; the unemployed, especially men in areas where unemployment is concentrated and long-term; and other – newcomers, committed churchgoers and community activists, for example – who are likely to have an interest in 'political' movements and/or voluntary associations of various kinds organised on a neighbourhood basis.

We would argue that the demographic forces affecting neighbourly help referred to above are not necessarily to be regretted, and that the negative effects they have upon informal care by neighbours have therefore to be accepted. There is little prospect of non-kin-based neighbourhood networks naturally or informally playing a major part in the provision of social care. We need, therefore, to look to formally organised methods of stimulating and providing neighbourhood care. If mobility and choice are two distinctive, though by no means universal, social effects of industrialisation, formal organisation can certainly be considered a third. Abrams (198U) has further singled out community politics or 'neighbourhoodism' as the most important example of the latter effect.

References

Abrams, P. (1980) 'Social change, social networks and neighbourhood care', *Social Work Service*, No. 22, February, pp. 12, 23.

Anderson, M. (1971) *Family Structure in Nineteenth Century Lancashire*, Cambridge University Press.

Bayley, M. J. (1981) 'Neighbourhood care and community care: a response to Philip Abrams', *Social Work Service*, No. 26, May, pp. 4–9.

Bulmer, M. (ed.) (1986) *Neighbours: the Work of Philip Abrams*, Cambridge University Press.

Hayes, R. and Knight, B. (1981) *Self-Help in the Inner City*, Voluntary Service Council, London.

Kuper, L. (1953) 'Blueprint for living together', in L. Kuper (ed.), *Living in Towns*, Cresset Press, London.

Litwak, E. and Szelenyi, I. (1969) 'Primary group structures and their functions: kin, neighbours and friends', *American Sociological Review*, Vol. 34, No. 4, August, pp. 465-481.

McGahan, P. (1972) 'The neighbour role and neighbouring in a highly urban area', *Sociological Quarterly*, Vol. 13, Summer, pp. 397–408.

Shulman, N. (1967) 'Mutual aid and neighbouring patterns: the lower town study', *Anthropologica*, Vol. 9, pp. 51–60.

Snaith, R. (forthcoming) 'Informal care and state intervention: choice in social policy' (Newcastle Upon Tyne: unpublished paper).

Walker, A. (ed.) (1982) *Community Care*, Blackwell/Martin Robertson, Oxford.

7

Neighbours

SUZY CROFT and PETER BERESFORD

Lil Curtis was in the community care system for quite a short time. It was just over three years from her GP arranging for her to have a home help and her dying, aged 80, in a psychiatric hospital.

We knew Lil for about 13 years. She was a warm and friendly woman. We lived in the same private rented block of flats in Battersea. She lived alone after her husband died when he was 40. They couldn't have children.

For a long time our relationship with her stayed the same. A wave or a nod when she was climbing the stairs to her flat or an occasional chat. Then things started to change. We saw her driven to distraction as she became increasingly confused. She sat rubbing her hands, crying, and said: 'What have I done to deserve this? What would my mother say if she could see me like this?

It started with things getting on top of her. Mrs Curtis came to us in confusion and tears about her gas bill. She'd had a final demand after she'd paid. Though she had been to the Gas Board to sort it out, it still worried her. 'Oh no, not Lil again!' they said when we went. She'd wanted a slot meter but they wouldn't fit one, and she kept getting estimated accounts because the meter reader didn't wait long enough for her to get down her stairs.

Other problems sapped her confidence and unsettled her more. Her pension book was stolen. 'A really nice smartly dressed young woman helped me carry my shopping home. She took the bag up the stairs and then asked for a glass of water. While I was in the kitchen, I heard the front door bang.' Later that afternoon Mrs Curtis found her pension book was gone, together with the £40 she'd just taken out. She cried and cried. Her sister told her she was a fool. 'That'll teach you a lesson.' She felt humiliated.

A week after she got her new pension book, Lil lost it. We looked everywhere. This was the first time we'd seen all over her flat. It was beautifully clean and tidy. There were ornaments everywhere going back years: brasses, pots, small plaster dogs and little framed pictures of flowers and cottage gardens. In the living-room, where she had her meals and watched TV, was the large old cabinet radio her husband had bought and colour photos of her great-nephews and nieces. 'He did all this', she told us about the brickwork surround of her fireplace behind her heater. This time we had to write a letter of explanation to get a new pension book.

Water kept coming in through her living-room ceiling. She had an outside lavatory and no bathroom. We've got a bad landlord. We had to phone the agent three times and go to the Citizens Advice Bureau before anything was done. Then it was no good and she had to keep a bucket and newspaper out to catch the water running down the wall.

Next we noticed that her train of thought was often interrupted. She'd lose her thread halfway through a sentence. At first she would see a funny side. Then she started to lose things, and finding them didn't help. She was frightened more and more of the time. She'd wander to the shops. She stopped cooking and washing herself regularly. Her nephew, Dave, and Cath, his wife, took on an increasing responsibility, coming to visit, arranging payment of her bills, taking her to lunch with her sister every other Sunday. People began to avoid her. She became more and more lonely. She came to see us at all hours.

One Saturday afternoon we found her shaking and crying. She didn't know why she was so upset. Making her a snack helped to calm her. She hadn't been eating. But as we were sitting down for Sunday dinner with Gran and the children, Mrs Curtis knocked and came in distraught again. We spent two hours talking to her, trying to sort out what was wrong and to calm her down.

At this point we really began to worry. The children had gone to bed late and we hadn't been able to take Gran home when she wanted. We were spending more and more time with Mrs Curtis while trying to bring up three small daughters on a low income. Our growing fears were confirmed when Mrs Curtis knocked on the door early next morning before we were up.

We decided we'd have to set limits. We would have to explain to Mrs Curtis if we had to do something else when she was with us. We told each other this was only realistic and we shouldn't feel guilty. But, of course, we still did. We were getting just a taste of the sometimes insuperable conflicts full-time carers know only too well. If you try to restrict your responsibilities, you feel mean and selfish; if you don't, you sacrifice yourself or someone else.

But our friendship with Lil wasn't all problems. We'd got to know her better. It was still a two-way relationship. She'd give pocket money and Christmas presents to the children. She played with them, singing 'Knees up Mother Brown' with Rebecca. We had shared interests. We talked about Latchmere Baths, where she had worked, and about how the area was changing. Where we live, gentrification meant there were fewer and fewer neighbours Lil could turn to for help.

Mrs Curtis's GP arranged a psycho-geriatric assessment after we phoned him. Then the community psychiatric nurse (CPN), Liz, started to call. The home help came twice a week. Meals on wheels were organised, but shortly afterwards Lil cancelled them. She didn't want to go to a day centre. Social services installed a telephone and intercom, but these only seemed to confuse Lil more.

We've been impressed by the professionals working with Lil. The psychiatrist took the trouble to phone us after making his assessment and spent time explaining the situation properly. Liz has kept in close touch. So has Annie, the home help. She's been a real support to Lil.

On New Year's Day we saw Lil on her doorstep in a terrible state. She said she hadn't been to bed the night before. There was no food in the fridge. She said she felt better after we made her some tea and toast. After the holiday, we phoned Liz. She feels that Lil is coping well generally, although she sometimes gets confused and depressed over a minor crisis like a light bulb going. She'll try and get meals on wheels again, but she'll only be able to have a home help a maximum of three times a week.

A few days later we saw Lil outside her front door again. We took her back upstairs. She was incoherent. She said: 'The water just came down my legs.' She's going to her next-door neighbour's more and more. She just can't bear to be on her own.

The CPN was on leave. We spoke to the team leader. We tried to convey how lonely and desperate Lil was, without making it seem that she couldn't cope. She said, 'It sounds like she needs to be in a secure place.' We repeated how much Lil clung to her home. She said she'd get on to social services straightaway.

A note was pushed through our door. Mrs Curtis was in hospital. Dave found her. She'd had a minor fall in her bedroom. She was in casualty all day. It was agreed she could stay for one to two weeks to get her walking and stronger again.

When we visited, she was sitting in a chair next to her bed, munching some chocolates that Dave had brought. Her face was content. She seemed happy. Her hair was clean and combed. But she also seemed confused. We weren't sure if she knew who we were.

All along, what Lil most wanted was to stay in her own home. She also wanted company. From the start, Liz seemed to understand this. She had appreciated that the stairs were difficult but said that if the time came when Lil couldn't manage, then she would press for more support so that she could still cope indoors. She had explained that no certain prognosis could be offered. Mrs Curtis wouldn't get any better, but she might be able to carry on in her home for years. Seeing our relief, she'd said:

'Oh I'm glad you feel like that. Lots of neighbours go, "Oh no!" when they hear that.'

Liz thinks that Lil still wants to be in her own home. The problem lies in the level of support she could have. Her chances of getting domiciliary support are 'very slim' – almost non-existent. Lil is 'too well' for that. There is a waiting list and this level of help is only offered to people who would otherwise definitely go into a home. It's also clear she won't get occupational therapy. She 'might possibly' get a home help up to four times a week. When Lil went home initially she'd see Liz two or three times a week, but then Liz's visits would have to drop back to once a month 'as I've got 30 Mrs Curtises'.

Dave phoned. He wants our support to get Lil into the old people's home just round the corner. He's been told there's a waiting list. He's been to see her every day in hospital. Sometimes she's happy, other times she cries and is confused. He seems worried that Lil will go home and he and Cath will end up having to do everything for her like before. He's frightened of being left with all the responsibility. They already have to look after his mother who is confused.

It was at this point that things really changed. Before, we'd been worried about how much responsibility we might have to take on for Lil. Now we realised more and more how little say Lil, her family and friends would have in what happened to her. Cath told us the news. Lil isn't coming home any more. She was taken to her flat for a home visit as planned. She went with the CPN, a nurse and a social worker. The visit was a failure. Mrs Curtis collapsed in tears. She said she did not want to be in her flat. She was unable to do anything like make a cup of tea. According to Cath, she now seems to be unable to do quite a lot of things for herself. Often she can't remember how to dress and she has started to be incontinent at times. Cath says she can no longer cope with going to see Lil. 'Anyway, she doesn't know who I am.' Dave goes every evening and she sometimes knows him. 'She knows he is *someone*. Sometimes she knows he is Dave. Other times she thinks he is her husband or her brother.'

She's going to Greenways, a home for 'confused elderly persons', 'for assessment'. She's staying there a fortnight, 'to see if she is suitable for a home'. We went to see Lil. The assistant officer-in-charge told us that it had been decided that Lil would stay there for six more weeks, then: 'if she wants to, she can stay here. . . . She's been fully assessed here.'

Lil was standing in the middle of a large lounge. Old women were sitting in chairs against the walls. Most were asleep. In one corner the television was on very loudly, showing children's programmes. Two old men were watching it. It was on all the time we were there. We went and sat in a corner of the lounge with Lil, next to a cage with two budgies in it. She looked very pleased to see us. She clearly recognised us, although we had to remind her of our names.

We asked Lil how she was. She shook her head and cried. She told us she didn't like Greenways. She didn't know how long she had been there. She wasn't sure who had been to see her. 'I know them when they're here, but I can't remember who they've been after,' she said. She thought the food was good and she said she did talk to people, but she didn't feel she had made any friends. She has to share a room. She thought she wasn't supposed to go out of the home. She told us it wouldn't 'be allowed'. She didn't know where the local shops were. We offered to take her out but she felt she wouldn't be up to it. She spoke to a woman with a walking frame who was just coming into the lounge, but they couldn't hear each other because of the television.

When we visit Lil and ask her how she is, she starts to cry almost at once. 'It's terrible, terrible.' She's been frightened to go to bed because the woman she shares with bullies her. She does less and less and cries more and more, in spite of medication. She told us: 'Sometimes I don't know what I'm doing. Sometimes everything can be so clear and then I don't know what I'm doing at all.' She's not allowed to make herself a cup of tea because 'someone might break a cup'. She showed us both her blue lacy long johns, something she'd never have done when she'd been our neighbour.

In the dining-room there's a large noticeboard which says 'Today is Tuesday. The month is April. The weather outside is dry. The next meal is supper.' All the workers, except the officer-in-charge, are black. All the residents are white.

We went to see Lil again with a picture we bought her on holiday. She was sitting in the same chair as last time. Her face lit up and she smiled when she saw us, although she didn't remember our names. She was very pleased to see Rebecca, our youngest daughter. She couldn't remember her name, but said she knew she wasn't 'one of Dave's children'. She was very pleased with the picture. She held it up and said how beautiful it was. Another woman sitting nearby said, 'How lovely.' We said we'd put it up for her. We'd brought a hammer and nails. She was pleased, but anxious that we check with the staff that it was alright to put it up.

She explained to Suzy that she wets herself now and has to wear a pad, 'like for a period'. It obviously upsets her a great deal. It took a long time to understand what she was saying. She cannot speak very clearly and seems to find it harder than ever to put sentences together. We wonder if she gets much chance to practice.

We asked the officer-in-charge how Lil seemed to be settling in. 'Well, very well at first but we had a lot of trouble with her a few weeks ago. She was very, very depressed, crying all the time.' Lil has been wandering out of the home. Apparently she is now on anti-depressants. 'Before, she was crying for days. She was unmanageable.'

We hadn't seen Lil for about a month. We called in. She was asleep in a chair. She woke up when we spoke to her and recognised us. She seemed far worse than we'd ever seen her. She looked crushed and was tearful almost as soon as we spoke to her. Then we noticed her legs. They were very swollen and the skin was red raw and peeling. We asked her what was wrong. A care assistant sitting nearby said that Lil had got water on her legs, caused by sitting down too much and not moving around. The care assistant said, 'Of course, it is difficult to get them to do anything here. They go from their rooms into the sitting room here and then from here into the dining-room and that's it.' We asked her what they could do. She said, 'Well, there isn't much they can do if they can't go out'.

Lil now goes to a day centre three times a week. 'She goes out in tears and she comes back in tears.' We asked Lil about it. She pulled a face but couldn't tell us what she did there. She didn't know where it was or how she got there. The care assistant said, 'At least it gets her out. It's better than sitting here all day.'

Lil can hardly walk now. We tried to help her to her room, but after a few steps she said that she would have to go back to her chair. She clearly didn't have the confidence. She also didn't feel up to going in the wheelchair. She has her own room now. The picture we bought her isn't there any more. Lil has deteriorated very rapidly in the last few weeks. She finds it even more difficult to talk than before.

We called in at Greenways today as we had heard that Lil is in the large local psychiatric hospital, Wellheath. She's been there a month now, in Victoria ward. She was at Greenways for nine months. A care assistant tells us there's a panel/case conference this week to decide whether she goes back. 'I hope she does as she is nice to have around. Not incontinent, can feed herself and all that. She's been on a diuretic to get rid of the water on her legs and a sedative to help her sleep'.

We visited Lil in Wellheath. She was sitting, asleep in a chair, in the ward. It took her quite a while to wake up. At first she didn't seem certain who we were. But after a few minutes she seemed to remember. she was slumped down low in her chair and looked uncomfortable. We asked if she would like to sit up and she said yes. She gets very distressed when she is moved. One of her legs is bandaged and the other looks red and painful. She said she doesn't walk around by herself. She cried out in little whimpers as we and a nurse helped her up.

She seems to be more herself in little flashes. When I said, 'It's Suzy. I used to live next door to you in Winders Road,' she said, 'No, not next door, down the road.' We share an orange. She is sitting next to a table with a plateful on it and she asked if we'd like one. We peel it and she did seem to enjoy it. Otherwise we didn't really understand what she was saying. This hasn't happened before.

While we sat there another old woman came and sat opposite. She said, 'Please help me. Can you help me?' We asked what was wrong, but she didn't answer. Later on she said, 'Oh, God help me.' We again said 'What's the matter?' But she didn't answer. She sat repeating 'Please help me' in a desperate tone of voice. Another old woman came to sit next to her and after a bit said fiercely, 'Shut up can't you.' She repeated this three times, but it had no effect. Then she said, 'Someone will come and help you in a bit. Try not to go on.' The woman continued to cry out until a nurse took her into lunch.

Before we left we spoke to the charge nurse about Lil. The panel/case conference was held yesterday. No one came from Greenways because of staff shortages, Mrs Curtis won't be going back. According to the charge nurse, she was admitted to Wellheath because of her demented behaviour. We said that we thought Greenways was for confused elderly people. She said yes but that her 'behaviour had deteriorated'. She was continually distressed, not eating or sleeping. She cried and wailed. We asked what treatment she has been receiving. 'Oh well, it was also thought that she might have been hearing voices' so she was put on a 'mild tranquilliser' and 'that has helped calm her down'. But she has a recurring urinary infection and we were told that increases her dementia. Lil will be admitted to a long-stay ward.

Today we phoned Greenways to ask if they knew which ward Mrs Curtis was in now. A man said he would check for us. After a few minutes he came back and said, 'I'm afraid I've got some bad news for you. We heard this afternoon apparently that Mrs Curtis is dead. She was buried last Friday.' He didn't know any more details.

We spoke to Cath on the phone. She said that Lil died of a urinary tract infection. Cath sounded bitter. Dave had not been at all happy for Mrs Curtis to be in Wellheath. 'They told us she was going in for two weeks for tests and then Greenways wouldn't have her back.' They both feel that Greenways 'slung' Mrs Curtis out. 'They pushed her out of there.' Lil was cremated and her ashes will be buried with her husband. Dave went to see her body. 'Her eyes were all sunken in like hollows and her temples had fallen in.' We wish we had been able to see her once more. We wish we'd known about the funeral so we could have gone.

After Dave closed up Mrs Curtis's flat, the builder who works for the landlord did it up. The roof was at last repaired. He showed us around. He'd put in wall-to-wall carpet throughout 'People like that.' The fireplace Mrs Curtis's husband made for her and of which she was so proud has gone. The builder has knocked out the outside lavatory and extended the kitchen. The boxroom has been converted into a bathroom. The walls have all been painted white.

A month before she died we saw a 'Sold' sign on the flat and a hired van parked outside. A young man called Charles and his parents were carrying furniture in. Now Lil's flat is his. The only sign of her is the metal hand-rail social services fixed on the outside stairs. It's still there as we write.

8

Two Views of Community Service

(a) Reflections of a Voluntary Worker*

MARGARET SIMEY

Everybody was taken by surprise by the sudden huge increase in the demands for the relief of families following the call-up of so many of the bread-winners [during the First World War]. No machinery existed which could cope with such a situation, apart from a fading organisation set up to deal with the relief of soldiers' and sailors' families during the Boer War. Sympathy ran away with sense and what had been a chaotic situation before became much worse. In despair, the Lord Mayor turned to his cousin, Eleanor Rathbone, who had for some years been training women for voluntary work under the auspices of the Victoria Settlement. Mary Stocks describes in her biography of Eleanor (Eleanor Rathbone, 1949) the astonishing speed and efficiency with which these cohorts of women rose to an opportunity such as they had never dreamed of. By the end of the war, two lessons had been learned. Firstly, a great increase in state intervention had to be accepted. Secondly, women, especially from the middle classes, must be allowed to play a far larger part in the world at large than ever before.

But what of voluntary work? Where did the social conscience of the individual come in? Burdened though they were, Eleanor and her colleagues on the working party never gave up their search for an answer. Many of the dreamers had been killed in the war, but the dream lived on. An increase in state benefits would have to be accepted, but they were wholly convinced that material relief was not the whole story. The more benefits the state provided for people's needs, the more compli- cated the machinery required for their administration. Such public assis- tance as was available was hedged about with a labyrinth of rules and

*This is an abridged extract from Fielding, N., Reeve, G., and Simey, M., *Active Citizens: new voices and values*, (1991) Bedford Square Press, London, pp. 5–11.

regulations which defeated many of those who applied. 'The poor' needed someone to be on their side, to advise them in their dealings with those in authority and, more subtly but none the less importantly, to care about their distress. Moreover, it was in meeting that need and maintaining a personal relationship between the community and those in need that all those who hungered to give service to others and to be of value to society would themselves find fulfilment.

The outcome was the setting up of a Personal Service Society (PSS), effectively a splinter group of members of the LCVA [Liverpool Council of Voluntary Aid] who banded together to defend the principle and practice of personal voluntary service. Their purpose was to provide the machinery whereby each and every citizen could voluntarily give and receive service, according to their capacity and their need. Out of that modest attempt to provide a counter-weight to what was one day to become the welfare state developed the nationwide service provided today by the Citizens Advice Bureaux.

The instant demand which deluged the little agency brought major difficulties. When Dorothy Keeling, who was appointed as organiser, wrote her autobiography, she called it *The Crowded Stair* because of the queues of applicants who chronically blocked the passage up to her office. The sheer bulk of poverty had always been a particular problem in Liverpool, but the aftermath of the First World War multiplied to unmanageable proportions. The agency had to face the fact that volunteers simply could not deal with such a volume of demand and that nucleus of paid staff would have to be employed. Moreover, the complexity of the problems brought by the clients demanded a response that was plainly beyond the capacity or the good-will of the average volunteer. Every worker would have to be trained and supervised. Casework, as it came to be called, could no longer be a matter for spontaneous charity; it must become a recognised profession. [. . .]

Eleanor Rathbone and her colleagues, who fought so hard for education and opportunities for women, can have had no idea of the far-reaching consequences of that apparently minor decision by a small voluntary society to pay women to do what they had previously done voluntarily, and to train them for it. As it turned out, opportunities for employment such as were offered by agencies like the PSS came as a heaven-sent chance for the regiment of 'superfluous women' left high and dry after the First World War ended. Their wartime service had enabled women to escape from domesticity. They had tasted independence. They had undertaken all kinds of jobs and knew that they could do them. But once the war had ended, they found themselves unwanted. There was no room for them. Men back from the forces inevitably claimed priority for such work as was available; the Great Depression was already casting its dark gloom over the economic scene. At the same time, there was no hope of retreating into marriage because of the slaughter of young men in the war. The option of staying at home as an unmarried daughter was no longer available in the changed economic climate.

[. . .] I had been reared in the tradition of the unpaid voluntary worker, my mother being an active member of the church women's section and I myself a Sunday School teacher. What more natural than that when I went to University, the first woman in the family to do so, I should be attracted to the prospect of earning my living as a social worker. [. . .]

Little did I foresee what a threat I and others like me were to become to the established order. I blush to remember with what condescension we regarded volunteers. We were professionals. We knew. Volunteers were of a lesser species, only to be tolerated as handmaidens, hopefully to be phased out as amateur dabblers who might well do more harm than good. Inevitably, the paid workers rose to the top, meekly though they might address the members of their Committees. The high-handed way Dorothy Keeling treated her voluntary chauffeur, the daughter of an important local family, became part of the folklore of students in training. As in the PSS so elsewhere, women flooded into this new and expanding job market. As fast as a new social need was uncovered, and a new specialism was devised to meet it, women swept in and took over. It could almost be said that women invented social work as a career in order to meet their own desperate need. There was little room here for amateurs.

It had been expected of me as a degree student that I would pioneer the entry of women into the expanding civil service brought into being by the increase in state welfare provision. What was, at the time, a high ambition held little attraction for me. I was even less tempted by the prospect of a career as a case worker: the closed-shop attitude of the professionals who dealt with the relief of the miseries of the poor repelled me. I was an out-going type, an enthusiastic folk-dancer who was essentially sociable. I had myself belonged to a curious little girls' club attached to a church, called the Camp Fire Girls. Without hesitation, I headed for what was called group work.

[. . .] The girls' club movement depended almost entirely on voluntary effort, although it had begun to attract a certain degree of official approval as a response to the 'youth problem' of the war years. [. . .]

It was on the back of the youth movement that voluntary work by local people for the benefit of the community as a whole began to develop. In particular, those men and women returning from the forces to the new housing estates found much to be desired in the land fit for heroes which they had been promised. These were people with no experience of voluntary work in the middle-class tradition of charitable effort, but quite spontaneously they began to come together in little local groups to struggle to improve conditions. Unhappily, the pressure of problems on big new estates deflected the energies of such groups into arguments with their landlord, the corporation of 'corpy', and this earned the community movement, as a whole, opposition from councillors and officials alike. [. . .]

To be fair, the official lack of appreciation has to be seen in the context of the Great Depression of the 1930s. Houses and jobs were not just a top priority; they were the only things that mattered. Demands for social facilities such as community centres or shops, or even churches, simply could not compete with that fearful urgency. Only public houses were available on the new estates and in those days women were not welcome in them. As official schemes for tackling the continuing distress multiplied, the drift to central control over their administration increased. There was little scope in those days of universal stress for the amateur endeavours of voluntary citizens, however active.

It was a drift which received a fresh impetus as a result of the evacuation of children from the inner cities on the outbreak of the Second World War in 1939. People living in the suburbs and affluent country dwellers were scandalised by the way of life of 'the poor' who invaded their orderly homes. The evacuees for their part, as in the case of the little family who arrived on my own doorstep, were equally dismayed by the lack of warmth or communal feeling in the welcome they received from the local community and quickly returned to wherever they had come from. I doubt if any increase of compassion or mutual understanding resulted from that entire exercise, but there was at least a fixed determination that 'something must be done' to improve conditions in the inner cities. So urgent was the need for action seen to be, that the Beveridge Plan for the setting up of the welfare state was actually published before the end of the war, in 1943. From then on, every energy was devoted to the preparation of the intricate legislation required to implement Beveridge's proposals and the setting up of the machinery necessary for their administration. Once again, as so often before, voluntary workers were left standing on the side-lines, bewildered and uncertain as to what to do next.

(b) Community as Service*

EILEEN and STEPHEN YEO

Local Liberal leaders first created this meaning [community as service] in response to the socialist practice of community. But it also featured in twentieth-century Labour Party politics and can be identified with politicians like Clement Attlee, Hugh Gaitskell, and with many would-be progressives in modern Britain. Community as service was important to professional men like doctors and lawyers, who grew rapidly in numbers from the mid-nineteenth century onwards, and who tried to establish their legitimacy by stressing their competence to treat social disease and their service to individual clients and to the community. Middle-class women, trying to move out of the home into public work, presented themselves as social mothers doing self-sacrificial service to the poor and to the community. These men and women also cooperated to reinforce each other's service role, especially in the area of public health, where women supposedly sweetened medical inspection, while doctors upgraded traditional philanthropic visiting into scientific activity. [. . .]

Mid-nineteenth-century civic leaders tried to transcend conflict and create community by making the municipality (as a city-state) into an object of service. Through service in local government and voluntary associations, public life was to bring 'the community', in the sense of everybody within the local state, into 'community' in the sense of a new kind of caring union. In the words of the Reverend Dale of Birmingham, where the 'civic gospel' received its clearest formulation in the 1860s, 'new ideas about municipal life and duty were pressed on the whole community'. The Reverend Dawson spoke of the Birmingham Public Library movement as

> capable of bringing about a better union of classes . . . There could not be anything more valuable than men [sic] finding rallying points at which they might forget sectarianism and political economy, which they did not half; understand, and find a brotherhood removed from the endless grovellings, and the bickerings . . . This then was the new corporation, the new church, in which they might meet until they came into union again.[1] [. . .]

Community was to be created by public facilities notionally available to all classes. These would displace or absorb similar facilities supplied

---

*This is an abridged extract from (1988) Yeo, S. (ed.) *New Views of Co-operation*, Routledge, pp. 234–57.

by working people for themselves. Bought for a song from the socialists, the Manchester Hall of Science became the first free Public Library in Britain and was hailed as the product of a 'common effort for a common purpose . . . that public domain for mental culture which is the joint heritage and ought to be the common enjoyment of rich and poor'.[2] These fine words must not obscure the fact that this idea of 'common' was displacing mutuality with hierarchy. [. . .] It is safe to say that in bringing the public facilities into being and then in running them, bourgeois men had decisive power. The Public Subscription Committee which often raised the funds was multi-class, but it was divided into a complement of wealthy donors, a large body of affluent subscribers and a separate 'Working Men's Committee'. The resulting hospitals, libraries, town halls, and parks were turned over to local government to be made into state 'services'. They were never controlled, or actively produced, by the users. This was very much a version of community provided through the service of middle-class governors and philanthropists for the people, however much energetic participation in it was urged and however much it was recommended with the rhetoric of mutuality.

Indeed a key feature of community as service and a clear contrast to working-class mutuality has been the continuing middle-class attempt to harmonise social relations without disturbing inequalities of class or gender power. A characteristic project of middle-class groups has been to marry the two oldest definitions of 'community' and to conceal, or, as they would see it, transcend, social antagonism. They have tried to force a union between the community as supplied from above with its basically unequal social structures and community created from inside with its supportive and more ethical human relations. The transforming agency was to be their own *voluntas* expressed in service to a formal entity (e.g. the municipality or a Community Association) together with equivalent though unequal working-class participation. This strand of community thinking has remained strongly committed to locality (the city rather than the nation) and to voluntary effort. But the emphasis has been on co-ordinating voluntary and state activity so that, despite the presence of democratic and visionary anti-state rhetoric, the state has been left in place and in control. Ernest Barker, a member of the National Council for Social Service and the chief ideologue of the Community Association movement, drew upon the whole radical rhetoric of essential Englishness (including the Saxon precedent and the Norman Yoke) to celebrate 'Voluntary Community and a New Democracy', even calling the Community Centre 'a "moot-stow" for their deliberations'. But however representative, Barker argued that a Community Association was 'not a unit of local government, and does not attempt to replace the Local Authority' (which usually, he noted, filled people with massive apathy).[3] This view differed from working-class anti-statism which sought to constitute a (new) state (of affairs) through its own associational activity. [. . .]

People seeing community as service have often been preoccupied with formal institutions and with constructions in the literal sense – buildings as the symbol and the location of community life. We have noted the mid-nineteenth-century bourgeois concern with public buildings. Community Associations put a lot of energy into fund-raising and into lobbying local Councils for a Community Centre or Community Hall. Not least, this building was necessary to provide a venue for middle-class service. [. . .]

The idea of community as service was usually located away from economic production, in leisure life after work. As Park of Chicago, an advocate of Community Centres, put it, 'politics, religion, and community welfare, like golf, bridge and other forms of recreation, are leisure-time activities and it is the leisure time of the community that we are seeking to organise'.[4] This was another contrast with the socialist vision, where production of every kind, including economic production and production of family life, was to be reorganised in order to embody community. [. . .]

Although situated where people had their homes, the middle-class view of community with its stress on service within formal organisations tended to restrict working-class women and to displace their communities. Women's informal networks of relatives and neighbours were a continuing experience of mutual aid. But Community Associations, while purporting to answer the sexism of Working Men's Clubs, had few women officers in their committee structures and few women writers for the CA newspaper. It is true that groups like the Women's Co-operative Guild and the Townswomen's Guild did affiliate, for example, to the Norris Green Community Association in Liverpool and that this Association started a benevolent fund to give members 'a little immediate help'. But the Community Associations never seemed to relate to the neighbourhood networks among women which provided economic and emotional support so important for survival.[5]

Sometimes middle-class women tried to absorb poor women's networks into a notion of community in which social workers and their service was indispensable. Helen Bosanquet was an activist in the Charity Organisation Society and, together with the Women's University Settlement, a pioneer proponent of training for social workers in Schools of Sociology and Social Economics. She argued that social workers would haves to coerce into being the very family and neighbourhood networks which were already there and on which the poor had always relied. She inflated the service of social workers at the expense of poor people's sacrifice:

the unceasing sacrifice of patiently unintelligent women and selfishly unintelligent men is of little use to the community. It does not rise to the level of self-sacrifice, for there is seldom anything voluntary about it; it is submission to the brute forces round them.[6]

Only much later, in the 1950s, did the pendulum swing the other way. Just when social services, public housing and private materialism seemed to be undermining the informal networks in fact, groups like the Institute of Community Studies resurrected these neighbourhood networks in theory as the 'traditional' (and desirable) working-class community.[7]

The example of Bosanquet and other women social workers illustrates a key feature of most of the middle-class practice of community. This was the inability to leave independent working-class mutuality alone and the recurrent attempt to absorb it or replace it with a practice designed to make middle-class service indispensable. This was the case even where the mutual aid was informed, as in the case of women's networks, and perhaps even more the case when mutuality was organised into formal and sometimes militant associations. Community as service has been continually invoked in and against situations of working-class militancy. [. . .]

Notes

1. Dawson quoted in E. P. Hennock, *Fit and Proper Persons Ideal and Reality in Nineteenth Century Urban Government*, Edward Arnold, London, 1973, p. 75.
2. Quoted in A. Briggs, *Victorian Cities*, Odhams, London, 1963, pp. 199–200.
3. *Norris Green Life*, June 1937, pp. 14–15, reprinting his address to the 8th Annual New Estates Conference in London.
4. R. E. Park, E. W. Burgess and R. D. Mackenzie, *The City*, University of Chicago Press, 1925, p. 117.
5. *Norris Green Life*, January 1937, p. 7. *The Wilbraham World: The Official Organ of the Wilbraham Association*, Vol. 1, No. 1, December 1932 – Vol. 2, No. 12, April 1935, in the Manchester Central Reference Library, is a rich source for the aspirations of a high-minded Community Association on a Manchester estate. From 1929 to 1935 their secretary was Emily J. Jenkinson; see her Utopian dream of what the Wilbraham estate could be like in 1999 in The Wilbraham World, Vol. 1, No. 3, p. 29, and her disappointed departing letter in *WW*, December 1934. 'A change of heart in their neighbours' seemed to be what the Wilbraham Association was trying to achieve, although there is also evidence, for example from Wythenshawe (*WW*, June 1934), of tenants' union/area impulses at work.
6. H. Bosanquet, *Rich and Poor*, Macmillan, London, 1899, p. 103; *Social Work in London, 1869–1912*, London, 1914, reprinted Harvester Press, Brighton, 1973, pp. 403–4.

7. E.g. P. Willmott, *The Evolution of a Community: a Study of Dagenham after Forty Years*, Routledge and Kegan Paul, London, 1963, p. 109, the follow-up study to Willmott and M. Young, *Family and Kinship in East London*, Routledge and Kegan Paul, London, 1957. S. Laing, *Representation of Working-Class Life, 1957–1964*, Macmillan, London, 1986, pp. 37ff., for genres of community study in the 1950s.

Part II

CARE

9

Introduction

This section begins with an anthology of care. The extracts in this anthology are drawn from fiction, research, autobiography, diary, oral history, newspaper articles and taped interview. They focus mainly on the personal and experiential dimensions of care, and cover a range of different groups who provide and receive care and support. From a different angle, the anthology also attempts to place 'care' in a historical and international context and to see it operating over a wide range of relations.

The first two chapters in this section open with a detailed look at caring processes. The first, an extract from Janet Finch and Jennifer Mason's work, explores the nature of obligation and responsibility to care within kin groups and looks at how far principles of obligation shape the care and support offered by daughters and sons to their elderly parents The second is drawn from Jane Hubert's searching, candid and closely observed research study of 20 families with young adults who have severe or profound learning difficulties or display challenging behaviour. She pieces together the complexity of reasons why parents in this situation find it difficult to let go of their adult children into care outside the home.

This is followed by work that in different ways opens up the field of research on caring. The first, by Yasmin Gunaratnam, fills an important gap. It looks at the experiences of black and ethnic minority carers, drawing on both her own research and her experiences as an Asian carer. She argues for the necessity to understand the needs of black and ethnic minority carers and the people for whom they care in a context wider than just 'care'. Many of the people she interviewed experienced poverty, poor housing conditions and racial harassment along with inappropriate and inaccessible service provision.

Hilary Graham continues with this theme of widening the context of care. She suggests that studies of caring need to account for the experiences of those who *receive* as well as those who *provide* care and to bring out more of the class and race differences in women's experiences of caring. Mike Fisher's chapter also represents an important refinement to research work on carers. Drawing upon more recent research, he maps the significance of *male* carers, particularly men who care for their wives.

Clare Ungerson's article looks at care in the yet wider context of social rights. The notion of *citizenship* has enjoyed a resurgence in the 1990s, but how far is it applicable to the needs and lives of carers?

In 1988 the publication of Gillian Dalley's book *Ideologies of Caring: Rethinking Community and Collectivism* represented a consolidation of feminist research and writing on care. We reproduce here a short extract from the second edition of this book, published in 1996, on the principles of collective care. The final extract represents a further significant development in work on caring. In this Jenny Morris, a disabled feminist, provides a critique of research on care which, she explains, has rendered invisible the experiences, perspectives and demands of those who receive care and support.

10

Anthology: Care

Compiled by FIONA WILLIAMS

These extracts have been grouped under five headings. The *process* of care focuses on the day-to-day experiences of those involved in caring for an older person. The *context* of care demonstrates the variety of historical, cultural and social sites and relations of care through extracts drawn from domestic service, institutional care, mothering, neighbouring and caring for a gay partner. In *struggles* of care both the carer and the person cared for describe the particular problems and difficulties that their situation gives rise to. Similarly, *dilemmas* of care illustrates the conflicts and constraints placed upon those committed to providing the best possible care. Under the heading of *rights* those who use care and support services give a powerful voice to the right to determine the kind of care and support they want. Overall, the anthology helps us to see care not only in terms of different contexts and relationships, but as a manifestation of different feelings and motivations: control, responsibility, obligation, altruism, love and solidarity.

10.1 The process

*An abridged extract from **Have the Men had Enough?**, a novel by Margaret Forster, Penguin, Harmondsworth, 1989, pp. 94–8.*

Adrian and I take Grandma to the chiropodist at the clinic. She, the chiropodist, would come to Grandma's home but it makes an outing for Grandma so we keep taking her. And it is what Mum calls a nice little job for Adrian. He does the driving. (Adrian is *very* proud of having passed his driving test first time last year.) He does the driving but for reasons unknown to me he cannot do the taking-into-the-clinic-and-divesting-of-stockings. Mum says Grandma would be embarrassed if Adrian took her stockings off. It would mean fiddling with suspenders – Grandma cannot be parted from her suspenders – and Mum says that is too much to expect. I can't see why but Mum also keeps saying Grandma would mind. How this could be proved I don't know. But I go as well, to be the stocking-taker-offer. Women's work, again.

Adrian has no idea how to get Grandma into the car. He just stands there, helpless, saying why can't she sit down and Grandma stands, equally helpless, and they stare at each other and Grandma asks Adrian if his name is Duncan. He says no, of course, and she says that's a pity because she knows a poem about Duncan Davidson that puts her in mind of him and it goes etc. etc. I say if we stand here any longer, we'll miss the appointment. Then I show off. I point to the floor of the car and tell Grandma to pick that sweetie up, it's going to waste. She bends slowly and, when she's nearly there, reaching into the front of the car, I put my hand on her head to protect it from getting knocked and I push her bottom sideways and she half-falls into the car and I lift her legs to join the rest of her. Mission accomplished. Adrian is aghast. He says I'm cruel. I tell him to shut up. He hasn't the faintest idea of how to manage Grandma. He drives slowly, as though he had a cargo of porcelain.

I sit outside. I suppose the chiropodist wouldn't mind if I stayed but when she asks would I like to wait outside, I always obey.

I go back in to put the stockings on. The chiropodist explains to me what she has done and what she will do next time. She refers to Grandma as 'she' and 'her', as though she was an idiot. When it comes to putting Grandma's shoes on, I have difficulty. They're very old shoes. They're made of brown leather, the sort that are laced and have good strong soles. The leather is very worn. In fact, there's a small hole, rapidly widening into a tear, where Grandma's largest bunion is pushing through. The chiropodist watches. She says maybe 'she' needs some new shoes. Grandma flares up. She says these are good shoes they cost a fortune, there is nothing the matter with them. I'm sweating. Grandma is not helping. She holds her foot rigid, won't even attempt to bend her toes. One shoe is on and laced but I can't get her left foot into the other. All this pushing and shoving is useless. Grandma is getting angry. She starts kicking her foot deliberately so that the shoe flies across the room.

> One, two, buckle my shoe.
> Grandma, behave.
> You mind yourself.
> You mind yourself, keep your foot still.
> I like a wee jig now and again.
> Not when you're putting your shoes on.

The chiropodist has retrieved the other shoe and comments sympathetically that she does feel sorry for me. Now I am angry. I snap at the chiropodist. Then I hand Grandma her shoe and I stand up and I tell her that if she doesn't hurry up, the men will be in for their tea and nothing ready. She proceeds to put her own shoe on, stumbling only over the tying of the laces which I bend and do quickly.

When we get home, I say to Mum straight away that Grandma must have new shoes, that her shoes are in a terrible state, that it's no wonder her walking is deteriorating. I put Grandma's slippers on her feet and then I flourish the offending shoes under Mum's nose. Mum says I'm not telling her anything she doesn't know. She has taken Grandma to a shoe shop and there is no such thing as a shoe which will fit her appalling misshapen feet. But she will mention to it Bridget and see if she has any ideas. Adrian chips in. He says how about men's trainers? I scoff but Mum nods. Adrian brings his new trainers and tries them on Grandma. They appear to go on quite easily. She looks so funny, sitting on the sofa with Adrian's white trainers plonked on the end of her lisle-stockinged legs. We're still laughing when Bridget arrives. Grandma is laughing too, she knows she's a good turn. She has taken the tea cosy off the tea pot – the tea cosy she crocheted herself years ago and loves to see on the tea pot, so Mum tries to remember to put it on – and she has put it on her head because she says she can feel a bloomin' draught. She has one ear poking out of the hole for the spout and the other out of the hole for the handle. The vivid reds, blues, greens and yellows of the tea cosy stripes straddle her large head. Adrian is crying with laughing and I am almost as bad. Then Bridget arrives. She snatches the tea cosy off Grandma's head. Grandma yelps and tells her to get lost. Bridget's face is red and angry. She *hates* Grandma to be a laughing stock even though Grandma loves to be the cause of mirth. Bridget says, 'Mother!' furiously and also yanks off Adrian's trainers. Now Grandma starts moaning her feet and head are both cold. Bridget grabs the tartan shawl from a chair and ties it round Grandma's head. She looks around and finds Grandma's shoes and forces them on. Mum looks annoyed. She says to Bridget it was only a joke. Bridget says some jokes go too far. Mum makes an exclamation of irritation and goes into the kitchen. I start to speak but Mum motions that I should say nothing. Really, Bridget is very odd.

10.2 The context

A home help talking about her job. An extract from an interview with Muriel Arncliffe, from the Open University course P654 **Working with Older People***.*

I used to enjoy me Fridays, that were a little old lady I had down there. She were great. She were crippled with arthritis but she was always right cheerful, you know, and she used to love me to go. [. . .] There is the type of people that appreciate whatever you do. I could have gone in there and just sat and she'd have never been bothered. [. . .] It's knowing you've achieved something isn't it? You've done that for them but they wouldn't be able to do it if you hadn't had time. [. . .] I mean it's alright sitting and talking but when you've gone they're still sit in a mucky house aren't they?

Mrs—, she was nasty. She couldn't understand why she had to have home help that's what it was. But she couldn't do it, you see, she'd got rheumatics, you know, arthritis. [. . .] You'd tell her why and then she'd forget and then she'd say well why are you here? And you'd tell her again and then ten minutes later she'd say but why are you here? And that's how it was all the time. [. . .] It gets you down. You know, I used to go back and say I think I need four hours there, it's driving me mad.

You panic when you go to the door and they don't answer . . . you look through t' letter box and if they're there on t' floor and they're not moving you do panic. You think, my God she's died, you know. Part of the job, isn't it?

————————————

Kevin Brompton, on caring for his lover, Alan. An abridged extract from **Who Cares? Looking after People at Home***, by Cherrill Hicks, Virago, London,1988, pp. 186–8.*

I suppose, looking at it now, all of last year on and off he was ill: there were lots of silly little things. If you're gay it's always at the back of your mind – every time you sneeze. He had had psoriasis, it got very bad; he had had problems with his bowels, as well as shingles and gout. He'd always been quite healthy before; he was the sort of person that everyone said: it will never happen to Alan.

I suppose, at first, we both sort of hoped we'd got a couple of years. We thought we had plenty of time for them to get a cure: in that situation, you grasp at any straw.

[Alan's parents, who live in a different part of the country, do not know that he is dead: there had been no contact between him and his family for years.]

There was a big bust up several years ago; they [Alan's parents] weren't happy because he was gay. At a later stage they said maybe they'd been a bit hasty, but it was too late for Alan. He got rid of everything to do with them: in all his belongings there was nothing, no papers or anything, not one reference to them. He didn't want them to know that he'd got AIDS, and he said they weren't to know about his death.

My own family have been as supportive as they could be. My father and stepmother: we're quite close, although we never openly discussed the fact that we were gay. It was referred to obliquely though. Just before Alan died, they guessed what was wrong.

We've got lots of very good friends, mostly gay, but some straight: they've been absolutely marvellous, and they still are. I don't think I could have done it otherwise, to be quite honest. In the last few months there were not enough hours in the day; I was working, but we had a rota of friends with keys who would all pop in.

Alan was always OK to be left. I used to give him his breakfast and leave a meal out, and a friend would drop by to see if he was OK; then he would snooze until I got home. I'd see to all the lotions and potions and ointments for his skin; he needed special cream for his fingers and feet. When he was in hospital I used to bath him.

When Alan first went into hospital, there was no proper AIDS ward. It was a fairly old ward and fairly crowded: not a very wonderful place. But later, when he went back, there was a new ward: they'd obviously spent a lot of money. Most of the time he had his own room with a shower, his own TV. The attention and love they got from the staff – it was quite exceptional. Especially the nurses. The doctors were good as well; but then, doctors have to be doctors, don't they?

I think it's affected all of us really. I can't speak for the whole of the gay community, of course; I can only speak for my circle. We all think we've got to live very much for today, but then most gay people have always felt like that.

He knew I'd look after him and I did, as best I could. That's all there is to it, really.

From A Woman's Place: An Oral History of Working-Class Women, 1890–1940, by Elizabeth Roberts, Blackwell, Oxford, 1984, pp. 189–91.

The neighbours were far better than they are today. They were not as clannish. If the next door neighbour was poorly we would go in and help. We'd do her washing, do her ironing, and we'd take them back and if they wanted any messages going we used to do it. They were always willing to help you. Now today, they're more clannish, they seem as if they want to be on their own.

When they were ill they used to get a sheep's head and a marrow bone and then twopennyworth of pot herbs and make a good pan of soup, and some split peas and barley and take them a good bowl of soup in at night. We perhaps used to take them their dinners. [. . .] Really they were better friends than what they are. They're good friends today but they're more for themselves. In the olden days it was sisterly love and more motherly love. I used to be knocked up time out of time when anybody died. They used to come and knock at the door at midnight and say, 'Will you come and lay the baby out? Will you come and lay so and-so out?' I used to go and lay them out.

---

*An abridged extract from **Life As We Have Known It**, edited by Margaret*
Llewellyn Davies, 1931; reprinted by Virago, London, 1977, pp. 20–5. The nar-
rator, Mrs Layton, was born in Bethnal Green in 1855.

Ten years of domestic service

When I was ten years old I began to earn my own living. I went to mind
the baby of a person who kept a small general shop. My wages were 1/6
a week and my tea, and 2d. a week for myself. I got to work at eight in
the morning and left at eight at night, with the exception of two nights a
week when I left at seven o'clock to attend a night school, one of a
number started by Lord Shaftesbury, called Ragged Schools. I was very
happy in my place and was very fond of the baby, who grew so fond of
me that by the time he was twelve months old he would cry after me
when I went home to my dinner and when I went away to school before
he was in bed. I felt very proud of my influence over my baby, and got
into the habit of taking him home with me rather than let him cry.

When I was thirteen years old I went into service at Hampstead where
I stayed twelve months. I had a very kind mistress and plenty of good
food. I was fairly happy, but had to sleep in a basement kitchen which
swarmed with black-beetles, and this made me very wretched at nights. I
was only allowed out on Sundays to go to church. Sometimes I got a
change by going on to the heath with the three children.

At the age of fifteen I had my first experience of maternity nursing. I
went to service at Kentish Town, where there were four children, and in
a few months another baby was born. A few days after the birth of the
child the mother died of puerperal fever. [. . .] From that time till I left,
two and a half years later, I had the principal care of the baby. I loved it
as I love my life.

'Bloodmothers, othermothers, and women-centered networks', an abridged extract
*from Patricia Hill Collins, **Black Feminist Thought**, Unwin Hyman, London,*
1990, pp. 119–20.

In African-American communities, fluid and changing boundaries often
distinguish biological mothers from other women who care for children.
Biological mothers, or bloodmothers, are expected to care for their children. But African and African-American communities have also recognised that vesting one person with full responsibility for mothering a
child may not be wise or possible. As a result, othermothers – women

who assist bloodmothers by sharing mothering responsibilities – traditionally have been central to the institution of Black motherhood.

The centrality of women in African-American extended families reflects both a continuation of West African cultural values and functional adaptations to race and gender oppression. This centrality is not characterised by the absence of husbands and fathers. Men may be physically present and/or have well-defined and culturally significant roles in the extended family and the kin unit may be woman-centered.

Organised, resilient, women-centered networks of bloodmothers and othermothers are key in understanding this centrality. Grandmothers, sisters, aunts, or cousins act as othermothers by taking on child-care responsibilities for one another's children. When needed, temporary child-care arrangements can turn into long-term care or informal adoption. Despite strong cultural norms encouraging women to become biological mothers, women who choose not to do so often receive recognition and status from othermother relationships that they establish with Black children.

In African-American communities these women-centered networks of community-based child care often extend beyond the boundaries of biologically related individuals and include 'fictive kin'. Civil rights activist Ella Baker describes how informal adoption by othermothers functioned in the rural southern community of her childhood:

> My aunt who had thirteen children of her own raised three more. She had become a midwife, and a child was born who was covered with sores. Nobody was particularly wanting the child, so she took the child and raised him . . . and another mother decided she didn't want to be bothered with two children. So my aunt took one and raised him . . . they were part of the family.

Even when relationships are not between kin or fictive kin, African-American community norms traditionally were such that neighbours cared for one another's children. Sara Brooks, a southern domestic worker, describes the importance that the community-based child care a neighbour offered her daughter had for her:

> She kept Vivian and she didn't charge me nothin either. You see, people used to look after each other, but now it's not that way. I reckon it's because we all I was poor, and I guess they put theirself in the place of the person that they was helpin.

Brooks's experiences demonstrate how the African-American cultural value placed on cooperative child care traditionally found institutional support in the adverse conditions under which so many Black women mothered.

An abridged extract from **A Price to be Born**, *New Directions, Colchester, 1981, pp. 91–3, the autobiography of David Barron, who spent many years in institutions. He was born in Leeds in 1925 in Street Lane Orphanage. At the age of 5 he went to a foster-mother who ill-treated him. He describes how at 14 he was removed.*

One evening' just as I was ready to go to bed! there came a knock on the front door and Miss Bellamy answered it to admit a lady and two gentlemen, one of whom asked my foster mother if they could see my bedroom.

The man turned to me, 'Come on David, you are to come with us.'

It might not have been so bad if they had let me get dressed again but before I knew what was happening they had taken me, still in pyjamas, to their care. I was never to see my foster mother again.

I was immediately placed in a home with children of my own age where I stayed for the next two days, but the worst was yet to come. From this short stay home I was taken to an institution which has to be very much my long stay home, and a very big home at that. The name of the Institution was the Mid-Yorkshire Institution, Wixley, near York. The reader might care to note that I was a mere fourteen years of age when I was taken to what was a mental institution, but in those days these places had to take in all kinds of homeless persons who were in no way mentally ailing. The Institution was to be my home for the next eighteen years, beginning as a so-called patient and finishing as a supervisor. It is now run by the Clifton Mental Hospital, York.

How my life proceeded from the formative years of early adolescence into adulthood is another story which may or may not be written, but the reader will appreciate that fate had decreed that the price to be born in my case was to go on being paid for right up to the present day.

10.3   Struggles

'Carers may be angels but does that make their dependents devils?', an abridged extract from the **Guardian**, *January 1991, by Kate Cooney.*

Maria's pale green eyes sparkle in the candlelight, ablaze with wine and desire. Slowly, carefully, she unzips the front of her dress. The black silk slips from her shoulders, caressing the lengths of her naked body as it rustles to the floor. Dropping to the bed, she slithers out of her shiny, thigh-high boots as a snake sheds its skin. She leans back, beckons to him and he obeys, stumbling and with shaking hands. At last, he is beside her, paralysed with anticipation. Turning boldly towards him, she whispers, 'Will you take my socks off, please?'

There is something terminally unsexy about not being able to take your own socks off – even if they're clean, without holes and have never belonged to your dad. It's been some years since I have been able to do it, yet it still rankles to see my partner peeling back those little black ones from M&S for me after a particularly sweaty day. It also peeves me that I need him to insert a suppository for me every night, that I've stopped wearing earrings because I don't want to bother him to put them in for me, that the air does not always smell of lavender when he has to help me off the loo.

I am 31 and have had rheumatoid arthritis since the age of 18. Like most people, I once plucked my eyebrows, made a cup of coffee when I felt like it, shaved my own legs. Slowly, the ability to do these things has been taken away from me.

Allowing someone else into the yuckier side of your life is hard. Even the most intimate of relationships do not contain the grossly earthy things that are par for the course in ours. I have next to no privacy. My partner knows my every nook and cranny, and I am left without a millimetre's worth of mystery.

No, it's *not* easy, being 'cared for'. It's not just the messy bits. It's no longer being able to nick a chocolate biscuit out of the fridge, or experiment with make-up, or grab just the right scarf to set off your jumper as you rush out of the door. Always, *always*, you have to ask.

These things may seem insignificant nit-pickings compared with the more obviously dramatic changes wrought by disability, but taken together they are as momentous as the arrival of the wheelchair or the loss of your job. As they are given up, a little bit of what outwardly makes you an individual is eroded.

Your carer has to run part of your body for you. If you insist it is run exactly the way you would have run it, you will be ridiculously demanding. But it still hurts to let go and it's still hard, getting used to the new, circumscribed you – should I ask for that or shouldn't I?

No one would deny that looking after another person can be tough. The current rash of articles written by and about carers bears witness to this. It is also often a job reluctantly undertaken. Knowing all this, reading all the accounts of ruined lives, it can be just as tough finding yourself in the position of having to receive all this 'care', – your self-esteem can easily be drowned out by guilt and gratefulness. If carers are way down the ladder, then those they care for are at the bottom, popularly seen as exacting tyrants, as indifferent to their helpers' feelings as pampered pet poodles.

Caring isn't just about changing incontinence pads and wheeling inert lumps of flesh, draped in tartan blankets, around the shops on Saturday mornings. Give the carers the recognition they deserve. Give them the money. But don't reduce those who depend on them to dehumanised burdens, don't let their handicaps cancel out their identities. After all, you are only one visit to the doctor, one dash across the road, one hair's breadth away from being one too.

---

*From **Carers at Work**, based on the National Carers' Survey, carried out by Opportunities for Women, London, 1990, p. 5.*

Carers in general face tremendous problems, fears. I mean just look at the financial worry, constantly trying to make sure bills are paid, trying to juggle the different incomes, make them stretch far enough.

And then there's the isolation. A lot of carers get sucked into isolation. It depends on the relationship they have with the person they are caring for. I mean I am very very lucky, I have a good relationship with my mother-in-law and she is very easy to care for considering her disability. Other people get bogged down, and people stop calling and they can't go out. You don't have much of a social life. You can't really roll home at two o'clock in the morning and then get up at 7 or 8 o'clock to breakfast people and things like that . . . there's lots of problems.

It would be good from the psychological point of view for carers to be able to go out to work, but they would need to have some very secure support system. Because you don't actually know from one day to the next what's going to happen or what's going to meet you when you get up in the morning, or if the person's going to be more ill than usual. Or if you're going to be up during the night. If you are, you're not going to be bright-eyed and bushy-tailed first thing in the morning. So halfway through the next day you would be very very tired. Then it would be difficult to work because your concentration would go. Carers in the main, the ones who work and who I have contact with, are generally in low-paid menial jobs, just very part-time hours and very very low wages, which is very unfortunate.

The support system and the benefits for carers at the moment are by no means adequate. I mean they just don't cover anything. There's nothing out there comparable to what it would cost to keep a person in a nursing home or in a long-stay hospital or whatever.

10.4   Dilemmas

*An abridged extract from A. Richardson and J. Ritchie, **Making the Break: Parents' Views about Adults with Mental Handicap Leaving the Parental Home**, London, Kings Fund, 1986, p. xx.*

Matthew is 36 and mildly handicapped as the result of an accident at birth. He can read, write, has an excellent memory and is a keen musician. According to his parents, 'he's definitely a character. He's an extrovert in every sense of the word, with a tremendous sense of humour.'

Matthew's parents are in their 70s and his father, after a major operation, is now in very poor health. They have a very close relationship with Matthew and both are quite devoted to him. They feel they are over-protective with Matthew, but there is clearly a real dilemma. 'Being a parent you automatically do for them – you can't help it. Partly you want them to look good all the time and partly it's because you just want to keep on doing things for them.' Again they are aware that they could have done more to encourage Matthew to be independent. 'You want him to be independent but at the same time it's difficult to put over this independence, and you are forced to do things that *they* want you to do although you know you shouldn't do it. For example, he won't tie his shoe laces so in the end we finally buy shoes for him that have *no* laces – slip-on shoes and that gets over the problem. Well it's wrong.'

Matthew's mother admits to it having been a wrench when her three older sons left home but saw it as a natural progression. With Matthew it's different. 'I always thought I'd look after him as long as I could. [. . .] I'd keep myself in good health and look after him, and I have done.' But at the same time, both parents are aware that it's not necessarily the best thing for Matthew. 'I mean, that's obvious . . . you think you're doing the best for them but deep down you know damn well he'd been better off in a place where they'd have given him a thorough education – but would they have looked after him? Would they have given him a home life?'

Because of his father's illness, Matthew's parents have begun very reluctantly to consider the issue of his move from home. They have written for information about village communities and asked around about the local hostels. They feel that life in the 'village system' would be best for him because of the small, family type living arrangements. But if a place became available, 'a lot's dependent on Matthew – if he puts his foot down and doesn't want to go – I can't go against that, can I?'

Matthew's parents think it is most likely that he will eventually go to live in one of the local hostels. Deep down, his father knows that they should be taking some steps to effect a move in the very near future. 'We're not youngsters any more . . . [if he agreed to try to live elsewhere] I would be happy; it would be so terribly important for him.' But his mother is less sure that she could ever part with Matthew. 'He's part and parcel of my life . . . my life is Matthew. It has been for such a long time that I can't visualise it any other way. And I don't think I would want to.'

An extract from Frank Thomas's diary in **The Politics of Mental Handicap**, *by Joanna Ryan and Frank Thomas, Free Association Books, London, 1987, pp. 36–7.*

Helping at meal times on my first day nearly drove me into getting my coat and heading for home. Standing at the patients' meal trolley, wearing my crisp white clinical uniform, hearing the high-pitched abuse, the constant shouting at the patients to sit down and shut up, was enough to make me jack it all in on the spot.

There was perhaps one staff, Bruce, who treated the patients as humans, as individuals. In the following days I jolted him out of the apathy and despair he was experiencing with the situation. He at the same time convinced me that if we worked together we might get a few things done. The potentialities of the situation could be exploited only if I chose to stay.

Could I help the lads get through the day without feeling too bad, soften the blows they constantly received, give a more humane aspect to their nursing care? With Bruce's help this seemed possible. The snag was of course that there were the other staff to contend with. What was needed was an attempt to break down the rigid staff/patient dichotomy, to be a friend of the lads, with all that entails. Completely reject the authoritarian side of my role as staff.

All the bizarre happenings on the ward would still go on, but at least I could define a purpose in being there. To stay meant to a certain extent accepting the situation, but at the same time not being part of it – an insider and an outsider simultaneously.

You change. Whether you change the system or the system changes you, you change. Circumstances change to change you. People hit other people. Horrific. A daily occurrence. A norm. You want to vomit at the ever present reek of urine. You get used to it. People swear, defile, bite themselves, scream incessantly, say nothing, do less, go beserk at you, dribble for ever, have dried food all over their clothes, look a terrible grey mess. A superficial overview. You get to know the lads, it doesn't take too long. Each lad is a highly individual person in his own right. Such relationships can be very satisfying, rewarding and enjoyable experiences.

As far as I could, every time I saw a patient being harassed or bullied or abused, I would attempt to relieve the suffering, for suffering it was. And with those lads who were up to it, we discussed their situation freely – the hospital, the staff, the food, what it was all about. It was an opportunity to take a look at their situation for themselves without the other staff interfering, an experience they had not had before. If this smacks of anarchy, well – maybe what these hospitals need is a revolution to sort them out.

10.5 Rights

Mukti Jain Campion defends the right of disabled women to be parents. An abridged extract from the **Observer**, *14 July 1991.*

'It's obscene, people like you shouldn't be allowed to have children.' These were the words of a complete stranger thrust at a young pregnant woman out shopping one day in her wheel-chair.

The assailant knew nothing about her disability, her domestic situation or about her preparations to become a parent. Like many people, she had made a lot of assumptions:

- Disabled women shouldn't have sex (young people with disabilities don't need sex education or family planning advice).
- Disabled women are ill (so the child will be too).
- Disabled women cannot be adequate mothers (so it's selfish).

They are prejudices which are no more true of most disabled women than they are of the able-bodied. What is worrying is that these misconceptions are so prevalent that even professionals, such as teachers, doctors and social workers, are often infected by them.

The result is that thousands of healthy, fertile women are put off having children or pressured into abortions. And if they decide to have children, they have to negotiate a painful series of obstacle courses. Few hospitals have staff trained in disability awareness or in signing for the deaf. Childbirth itself can be made more frightening because of the lack of accurate information and optimistic support.

Then when the child is born the mother is often labelled as either a pathetic victim in need of pity, or a courageous heroine with no need of help. Both labels deny the woman's right to be treated as normal. The threat of children being taken into care also looms when fitness to parent is questioned.

So are disabled women fit to be mothers? The question suggests there is a norm, established by able-bodied parents, that disabled parents have to match. This is ludicrous.

All the research shows that, as far as the welfare of the child is concerned, disability is not a bar to being a competent, caring parent. Disability takes so many different forms that no outsider can generalise on whether it might prevent mothers from being fit to look after their own children. Thousands of women – with arthritis, multiple sclerosis, spina bifida, women who are blind or deaf, disabled since birth or in later life – have successfully borne and brought up children. Each has contributed her own version of normality and in the process enriched our society.

Some disabled women may need additional medical help in pregnancy or practical help with childcare, but then so do many able-bodied mothers. If disadvantages arise, they are often due to social repercussions of disability, such as poverty, poorly-adapted housing, isolation and, above all, public attitudes. These are society's failings, yet it is disabled mothers and their families who are penalised.

Things are changing slowly. Peer networks such as the one run by ParentAbility are springing up all over the country. These enable prospective mothers to tap into the wealth of advice and experience of others with similar disabilities.

Professionals, too, are putting disability and parenthood on their agenda.

It is often argued that not everyone has a right to be a parent. But if that is the case, selection criteria should be agreed and applied to everyone, not just to those who appear different.

In a historic case in the US, a judge returned a child to the care of a disabled mother whose fitness to be a parent had been questioned. He suggested that other people, as well as parents, could help with the physical aspects of childcare, but said the essence of parenting 'lies in the ethical, emotional and intellectual guidance the parent gives to the child throughout the formative years and beyond'. In this, he judged, the mother was thoroughly able.

Mike Lawson, from Survivors Speak Out, an organisation for people who use psychiatric services, and Jane Campbell, from the British Council of Disabled People, discuss the meaning of care to them as users of services. Extract from an interview for the Open University course K259 **Community Care**.

Mike:
I want the choice when I want to be cared for and when I want to be left alone like any other human being would and I don't want a special set of circumstances to be considered simply because I've been labelled as psychiatrically ill or whatever and I assume that this is a mutual sort of feeling.

Jane:
I'd say we don't want to be cared for at all. I would say that we want to be facilitated, supported and empowered. Care to me has connotations of custody and of lack of control and of looking after somebody who is sick and getting worse basically. Several people have actually become more and more to actually loathe the term care because it is being used in such a way to fudge the issue. You know, we have care and repair for all these

wheel-chair companies; now we have the caring government that really is going to look after us and make sure that care in the community really works well. Nothing could be more far from the truth. Then there's the carers – you know these paragons – these people who who care at the expense of their own lives, the burden of the disabled person who they look after. I'm just quoting some of the tabloids. This has actually made disabled people become very touchy around the whole notion of care because it's not what they want. What they want or what we want or what I want is to have control over my life, but at the times when it's difficult to do that then I want the support to actually get through that particular time. I would say caring and care in the community is about control – maintaining us in a certain position – and it's about seeing disabled people as people with individual problems. It's not empowering at all.

Filial Obligations and Kin Support for Elderly People*

JANET FINCH and JENNIFER MASON

11.1 Introduction

Research on the family care of elderly people has been a major growth area in recent years, in Britain as elsewhere. Underlying much of it – but often not addressed directly – are questions about the nature of obligation and responsibility within families, and how far these underscore the support which may be offered to elderly people who can no longer fully care for themselves. Research which has attempted to encompass these issues has tended to be conducted on a fairly small scale.[1]

This chapter is based on a large research project, which includes qualitative and quantitative data on kin obligations and support. We are confining ourselves to discussing data upon the care of elderly people and upon the obligations of children in particular. The central focus of our research is support which passes between kin and adult life, and how far this is underpinned by concepts of obligation, responsibility and duty. We are therefore concerned with issues about norms and morality in family life, and how far these constitute explanations of what people do, or do not do, for their relatives. Other explanations of what people do are possible, of course: personal preference or liking, pragmatic considerations or patterns of exchange built upon reciprocity over a lifetime. We are not excluding any of these – indeed we are very interested in trying to understand how they mesh together – but our central concern is the issue of normative obligations and how they operate. To put it very simply, in what

*This is an abridged version of a paper that was first published in *Ageing and Society*, Vol. 10, 1990, pp. 151–73.

sense do people support their kin because they see it as 'the proper thing to do'?

Our discussion locates these issues in the context of contemporary Britain, because the study upon which we draw was based in the north west of England. However, the issues which we raise are fundamental to understanding the nature of final obligations in any society. Existing literature on kinship in Britain would suggest that if we are going to find a strong sense of duty or obligation anywhere, we will find it in parent–child relationships. It is variously described in this literature as the central kinship bond, the least ambiguous of adult kin relationships and the relationship most clearly founded upon a sense of obligation.[2]

The classic kinship literature indicates that it is widely seen as legitimate for parents who are elderly to make demands on their adult children, but that literature also suggests that it is possible for parents to overstep the mark by demanding *too much* and also by making demands in the *wrong way*. Alongside this we also have to place the substantial evidence that a situation of total dependence of elderly people on their children seems to be widely regarded as undesirable. Townsend's classic study of the family life of old people[3] popularised the phrase 'intimacy at a distance' to describe the desired relationships between elderly people and their children, and later studies do seem to keep confirming that.[4]

There are also predictable sources of variation in the support which passes between elderly people and their children, most obviously related to gender and ethnicity. The classic kinship literature documents the central role which women play in the maintenance of family relationships ('kin keeping'), and there is also ample evidence that when it comes to the more arduous of the practical tasks, these are usually performed by daughters, or indeed daughters-in-law, rather than sons.[5] Clearly that reflects the gender division of responsibility and labour in the performance of domestic tasks more generally, a division which itself varies in different ethnic groups. There is a separate, but linked question about whether women and men display a different sense of obligation and duty towards their parents, or their relatives more generally. Some feminist writers have argued persuasively that 'a sense of responsibility' permeates women's approach to family relationships in a way which is not replicated for men.[6]

These then, are the kinds of issue which form the background to our study. The questions which we are raising are:

(1) Do people in contemporary Britain clearly acknowledge that parent–child relations are founded upon norms of obligation (rather than personal preference, pragmatic considerations, etc.)?

(2) What is the substance of these norms? Is there anything

approaching a consensus about what parents can expect from their children?

(3) How do norms operate in practice?

11.2   Public norms about filial obligations

We begin with some of the data from the Family Obligations survey. This was conducted in the Great Manchester area in late 1985 and involved interviews with 978 adults of all ages.

The purpose of the survey was to investigate how far it is true to say there is a public normative consensus about obligations between adult kin. We wanted to see if there is any level of agreement among a random sample of the population about what counts as 'the proper thing to do' for relatives in specified circumstances. We were not trying to use the survey to generate data about what people *actually* do for their own relatives – that came at the second stage of the study, which was based on in-depth interviews with some of the people who had been in the survey, and some of their relatives. Nor were we wishing to make any prior assumptions about the relationship between beliefs and values expressed in our survey and the ways in which people arrive at commitments to their own relatives. Again, it is in the second stage of the study that we have tried to explore the extent to which people are guided by a sense of 'the proper thing to do' in relationships with their own relatives.[7] In the survey, our method was to assess whether there is agreement about proper forms of obligation between kin, mainly by using questions about hypothetical situations concerning third parties, in which people were invited to indicate what the participants 'should' do.

11.2.1   Do people give assent to the idea of filial obligations?

At the most general level, our survey data suggest that most people do give assent at this normative level to the idea of filial obligations (i.e. that adult children are obligated to their parents), but that this assent is neither universal nor unconditional. When presented with a bald attitude statement: 'Children have no obligation to look after their parents when they are old', 57 per cent of our sample disagreed and 39 per cent agreed. Disagreement with this statement indicates assent to the idea of filial obligations, and we can see that although a majority fall into this category, a sizeable minority do not.[8]

In various other more specific questions concerned with examples of middle-aged or elderly people needing assistance, again a majority seemed to give approval to the idea of filial obligations. We had a whole series of questions in which we spelled out a situation, asked respondents to presume that some relative was going to provide assistance and invited them to say *which* relative this should be. Respondents were not presented with a list of options so that, in effect, they could propose any permutation of relatives they wished. In all circumstances where a child could be presumed to exist, children were the clearest targets. Tables 11.1–11.4 give some examples from these questions, which are concerned both with financial and practical assistance.

A number of points could be explored in relation to these tables – for example, the variations in people's responses according to the type of assistance needed. However, we use them here for a fairly limited purpose: to focus upon what is being said about who should offer help. Although there is some variation in the preferences expressed, it is noticeable that they remain concentrated in a very narrow genealogical range. Of course there is nothing startling about this pattern, but it does confirm empirically that, at the level of publicly expressed norms, most people do see children as the people who should step in first and offer assistance even when other relatives are presumed to be available. A few people did mention siblings, grandchildren or more distant relatives, but they were in a very small minority.

Thus the data contained in these tables suggest fairly strong support for the idea of filial obligations specifically – the special responsibilities of children over other relatives. This seems to hold for all the questions where we asked our respondents to assume that *some* relative was going to provide assistance for an elderly person. These answers have to be understood in the light of knowing that a sizeable minority of our survey population would not necessarily have wanted care to come from relatives at all – or at least did not regard this as the optimum solution. That is illustrated in Table 11.4, for example, where 35 per cent thought that relatives definitely should not offer money to pay for decorating. In relation to the situations posed in Tables 11.1–11.3, earlier in the interview between 56 per cent and 70 per cent of our respondents had opted for some solution other than family care, when they were given the choice of state care, privately paid for care, care by relatives or care by friends. Presumably what these respondents were telling us is: I would prefer the responsibility not to fall on the family, if it has to be relatives, then it should be children.

However, although our data suggest that people generally see it as appropriate that adult children should do *something* to support their parents, there is less broad agreement as to exactly what children should do. In fact, our data often point to different ways of fulfilling obligations legitimately. One of our questions which illustrates this particularly well is concerned with a middle-aged couple facing the dilemma of what to do about the husband's parents who live several hundred miles away, and who have been seriously injured in a car accident. Proportions of our

TABLE 11.1 Caring for an elderly woman: which relatives should offer assistance?

Introductory statement to Tables 11.1 to 11.3

I would like to ask you about some situations in which people might need personal care. This time, let's suppose that the help is going to come from a relative.* In each case, the person has a lot of relatives living nearby who could help.

An elderly woman who can manage well living alone but who needs help getting up and going to bed. Which relative should be the first to offer help?

	Number of respondents	%
Daughter	663	67.8
Children	102	10.4
Son	43	4.3
Sister	42	4.2
Brother/sister	10	1.0
Other named relative	18	1.8
Whole family/all equally	33	3.3
Immediate/closest	9	0.9
Who is available/can cope	8	0.8
Other	16	1.6
Don't know/not applicable	34	3.4
Total	**978**	**100.0**

*Respondents had been asked to consider these same situations earlier in the interview, but had been asked different questions about them.

TABLE 11.2 Caring for a woman recovering from a hip operation: which relatives should offer assistance?

An elderly woman who lives alone and who has to stay in bed all day for the next few months following a hip operation. Which relative should be the first to offer help?

	Number of respondents	%
Daughter	646	66.0
Children	94	9.6
Son	33	3.3
Sister	59	6.0
Brother/sister	9	0.9
Other named relative	12	1.2
Whole family/all equally	53	5.4
Immediate/closest	12	1.2
Who is available/can cope	4	0.4
Other	13	1.3
Don't know/not applicable	43	4.3
Total	**978**	**100.0**

TABLE 11.3   Caring for an elderly and confused man: which relatives should offer assistance?

An elderly man who can move about well, and who lives alone, but who gets confused and who needs someone to go in regularly several times a week to check that everything is safe. Which relative should be the first to offer help?

	Number of respondents	%
Son	382	39.0
Daughter	299	30.6
Children	90	9.2
Brother	46	4.7
Sister	28	2.8
Brother/sister	7	0.7
Other named relative	19	1.9
Whole family/all equally	43	4.3
Immediate/closest	9	0.9
Who is available/can cope	7	0.7
Other	15	1.5
Don't know/not applicable	33	3.3
Total	**978**	**100.0**

TABLE 11.4   Decorating an elderly couple's house: should relatives help to pay?

(*a*) Suppose an elderly couple need money to redecorate their home. Do you think that relatives should offer to pay to have the work done?

	Number of respondents	%
Yes	538	55.0
No	342	35.0
Depends	98	10.0
Total	**978**	**100.0**

(*b*) Respondents who said 'yes' or 'depends' – up to three answers post-coded. Assuming that they could all afford to help which relatives, if any, should be the first to offer money?

	Number of respondents	%
Son	247	38.8
Children	138	21.7
Daughter	27	4.2
Other named relatives	24	3.8
All equally/whole family	113	17.7
Whoever can afford it	32	5.0
Immediate/closest family	11	1.7
Don't know/not applicable/other answer	44	6.9
Total	**636**	**100.0**

sample choosing the various options were as follows: move to live near the husband's parents 33 per cent; have the parents move to live with them 24 per cent; give the parents money to help them pay for daily care 25 per cent; let the parents make their own arrangements 9 per cent. Only the last option suggests that the couple have no filial responsibility, and even there people may well have expected that they would, in fact, provide some kind of support. Viewed in this way, we can say that 82 per cent of our sample were assenting to the notion of filial responsibility, but were acknowledging different ways of fulfilling it.

11.2.2   Do people distinguish between children in relation to their filial obligations?

We did not have any questions in the survey which explored in detail whether people distinguish between different children when allocating responsibility for parents, but our data do give us some clues here.

First, there does not seem to be any significant inclination to distinguish children by birth order. We had expected that people might see the obligations of an eldest son or daughter as 'stronger' than the rest, but very few specified this on those open-ended questions where we invited them to name a relative (as above).

Second, there is a clear sense in the data of people wanting to follow an 'equal shares' principle if at all possible. Tables 11.1–11.4 all have substantial proportions of respondents who say that the 'children' should assist the elderly people in question, without making any further distinction, or who specify that it should be 'the whole family' or 'all equally'. This occurs in questions where people were asked to say who should offer *first*, directing them to name a single individual, so we take this to be quite a strong response.

Third, there is clearly some tendency to distinguish between sons and daughters in the allocation of responsibilities, although this is not as straightforward as stereotypes would predict. The equal shares principle suggests that many people see both sons and daughters as targets for providing assistance to parents, although in the case of providing money (Table 11.4) a substantial proportion of our respondents specify that it should be a son. When it comes to providing care (Tables 11.1–11.3), the question of where the responsibility should fall apparently depends upon the gender of the person needing care, at least for some of our respondents. Where an elderly woman needs care (Tables 11.1 and 11.2), a daughter is the clear preference of two-thirds of our respondents. For an elderly man both daughters and sons are regarded as appropriate to take prime responsibility. (What 'taking responsibility' means could, of course, be different for daughters and sons, but we cannot explore that on the basis of these data.) This pattern is repeated elsewhere in all these questions is quite complex, and certainly does not just follow gender stereotypes, there are some situations in which gender does seem to have a clear impact upon people's normative judgements: daughters are rarely chosen as the appropriate people to provide money, and sons are rarely chosen as the people who should provide care for an elderly woman.

11.2.3   Do filial obligations have limits?

One important way to test out the significance of publicly expressed norms about filial obligations is to consider whether they have limits and, if so, of what kind. Our data enable us to make two points about this.

First, the quality of the relationship between a parent and adult child does not seem to have much impact upon the way responsibilities are allocated – at least not at this level of publicly acknowledged norms. We asked one question about whether a person should be prepared to make daily visits to look after his or her elderly father, even if they have never got on well together (Table 11.5); 72 per cent of people said 'yes'. Neither respondents' gender nor their social class was apparently related to the answers they gave, although there was a small tendency for people over the age of 65 to answer 'yes' more frequently than younger people. Table 11.5 also shows that, for about half of the respondents who thought that a child should visit despite a poor relationship, a key consideration was the fact that the relative in question was a *father* since, when we substituted 'uncle' for 'father', the proportion saying 'yes' dropped to 40 per cent.

This 'strong' view of filial obligations is supported elsewhere in our survey data. For example, one of our examples concerned an elderly woman and her daughter, who had never got along well. They had quarrelled, and the older woman had cut the daughter out of her will. Yet in this case, 37 per cent of people still thought that the daughter should offer her mother a home when she needed it – a proportion very similar to answers given in other questions about children giving a home to elderly parents, where the circumstances were less contentious. So it appears that the particular circumstances in this question, including a very poor relationship between mother and daughter, have little effect on the number of people prepared to endorse the principle of filial obligations. In general, people do not seem to 'count' the quality of the relationship as a factor which legitimately puts limits upon the obligations of children to their elderly parents.

Second, the fact that the quality of the relationship does not set limits does not mean that there are no limits at all to filial obligations. In another of our examples, we set up a situation where a middle-aged couple would be torn in two directions – between moving several

TABLE 11.5   Obligation to visit and 'getting on'

(*a*) Should a person be prepared to make daily visits to look after his or her elderly father, even if they have not got on well together?

	Number of respondents	%
Yes	704	72.0
No	220	22.5
Depends	49	5.0
Not applicable	5	0.5
Total	**978**	**100.0**

(*b*) And should a person be prepared to make daily visits to look after his or her uncle, even if they have never got on well together?

	Number of respondents	%
Yes	390	39.9
No	486	49.7
Depends	90	9.2
Don't know / not applicable	12	1.2
Total	**978**	**100.0**

hundred miles away to care for the husband's parents, or staying put because their own children were at a crucial stage in their education (coming up to O-levels). Here there was much clearer agreement about the proper thing to do: 78 per cent said that they should stay put, and 20 per cent that they should move, which we interpret to mean that four out of five of our respondents thought that the needs of the younger generation should take precedence over the older. Thus there *are* normative limits upon filial obligations and, in this instance, these are set by the need to fulfil other responsibilities which are seen as taking precedence.

In summary, our findings do seem to confirm the normative strength and importance of filial ties, but also underline that they do not entail unconditional responsibilities. It seems then that there is a degree of public normative consensus (although by no means universal) that children should do *something* to assist their parents in these types of circumstances, but it is not always clear what that should be, who should do it, or what limits might apply to filial obligations.

If various different courses of action *could* constitute the 'proper thing to do', then two consequences follow. First, on an individual level, each person necessarily has to engage in a task of 'working out' what to do for his or her own parents in a given set of circumstances. The appropriate course of action does not present itself as obvious, as if it were a well-defined rule where the only choice left to the individual is to obey it or break it. Second, there is the task of presenting one's actions publicly and getting other people to accept that they lie within the legitimate range of filial obligations. These two processes might be consecutive (you decide what you are going to do first then you sell it to other people), but equally they might operate in parallel (your assessment of what other people will accept as legitimate may well influence precisely what you decide to do for your parents).[9] On the basis of our survey findings, it seems likely that both processes have to be worked at actively, but clearly we need quite different kinds of data to get further with understanding that.

We can say that relationships between parents and children *are* importantly founded on a sense of obligation, but one which recognises definite limits. there is not a clear consensus about what it is reasonable to expect. However, there are well understood principles which can be mobilised when you are working out 'the proper thing to do' in practice. People do have an understanding of what would be generally accepted as proper, but they use it as a resource with which to negotiate rather than as a rule to follow.

Notes

1. For example, Ungerson, C., *Policy is Personal*, Tavistock, London, 1987; Lewis, J. and Meredith, B., *Daughters Who Care*, Routledge, London, 1988.
2. Morgan, D. H. J., *Social Theory and the Family*, Routledge and Kegan Paul, London, 1975.
3. Townsend, P. *The Family Life of Old People*, Routledge and Kegan Paul, London, 1957.
4. Firth, R., Hubert, J. and Forge, A., *Families and their Relatives*, Routledge and Kegan Paul, London, 1969; Allan, G., 'Kinship, responsibility and care for elderly people', *Ageing and Society*, Vol. 8 (1988), pp. 249–68.
5. Firth *et al. op. cit.*; Wenger, G. C., *The Supportive Network*, Allen and Unwin, London, 1984; Qureshi, H. and Simons, K., 'Resources within families: caring for elderly people', in Brannen, J. and Wilson, G. (eds), *Give and Take in Families*, Allen and Unwin, London, 1987.
6. Graham, H., 'Caring: a labour of love', in Finch, J. and Groves, D. (eds), *A Labour of Love: Women, Work and Caring*, Routledge and Kegan Paul, London, 1983; Cornwell, J., *Hard-Earned Lives*, Tavistock, London, 1984; Ungerson, *op. cit.*
7. The findings from this aspect of the study have not been included in this extract.
8. This and other attitude statements in our survey were taken from another study, in Scotland in 1982, directed by Patrick West. Patterns of response to this question were similar on both surveys. (See West, P., 'The family, the welfare state and community care: political rhetoric and public attitudes',

Journal of Social Policy, Vol. 13, No. 4 (1984), pp. 417–46). There were some differences among our survey population in answering the attitude statement about filial obligations. Notably, older people were more divided in their views than younger people. In the 18–29 age group, 65 per cent supported the principle of filial obligations.

9. Finch, J., *Family Obligations and Social Change*, Polity, Cambridge, 1989.

Acknowledgement

The project discussed in this paper was funded by the Economic and Social Research Council 1985–89 (Grant number GOO 23 2197).

12

At Home and Alone: Families and Young Adults with Challenging Behaviour*

JANE HUBERT

This chapter is based on an intensive study of 20 families with teenagers or young adults who have severe or profound learning difficulties and challenging behaviour living in one county of southern England. . . . The 20 young people are between the ages of 14 and 22 years old, have little or no speech and have few basic skills. Some are very physically disabled, and spend much of the time in wheelchairs, whereas others are highly mobile. Most are subject to epilepsy, and the majority are incontinent. Their challenging behaviour, where it exists, ranges from aggression and self-injury to destructiveness and non-compliance.

[. . .] Since the birth of their children, the parents had been waging an almost continuous battle to keep going, with help and support from the local health and social services often proving unreliable and inadequate. Many of them, determined to keep their child at home in spite of the enormous problems this often caused to themselves and to their families, found that other people, including professionals, often responded to their crises and their cries for help with defeatism, suggesting that permanent care away from home would 'solve' the problem. To parents who are asking for help to do just the opposite this response is unhelpful, and indicates a lack of understanding of what they actually want and feel. It also tends to add to their sense of frustration, since it

*This is an abridged extract from a chapter in Booth, T. (ed.) (1990) *Better Lives: Changing Services for People with Learning Difficulties*, Social Services Monograph, pp. 105–14.

appears to them that they are fighting a battle which the professionals already consider to be a losing one. [. . .]

Almost all the mothers find it difficult to manage if their young adult child is at home all day every day – which often happens during holidays or bouts of illness. The daily routine is already extremely demanding. In addition to all the usual day-to-day tasks involved in family life, they must attend to the almost continuous basic needs of a young adult – washing, dressing, toileting and changing incontinence pads, feeding, carrying and in most cases having to be in the same room for almost every minute of the- day. For many the task continues at intervals throughout the night – in response to cries of discomfort, to change wet bedclothes, or to hold and comfort their child through each epileptic fit.

Families such as these walk a narrow tightrope, and any upheaval or crisis within the family – not necessarily related to the disabled young adult – can upset a delicate balance between managing or not managing to get through each day. Most of the mothers work to a precise and precarious schedule, easily thrown out of gear by any lack of response by professionals to relatively simple requests for such things as more incontinence pads, wheelchair repairs, dressings or even a lift to the hospital, let alone requests for more major help, such as the provision of a downstairs toilet or bedroom, a stairlift or the widening of a bathroom door.

The most essential service, according to most parents, is access to short-term residential care, which allows them at least an occasional night without their disabled child at home. Many say it is these breaks that make it possible to keep going, although two families have found their experience of the units so unpleasant, for them and for their children, that they no longer make use of the service. In the county under study, short-term residential care is available in long-term National Health Service residential units, run by senior, qualified nurses, with a staff of trained and untrained care assistants. In most cases the young adults spend a weekend away at regular intervals, with perhaps a week or two in the summer holidays.

Many parents spoke of the children's residential units as sympathetic and friendly places, but at the age of 16 their children have to leave these, and the transition to adult units is often abrupt and distressing for both parents and children.

Apart from this unwelcome change from children's to adult services, parents are often, at this stage, facing all kinds of other changes and crises: for example, other children in the family having adolescent problems or leaving home, mothers facing hysterectomies, grandparents slipping from potentially useful roles into increasing dependence. Altogether, it is often a trying time during which parents feel they need greater support than ever before. Instead, many of them find there is less support, less interest in their children and a correspondingly greater battle to get an acceptable level of care for them.

The transition from children's to adult units is considered by most parents to be too early, and in most cases far too abrupt. Ideally there would be no administrative switch, but if there must be one then it should happen a few years later. Such a move should also be made gradually – preferably with others of the same age group to reduce any sense of isolation – so that the young people can grow accustomed to the new environment before being finally cut off from the children's unit. Few parents feel their 16-year-olds are ready to be plunged into an adult environment. Not only are adult residential units very different from the children's unit, but they are also full of many older people who may have been institutionalised for most of their lives. Parents would prefer small, home-like units which cater for short-term residents only.

Although almost all of the parents in this study do make use of short-term care facilities, many still feel guilty about letting their children go away even for one night, mainly because they feel that the level of care is inadequate. In spite of this dissatisfaction with the quality of the care, they know that they need occasional breaks even though for many of them these few days are spent worrying about what might be happening to their child, rather than enjoying a recuperative and stress-free period of rest.

In fact the demands that parents make of the short-term residential care services are very basic, and all are aspects of the same thing – quality of care. This is the fundamental issue, and one that is determined by a wide range of policies and people from national policy makers and health authority administrators to the care staff working in the units.

An important part of this care is basic physical care: the provision of adequate and appropriate food, warmth and rest. It also includes the right to cleanliness and comfort, which may involve constant vigilance and work with those young people who are incontinent or who are unable to move or who dribble continuously. It is the inadequacy of this physical care that angers and saddens many of the parents, especially those whose sons and daughters cannot walk and are sometimes left sitting in their urine, even in faeces, their tee-shirts stiff with dried dribble. Parents believe that attention to such basic needs is an essential right of their young adult children, and that they are only treated in this way because they are unable to protest or to express their discomfort.

Another aspect of care that concerns parents is the protection of their children from harm of any kind. Few of these young people are able to protect themselves from the actions of others, whether these are direct acts of aggression or merely mistakes made by the staff responsible for their well-being. Mistakes of this kind do occur – in such things as the preparation of food for those who cannot chew, or in the administration of drugs. Often it is the latter – the prescription and administration of drugs – that causes the most acute concern to parents.

Almost all the young people concerned are on regular medication of one or more kinds. Three-quarters are on anti-convulsants to control their epilepsy, the majority on more than one. Other drugs include anti-psychotics, anti-depressants and hypnotics. Apart from general anxiety about the number and levels of regular drugs, parents are particularly worried, when their children are in short-term care, by the possibility of unacceptably high dosages of drugs being given, either deliberately – to suppress violent behaviour or to deal with sleep problems – or by mistake. Such overdosages have occurred, and tend not to be adequately explained or excused.

Parents are well aware that mistakes are easily made in a situation where there are few staff and many people to be cared for, each with specific individual needs. However, when such accidents happen, they are justifiably angry and become even more unwilling to let their children out of their sight. They may not blame the members of staff involved, but this does not affect their basic complaint that their adult children are receiving inadequate care.

As their children grow older and become adult, parents know there will be even fewer people who will want to look after them and who will be concerned with their individual needs. To them it is a labour of love, but they have few illusions about the nature of the task. Moreover, parents sometimes feel that because their physical needs are so time-consuming care staff only respond to the young people at this basic level and seldom pay attention to their emotional or intellectual needs. The young people are often left to sit alone, or to wander around the building for most of the day, receiving very little affection or understanding, and with few opportunities to try to communicate in whatever way they can.

Many parents feel that care staff do not respond to the changes that are taking place in their children, and that they often disregard their intellectual, perceptual and emotional development – including sexual awareness. They consider that carers should take account of this as they attend to the personal needs of these young people. Allowances should be made for feelings of embarrassment and pride, even if they cannot be expressed. Carers should act on the assumption, for example, that those they care for would prefer their incontinence to be treated as a private matter, and would rather not be seen to be sitting in wet clothes, or be changed in front of other people.

At the same time, one of the criticisms parents level at the adult residential units is the apparent assumption that those who are transferred to them for short-term care at 19 suddenly cease to be children altogether, and become fully-fledged adults. Often they are deprived of the physical and emotional comforts that they are used to at home and used to have at the children's unit, but which are no longer considered 'age-appropriate' – a concept which, in this context, seems to override individual needs and desires.

Through their intimate experience with their children since birth, parents are aware of the infinite complexity of their abilities and disabilities, of their likes and dislikes, and recognise the many different 'ages' they may be at any one time. The fact that someone enjoys sensations such as chewing, squeezing and banging does not mean that this source of enjoyment is the sum total of their intellectual and physical needs.

Because of their disquiet about the quality of care for their young adult children, the parents in this study are faced with a very real dilemma. Two families resolved this by refusing to allow their children to go into short-term residential care at all, whatever the cost to the main carer and the other members of the family. For the other 18 families, the choice has been to make use of the service, however distressing this may sometimes be. In fact, most feel they must have these breaks to survive, and as a result consider it essential that they should be able to count on a reliable short-term care service. The survival of these families has often relied upon a fragile balance between the various needs of different members of the family, including agreements – whether explicit or not – between husband and wife. For this balance to be maintained it is essential that there is a reliable agreement with the service agencies. Any unexpected gaps in availability of short-term care, or changes in frequency of breaks, or in agreed dates, may threaten the stability of the families concerned.

One of the major penalties paid by many families, especially the mothers, of keeping a highly dependent child at home is the loss of any social or community life, and a gradual erosion of relationships with friends and kin outside the household. This is especially true when there is also very challenging behaviour to contend with. The problems involved in maintaining relationships are less acute when the children are small. They are more portable, more easily contained by car seats and pushchairs. As they grow older, behaviour that is tolerated in a young child may, in an adult, be seen by other people as threatening or even dangerous. Even trips to local shops or to a neighbour's house may be too daunting to contemplate with a teenager who is likely to start shrieking, 'throw a wobbly', or kick and grab at people and objects within reach.

Apart from the problems involved in taking their young adults out, it is also difficult to leave them at home. Few of them can be left at home with a 'sitter'. Thus any outing has to be planned far in advance and often depends on the availability of a short-term bed for the night. Ordinary social relationships, based on mutual visits and joint outings, often lapse to the point that mothers, at least, sometimes cease to have any social life whatsoever. In many cases fathers, or partners, may well continue to have an outside life, at least during the day.

Thus, ironically, by keeping their children at home 'in the community', the families as a whole and the mothers as individuals may, in effect, cut themselves off from the community. This is not only the result of practical problems and lack of mobility. Relationships may well be affected by infrequency of contact, but many mothers in the study also feel their isolation is greater because, as the years pass, they have less and less in common with their kin and friends who have children of the same age. It is when other people's children are beginning to live adult lives – getting jobs, going to college, leaving home and getting married – that these parents feel particularly excluded. The things that happen to them in their daily lives, and the successes and failures that they experience in connection with their children, have no counterpart in the lives of their relatives and friends.

In spite of such social isolation, and the awareness of a potentially very different life, these parents continue to resist pressure to put their adult children into permanent care. Most of them are used to this sort of pressure, whether it be from kin or friends or professionals, but as their children become adults there is often a new wave to overcome. Professionals tell them it is normal for teenagers to leave home, to become independent of their parents, and abnormal for a mother to devote her life to an adult child. But these parents know their children will never have any real independence and will remain totally dependent on other people for their most basic needs. In fact, if they left home, they would move into an environment in which they would be even less autonomous than they are now, since their needs and wishes would be less understood by those around them, and in most cases there would be no one prepared to try to interpret the often minute signs that parents have learnt to understand. Thus many would probably live the rest of their lives without ever having another close and reciprocally satisfying relationship.

Many of these parents would be pleased to let their children live away from home, at least for longer periods of time, if they knew there was any *viable* alternative for them somewhere else. So far, all their experiences have proved to them that there is no acceptable alternative to keeping them at home. In particular, their wide and varied experience of short-term respite care has convinced many of them that, judged by the low standards and level of neglect suffered in a week away, the prospect of a life in residential care is intolerable.

This chapter has only covered a small part of the results of the research carried out with these families but it will, perhaps, have given some idea of the sorts of problems faced by parents who want to keep their adult children at home. Because they see no acceptable alternative they are determined to continue, whatever happens, to have their children living at home. Three-quarters of them say they would rather their children should actually die than go into permanent care away from home.

There are many conclusions to be drawn. Among the most obvious is that services to families should be better co-ordinated, and so arranged as to make it possible for them to keep a young adult at home for as long as they choose. This calls for simple and quick ways of getting help when necessary both at the basic level (of having incontinence pads delivered, wheelchairs mended, support at home in crises and so on) and also at the level of providing alternative care of an acceptable quality away from home as regularly and as frequently as individual parents required.

Increased funding and adequate staffing (in terms of numbers, training and quality) would go a long way towards achieving this goal, but this is only part of the answer. This study has revealed that it is not only adequate staff and funding that is lacking. Most parents feel that once their children are adult no one – except their families – really cares about them or what happens to them. As they become adult, it is as though their learning difficulties and challenging behaviour are all that most people see and react to. They often cease to be treated as fellow human beings, with the same needs, preferences and dislikes as other people. Even more disturbing is the lack of understanding of these young people's doubts, confusions and fears.

The professionals may consider parents' 'overprotective' of their young adult children, but such protectiveness generally arises from an intimate knowledge and understanding of them as whole people, who lack only the ability to care for themselves and to communicate their own needs and fears to others.

Until there is a major change in attitudes towards adults with severe and profound learning difficulties, these families will continue to watch and worry, and will be forced to continue to fight their own individual battles for the basic rights of their adult children.

Breaking the Silence: Black and Ethnic Minority Carers and Service Provision

YASMIN GUNARATNAM

Since the 1970s a significant body of research on 'informal' care within the family has emerged, which has also held implications for wider social policy developments. Yet more than twenty years later, much of the literature is still largely ethnocentric, with a conspicuous lack of research that systematically recognises and explores how ethnicity can shape caring relationships. Within this context, this chapter has two main aims: first, at a practical level, it aims to identify and address some of the ways in which ethnicity can affect social relations of caring, and in particular experiences of service provision; secondly, at a more conceptual level, it suggests that the process of addressing 'race' can significantly expand and build a dynamism into the way we see and think about caring relationships.

In examining experiences of caring, this chapter also draws upon my own research for the King's Fund, on a project to produce information for Asian carers of elderly people (Gunaratnam, 1991). The project involved semi-structured interviews with 33 Asian carers, mainly in London, Birmingham, Bradford and Derbyshire.

13.1 Attending to diversity

In examining the ways in which ethnicity can affect caring, I will be looking at a range of experiences and social situations. As such, it is important to begin by addressing the analytical clumsiness of conceptualising 'black and ethnic minority' carers as an undifferentiated, homogeneous group of people who share the same experiences and needs. Not only are there significant variations *between* the experiences of different ethnic groups, but there are also differences *within* groups, and both can be influenced by factors such as class, migration history, gender and the disability of the person requiring care.

For example, drawing upon both general and specific data on black and ethnic minority people and class, it is possible to identify the complex interactions between ethnicity, class, health status and caring. Thus data from the Labour Force Survey (OPCS, 1991) show that minority workers occupy a vulnerable position in the labour market, being more likely to be in manual or working-class occupations than white people. More general data have further suggested that working-class people have higher rates of physical impairment and poor health status (Townsend *et al.*, 1988) and that, as carers, they are more likely to be coresident carers, with a greater level of caring responsibilities than middle-class people (Arber and Ginn, 1992). As Patel (1993) has also argued, labour market marginalisation can compound poverty in retirement through reduced levels of pensionable income.

With these findings in mind, it is important to note that there are significant class differences between ethnic communities. For example Afro-Caribbean people are particularly marginalised within employment, with over 70 per cent being in manual occupations, compared with 54 per cent of white workers (OPCS, 1991). However data on Asian communities are more complex, and serve to illustrate the influences of class and migration history within communities. Thus it appears that, of the different South Asian communities, Pakistani and Bangladeshi people are disproportionately concentrated in manual occupations (OPCS, 1991; Employment Department, 1994). In terms of caring, what such data point to is the need to recognise a diversity of both experiences of disability and of caring within different communities. Therefore, while this chapter will seek to make links between experiences of caring based upon ethnicity, it will also address diversity.

13.2   Families and caring: myths and stereotypes

For a Black family (irrespective of 'ethnicity') the popular image is one of an extended family network, 'families' within families', providers of care and social and psychological support.

(Patel, 1990, p. 36)

Perhaps the most dominant stereotype of black and ethnic minority communities, and in particular Asian communities, is that they do not make use of support services because of a preference for 'looking after their own' (Walker and Ahmad, 1994; Yee, 1995). Such assumptions are closely tied up with images of minority extended-family and household structures, where caring for ill or disabled family members is a 'natural' function. As Walker and Ahmad (1994) have argued, such images of caring gain a particular resonance within the broader discourses of community care: 'The resilience of the stereotype goes to the heart of thinking about community care, encapsulating the 'natural' morality of familial caring for the vulnerable' (p. 634).

While there is insufficient empirical data to allow us to deconstruct stereotypes of family structures and caring, it is apparent that there are more subtle and complex relations of caring within communities. For example, at a broad level, research has shown that patterns do exist in household composition between communities, with South Asian peoples having larger families and Afro-Caribbean and African peoples having a greater proportion of single-parent households (Berrington, 1994). However such data need to be addressed cautiously, since information on household structure and size does not actually tell us anything about the nature of caring relationships, or how they vary between the different generations. Indeed a series of studies of the Chinese community in Liverpool (Au and Au, 1994) found that of a sample of 46 Chinese elders, only 11 of the 31 people who had children were actually living with them.

My own research revealed a variety of relationships and patterns of care, including elderly couples living alone in reciprocal caring relationships; elaborate systems of shared secondary care by relatives and friends living separately from the person requiring care; and lone carers whose relatives either did not live in this country or lived some distance away. In fact only 8 of the 33 carers lived in 'extended', multi-generational families.

One of the most important issues, however, that appears to have got lost in debates about family structures and caring within minority communities, is a concern for understanding the meaning and nature of caring within families. For example research on 'black' (African-American) and white elders in the United States (Groger and Kunkel, 1995) suggests that there were important differences in the meanings attributed to similar forms of caring and support between the black and white elders in the study:

> food exchanges among Blacks were important subsistence activities, as are the frequent exchanges of small amounts of money. Among whites, food exchanges serve as vehicles for expressing affect, while their more infrequent

exchanges of relatively significant amounts of money serve to transfer wealth to the next generation.

(Groger and Kunkel, 1995, p. 284)

In terms of carers, what my research also highlighted was that carers' gendered identity within the family, and their own perceptions, were critical in determining the nature of caring. These factors were particularly significant with regard to the distinction between the simple presence of family networks and the actual practical support available and how it was received. For example, in the following two extracts it is useful to consider the elderly Punjabi woman's reluctance to 'trouble' her son for help in the first case, and the second younger Pakistani woman's feelings of isolation and frustration with the lack of support from her wider family:

> We live in my son's house. The toilet and bathroom are upstairs and we live in the downstairs. So every time he [husband] wants to go to the toilet, my son has to take him up and down. I can't do it. I'm too old and I haven't got my eyesight. I would like to live near my son in another house. We are too much trouble to him and he has three small children to look after.

> My brothers and sisters-in-law don't want to look after my Mum because they think she is too demanding on them. They can't take looking after her, it would take up too much of their time and energy. So they have left it all to me.
>
> I'd like to spend more time with my Mother . . . but it is difficult. I have so much pressure from my husband, my in-laws and the business. I don't know what to do . . . I'm the only daughter and I should be looking after my Mother, and I want to, it is just all the circumstances that are making it difficult.
>
> I think it's probably easier for men. My brothers do not see my Mother as their responsibility. But I am the only daughter, how can I turn my back on her?

What such examples illustrate is the need for both researchers and service providers to explore the nature and meanings of caring within black and ethnic minority communities. Ill-informed assumptions about the greater caring resources within minority families have served to limit service provision and support (Walker and Ahmad, 1994), and are a particular cause of concern. However, in challenging such discriminatory stereotypes, anti-racist researchers and practitioners have failed to grapple with the complexities of how caring relationships can be influenced by individual identity, cultural prescriptions and wider socio-economic conditions.

13.3   Service provision: accessibility and appropriateness

There is much evidence to show that poor take-up of service provision by
Black carers is due to the difficulties of getting to services and the way services are publicised, organised and prioritised.

(Yee, 1995, p. 33)

Closely related to the stereotype about greater caring resources within
black and ethnic minority communities is a 'common sense' generalisa-
tion that minority communities are insular and self-servicing and therefore do not 'need' service provision. It is certainly true that black and
ethnic minority communities' take-up of services is comparatively low,
but this appears to be related to a lack of knowledge about services. For
example a study of Asian, Afro-Caribbean and European elders in
Birmingham (Bhalla and Blakemore, 1981) found that 64 per cent and 35
per cent of the Asian and Afro-Caribbean samples respectively had not
heard of any of the services mentioned in the study (such as home-help,
day centres and meals-on-wheels), compared with just 2 per cent of the
European sample. Similarly, research with Asian, Afro-Caribbean and
Vietnamese carers in a London borough found that 'In most cases carers
were unable to say whether services were suitable to their needs, because
they did not know about them or use them' (McCalman, 1990, p. 10).

The accessibility of services is thus a critical issue in determining the
take-up of services by black and ethnic minority carers. Two main factors
that can affect access are awareness about services and the appropriateness of services to the needs of minority carers. In relation to the former,
some carers have found that the ways in which services are publicised
can exclude them from making choices about their use of services. For
example in some black and ethnic minority communities, particularly
among elderly people and women, inability to speak English and illiteracy in their first language can directly affect awareness of services.
Thus in a Liverpool study of 60 Chinese carers, only six (10 per cent)
were fluent in English and 24 (40 per cent) said they could not understand translated Chinese information because of illiteracy (Au and Au,
1994). In my research, 10 of the 33 carers were illiterate, all being women
over the age of fifty: five were Bangladeshi and five were Punjabi. For
these carers even translated information in their first language was of
limited value, and information about service provision was exclusively
gained through 'word-of-mouth' from relatives, friends and community
organisations.

However, while there is a need for service providers to develop more
imaginative forms of information-giving to black and ethnic minority
communities, it is equally important that consideration is given to differences in attitudes towards the use of services and, more fundamentally,

to caring itself. For example in the Liverpool carers' study it was found that many of the carers were reluctant to ask for support from services because 'They thought that asking for help was a form of begging and it was shameful for the family as a whole. They did not want outsiders to know what the difficulties were within their family' (Au and Au, 1994, p. 38).

Although such differences in attitudes towards the use of services are frequently attributed to cultural 'traditions', black and ethnic minority peoples' perceptions of services can also be affected by wider racist ideologies. As a young Bangladeshi carer in my research commented about his father's non-use of services:

> Just because they [services] are there, doesn't mean that they are available to him. . . . He doesn't like to ask. Why should he? He also has a real attitude about not wanting to scrounge, which is something that gets instilled in you. This country doesn't encourage you to get your entitlements. It is not just a case of knowing what is available.

A particular challenge for service providers is thus not only raising awareness of service provision among black and ethnic minority communities, but also of empowering carers to make demands upon services. These two points are also related to very basic issues concerning the perceptions and identifications of carers. As Rose and Bruce (1995) have suggested, many carers do not actually see themselves as 'carers', but reframe caring as a 'normal' part of family life as a means of coping with caring. In addition, for minority carers the concepts of 'caring' and 'carers' are also highly ethnocentric. For example in some Asian languages there is no precise translation of the word 'carer'. As one carer in my study pointed out: 'I think that it is difficult for us Asian people to see ourselves as 'carers' . . . the idea is not something that is a part of our culture or language, it is just another part of family life' (Gunaratnam, 1991, p. 2).

It is not surprising, therefore, that outreach workers working with black and ethnic minority communities have found that the unfamiliarity of both the word and the concept of 'carer' has presented particular difficulties for local initiatives aimed at supporting minority carers (Griffiths, 1992). The limitations of 'dominant' terminology in cross-cultural use and interpretation thus necessarily also raise questions about the versatility of basic service conceptualisations in dealing with, and recognising, diversity in caring experiences.

At a conceptual level, an area for further exploration is an examination of how black and ethnic minority people give meaning to their caring relationships and how these relate to the 'dominant' discourses of caring employed by both service providers and researchers.

The second main issue affecting black and ethnic minority peoples' use of service provision is related to the extent to which services are seen to meet their specific needs. In a survey of care providers' attitudes to community care for black and ethnic minority elders in Bradford (Walker and Ahmad, 1994), examples of inappropriate service provision included services failing to cater for different dietary needs, inadequate interpreting provision and an under-representation of minority staff within services. The authors suggest that for black and ethnic minority people: 'The combined effect of all these factors is to foster the conclusion that "these services are not for us" (mental health worker)' (p. 641).

An issue that has been neglected in wider debates about caring in relation to service provision is that home-based care for many black and ethnic minority people can often include vital forms of cultural affirmation and support that are frequently missing from services. For example, drawing upon her experiences of working with elderly people in long-term care settings, Jones (1992) has highlighted how the common loss of second language in people with dementia, together with staff lack of awareness of interpreting services, have led to situations in which some (European) ethnic minority people have not spoken to anyone in over six months. What such an example serves to highlight is how inequalities in care can arise through mono-culturalism within institutions, and how 'choices' about service provision can be directly restricted by the ability of services to meet specific needs.

Although increasing attention is being focused on the requirement to provide services that meet the differing cultural and religious needs of service users, there is less recognition that the experiences of black and ethnic minority carers and disabled people are more complex and extend beyond cultural issues (Begum, 1995). As Gilroy (1992) has argued, 'coat-of-paint' analyses, which only address racism at the surface of social life, are restrictive and end up defining black and ethnic minority people solely in terms of 'cultural' differences. As the discussion on diversity at the beginning of this chapter suggested, structural issues such as class, poverty and racism within employment can all interact with the influences of ethnic identity to shape the needs of minority carers.

In talking to Asian carers I found that caring issues were rarely identified in isolation, and for some carers were not even a priority in determining their service needs. Issues raised by carers included poverty, poor housing conditions and racial harassment, which directly related to the wider social and economic position of minority communities in this country. For many carers, it was a cause of concern that service providers had failed to recognise the relationship between caring and the wider experiences of racism and discrimination and to respond accordingly. Appropriate service provision for these carers was thus also related to the extent to which services were able to assess and respond to the needs of black and ethnic minority carers in a holistic way.

In fact, in terms of race equality initiatives in service provision, it appears that awareness of the effects of racism on the lives of black and ethnic minority service users can positively enhance service developments. For example a survey of health and 'race' initiatives among 45 purchasing health authorities (Jamdagni, 1996a) found that 'a certain type of awareness of racism, and of its potential impact on the health of the black population, is more likely to lead to a level of political commitment which brings about positive change' (Jamdagni, 1996b, p. 31).

13.4 Conclusion

This chapter has examined black and ethnic minority peoples' experiences of caring within the context of service provision. Several issues emerge from such an exploration. At a fundamental level, it is suggested that there is inadequate knowledge and understanding of the nature and meaning of caring within minority communities. In particular, there is still a lot we don't know about how caring relationships can be shaped by experiences such as ethnic identity, gender, class and disability. Such an examination of caring within black and ethnic minority communities would be beneficial in both deconstructing stereotypes about minority carers and also in developing services that are relevant to the specific needs of a range of different carers.

In terms of actual service provision to black and ethnic minority carers, research suggests ambivalent developments. The 1990s have certainly seen a growth in specific projects and initiatives aimed at minority carers (Carers National Association, 1995; Yee, 1995). However, many of the initiatives have been both marginalised and guarded. For example, many imaginative services have been developed within the voluntary sector, while race equality initiatives within the statutory sector have been piecemeal and inconsistent. Of particular concern is the fear by both health (Jamdagni, 1996b) and social care agencies (Walker and Ahmad, 1994) that increasing access to services for minority communities will lead to unmanageable demands: 'There is an awareness that, if we target groups to uncover their potential unmet needs, we shall not be able to meet the demand and will destabilise existing services' (county health authority representative, quoted in Jamdagni, 1996b, p. 30).

So although the provision of accessible and appropriate services to black and ethnic minority communities is not simply a matter of good practice, but is also a matter of law (Race Relations Act, 1976), lack of strategic commitment to race equality and budgetary restrictions can conspire actively to constrain service developments. It is at this level that

the realities of institutional racism are often unmasked, posing fundamental questions about the very ways in which 'need' is defined and services are organised. As Jenny Alphonse has argued:

> Part of the problem lies with the way in which organisational structures per-
> ceive and prescribe needs and services respectively. Once again, there appears
> to be a problem of letting go of a paternalistic, prescriptive approach. After all,
> can Black people in their communities really manage themselves, identify their
> own needs – which may not fit into a white perspective of what a carer is –
> and seek to have these needs met appropriately?
>
> (Alphonse, in Yee, 1995, p. 27)

The challenge for service providers is thus twofold: first, there is a need
to develop flexible and imaginative services in collaboration with black
and ethnic minority service users, which will empower self-determined
choices; secondly, there is a need for a strategic approach to race equality
that recognises that service developments will require a radical rethinking of basic conceptualisations of caring and also of power relations
between service users and providers.

References

Arber, S. and Ginn, J. (1992) 'Class and Caring: a forgotten dimension', *Sociology*,
Vol. 26, pp. 619–34.
Au, W. and Au, K. (1994) *Care in the Chinese Community: the way ahead*,
Merseyside Chinese Community Development Association, Liverpool.
Begum, N. (1995) *Beyond Samosas and Reggae: A guide to developing services for Black
disabled people*, King's Fund, London.
Berrington, A. (1994) 'Marriage and family formation among white and ethnic
minority populations in Britain', *Ethnic and Racial Studies*, Vol. 17, No. 3, pp.
517–546.
Bhalla, A. and Blakemore, K. (1981) *Elders of the Ethnic Minority Groups*, All Faiths
For One Race, Birmingham.
Carers National Association – London Region (1995) *Directory of Projects
Supporting Carers from Black and Minority Ethnic Communities in Greater London*,
Carers National Association, London.
Employment Department (1994) *Ethnic Groups and the Labour Market*,
Employment Gazette, May, p. 147–159.
Gilroy, P. (1992) 'The end of antiracism', in Donald, J. and Rattansi, A. (eds),
'Race', Culture and Difference, Sage Publications, London.
Groger, L. and Kunkel, S. (1995) 'Ageing and exchange: differences between
black and white elders', *Journal of Cross-Cultural Gerontology*, Vol. 10, pp.
269–287.
Griffiths, K. (1992) 'The silent minority', *Carelink*, 16, p. 3.
Gunaratnam, Y. (1991) *Call For Care*, Health Education Authority/King's Fund
Centre, London.

Jamdagni, L. (1996a) *Purchasing for Black Populations*, King's Fund, London.

Jamdagni, L. (1996b) 'Race against time', *Health Service Journal*, 7 March 1996, pp. 30–31.

Jones, G. (1992) 'A nursing model for the care of the elderly', in Jones, G. and Miesen, B. (eds), *Care-Giving in Dementia: Research and applications*, Routledge, London.

McCalman, J. (1990) *The Forgotten People: Carers in three ethnic minority communities in Southwark*, King's Fund Centre, London.

OPCS (Office of Population Censuses and Surveys) (1991) *Labour Force Survey 1988 and 1989*, HMSO, London.

Patel, N. (1990) *'Race' Against Time: Social Services Provision to Black Elders*, Runnymede Trust, London.

Patel, N. (1993) 'Healthy margins: black elders' care – models, policies and prospects', in Ahmad, W. (ed.), *'Race' and Health in Contemporary Britain*, Open University Press, Buckingham.

Rose, J. and Bruce, E. (1995) 'Mutual care but differential esteem: caring between older couples', in Arber, S., and Ginn, J. (eds), *Connecting Gender and Ageing*, Open University Press, Buckingham.

Townsend, P., Davidson, N. and Whitehead, M. (1988) *Inequalities in Health: the Black Report and the Health Divide*, Penguin, Harmondsworth.

Walker, R. and Ahmad, W. (1994) 'Asian and black elders and community care: A survey of care providers', *New Community*, Vol. 20, No. 4, pp. 635–646.

Yee, L. (1995) *Improving Support for Black Carers: A source-book of information, ideas and service initiatives*, King's Fund, London.

Feminist Perspectives on Caring

HILARY GRAHAM

14.1 Introduction

Since the late 1970s, feminist researchers have been engaged in a sustained critique of government policies on community care, speaking out against the orthodoxy that communities should be the major source of care for people with long-term needs for support. While questioning the orthodoxy, feminist perspectives have themselves been subject to little by way of development or critique. Instead the perspectives appear to have become fixed in the form in which they developed in the early 1980s. They have remained largely untouched by recent debates within and beyond feminism, debates that challenge many of the assumptions upon which feminist approaches to care have been based.

This chapter reviews the British feminist literature on caring, focusing on some of the complex issues raised and obscured by this important body of research. It begins by outlining what feminists have added to the debate community care before exploring dimensions of care that are neglected in feminist accounts. The chapter moves on to highlight how, along with gender, other social divisions are built in to the exchange of care within communities. It pays particular attention to class and 'race' as axes of difference among women that are reflected in their experiences of giving and receiving care.

14.2 Challenging the orthodoxy: feminist perspectives on caring

Care by families and within communities has long provided the cornerstone of Britain's welfare system. The centrality of such care has been highlighted in recent debates on the support of those who need help with day-to-day living. Here, the 'community' figures prominently, linked to 'care' in ways that convey the sense that they go naturally together. In this linking of community and care, communities are seen as both the major and the best source of care for people with physical disabilities, with physical and mental illnesses and with learning difficulties As the Griffiths report on community care put it, 'families friends, neighbours and other local people provide the majority of care . . . this is as it should be' (Griffiths, 1988, p. 5).

The assumption that communities are the major and best source of care has informed, in increasingly explicit ways, welfare policy since the 1970s. Both Labour and Conservative governments have seen community care as self-evidently the right way to support individuals who find it difficult to live independent lives. While a question mark has hung over its resourcing, few have spoken out against the principle of care within communities. One of the most sustained and systematic critiques has come from feminist researchers, in a steady stream of studies over the last decade. Their critiques were developed in a series of empirical studies that described the experience of looking after people with long-term health and mobility problems. Alongside these empirical studies were theoretical papers, which tracked the impact of caring on women's lives. This seam of empirical and theoretical research has continued into the 1990s, with the result that there is now a sizeable feminist literature 'on caring'.

This literature has pointed to ways in which community care is resourced by women's unpaid labour. It notes how care within communities is largely care by families, which in turn is largely care by female kin. Using a definition of care that may well underestimate the extent of care by women, the recent national study of informal carers nonetheless reminds us that women make up the majority (two in every three) of those caring for at least 20 hours a week. Underlining the kinship-base of community care, the survey suggests that the majority of female carers (over 70 per cent) are caring for relatives (Green, 1988).

In explaining these patterns, feminists have pointed to the way in which gender divisions take shape within families. They have pointed in particular to the fact that family life is sustained by the responsibility that women assume for the health and care of children and for the welfare of male partners. Women's care of those with long-term needs, they suggest, builds on and extends these private caring responsibilities. Low-waged and part-time work limit the opportunities most women have to pay for high-quality and reliable care from others, while their caring role restricts their employment opportunities. Presented by policy makers as a way of supporting the social independence of those receiving care, community care is recast by feminists as a policy that reinforces the economic dependence of women.

This critique of community care developed in the late 1970s and early 1980s. Since then the frameworks that informed the critique have themselves become the focus of intense debate within feminism. It is to these debates that the chapter now turns.

14.3   Feminist perspectives on caring: recent critiques

Feminist research on caring is marked out by a uniformity of perspective. Instead of the sharp lines of theoretical division that characterise other fields of feminist enquiry, it is consensus that is the hallmark of feminist studies of caring. This consensus can be traced back to a series of articles published in the early 1980s, which opened up women's experiences of caring to feminist analysis (for example Finch and Groves, 1980; Stacey, 1981; Graham, 1983). These articles articulated a common perspective, one that defined caring in terms of the unpaid responsibility that women have for the welfare of their families. As the previous section suggested, such an approach identifies gender divisions as determining the organisation and the experience of care within families.

The perspectives developed over a decade ago have continued to inform feminist studies, both empirical and theoretical (see for example, Dalley, 1988; Lewis and Meredith, 1988). The enduring influence of the early critiques gives this literature a somewhat dated feel, speaking to past rather than present currents in feminism. Recent debates appear to have largely passed it by. As a result, feminist research on caring has become distanced from the arguments that made the 1980s such a difficult but productive period for feminism as an intellectual and political movement. It has yet to engage in a systematic way with the debates about differences and divisions among women, with the critiques that accuse academic feminism of masking 'race' and class, sexuality and disability as crucial dimensions of women's lives. Yet many of these arguments – which were emerging at around the time when feminist research on caring was developing its frameworks – apply directly to the organisation of care within families (see for example Carby, 1982; hooks, 1982; Mama, 1984). They suggest that, while couched in terms of women in general, feminist research on caring has a more exclusive focus. An inclusive language that speaks of 'women's lives' and 'women's experiences' hides the fact that perspectives are grounded in the lives and experiences of some, rather than all, women. Specifically perspectives are grounded in studies where most (if not all) of the respondents are white, heterosexual women whose lives are structured by the giving of care within their families. As a result some relationships and experiences find a secure place within feminist research, while others are left on the margins of analysis Three examples may help illustrate what has been eclipsed in feminist perspectives on caring.

First, the emphasis in most feminist studies of caring is on the experience of providing care. Like the orthodox perspectives on community care that they critique, feminist studies tend to see 'care' and 'caring' services as that carers give rather than others receive. When studies talk about 'the meaning of caring' and 'the cost of caring', when they describe 'caring relationships' and 'the experience of care', the frame of reference is typically that of care-providers. It has been left to women excluded from this frame of reference to point to the tacit alignment of feminist and carers' perspectives. This exclusion is powerfully conveyed in the juxtaposition of 'feminists' and 'women with disabilities' in Nasa Begum's account of women receiving personal care. She notes that:

> *To feminists* community care is a means of reinforcing women's oppression. It traps women within the private domain of the family home and leaves the carers struggling with the emotions of love and duty.
>
> *To women with disabilities* community care is a policy which can perpetuate oppression and/or promote their right to independence. It is the mechanism which enables them to receive personal care outside institutional settings; yet it is also the tool that can leave them dependent for intimate personal care at the mercy of others.
>
> (Begum, 1990, p. 18; italics added)

Recognising the contradictory position that women with disabilities occupy in caring relationships, other studies have also argued for perspectives that reflect the experiences of those receiving as well as giving care (Campling, 1981). They have argued, too, for a recognition that 'receivers' and 'givers' are not rigid, mutually exclusive groups. Many women with disabilities are heavily involved in both self-care and in servicing other family members. For women who were carers prior to the onset of their disability, this involvement can have a deep psychological significance. As Morris notes, many women who experience disability in their adult lives measure their progress towards independent living 'in terms of whether or not they are still able to look after their families' (Morris, 1989, p. 48, see also Morris in this volume).

Second, in exploring the lives of those who give intimate personal care, feminist studies are populated primarily by white, heterosexual women in established family networks. On the basis of their experiences, researchers in the UK have identified a 'hierarchy of caring', which runs from spouse (first choice) through daughters (second choice) to other close relatives (Qureshi and Walker, 1988). The importance of marriage and the nuclear family is borne out by the national survey of informal carers, which confirms that these social relationships provide the setting for most caring relationships. However, while feminist studies of caring have explored the consequences of having family ties, they have paid less attention to the experiences of lesbians seeking and providing care for women outside the nuclear family. These studies have paid little attention, too, to how 'race' structures the hierarchy of caring. Yet black feminists have argued that it is the absence rather than the presence of family networks that has shaped the domestic lives and health experiences of many black women in Britain. The struggle was, and is, to build families and to care for, and be cared for by, one's kin. Thus while caring can be a negative and oppressive experience, it can also be experienced as a way of resisting the divisions of class, 'race' and sexuality, which have worked to separate women from those they care about.

Third, like policy makers, feminist studies typically define 'care' and 'caring' in terms of the unpaid health-related activities that go on at home and between relatives (and, more rarely, friends). Caring is seen primarily as being about the unpaid work of those who are related to each other through birth or marriage. This kind of definition makes it hard to see forms of home-based care that are not shaped by marriage and kinship obligations. One major example is domestic service, a relationship that constrained the lives of many white and black working-class women in eighteenth- and nineteenth-century Britain. Its influence continues today in the divisions within women's paid work, which mark out 'caring' work, such as nursing and social work, from 'service' work, such as laundry, catering and domestic work.

These three examples suggest that gender alone can not explain the patterns of care within families and communities. Women occupy different positions, both in terms of their access to and responsibilities for care, with these positions linked to their experiences of disability and their place in the hierarchies of 'race', class and sexuality. The next section looks in more detail at two of these dimensions, focusing on how the social divisions of 'race' and class are reflected in women's need to receive and opportunities to give care within their families.

14.4   Social divisions and the patterns of care within

The social divisions of class, 'race' and gender are etched into the patterns of care within families and communities in ways that, as yet, are only partially understood. While research remains limited, the available studies highlight three important aspects of the relationship between these social divisions and family care. The aspects relate to the distribution of illness and disability, the patterns of access to informal networks and the forms of care within families.

First, social divisions are reflected in people's exposure to illness and disability, with prevalence linked to gender and socio-economic status and rising sharply with age. Thus, the proportion of adults reporting a long-standing illness or disability that limits their activities ranges from 10 per cent among men aged 16 to 44 years in non-manual households to 51 per cent among women aged 65 and over living in manual households (Office of Population Censuses and Surveys, 1990). While national surveys such as the General Household Survey and the OPCS surveys of disability do not address 'race' as a dimension of disadvantage, small-scale studies have begun to compare the experiences of white and black ethnic minority populations. These studies remind us that 'white' and 'black' are not homogeneous groups – the patterns of health and illness vary both within and between ethnic groups. However they do point to a high incidence of chronic ill-health and physical and sensory disability among Afro-Caribbean and Asian elders (Glendinning and Pearson, 1988).

Second, the social divisions reflected in the distribution of illness and disability emerge again in the family networks that govern access to care within the community. These networks have long been recognised by governments as the 'irreplaceable' and 'principal source of support and care' in old age (Department of Health and Social Security, 1981, p. 37). As the Griffiths report put it, they are 'the primary means by which people are enabled to live normal lives in community settings' (Griffiths, 1988, p. 5). Yet the evidence suggests that this primary and irreplaceable resource is unequally distributed. Resources in 'the community' are not universally available. Like access to health, access to communities of carers appears to be linked in systematic ways to racial and class divisions. Studies have highlighted how poor employment prospects have combined with the progressive tightening of controls on immigration to leave many black elders without access to kin. In one study of 400 older people, one third of the Asian respondents and one half of the Afro-Caribbean respondents had no family in the neighbourhood. One quarter of the Asian respondents had no family in Britain (Bhalla and Blakemore, 1981). Other studies, too, have described the isolation experienced by those who have no family here and for whom family reunification is no longer seen as a real possibility (Fenton, 1985; and Gunaratnam in this volume).

It is not only black elders who find themselves denied access to the family networks that government policies have defined as irreplaceable. White people, too, can find themselves without informal sources of support for the tasks they find it difficult to perform alone. The OPCS survey of disability, for example, found that four in ten (44 per cent) of disabled adults were not receiving informal support with the everyday tasks where help was needed (Martin *et al.*, 1989). As the studies of black elders suggest, low social class, and poverty in particular, is associated with restricted access to informal sources of help. In one recent study of working-class older people living alone, four out of five were women and the majority lived on social security benefits. A large proportion of the respondents (over 50 per cent) were housebound. Yet despite their location 'in the community', 45 per cent had no living children. Only one in three had a relative living in the neighbourhood (Sinclair *et al.*, 1988, p. 25).

The social divisions of class, gender and 'race' are reproduced in the patterns of family care in a third way. As a number of feminist historians have noted, the lives of many women have been shaped by colonial labour patterns in which women's care of other families took precedence over the needs of their own families. 'The family' was the setting for domestic service as well as the care of kin.

In the seventeenth and eighteenth centuries, black slaves were brought to Britain from Africa and the West Indies to work as personal and household servants: as cooks, maids and valets (Fryer, 1984, p. 72). Through the nineteenth century, Afro-Caribbean women in Britain continued to be employed as servants, while colonial expansion beyond Britain established domestic service as a major source of employment for black women in India and the Caribbean.

For white English working-class women, and for Irish and other ethnic minority groups, the maintenance of white middle-class families has also been a major source of paid employment. In the 1880s, it is estimated that one in three women aged 15 to 20 had entered domestic service (Lewis, 1984, p. 56). In London in 1861, 55 per cent of women in employment were engaged in personal service (Stedman Jones, 1984).

Residential domestic service remained the largest single occupation for women well into the twentieth century, with over 1 000 000 women in service' in the 1930s. Today domestic work continues to characterise the labour market position of many black and white working-class women engaged in low-paid, low-status work that services the needs of those working in more privileged positions in the household/organisation. Within the health service, an organisation centrally concerned with meeting daily needs for care, racial hierarchies are in evidence in the organisation of women's care and service. For example, the evidence suggests that Afro-Caribbean women are disproportionately placed in posts where the emphasis is on domestic and personal service rather than on nursing care (London Association of Community Relations Councils, 1985).

In looking at the building of families and kinship networks, it appears that white middle-class women have had greater access to a family life sustained by their care. Many white working-class women and black and ethnic minority women have found their care arrangements structured by employment opportunities and immigration restrictions in ways that restrict their opportunity to receive and give care within their families.

While not underestimating the difficulties, women have emphasised their resistance to the restrictions placed on them by racism and poverty. In their accounts of their lives, many women have described the strategies they use to protect their own health and the health of those they care about. They emerge not as the passive recipients of oppression, but as agents struggling actively to get help and to achieve change for their families (Fenton, 1985; Lewis and Meredith, 1988; Eyles and Donovan, 1990; Phoenix, 1991). They are, in Linda Gordon's evocative phrase, 'heroes of their own lives' (Gordon, 1988).

14.5 Concluding remarks

This chapter has been concerned with a seam of British feminist research on caring that has emerged over the last decade. This research provides a critical commentary on community care, highlighting the way in which both the ideology and the practice of community care rests on, and reinforces, gender divisions. While offering a critical review of policy, feminist perspectives on caring have become strangely insulated from recent critiques of feminism. These critiques challenge the assumption that gender divisions provide a catch-all explanation of care within families. They suggest that other social divisions are also deeply embedded in the past and present organisation of family care.

What are the implications of recognising that the day-to-day care for people in families is structured by many, rather than one, social division?

First, it suggests the need for a broader understanding of 'care' and 'caring'. This understanding should take account of women's experiences of receiving care within families, as well as their experiences of giving it. A more inclusive concept of care also needs to confront women's differential need for, and access to, the communities of kin who provide day-to-day support.

A feminist concept of care should recognise that unpaid care between relatives and friends is not the only kind of home-based care that has defined women's place in British society. Other forms of care have played a crucial part in the reproduction of gender as an identity that has class and racial divisions embedded within it. A focus on care and service within the home provides one way of recognising that the everyday reproduction of families is linked to the reproduction of class and racial differences among women.

Broadening the concept of care highlights a second issue for future analysis. It suggests the need to approach the concept of women critically. Feminists should be wary of treating 'women' as a homogeneous group, with identical interests born of their common experience of gender oppression. Black feminist and lesbian researchers, together with those describing the lives of women with disabilities, have pointed to the profound differences between women. These differences affect, in direct and powerful ways, the kinds of caring relationships that women experience.

Differences and conflicts are part of the reality of many women's lives. As the black feminist researcher bell hooks has put it, 'none of us experience ourselves solely as gendered subjects. We experience ourselves everyday as subjects of race, class and gender' (Childers and hooks, 1990). Her comments suggests that a woman's experience of caring is mediated through her multiple (and potentially conflicting) identities. She is a carer, but she is also middle class, she is black, she is a mother, she is disabled, she is heterosexual, she is in paid employment. These different dimensions of her life are likely to shape, in complex ways, the choices she can make about how she cares for her family.

Third, and finally, the arguments of this chapter suggest that the development of one all-embracing feminist perspective is an inappropriate as well as an unachievable aim for those concerned with community care policies. Instead it suggests that the strength of future feminist analyses of caring is likely to lie in their tolerance of the uncertain and unfinished business of understanding women's lives. I anticipate – and hope – that these analyses will more explicitly recognise that feminism is a changing landscape of ideas, with feminist perspectives on caring representing not a fixed intellectual position but a provision body of knowledge under continual review. With these more fluid and open-ended frameworks, feminist research on caring may be better able to take up its rightful place, at the centre rather than on the margins of contemporary feminist thought.

References

Begum, N. (1990) *Burden of Gratitude: Women with Disabilities Receiving Personal Care*, University of Warwick, Social Care Practice Centre/Department of Applied Social Studies.

Bhalla, A. and Blakemore, K. (1981) *Elders of the Ethnic Minority Groups*, All Faiths for One Race, Birmingham.

Campling, J. (ed.) (1981) *Women with Disabilities Talking: Images of Ourselves*, Routledge, London.

Carby, H. (1982) 'White women listen! Black feminism and the boundaries of sisterhood', in Centre for Contemporary Cultural Studies, *The Empire Strikes Back: Race and Racism in 70s Britain*, Hutchinson, London.

Childers, M. and hooks, b. (1990) 'A conversation about race and class', in Hirsch, M. and Fox Keller, E. (eds), *Conflicts in Feminism*, Routledge, London.

Dalley, G. (1988) *Ideologies of Caring*, Macmillan, London.

Department of Health and Social Security (1981) *Growing Older*, HMSO, London.

Eyles, J. and Donovan, J. (1990) *The Social Effects of Health Policy*, Avebury, Aldershot.

Fenton, S. (1985) *Race, Health and Welfare: Afro-Caribbean and South Asian People in Central Bristol*, University of Bristol.

Finch, J. and Groves, D. (1980) 'Community care and the family: a case for equal opportunities?', *Journal of Social Policy*, Vol. 9, pp. 487–511.

Fryer, P. (1984) *Staying Power: the History of Black People in Britain*, Pluto Press, London.

Glendenning, F. and Pearson, M. (1988) *The Black and Ethnic Minority Elders in Britain: Health Needs and Access to Services*, Health Education Authority, London, in association with the Centre for Social Gerontology, University of Keele.

Gordon, L. (1988) *Heroes of Their Own Lives*, Virago, London.

Graham, H. (1983) 'Caring: a labour of love', in Finch, J. and Groves, D. (eds), *A Labour of Love: Women, Work and Caring*, Routledge and Kegan Paul, London.

Green, H. (1988) *Informal Carers: General Household Survey 1985*, HMSO, London.

Griffiths, R. (1988) *Community Care: Agenda for Action*, HMSO, London.

hooks, b. (1982) *Ain't I a Woman: Black Women and Feminism*, Pluto Press, London.

Lewis, J. (1984) *Women in England 1870–1950*, Wheatsheaf, Brighton.

Lewis, J. and Meredith, B. (1988) *Daughters Who Care: Daughters Caring for their Mothers at Home*, Routledge, London.

London Association of Community Relations Councils (1985) *In a Critical Condition: a Survey of Equal Opportunities in Employment in London's Health Authorities*, LACRC, London.

Mama, A. (1984) 'Black women, the economic crisis and the British state', *Feminist Review*, Vol. 17, pp. 21–35.

Martin, J., White, A. and Meltzer, H. (1989) *Disabled Adults: Services, Transport and Employment*, OPCS Surveys of Disability in Great Britain, Report 4, HMSO, London.

Morris, J. (ed.) (1989) *Able Lives: Women's Experience of Paralysis*, Women's Press, London.

Office of Population Censuses and Surveys (1990) *The General Household Survey 1988*, HMSO, London.

Phoenix, A. (1991) *Young Mothers?*, Polity Press, London.

Qureshi, H. and Walker, A. (1988) *The Caring Relationship*, Routledge and Kegan Paul, London.

Sinclair, I., Crosbie, D., O'Connor, P., Stanforth, L. and Vickery, A. (1988) *Bridging Two Worlds: Social Work and the Elderly Living Alone*, Gower, Aldershot

Stacey, M. (1981) 'The division of labour revisited or overcoming the two Adams', in Abrams, P., Deem, R., Finch, J. and Rock, P. (eds), *Practice and Progress: British Sociology 1950–1980*, George Allen and Unwin, London.

Stedman Jones, G. (1984) *Outcast London: a Study in the Relationship between Classes in Victorian Society*, Penguin, Harmondsworth.

15

Older Male Carers and Community Care

MIKE FISHER

15.1 Introduction

We are in the sitting room of a small bungalow in a seaside town in England. Bill, aged 82, is explaining his day, while Mary, his lifelong partner, listens with a pleasant smile. She has Alzheimer's disease, and likes to be included in conversations, even if she does not actively participate. Bill started work at 5 a.m., dealing with the laundry from Mary's bed, then it was time for Mary's shower, a long struggle to get her dressed, then breakfast and more cleaning up, before Mary was assisted from her wheelchair into her favourite armchair. Expanding on an earlier comment about the work he was doing not being 'man's work', Bill says:

> I think that a woman should look after a woman but I've learned that a woman relies on a man . . . once those little cogs go, you can't put them back and you've got to help them out. She gets very obstinate and some of the chaps get very out of bed about it. But what's the good of that . . . My mum was blind for years and I used to look after my mum. I loved my mum and love Mary and my love for Mary is to see that she's right.

Bill's caring for Mary is evidence of a sea-change in our understanding of caring in general, and of caring by older men in particular. We are so used to conceptualising personal care as women's work that it seems surprising to encounter a man doing it at all, let alone quoting love as the motivation. And we are so used to arguing for equity in community care policy in the name of women, that we are surprised to find the need to integrate older men into this argument. This chapter investigates the reasons why older men, like Bill, are involved in personal caring, and explores the implications for our understanding of caring and for community care policy.

This chapter is also about personal care for adults, rather than the more general notion of caring or the personal care given by parents to their children. By personal care for adults I mean the provision of physical and emotional support assisting adults with the activities of daily living. It involves helping people with such activities as getting up and going to bed, with bathing and toileting, and with eating. Emotional care is included in this definition primarily to recognise the substantial care given to people with mental health problems to enable them to get through their daily lives, and is not meant to encompass the general notion of 'caring about' someone.

15.2   Who are the carers?

Establishing the numbers of carers is a political question involving how caring is defined. Most commentators now suggest that the figures published in 1988 from the General Household Survey (GHS), estimating that there were about six million carers – 3.5 million women and 2.5 million men (Green, 1988) – are an unreliable guide to personal caring because the question used was too inclusive. The main question asked in the survey was whether people had 'extra family responsibilities because they look after someone who is sick, handicapped or elderly', and this might include activities such as looking after money. Parker and Lawton (1994), in their analysis of the 1988 GHS figures, suggested that care should be divided into six categories: (1) personal and physical care, (2) personal *not* physical care, (3) physical *not* personal care, (4) other practical help, (5) practical help only, (6) other help. They argued that only the first two involved the provision of personal care representing about 1.29 million people. They also suggested that 67 per cent of people providing 'personal and physical care' and 74 per cent of those providing 'personal not physical care' were women. Since this analysis, the 1992 figures for the GHS show a 15 per cent increase in the overall number of carers between 1985 and 1990, suggesting an upward revision of the figure of 1.29 million providing personal care (Office of Population Censuses & Surveys, 1992).

The proportion of men and women caring is of extreme importance to the question of equity in community care. There are critical questions, of course, about how the state supports people who need care and those who provide it, and the current pattern of residualisation and diminished commitment to collective welfare provides an important backdrop to the search for solutions. No-one is in any doubt, however, that the majority of care is undertaken by women, and that insofar as it is unpaid, unrecognised and restricting of women's aspirations, it should be a target for equity in social policy. Sharing the caring task more equally between men and women could therefore be a major way of providing greater equity in community care.

Attention to older carers grew partly out of the GHS figures that 20 per cent of carers were themselves over 65 years. The question of how to tackle gender inequality was further illuminated by the finding that, in this age group, caring was more equally shared between men and women. The 1992 GHS shows that, although overall 10 per cent of women and 6 per cent of men defined themselves as carers, over the age of 65 the figures were 13 per cent and 14 per cent respectively (see Table 15.1). Disentangling proportions and numbers is important here: although the proportion of men over 65 undertaking caring is higher than that of women, there are still more women undertaking caring in this age group, simply because the total number of women over 65 is greater than that of men. If we are looking for instances of equitable sharing of the caring task, we have to take account of whether proportionately to their numbers, men are caring as much as women. The GHS suggests that we should look at older people, and in particular spouse care. It should be noted that the GHS does not provide figures for carers from minority ethnic groups, on the ground that the numbers in its survey are too small to provide a reliable basis for analysis.

TABLE 15.1   **The percentage of women and men undertaking caring, by age**

Age	Women %	Men %
16–29	9	7
30–44	18	12
45–64	27	20
65+	13	14
All ages	10	6

Derived from Office of Population Censuses & Surveys, 1992, p. 4, Table 4.

15.3   The gender and caring debate

I have argued elsewhere that the legitimate concern to identify the major task of caring as falling on daughters has had the unintended effect of blurring the picture of the care given by older people to other older people, and thus by husbands to wives (Fisher, 1994). The debate on women and caring has largely focused on the circumstances of white women in their middle years, the 'women in the middle' (Brody, 1981) with caring responsibilities both to their immediate family and to their parents. Caring was conceptualised as a 'burden', with negative connotations for those receiving care (Baldwin and Twigg, 1991; Morris, 1991), who are mainly women of course. The idea that caring might be rewarding (Fitting *et al.*, 1986; Motenko, 1989) was largely absent from the debate. This perspective also concealed the notion of mutual care, where both people in a caring relationship offered care to each other. If care receivers were conceptualised as merely passive recipients, their role in determining care was not analysed. For example it was assumed that if women undertook care where a man was also available, this was solely because of the preferences of the carers, and any possibility that the care receiver might have a say was overlooked. This is highly relevant to questions of choice and equity in community care, since personal care often involves intimate physical contact (Qureshi and Walker, 1989; Askham and Thompson, 1990) and it might be expected that women and men would have preferences about same-sex or cross-sex caring, and that they should be heeded. Indeed it is only in the context of policy that prioritises the needs and wishes of carers over those of the recipients of care that such a dominant feature of the caring landscape as the 'gender boundary' (Fisher, 1994, p. 675) could be overlooked.

The focus on white women led to a lack of attention to the differences in experiences of carers in minority ethnic groups. The different age profile among some minority ethnic groups and the different social construction of family responsibility combine with black people's experience of personal and institutional racism to lead to specific and unique experiences of caring (Cameron *et al.*, 1989; Atkin and Rollings, 1992, 1993; Blakemore and Boneham, 1993; Butt and Mirza, 1996). In particular we may have to look very closely at how caring responsibility is constructed among people with Asian backgrounds, given evidence of a cultural expectation that men will take responsibility for dependent members but exercise it by arranging care, rather than undertaking it directly (Finch and Mason, 1990). Different patterns of housing and other socio-economic factors will also affect how care is provided (Sinclair *et al.*, 1990; Atkin and Rollings, 1993). Assumptions have been made about the support available within minority ethnic communities, but as Yasmin Gunaratnam's research suggests, it is perfectly possible for black and Asian carers to be as isolated as white carers (see Chapter 13). Furthermore the priority given to able-bodied carers has been criticised by disabled feminist writers, from the perspective both that it fails to recognise the mutuality of care and that equity requires the rights of disabled people to be respected when formulating solutions (Keith, 1990; Morris, 1991).

In terms of gender inequality, the debate assumed fundamental differences in women's and men's motivation and ability to care. Graham's concept of a 'labour of love' was intended to capture the unique mixture of love, affection, duty and hard work that characterises women's commitment to caring (Graham, 1983). The work of Chodorow (1978) and Gilligan (1982), which suggests that there are basic differences between women and men in their approach to maintaining connectedness between human beings, has influenced the debate. In particular it locates the technical and emotional capacity to care in the experience of mothering and suggests that women are more morally adept at recognising and meeting needs (for example Finch, 1989). This considerably complicates the question of equity and caring, since it might suggest recognising the better caring capacity of women by paying for their care, rather than altering the gender balance of caring. It might also be taken to mean that, if women are more 'naturally' suited to care, that it costs women less emotionally, and therefore runs the risk of blunting our sensitivity to the stress women experience as carers, and of reinforcing gender stereotypes in provision of support. These theoretical perspectives also have the effect of marginalising men's caring: the possibility that men might combine love and duty in the same way as women becomes remote, and men who do care are seen as exceptions, requiring special recognition for 'going against the grain'.

15.4   Men who care

When the figures on the proportion of male carers first emerged in 1988, commentators suggested that the result had been influenced by the wording of the question. It was argued that the phrasing characterised caring as an additional and special task and that women were less likely to think of their caring in these terms than men (Arber and Ginn, 1992; Grundy and Harrop, 1992). As I pointed out in 1994, there is no empirical evidence that this is so, and it is equally conceivable that men would be reluctant to characterise what they do in terms commonly thought of as 'women's work' (Fisher, 1994). In the absence of direct evidence, this argument remains as an example of the tendency to discount the possibility of similarities between men and women in their caring.

When researchers encounter men like Bill, it appears that the first approach is to explain away their behaviour. The first and most common explanation is that men who care are trapped, and do it because they have no option. Qureshi and Walker adopt this approach when they discuss how caring tasks were more equitably distributed when the male carer was a spouse (and thus in the same household): 'Thus it might seem (uncharitably perhaps) that men, especially husbands, were being forced into caring by their spouses' disability' (Qureshi and Walker, 1989, p. 91). Other commentators suggest that men's care is not really the same as women's care because it does not involve intimate physical care. Ungerson (1987) and Finch (1984) both theorise a taboo on men's involvement in this aspect of care. Toileting, bathing and cleaning up the results of incontinence are held to be beyond the boundary. The way men organise their care has also been subject to criticism, from the point of view that men seem to use patterns of dealing with the work that draw on their previous work experience. Thus Ungerson suggests the men she studied imported concepts of 'business efficiency', and that as a result their care was less imbued with moral commitment than that of women (1987, pp. 103–9).

The clearest example of this unsympathetic approach to under-standing men's caring is the analogy used by Rose and Bruce to describe the relationship they observed between husbands and the wives for whom they cared. They contrast men's getting-on-with-the-job approach with that of women 'grieving for lost persons and for a diminished rela-tionship' and suggest the analogy of a 'pet rabbit relationship'.

> A pet rabbit's survival requires conscientious care: indeed its condition is a source of pride for its carer, and the well-cared for pet, or rather its owner, receives much admiration. For women, the husband with Alzheimer's fails to become an equivalent pet, so they grieved. Their equally conscientious care – which gave them little or no respite – produced little of the real, if subdued, sense of pride that the men displayed.
>
> (Rose and Bruce, 1995, p. 127)

The analogy characterises the love and devotion between a husband and his wife as equivalent to that between an animal kept for personal plea-sure and its keeper, a parallel as damaging to women with Alzheimer's as it is to husbands who care. In a later part of the same paper, Rose and Bruce give a sensitive account of the way gender stereotypes operate to reward men who care as 'Mr Wonderful', while women are simply expected to cope. This is an important and helpful insight, but the pet rabbit analogy does no such service to either older men or older women.

These kinds of approach appear to discount even the remotest theoret-ical possibility that older men might offer care that resembles that of women in terms of emotional content and motivation. In contrast, the few studies of older men's care do suggest similarities between men's and women's care. Bytheway's studies of family care among redundant Welsh steelworkers show that men adopt a primary caring responsibility even when female kin are available, and are motivated by a deep sense of obligation (Bytheway, 1986, 1987). A man caring for his wife responded to a query about how he managed to offer what appeared to be nursing care in the following terms:

> It really astonished me because I found I've got an enormous amount of patience. . . . She was a marvellous housekeeper. . . . But then, when it came to my turn, I had no regrets because she had looked after me for over thirty years

and I thought well she can't do it now, I have to do my best, I didn't prevaricate, I didn't think it was the wrong thing to do. I was glad of the opportunity to pay her back . . . I accepted that. Put it as a labour of love more than anything else.

(Bytheway, 1987, p. 56)

Large-scale studies of caring in North America suggest that 70 per cent of husbands and 78 per cent of wives assist with personal care and hygiene (Stone, *et al.*, 1987, p. 623). Although not specifically about older men, studies of gay carers suggest that no boundary is drawn to avoid intimate personal care (Small, 1993). If such boundaries do influence cross-sex caring, they reflect the same preference of older women for same-sex intimate care highlighted by Wenger (1984, 1990). Thus Kaye and Applegate (1990a) show that, in their sample of North American couples, women prefer their 'bathroom needs' to be met by other women, and men do not see this as their forte, but in the absence of choice, both get on with it. They also challenge Gilligan's notion that men operate from sets of rules rather than a sense of duty (Kaye and Applegate, 1990b), and highlight what they call a 'family caregiving orientation' among older men (Kaye and Applegate, 1994). They argue that older men are beginning to show very different patterns of behaviour than might be predicted from gender stereotypes, echoing perhaps the point made by Bengtson *et al.* (1995) that generations need some rehearsal time before new behaviour is established.

In short, the studies of men who care, particularly older men caring for their spouses, suggest that men are capable of choosing to care (rather than being forced to do so), of investing care with emotional depth (instead of regarding it as a job of work), of undertaking intimate personal care (rather than shirking this responsibility). Again, we must stress that most of the studies have focused on white samples, and any differences in the preferences of black and Asian elders receiving care and the ability of older black and Asian men to provide it has not yet received sufficient attention from researchers.

15.5 Conclusion

One of the great successes of the debate on women and caring has been to question the gender assumptions underlying the provision of community care. Although there is a long way to go, this questioning approach now underpins a great deal of the thinking about community care and the training of community care professionals. Just as community care can no longer be planned on the basis of gender stereotypes of women, stereotypes of some men also need to be questioned. Some men, particularly older husbands, can and do care, and they need appropriate support that recognises this. Excessive praise (the 'Mr Wonderful' approach) is as unhelpful to older men as the assumption of coping is to women. Services that are directed at older men 'because they can't be expected to cope' are as discriminatory and unlikely to mesh with the carers' and care receivers' needs as services withheld from women 'because it's their job to care'.

Furthermore, if we want to address the inequity between the amount of caring undertaken by women and men, we must recognise some of the similarities between women's and men's caring, as well as the differences. The caring relationship between older men and their wives and partners provides a starting point for this work.

References

Arber, S. and Ginn, J. (1992) *Gender and Later Life: a Sociological Analysis of Resources and Constraints*, Sage Publications, London.

Askham, J. and Thompson, C. (1990) *Dementia and Home Care*, Age Concern Institute of Gerontology, Research Paper No. 4, Age Concern, Mitcham.

Atkin, K. and Rollings, J. (1992) 'Informal care in Asian and Afro-Caribbean communities', *British Journal of Social Work*, Vol. 22, pp. 405–418.

Atkin, K. and Rollings, J. (1993) *Community Care in a Multi-Racial Britain*, HMSO, London.

Baldwin, S. and Twigg, J. (1991) 'Women and community care-reflections on a debate', in Maclean, M. and Groves, D. (eds), *Women's Issues in Social Policy*, Routledge, London, pp. 117–35.

Bengtson, V., Mills, T. and Parrott, T. (1995) 'Aging in the United States at the end of the century', paper presented at the International Conference Aging in the East and West: Demographic Trends, Sociocultural Contexts and Policy Implications, 21–2 September, Seoul, Korea.

Blakemore, K. and Boneham, M. (1993) *Age, Race and Ethnicity*, Open University Press, Buckingham.

Brody, E. (1981) 'Women in the middle and family help to older people', *The Gerontologist*, Vol. 21, pp. 471–80.

Butt, J. and Mirza, K. (1996) *Social Care in Black Communities*, HMSO, London.

Bytheway, W. R. (1986) *Early Retirement and the Care of Elderly Dependent People*, Conference Paper, British Sociological Association Annual Conference, Loughborough UK.

Bytheway, W. R. (1987) *Informal Care Systems: an exploratory study within the families of older steel workers in South Wales*, Report to Joseph Rowntree Memorial Trust, York, UK.

Cameron, E., Evers, H., Badger, F. and Atkin, K. (1989) 'Black old women, disability and health carers', in Jefferys, M. (ed.), *Growing Old in the Twentieth Century*, Routledge, London, pp. 230–48.

Chodorow, N. (1978) *The Reproduction of Mothering*, University of California Press, Berkeley.

Finch, J. (1984) 'Community Care: developing non-sexist alternatives', *Critical Social Policy*, Vol. 3, No. 3, pp. 6–18.

Finch, J. (1989) *Family Obligations and Social Change*, Polity Press, Cambridge.

Finch, J. and Mason, J. (1990) 'Filial obligations and kin support for elderly people', *Ageing and Society*, Vol. 10, pp. 151–75.

Fisher, M. (1994) 'Man-made care: community care and older male carers', *British Journal of Social Work*, Vol. 24, pp. 659–68.

Fitting, M., Rabins, P., Lucas, J. and Eastham, J. (1986) 'Caregivers for dementia patients: a comparison of husbands and wives', *The Gerontologist*, Vol. 26, No. 3, pp. 248–52.

Gilligan, C. (1982) *In A Different Voice*, Harvard University Press, Cambridge Massachusetts.

Graham, H. (1983) 'Caring: a labour of love', in Finch, J. and Groves, D. (eds) *A Labour of Love*, Routledge and Kegan Paul, London, pp. 13–30.

Green, H. (1988) *Informal Carers: General Household Survey 1985*, HMSO, London.

Grundy, E. and Harrop, A. (1992) 'Co-residence between adult children and their elderly parents in England and Wales', *Journal of Social Policy*, Vol. 21, No. 3, pp. 325–48.

Kaye, L. and Applegate, J. (1990a) *Men as Caregivers to the Elderly: Understanding and Aiding Unrecognized Family Systems*, Lexington Books, Lexington MA.

Kaye, L. and Applegate, J. (1990b) 'Men as elder caregivers: a response to changing families', *American Journal of Orthopsychiatry*, Vol. 60, No. 1, pp. 86–95.

Kaye, L. and Applegate, J. (1994) 'Older men and the family caregiving orientation', in Thompson, E. H. (Jnr.) (ed.), *Older Men's Lives*, Sage Publications, London, pp. 218–36.

Keith, L. (1990) 'Caring partnership', *Community Care*, 22 February.

Morris, J. (1991) *Pride Against Prejudice: Transforming Attitudes to Disability*, Women's Press, London.

Motenko, A. (1989) 'The frustrations, gratifications and well-being of dementia caregivers', *The Gerontologist*, Vol. 29, No. 2, pp. 157–65.

Office of Population Censuses & Surveys (1992) *General Household Survey: Carers in 1990: OPCS Monitor SS 92/2*, HMSO, London.

Parker, G. and Lawton, D. (1994) *Different Types of Care, Different Types of Carer*, HMSO, London.

Qureshi, H. and Walker, A. (1989) *The Caring Relationship: Elderly People and their Families*, Macmillan, Basingstoke.

Rose, H. and Bruce, E. (1995) 'Mutual care but differential esteem: caring between older couples', in Arber, S. and Ginn, J. (eds), *Connecting Gender and Ageing: A Sociological Approach*, Open University Press, Buckingham, pp. 114–28.

Sinclair, I., Parker, R., Leat, D. and Williams, J. (1990) *The Kaleidoscope of Care: a Review of Research on Welfare Provision for Elderly People*, HMSO, London.

Small, N. (1993) *AIDS: The Challenge: Understanding, Education and Care*, Avebury, Aldershot.

Stone, R., Cafferata, G. and Sangl, J. (1987) 'Caregivers of the frail elderly: a national profile', *The Gerontologist*, Vol. 27, pp. 616–26.

Ungerson, C. (1987) *Policy is Personal*, Tavistock, London.

Wenger, G. C. (1984) *The Supportive Network: Coping with Old Age*, Allen and Unwin, London.

Wenger, G.C. (1990) 'Elderly carers: the need for appropriate intervention', *Ageing and Society*, Vol. 10, pp. 197–219.

16

Caring and Citizenship: A Complex Relationship

CLARE UNGERSON

16.1 Introduction

The idea of citizenship has a long and distinguished history; but like any idea with historical antecedents it has, as a notion, become more and more complex and therefore eventually vague. Different groups and political associations claim they hold the true notion of citizenship, but all too often their definition turns out simply to be the one that suits their particular interests. But one thing about the idea is clear: it is always concerned with the relationship between the individual and the state. Of course we can and do argue about the nature of that relationship: whether, for example, it contains a notion of reciprocal rights and duties between state and citizen, whether citizens' rights are more important than citizens' obligations, whether there are different kinds of citizens' rights – such as legal, civil and social rights – and whether these can be placed in historical sequence and/or normative hierarchies. We can also argue, as we shall see later, about whether the notion of citizenship is essentially masculine. But the one immovable feature of the idea of citizenship is that it is placed in the public domain: it is concerned with how the individual and the state relate to each other across public concerns, and how public institutions, such as the judiciary and the polity, mediate that relationship.

16.2 Public rights and the private domain

In Britain an important movement of carers, often combined with feminists, has over the last twenty years managed to make informal care a public and political issue. No current government report would dare discuss policies for community care without giving at least some space to the needs of informal carers (for example the 1989 White Paper on community care, CM 849, para. I.11). However, if in the context of this article we take the word 'care' to mean the care – by relatives, neighbours or friends – of dependent people in their own homes or in the homes of their carers, then there are a number of problems about extending a general notion of citizenship into the world of 'informal care'. The fact that the notion of citizenship is essentially placed in the public domain and that, in the twentieth century at least, it has come to contain within it a very strong emphasis on rights, particularly 'social rights' to personal security and welfare, poses two particular problems. The first problem is that carers are not in the public domain; they are physically located within the so-called 'private' world of hearth and home. Moreover there is a panoply of ideology that reinforces this idea that caring is essentially a private activity, since – it is often and easily argued – the motivation to care commonly arises out of love or, if not love, then obligations based on kinship and reciprocal biography. But love and kinship are particularistic, internal and domestic – unlike citizenship, which is most often taken to be general, external and public. Hence, logically, these essentially private constructs of love and kinship do not sit easily within the public construct of citizenship.

The second problem that arises when we try to link care with citizenship is that, particularly when we adopt a notion of citizenship that emphasises rights, we run into difficult water as soon as we try to operate a notion of rights within the domestic and private domain. It is notoriously difficult and controversial to operate and ultimately to enforce rights within the domestic domain, and if attempts are made to do so, these attempts are often sexist. For example the question of the right to sexual intercourse in marriage and the related issue of married women's right over their own bodies, and the question of women's right to live free of the threat or actuality of their partner's violence are both issues that demonstrate how generally complicated it is to translate the essentially public issue of rights into the domestic domain, particularly when the state and its agencies, in the process of both defining and enforcing rights, very frequently act in a patriarchal manner. One can immediately see similar difficulties when it comes to caring: do children have a right to their parents' or, more particularly, their mother's continual attention? Do parents, once they have grown frail and elderly, have a right to be cared for by their children and a right to be financially maintained by their better-off kin? Do people with schizophrenia have a right to be looked after by their parents or, conversely, a right not to be looked after by their parents? One can imagine deep controversies around these issues, and one can even imagine such 'rights' being placed on the statute book,[1] but it is extremely difficult to understand how they could be enforced except within an exceptionally authoritarian state –

which would in itself be in antithesis to the civil-rights aspect of the idea of citizenship. Moreover one can all too easily imagine how the operation of such 'rights' to be cared for would make those caring relationships extremely fraught and even dangerous.

A further difficulty surrounding the issue of rights in the domestic domain is that, particularly within a caring context, people locked into caring relationships with each other may well have conflicts of interests, such that they want different rights. For example it is arguable that it is in carers' interests, and that they should have the right, to be freed of caring at least for (say) one week in six by placing their dependent persons in respite care, or having someone to replace them in their own homes while they go away. But it could equally well be argued that dependent people should not have to suffer the disruption of continuously changing where they live, or having strangers enter their homes in order to care for them in the most personal and intimate ways. In other words carer and cared-for may well have conflicts of interest, and want to claim rights to quite different types of resource and conditions for autonomy.

16.3   Citizenship and women

These problems of using an essentially public notion of citizenship to deal with the rights of people who spend most of their physical and psychic time in the private world of the home are not new. Such problems have been largely considered in relation to the question of how to integrate women as citizens. One aspect of this discussion has been a general feminist critique of the idea of citizenship within political theory, suggesting that it is essentially masculine – an analysis powerfully developed by the political theorist Carole Pateman (1988, 1989). Other feminist writers such as Cass and Lister have developed a feminist critique that contains suggestions as to how – in practical ways – women's social rights within a framework of citizenship might be underwritten. The basic question they have attempted to answer is how, given women's domestic roles and responsibilities, social policy can be used to guarantee women's autonomy so that women attain social rights quite independently of men (in particular their husbands), and irrespective of their civil and legal status as wives, mothers or carers (Cass, 1990; Lister, 1990). Clearly such critique and analysis is relevant when it comes to considering caring and citizenship, for at least two reasons. First, this feminist literature on citizenship is dealing with overlapping categories: most – although, as we shall see later, by no means all – carers are women. Second, this tradition of feminist commentary on social policy has critiqued the way the state has treated as natural and unproblematic the contribution that women make as unpaid reproducers at home (Land, 1978). It is out of this twenty years of more general feminist critique that a considerable feminist literature focused particularly on caring has developed. In other words, much of the existing caring literature owes its origins to the general feminist claim that caring is a form of domestic labour.

Thus the feminist commentary on the issue of the integration of women as citizens is important for the purpose of putting caring and citizenship together; but, I shall argue, it is not wholly adequate for our purposes. There are a number of reasons for this. For a start, the main focus of this literature has so far been concerned with finding ways of guaranteeing women's income in a way that loosens, if not does away with altogether, their dependency on men. This commentary stresses the way in which social policy can be used to underwrite women's full participation in the labour market. Secondly, the feminist critique talks about 'women' but usually, in the citizenship context, talks most particularly about mothers. Often the feminist commentary on citizenship conflates mothering with caring, and treats mothers and carers as though they are in identical positions (Cass, 1990). But the difficulty is that, while mothers and carers may share a sex, they are also rather different, and they have different needs.

One of the important differences between mothers and carers is the question of age. Of course there are mothers who are carers too, and they have particular problems (Ungerson, 1987); but it is interesting to note that most carers are beyond child-bearing age (if they are female) and that for many of them the period of their lives devoted to child-caring is also probably over. In 1985 a national sample survey found that of carers looking after someone dependent for at least twenty hours a week, 69 per cent were aged over 45, and 26 per cent were aged over 65. Moreover, given feminist literature on caring that claims that caring is very largely undertaken by women working on their own, it would appear that a surprisingly high proportion of carers – 36 per cent – are men (Green, 1988, Table 4.4).

Thus the literature on women and citizenship, while claiming to be relevant to carers, has to be somewhat refined and qualified in order properly to take account of carers' needs. The first point is that, if citizenship is to be operationalised to mean economic independence underwritten by participation in the labour market supplemented by benefits, then, for many if not most carers the labour market, and participation within it are no longer relevant since they are largely beyond that point in their life course. Secondly, while it is the case that carers are often in desperate need of income, partially to cover the additional costs of caring but also simply to maintain themselves while outside the labour market, it is also the case that most carers have very pressing problems to do with the actual nature of caring – for which income may only be a limited answer. Obviously money, particularly lots of it, might help alleviate some of these problems if carers can use the money to buy in support services, but such private-sector services may be difficult to find, unreliable, and create further problems for the carer who has to organise and manage them. Thus an employment- and income-related discourse, which clearly has much salience to the general question of women and citizenship, and to the more particular question of mothers and citizenship, has to be qualified when it comes to the issue of carers and citizenship.

Carers and mothers also experience their caring in different ways and have different needs for support. Mothers need help with the socialisation of their children, their feeding, clothing and washing, their education and recreation; but mothers can expect the State to take over aspects of this socialisation – particularly education and some recreation – at a particular point in their children's lives. In other words, the life course of a normally developing child is relatively predictable, and although the care of that child will demand a great deal in terms of time and emotion from the mother, at least she can make plans for herself within a fairly ordered universe, as can the state. Carers' need for support is ostensibly fairly similar to that of mothers. They too have to feed, clothe and wash their cared-for, and provide for their recreation and (for younger people) education. But the one thing about caring, particularly where elderly people are concerned, is that it is unpredictable. A carer may expect to care for someone who appears to be close to death for a brief period, only to find that the person they are looking after recovers to live for many more years but in a highly dependent condition. Moreover, just as there is no predictability whatsoever about when, if at all, the State will step in to take over some of these caring functions, so there is no predictability for the state as to when, for example, a once employed carer might return to work. Hence the development of rights to, for example, carers' career breaks is much more problematic than the development of rights surrounding maternity.

Moreover, if we are to operationalise rights in the context of informal care, then in effect we have to lay down standardised, minimum rights for carers and their cared-for, irrespective of their circumstances. But it would be quite wrong to standardise rights to services across all dependencies: young disabled adults clearly have quite different needs from older people who are mentally infirm. Similarly the needs of carers will vary, partially reflecting the particular dependencies of the persons they care for, but also carers themselves vary widely in terms, for example, of age, length of time spent caring and additional costs of caring. Not surprisingly, in the field of community care we are constantly trying to find ways of dealing with a variety of needs: hence all the talk of flexibility of care, and packages of care tailored to the particular needs of individual dependent people (Griffiths, 1988). I do not wish to rule out altogether the question of carers' rights to services; it is simply to recognise that there is bound to be a problem of matching highly various needs to standardised rights to services, and that there will always have to be a considerable place for the exercise of discretion.

16.4   Rights for carers

So how might care and citizenship be put together, as far as carers are concerned? As I have argued, the situation is extremely complicated, and the concept of rights in this context is a slippery one. This is both because it is very difficult to translate the public notion of rights into the private world of relationships, and also because carers and the situations in which they find themselves are very heterogeneous. However a number of suggestions as to how to underwrite carers' citizenship are currently under discussion, and indeed are being placed on the statute-book. The first concerns the development of employment rights for carers (such as so many days off a year to care for someone, protection of pension rights, career-break rights) or social service rights (such as the right to a certain number of hours or weeks of respite care, the right to access to a social worker or care manager, the right to a care allowance). A somewhat watered-down version of this idea of carers' rights has now been enshrined in the 1995 Carers (Recognition and Services) Act, which gives carers the right to have their own needs assessed alongside, but separate from, the needs assessment of the person for whom they are caring. Such assessment does not provide the basis for carer's right to services, and indeed has been criticised for not so doing (Arksey, 1996), but it does introduce a right to speak, and be heard.

Another set of rather more radical proposals queries the direction of community care altogether, suggesting that residential care for dependent people remains the better alternative (Finch, 1984) or that forms of collective care, which might include high-quality residential care, should be developed (Dalley, 1988). The difficulty here is that institutional care is notoriously vulnerable to the risk of becoming authoritarian and even brutal. Within a citizenship framework, if institutional care is to avoid this danger, then the right of residents and their families to high-quality and safe care has to be underwritten and enforced by widespread inspectorates, with teeth. Perhaps the best way of ensuring high-quality institutional care is to make it attractive to carers as well as their cared-for: Christmas for the family in 'the' home, rather than 'at' home.

Other radical proposals accept that community care policies should continue, but at the same time acknowledge that the burden on carers is very considerable, and that they should be compensated in some way.

Two different kinds of proposal then emerge: the first is the 'basic income guarantee', which would be a benefit payable to all citizens, irrespective of their employment or marital status. Everyone over a certain age would receive the same amount, which they could then supplement by earnings, which in turn would be highly taxed. This is not specifically a carers' benefit, although those who support this proposal often argue that one of its main advantages is that it recognises the unpaid labour of housewives, mothers and carers and provides them with an independent income (Parker, 1990). Basic income has also been adopted by many commentators as the way of operationalising the concept of citizenship (Jordan, 1989; Dahrendorf, 1990; Pateman, 1989). The difficulty here, as far as carers are concerned, is that if everyone gets the same, then the specific work of caring in effect remains unrecognised. There is also the more general problem that basic income proposals are extremely expensive, and in the current political climate are thought not to be feasible.

The second proposal along these lines is that carers should be paid for the work they do. The feasibility of such a proposal is not so open to question since there are already systems of payment in place for, in particular, foster parents (Leat and Gay, 1987), and there are comparable developments for carers nationally and internationally (Evers *et al.*, 1994: Glendinning and McLaughlin, 1993; Ungerson, 1995). Of course such a proposal commodifies care, and the effect is that it might alter, quite possibly for the worse as much as for the better, the relationship between carer and cared-for. It is not that difficult, for example, to imagine people assuming they have an infinite right to their carers' time and patience because their carers' time and patience is being paid for by the state.

16.5   Conclusion: a growing rights-based discourse

This chapter has presented a somewhat sceptical view of the position of carers *vis-à-vis* citizenship in general and rights in particular. On the whole I have pinpointed the dilemmas and complexities that arise when we try to put caring and citizenship together, and the difficulty of operating a public concept of rights within the caring relationship. It is nevertheless the case that the policy discourse on community care is increasingly couched in terms of 'rights' for both carers and care users. Both the Carers (Recognition and Services) Act 1995 and the Community Care (Direct Payments) Act 1996 introduced statutory intervention into the care relationship, and potentially provided the foundation for further rights-based developments in the operation of community care. In the case of the Carers (Recognition and Services) Act, this gives carers the right to an assessment but not to services; it nevertheless imposes on local authorities a statutory duty to take into account carers' needs when making their assessment of users' needs and deciding on appropriate services for users. Thus a space is provided where a politics of carers' rights may well develop, supported not just by carers' pressure groups (such as the Carers National Association), but also by social services department care managers who, once they start hearing what carers want, will begin to see carers' rights as a way of providing support for effective informal care relationships. This is particularly likely to be the case with rights to employment protection, paid leave and so on, which, for local authority care managers are cost-free. In the case of 'direct payments', where care users are given the right to opt for cash rather than services, such organisation of service delivery through cash and the market rather than through the discretionary judgement of professionals and managers at first glance looks rather more like the extension of effective demand than the expansion of social rights. However there is no doubt that disabled people themselves see direct payments as an extension of their social rights (Morris, 1993). Moreover the introduction of contractual arrangements between disabled people and the people who care for them will begin to surround the care relationship with rights protected by contract and employment law. While, for the moment, direct payments to kin are specifically excluded by the legislation, it is noticeable that there is already a groundswell of opinion (writing in early 1996) coming from the carers' lobbies that Social Services Departments should have the discretionary power to allow disabled people to use direct payments to employ their kin when care managers think it appropriate (Carers National Association, 1995). Thus slowly but surely the language and practice of rights, on the part of both carers and users, is beginning to frame the caring relationship. What remains to be seen is whether, through these developments, the quality of the care relationship and the citizenship of carers and users are enhanced.

Note

1. The German principle of 'subsidiarity', laid down in the German Social Assistance Act, states that before individuals can qualify for state social assistance they have to have tried – and demonstrate that they have failed – to change their own circumstances and to get support from their immediate family or voluntary organisations (Jamieson, 1990).

References

Arksey, H. (1996) 'Missed target', *Community Care*, 29 March–3 April.
Carers National Association (1995) *Community Care (Direct Payments) Bill*,

Response to the Government's Consultation Paper, Carers' National Association, London.

Cass, B. (1990) 'Gender and social citizenship: the politics and economics of participation and exclusion', paper given at the Social Policy Association annual conference, University of Bath.

Dahrendorf, R. (1990) 'Decade of the citizen', interview with J. Keane, *Guardian*, 1 August.

Dalley, G. (1988) *Ideologies of Caring: Rethinking Community and Collectivism*, Macmillan, London.

Evers, A., Pijl, M. and Ungerson, C. (1994) (eds) *Payments for Care: A comparative overview*, Avebury, Aldershot.

Finch, J. (1984) 'Community care: developing non-sexist alternatives', *Critical Social Policy*, No. 9, pp. 6–18.

Glendinning, C. and McLaughlin, E. (1993) *Financial Support for Informal Care: A European Study*, HMSO, London.

Green, H. (1988) *Informal Carers: a Study*, Office of Population Censuses and Surveys, HMSO, London.

Griffiths, R. (1988) *Community Care: Agenda for Action*, HMSO, London.

Jamieson, A. (1990) 'Informal care in Europe', in Jamieson, A. and Illsley, R. (eds), *Contrasting European Policies for the Care of Older People*, Gower, Aldershot.

Jordan, B. (1989) *The Common Good: Citizenship, Morality, and Self-Interest*, Blackwell, Oxford.

Land, H. (1978) 'Who cares for the family?', *Journal of Social Policy*, Vol. 7, No. 3, pp. 257–84.

Leat, D. and Gay, P. (1987) *Paying for Care: A Study of Policy and Practice in Paid Care Schemes*, Policy Studies Institute, Research Report No. 661, London.

Lister, R. (1990) 'Women, economic dependency and citizenship', *Journal of Social Policy*, Vol. 19, No. 4, pp. 445–67.

Morris, J. (1993) *Independent Lives?: Community care and disabled people*, Macmillan, Basingstoke.

Parker, H. (1990) 'Terminology', *Basic Income Research Group Bulletin*, No. 12, February.

Pateman, C. (1988) *The Sexual Contract*, Polity Press, Cambridge.

Pateman, C. (1989) *The Disorder of Women: Democracy, Feminism and Political Theory*, Polity Press, Cambridge.

Ungerson, C. (1987) *Policy is Personal*, Tavistock, London.

Ungerson, C. (1995) 'Gender, cash and informal care: European perspectives and dilemmas', *Journal of Social Policy*, Vol. 24, No. 1, pp. 31–52.

The Principles of Collective Care*

GILLIAN DALLEY

17.1 Essential principles of collective care

Home Life, a code of practice for residential care published in 1984 and updated in 1996 (Centre for Policy on Ageing, 1984, 1996), outlines a set of principles that should underpin good care: fulfilment, individuality, dignity, autonomy, respect and esteem. These provide a useful starting point for developing a coherent and principled approach to organizing residential care.

'Building on this approach, it is possible to identify further essential principles that must be observed in the development of any form of care. Responsiveness to individual need and inclination is clearly one, but perhaps overriding that and all others from the cared-for person's perspective is the ability for that person to be responsible for his or her own life. This is a theme that emerges from many studies of disability and dependence (Blaxter, 1976; Shearer, 1982a; Morris, 1991, 1993), and it is precisely this quality that current provision too often denies. Disabled people recognize quite clearly that, to varying degrees, they require assistance or support (Morris, 1991; Wood, 1991) from other people for the performing of certain basic tasks. They acknowledge that independence, in the sense that this might imply freedom from such reliance on other people, is not an option for them, however sophisticated mechanical aids and adaptations might become. What they are concerned with is to be able to control the way in which they manage that dependence and the degree to which they have options from which to choose. Dependence and interdependence are a part of ordinary life (Shearer, 1982b); a life of total *independence* would mean isolation and separation. In the view of one disabled person, disabled people are victims of an

---

* This is an abridged extract from *Ideologies of Caring*, 2nd edn, Macmillan Press Ltd, 1996, pp. 121–8.

'ideology of independence' whereby a disabled person is penalized by exclusion from society if he or she is unable to accomplish the tasks of daily living; for the disabled person, independence means control rather than accomplishment of this kind (Brisenden, 1989, quoted in Morris, 1993).

For collectivists, it is the recognition of dependence and interdependence as facets of all human relationships that validates their approach to the issue of caring. By the collectivity taking on responsibility for the provision of care, the tensions, burden and obligation inherent in the one-to-one caring relationship, which are the product of the family model of care, are overcome. Particular individuals are not forced into particular caring and cared for roles, dictated by their social and biological relatedness, for it is in those relationships that dependence becomes a warped and unhealthy pressure on the actors involved. In collectively shared relationships of caring, the burdens are dispersed and fewer pressures arise. The individuals who are being cared for are not forced into dependence on certain other individuals with whom they might have other kinds of relationships (of love, dislike, intellectual partnership, parenthood, siblingship, and so on).

Thus the first principle of collective care, which is also applicable to any form of care provision, must be for the disabled and/or dependent individual to be in a position to be responsible for his or her life choices. These should not be once-and-for-all choices – the possibility for change has to be incorporated. Equally, those who provide care should also be in a position to be responsible for decisions about their role in providing care. Women should not be forced into the position of having to care at the cost of other choices, and the status and economic rewards of caring should be comparable with those of alternative activities.

A second principle should be that the system of care should be responsive to the needs and inclinations of the individuals receiving care. This must mean that forms of care should be flexible in themselves – rigid routines and fixed expectations should play no part – and movement between different forms of care *when appropriate* should be possible. However, this should not be mandatory; concepts such as the continuum of care, which sees dependent people moving from one form of care into another as their dependency-related conditions improve or deteriorate, often fail to recognize the regimentation which that may involve. Existing care should be responsive, as far as possible, to accommodate such changes, rather than the dependent person being expected to change location.

A third principle must be maximal opportunity to form as wide and varied a range of personal relationships as the individual might wish. This might be coupled with a fourth principle – an equally maximal opportunity to develop skills and talents in any way that the individual chooses. It is important to recognize the multiplicity of skills and talents that every individual has and – in the case of older people – has developed and nurtured over a lifetime. Room must also be given for the expression of joy and sorrow and for the capacity for intimacy (Brown and Thompson, 1994). These principles relate closely to concepts of integration, ordinary life and normalization, although the normative and, indeed, prescriptive implications of the latter concept may be inappropriate (Dalley, 1992) if one of the objects of this alternative approach to care is to open up new ways of being and doing. Dependent individuals should not be cut off from other areas of social life if they choose not to be; on the other hand, they should be free to develop their own social environment in the way they wish. An ordinary life means precisely that – that the lives of dependent people should be unremarkable, should not be *ab*normal.

A fifth principle should underwrite all the others: dependent people should be economically secure, to ensure that the other principles have real meaning. Berthoud (1991), Shearer (1982a) and Blaxter (1976) examine the effects that economic constraints have on disabled people endeavouring to live independently. Indeed, Williams (1983) notes that Shearer suggests direct monetary assistance to be the most important resource permitting some people with disabilities to live independently. This has been substantially confirmed by recent studies of the Independent Living Fund, set up specifically to enable disabled people to pay directly for forms of support of their own choosing (Kestenbaum, 1993; Lakey, 1994). There can be no ordinary life and no control over choice or exercise of responsibility in conditions of poverty. In Britain, the level of income maintenance for disabled people is notoriously low, despite recent changes in the benefits system with the introduction of the disability living allowance, which is ostensibly intended to improve the position (Rowlingson and Berthoud, 1994). Arbitrary limits are put on the levels of state support available for people in residential care, unrelated to the actual costs, and, furthermore, the trend in recent years has been for the state to transfer financial responsibility to individuals and their families. Comparison of state retirement pension levels between current and past provision and between Britain and other countries, reveals how far Britain is from guaranteeing those who are not economically active a secure standard of living.

17.2 Contrary views

When disabled people read discussions about their position written by people who are not disabled, they respond forcibly. When this chapter was first published (Dalley, 1988) it provoked strong criticism from disabled writers, notably Jenny Morris (1991).[1] The principal focus of their criticism is that non-disabled commentators write from a viewpoint that, while using them as subjects, excludes disabled people from the analysis. This then leads to a failure to understand disabled people's own perspective. Essentially, their argument is that non-disabled writers see disabled people as a burden and as dependent on society in general and their carers in particular, instead of seeing them as full citizens with the same rights to develop their potential as all other citizens. Rejecting the medical model of disability, which focuses on the extent of their physical or mental impairment, they regard disability as socially defined. While they have impairments that may inhibit their mental or physical functioning, it is society that disables them by refusing to make buildings and transport systems accessible, by excluding people with impairments from employment and by refusing to provide sufficient personal support services for them. They favour the term 'disabled people' because it draws attention to the fact that the disabling comes from society and not from themselves.

Those who adopt this perspective have a particular hostility towards institutional care for disabled people. For them, it represents the way in which society excludes them and herds them together out of sight and out of mind. They believe it emphasizes the model of disability that locates the problem with disabled people themselves – they require full-time care because they cannot look after themselves, they are dependent on others. For the same reason, disabled people have attacked the current emphasis on protecting the interests of carers. Disabled people see an ideological collusion between policy makers and carers, which, again, focuses on the notion of disabled people as dependent, as burdens, as encroaching on the freedom and autonomy of those upon whom they are dependent.

Activists in the disability movement – for example, the British Council of Organisations of Disabled People – campaign powerfully for the right to control their own lives through a variety of strategies. They argue for antidiscrimination legislation (Oliver, 1991; Wood, 1991) as a means of strengthening their position in relation to their participation in the public sphere. They also argue for economic and financial autonomy. Instead of being provided with inadequate services, allocated by uncomprehending professional state employees, disabled people want to receive cash allowances with which to buy the personal assistance they themselves choose. Only in this way, they argue, will they be able to live independent lives – independent in the way *they* define independence (Morris, 1993) – in control of their life circumstances.

In the light of these views, it is hard to present a counter argument. Morris is particularly critical of feminists who try to do so. While she accepts that feminist analysis has an important contribution to make to

disability theory – through accepting the personal experience of impairment as a valid component of the disabled person's perspective (rather
than focusing on disability as a wholly social creation) (Morris, 1991) –
she criticizes feminists for treating 'women' and 'dependent people' (disabled people) as completely separate groups with conflicting interests.
This separation extends, in much feminist analysis, she suggests, to
working-class women and to black women. It is thus fatally compromised.

When feminists argue for the extension of collectivist principles to the
field of care, disabled people find the argument especially hard to accept.
For them, even the concept of care is inappropriately applied to their situation. They do not seek care; rather, they require personal assistance or
support. Morris calls for the term 'care' to be restored to its rightful
meaning of caring 'about' and not caring 'for'. They resist the idea that
one option might be for personal support to be provided on a collective
basis. The memories of institutional care in the past preclude any consideration of new possibilities.

It could be argued, however, that this view is too narrow. There may
be circumstances in which collective systems of care are valid, both in
terms of basic principles and in relation to the people who might benefit
from them. It is significant to note that the priority groups who are the
focus of current community care policies are not homogeneous either in
type and degree of impairment or, thus, in their need for support. The
pertinence of the principles established may vary accordingly. A young
person who is physically impaired is in a very different situation from a
very elderly person suffering from senile dementia; likewise, a mentally
ill, middle-aged individual has different needs and wants from a child
who has severe learning difficulties. Young people at the beginning of
their lives may be eager to develop social networks; old people facing the
end of their lives may be more concerned with consolidating and maintaining existing social networks than seeking new ones. Physical disability requires physical care, especially related to problems of mobility-
mental disability requires different forms of supportive care, and chronic
sickness may require constant nursing care. These differences have major
consequences for the expectations that individuals themselves have of
their own lives and for the varieties of care that should be available.
Williams (1983) makes a pertinent comment on the heterogeneity of
dependency in his critique of the independent living movement in the
USA:

> The core constituency of the independent living movement is young, male and
> 'fit' as opposed to 'frail', whereas a major feature of the social reality of dis-
> ablement is the elderly female, lacking in robustness and living far from the
> supportive confines of university campuses [where the independent living

movement originated]. It may well be that the disadvantage and needs of an elderly arthritic in an urban slum have more similarity to the problems of her able-bodied neighbours than to the values of the movement for independent living.

There may be a danger, then, if the heterogeneity of dependency is ignored, that certain groups may be excluded from benefiting from developments in patterns of care. In policy and administrative terms, it is relatively straightforward to talk about priority groups as a whole, but the reality of the lives of the people who form those groups is far from straightforward. The flexibility and responsiveness to need, discussed above, has to include the policy and administrative levels, and from there permeate the whole system, involving from the outset the people who are to be in receipt of care (or personal assistance) or their advocates. Indeed, some might argue that only those in receipt of care have any conclusive right to determine types and standards of care. If this is so, the right should also be extended to the other potential partner in the caring dyad – those who provide the care, both paid and unpaid, and who are predominantly women.

Note

1. In Chapter 18 we reproduce an extract from *Pride Against Prejudice* by Jenny Morris which articulates these criticisms.

References

Berthoud, R. (1991) 'Meeting the costs of disability', in Dalley, G. (ed.), *Disability and Social Policy*, Policy Studies Institute, London.

Blaxter, M. (1976) *The Meaning of Disability*, Heinemann, London.

Brisenden, S. (1989) 'A charter for personal care', *Disablement Income Group Progress*, 16.

Brown, C. and Thompson, K. (1994) 'A quality life: searching for quality of life in residential services for elderly people', *Australian Journal on Ageing*, Vol. 13, No. 3.

Centre for Policy on Ageing (1984) *Home Life: A Code of Practice for Residential Care*, Centre for Policy on Ageing, London.

Centre for Policy on Ageing (1996) *A Better Home Life*, Centre for Policy on Ageing, London.

Dalley, G. (1988) *Ideologies of Caring*, 1st edn, Macmillan, London.

Dalley, G. (1992) 'Social welfare ideologies and normalisation: links and conflicts' in Brown, H. and Smith, H. (eds), *Normalisation: A Reader for the Nineties*, Tavistock/Routledge, London.

Kestenbaum, A. (1993) *An Opportunity Lost? Social Services Use of the Independent Living Transfer*, Disablement Income Group, London.

Lakey, J. (1994) *Disabled People and the Independent Living Fund*, Policy Studies Institute, London.

Morris, J. (1991) *Pride Against Prejudice*, The Women's Press, London.

Morris, J. (1993) *Independent Lives: Community Care and Disabled People*, Macmillan, London.

Oliver, M. (1991) 'Speaking out: disabled people and state welfare', in Dalley, G. (ed.), *Disability and Social Policy*, Policy Studies Institute, London.

Rowlingson, K. and Berthoud, R. (1994) *Evaluating the Disability Working Allowance*, Policy Studies Institute, London.

Shearer, A. (1982a) *Living Independently*, Centre for the Environment for the Handicapped and King Edward's Hospital Fund for London, London.

Shearer, A. (1982b) *An Ordinary Life: Issues and Strategies for Training Staff for community Mental Handicap Services*, King's Fund Project Paper, No. 42, King's Fund Centre, London.

Williams, G. H. (1983) 'The movement for independent living: an evaluation and critique', *Social Science and Medicine*, Vol.17, No.15.

Wood, R. (1991) 'Care of disabled people', in Dalley, G. (ed.), *Disability and Social Policy*, Policy Studies Institute, London.

18

'Us' and 'Them'? Feminist Research and Community Care*

JENNY MORRIS

Community care is a major area of concern for feminist academics, yet the experiences of disabled and older women are missing from the debate, from the research and from the development of theory. This has meant that, in attempting to explore forms of care which do not depend on women's unpaid work within the family, non-disabled feminists have advocated residential care. Thus Janet Finch writes, 'On balance it seems to me that the residential route is the only one which ultimately will offer us a way out of the impasse of caring' (Finch, 1984, p. 16).

Disabled and older people experience daily the inadequacies of 'community care'. However, as individuals and through our organisations we have put our energies into achieving a better quality of life *within* the community. How has this conflict between non-disabled feminist academics and organisations of disabled people come about?

18.1   Us' and 'Them'

For feminists writing and researching on carers, the category 'women' does not include those who need physical assistance. When Janet Finch asked 'Can we envisage any version of community care which is not sexist?' she went on, 'If we cannot, then we need to say something about how we imagine such people *can* be cared for in ways which we find acceptable' (1984, p. 7). In order to understand how she, and other feminists, answer this question we need to recognise who Janet Finch means

* This article is an edited version of a chapter in *Pride Against Prejudice: Transforming Attitudes to Disability*, The Women's Press, 34 Great Sutton Street, London, 1991.

when she says 'we' and whether 'we' are included in the term 'such people'.

The latter term refers to 'people . . . whose physical needs require fairly constant attendance' (p. 7). Throughout Finch's writing it is clear that the term 'we' does not include 'such people'. When Finch and others are assessing what policies would be acceptable to 'us' she means what policies would be acceptable to non-disabled feminists.

Feminist research on caring explicitly separates out non-disabled women from disabled women. This distinction has major implications for the issues which feminists consider important. Finch and Groves, for example, identified that the equal opportunity issues around community care concerned the sexual division of labour between men and women as carers (Finch and Groves, 1983). In none of the research is there any analysis of equal opportunity issues for disabled and older women.

This separating out of disabled and older women from the category of 'women' comes about because these feminist researchers fail to identify with the subjective experience of 'such people'. The principle of 'the personal is political' is applied to carers but not to the cared for. This is articulated by Clare Ungerson's account of why the issue of caring is of personal significance. She writes 'my interest in carers and the work that they do arises out of my own biography. The fact that my mother was a carer and looked after my grandmother in our home until my grandmother's death when I was 14 combines with the knowledge that, as an only daughter, my future contains the distinct possibility that I will sooner or later become a carer myself' (Ungerson, 1987, p. 2). Lois Keith, a disabled feminist, commented on Ungerson's inability to see *herself* as potentially a person who needs physical care, 'Most of us can imagine being responsible for someone weaker than ourselves, even if we hope this won't happen. It is certainly easier to see ourselves as being needed, than to imagine ourselves as dependent on our partner, parents or children for some of our most basic needs' (Keith, 1990).

Ungerson's failure to identity with those who need care is then carried over into her feminist analysis, which must remain incomplete while she considers only one part of the caring relationship. Yet again disabled and older women are marginalised – but this time by those who proclaim their commitment to 'women-centred issues'.

18.2 Gillian Dalley's 'Collectivism'

Gillian Dalley presents the most fully developed feminist critique of community care, arguing for the development of social policy based on the principle of collectivism rather than that of familism and possessive individualism which she says motivates community care policies (see Chapter 17).

Most disabled people would thoroughly endorse Dalley's promotion of the principles of collectivism and mutual support. We would also welcome her insistence that disabled and older people should 'be in a position to be responsible for his or her life choices' (Dalley, 1988, p. 115). The problem is that she reaches a decision about which policies should be supported without allowing our voices to be heard.

One of Dalley's reasons for arguing against community care policies is that she believes that these policies are not necessarily supported by 'dependent people'. Unfortunately, the only evidence that she produces to back this up is from non-disabled people. The only time she cites the opinion of a disabled person, she quotes him out of context to support a position which he would never have agreed with. In advocating group living for disabled people, Dalley quotes Bernard Brett (whom she describes as 'heavily dependent') on the advantages of having more than one person providing personal care. 'Nothing is quite as corrupting for all concerned as being completely dependent on too few people' he says. 'I can promise you, there are few less pleasant things than to be cared for by somebody who is constantly tired and under too much strain. This makes life tense, unpleasant and unfulfilled' (quoted in Dalley, 1988, p 120).

Far from advocating some kind of residential, group-living situation (which is how Dalley uses this quote), Bernard Brett was describing a set-up where he had bought his own house, let rooms in it to non-disabled lodgers and employed a number of different carers. Like many disabled people, Bernard Brett described residential care as 'a form of living death' and like most non-disabled people he wanted a home of his own (see Shearer, 1982, pp. 37–48).

Bernard Brett was not, of course, receiving 'family care'. He was instead able to choose to pay (in cash and in kind) those who provided assistance to him. However, feminists such as Dalley and Finch have dismissed this as an option, arguing that even where assistance within the home is provided by a paid carer that carer is still likely to be a low-paid, low-status woman and, although this is also true for care workers employed in residential establishments, residential workers are more likely to be able to campaign for better pay and conditions. They see the removal of caring for disabled and older people from a family setting as a crucial part of undermining women's dependency.

Dalley dismisses the demands that have been made by disabled people and their organisations for good quality services to enable them to live in their own homes, insisting that such demands are merely expressions of dominant ideology.

She argues, 'Propounders of the familist ideal favour it [a community care policy] because for them it embodies notions of the family as haven, as repository of warm, caring, human relationships based on mutual responsibility and affection and thus a private protection against a cold, hostile, outside world' (Dalley, 1988, p. 25). When disabled and older people express an aversion to residential care, according to Dalley, this must be set in the context of the strength of the ideology of the family.

There is no recognition here that disabled people are often denied the family relationships that she takes for granted. Insult is then added to injury by the assumption that for a disabled person to aspire to warm, caring human relationships within the setting where most non-disabled people looked to find them is a form of false consciousness.

Dalley also insists that disabled people's organisations are not representative. Anti-feminists often seek to undermine feminism by claiming that most feminists are white, young and middle-class. Dalley echoes this sort of divisiveness by quoting a critic of the Independent Living Movement (ILM). 'The core constituency of the independent living movement is young, male and "fit" as opposed to "frail", whereas a major feature of the social reality of disablement is the elderly female, lacking in robustness and living far from the supportive confines of university campuses [where the American ILM originated]' (G. H. Williams, quoted by Dalley, 1988, p. 117).

It is certainly true that the ILM is dominated by men. However, to use this to undermine the principles of the movement is to deny the basic human rights for which it stands. The aims of the ILM are not only relevant to young, middle-class, white men. Such men are merely demanding what young, middle-class, white, non-disabled men take for granted. The economic and social advantages of this latter group normally enable them to achieve such things – and this is why it is common for white, middle-class young men to react with such outrage when their social and economic privileges are suddenly threatened by disability. Why shouldn't those of us whose class, race, age, gender and disability mean that we are denied such advantages, insist on the same rights?

Given non-disabled feminists' inability to identify with our subjective experience, perhaps they should be wary of prescribing the kind of care that would be best for us. Dalley, however, is not inhibited by this. Dismissing the demands of the Independent Living Movement, she advocates new forms of residential provision on the grounds that it is only by removing caring and servicing functions from a family setting that the sexual division of labour (in both the private and public sphere) will be fundamentally undermined. A sceptical disabled feminist may comment that if communal living is such a liberating force for women, then perhaps non-disabled women should try it first.

Dalley argues that a group home would make it possible for a 'bed-bound' young mother to develop an 'ungendered' role. Such a woman, says Dalley, will not expect to 'take up a domestic role *vis-à-vis* house-work and child-rearing as she would (because of normative attitudes at large) if she were able-bodied' (1988, p. 122). Others would perform this role for her and the advantage of a 'collective' setting, according to Dalley, is that her role would be performed by men or women, depending on who was employed.

Such a solution to accommodation and personal assistance needs would be firmly rejected by disabled mothers like Sheila Willis, whom I interviewed when writing *Pride against Prejudice: Transforming Attitudes to Disability* (Morris, 1991). Her aim after learning that she had multiple sclerosis was to remain living in her own home continuing her role of a mother caring for her daughter. Sheila rejected the term 'bed-bound' 'What me? *Bound* to a bed?'. During the last years of her life, she spent most of the time on her bed, organising and taking responsibility for not only her own household but also setting up a voluntary organisation which would provide help to other disabled people. A feminist for 15 years, her role as a mother and her ability to run her own home were intensely important to her; to deny this would be a denial of her funda-mental human rights – and those of her daughter.

18.3   Different questions, different answers

Feminists cannot claim to have developed a full analysis of and adequate strategies on community care until the experiences of disabled and older people are included within the research. Nasa Begum, a disabled femi-nist, recently carried out a piece of qualitative research into ten disabled women's experience of receiving personal care which illustrates some of the ways that this subjective experience can be incorporated into a femi-nist analysis of community care (Begum, 1990).

Disabled feminists (were they properly represented within the acad-emic and research community) would raise new questions when car-rying out research on community care and would not be faced with the stark choice which Finch has posed between community care or residen-tial care.

Instead of focusing on the 'taking charge of' part of Hilary Graham's definition of 'caring about' (Graham, 1983, p. 13), such research would focus more clearly on the reciprocity involved in caring relationships and the threats to that reciprocity. Loss of reciprocity brings with it a vulnera-bility to abuse.

Little attention has been paid to disabled and older people's experi-ence of physical and emotional abuse, which occurs within both residen-tial and community care. Unfortunately feminism's concern with the various forms of abuse experienced by non-disabled women has generally failed to incorporate the experience of disabled women.

We should ask whether people want to receive physical care from someone they care about and who cares for them. For someone like Clare Robson, who has multiple sclerosis and lives with her lover and her children, the answer is clear 'I know that I am loved and that I love her. I feel very privileged and secure. I never, ever, anticipated a relationship that was so wonderful and loving. Obviously there are difficulties. There are, in effect, three of us – me, her and the MS – and we have to take account of the uninvited guest, the squatter' (Morris, 1991, p. 164).

On the other hand, Simon Brisenden identified that where there are no options other than dependence on a relative or partner, then this can be 'the most exploitative of all forms of so-called care delivered in our society today for it exploits both the carer and the person receiving care. It ruins relationships between people and results in thwarted life opportunities on both sides of the caring equation' (Brisenden, 1989, pp. 9–10).

Research must examine what makes 'caring for' in a 'caring about' relationship possible in a way which meets the interests of both parties. Many disabled people have identified that 'caring for' in a 'caring about' relationship cannot work unless there is real choice based on real alternatives. Such a choice cannot exist where the only alternative to assistance by a partner or relative at home is residential care.

Feminist research which incorporated the experiences of disabled and older people might also raise the question of the meaning of the word 'home', separating this out, in a conceptual and political sense, from the feminist critique of the family. Disabled feminists should be able to assert their right to live in their own home without being accused of supporting the oppression of women within the family.

Feminist research on caring emphasises that most carers are women. There are in fact 2.5 million male carers and 3.5 million female carers, although women are more likely to be full-time carers (Green, 1988). It is of fundamental concern to (particularly heterosexual) disabled women to challenge the assumption that men will not 'care for' in a 'caring about' relationship.

This assumption is often experienced as oppressive by disabled women, confronted by health and social services professionals who undermine the ability of such women to sustain heterosexual relationships. For example, it seems to be common for married women entering spinal injury units, particularly if they are tetraplegic, to encounter a negative attitude towards the chances of their marriages surviving their disability (Morris, 1989, p. 83).

If men are carers they are most likely to be caring for their wives. In 1986, 46 per cent of British women in the 45-64 age group reported long-standing illness and for 28 per cent their illness limited their activities

(General Household Survey, 1989, p. 147). We need to know more about the experiences of the significant number of women in both this age group and in older age groups who rely on their husbands for care.

Roughly the same levels of long-standing illness are found amongst men in these age groups, which must mean that there are many households where both partners require some level of care. Amongst the elderly population there is evidence that significant numbers of carers are also in need of care. We need to know what factors enable or prevent women from getting the care they need.

Feminist research tends to draw very distinct lines between carers and those who are cared for, so the extent to which older and disabled women are also carers is obscured. Research on women who have experienced spinal cord injury found that 'women are primarily the carers within a family and most of us continue in this role. Yet too often it is assumed that we will be the passive recipients of care' (Morris, 1989, p. 188).

The failure of feminist researchers and academics to identify with the subjective experience of those who receive care has meant that they have studied caring situations where there are seemingly very clear distinctions between the person who cares for and the person who receives care. The most common source of identifying potential interviewees has been organisations to whom people have identified themselves as carers. However, a situation in which one party to a relationship has a clear identity as a carer while the other is clearly cared for can only represent one type of caring relationship. It may be that in other situations the roles are blurred, or shifting. We may also want to expand our definition of caring for to encompass not just physical tasks but also the emotional part of caring-for relationships. Research carried out by disabled feminists would, therefore, focus not so much on carers as on caring.

Disabled people would join with non-disabled feminists in rejecting the way that 'community care' too often means 'family care'. But we would assert our own political demand – a demand for the right to live within the community in a non-disabling environment with the kind of personal assistance that we would choose. In doing this, we are not only pursuing the human rights of disabled and older people but also launching an attack on the form that caring currently taxes. Such a strategy should therefore also be clearly supported by feminists who wish to undermine women's dependency within the family.

References

Begum, N. (1990) *The Burden of Gratitude*, University of Warwick and SCA, Warwick.

Brisenden, S. (1989) 'A charter for personal care', *Progress*, 16, Disablement Income Group.

Dalley, G. (1988) *Ideologies of Caring: Rethinking Community and Collectivism*, Macmillan, London.

Finch, J. (1984) 'Community care: developing non-sexist alternatives', *Critical Social Policy*, Vol. 9.

Finch, J. and Groves, D. (eds) (1983) *A Labour of Love Women, Work and Caring*, Routledge and Kegan Paul, London.

Graham, H. (1983) 'Caring: a labour of love', in Finch, J. and Groves, D. (eds), *A Labour of Love: Women, Work and Caring*, Routledge and Kegan Paul, London.

Green, H. (1988) 'Informal Carers', *General Household Survey 1985*, Supplement A, HMSO, London.

Keith, L. (1990) 'Caring partnership', *Community Care*, 22 February 1990.

Morris, J. (1989) *Able Lives: Women's Experience of Paralysis*, Women's Press, London.

Morris, J. (1991) *Pride Against Prejudice: Transforming Attitudes to Disability*, Women's Press, London.

Shearer, A. (1982) *Living Independently*, CEH and King's Fund, London.

Ungerson, C. (1987) *Policy is Personal*, Tavistock, London.

Part III

POLICY

19

Introduction

This section provides material on the policy aspects of community care. There is always a tension between policy and practice. Expressed somewhat contentiously, policy is what happens in theory, whereas practice is what happens in reality. Be that as it may, policy is important because it represents how people think, what society values, what is intended to happen and how governments endeavour to engineer change.

The section begins with an anthology of extracts from a variety of documentary sources since the early nineteenth century. Most are from policy documents, but we also include extracts from a powerful series of research studies that were carried out during the late 1950s and 1960s on institutional care. These studies certainly fuelled the flames of future community care policies. Following the anthology are a series of articles that raise a number of fundamental issues about community care policy at the turn of this century.

In the opening article, Len Doyal argues that, on the basis of human need, people have a moral right to optimal community care. This philosophical treatment of community care policy introduces a moral dimension to debates about need and provision. At a time when community care decision making tends to be driven by notions of targeting, budget management and cost-effectiveness, his humanistic perspective is particularly important. Community care policy is focused on those deemed to be in need, who are often described as 'dependent'. Peter Townsend's chapter is an influential article from the early 1980s that demonstrates how the 'dependency' of older people is socially created through social and economic policies that deprive people of equal access to resources.

It is important to consider the historical context of community care policy and the social and economic imperatives that drive policy development. Alan Walker presents a challenging analysis of the development of community care policies in the 1980s and 1990s, particularly in relation to older people. He disputes the claim that changes over this period have promoted more choice for services users and puts forward an alternative strategy for a progressive community care policy that would create new options and guarantee the right to good quality care. David Pilgrim also considers alternative approaches to community care and suggests how mental health services can be user-led as opposed to professionally dominated. A further review of the development of community care policy is provided by Joan Busfield. Her focus is on mental health policy and she offers competing explanations as to why there was a shift from institutional care to community care.

Community care policy for people with learning difficulties has long been underpinned by the principle of normalisation. Hilary Brown and Jan Walmsley take a critical look at how this principle has been interpreted and put into practice. Is normalisation an inclusive concept that values us as we are, or is it an exclusive concept that requires us to fit socially accepted norms?

Community care is not just about the provision of care services to those in need of support; it is also about having an adequate income and suitable housing to lead a 'normal' life in the community. The final chapter of this section focuses on housing, a somewhat neglected aspect of community care policy. Judith Hudson, Lynn Watson and Graham Allan, on the basis of their own research, report on what housing choices people with support needs have and make. As they point out, suitable accommodation is usually a priority for people, to be followed by negotiations over support services. This echoes Len Doyal's argument that housing and income are essential to meeting basic human need. In the debates on community care policy, it is all too easy to overlook the building blocks of a sound community care policy – shelter and economic security.

20

*Anthology: Policy**

Compiled by DAVID PILGRIM and JULIA JOHNSON

This anthology of extracts, mainly from official documents, starts with the 1834 Poor Law, which enunciated the principle of 'less eligibility'. This ensured that those not in work were inevitably going to be poor, as they had to receive less than the lowest-paid worker. The Law also ushered in the end of outdoor relief and the central regulation of Poor Law institutions. The latter were workhouses for sane, able-bodied adults, or specialist institutions for others. The Poor Law administrators conceived of five groups in need of special provision: children, the sick, the insane, the 'defective' and the 'infirm and aged'. Gradually other legislation (for example the 1845 Lunacy Act) formalised the separation of these groups after the general principle of segregation was announced by the Poor Law.

The sections from the Radnor and Wood reports demonstrate the interplay between a segregative policy in the first part of this century and, prevailing eugenic ideas. These included the notion that a variety of groups – pauper lunatics, criminals and mental defectives – were a product of a 'tainted' genetic stock, which threatened the quality of the British race.

The extracts from the mid-twentieth century give some sense of the transition from the old segregative policy to one moving out to the community. The moral and political arguments for desegregation intensified following the Second World War in the wake of the Nazi concentration camps and in the context of an egalitarian ethos associated with the new National Health Service.

The material from the 1980s reveals a strong consensus in documents from and for government, as well as those from trade unions and voluntary bodies, about a positive approach to care in the community. Even the Wagner Report, which points to a new version of residential care as part of community care, strongly marks itself off from the old segregative philosophy. However the role of enforced segregation is still apparent within this consensus. Examples of this are shown in sections of the 1983 Mental Health

---

*Comparisons of public policy documents applying to England, Wales, Scotland and Northern Ireland are made in the following texts: D.J. Hunter and G. Wistow, *Community Care in Britain: Variations on a Theme*, King's Fund, London (1987); M. Titterton, 'Community care policy in the United Kingdom: conformity and diversity', in *Community Care*, K259 (Workbook 2), Open University, Milton Keynes, pp. 104–21.

Act. The powers of the 1948 National Assistance Act quoted are also still in force. (Its revision, in 1951, actually increased the speed at which local authorities can effect segregation.) Thus at the end of the twentieth century, legislation prescribes continuing local state *powers* to segregate people but also *obligations* to provide services for those defined to be in need, whether they are at home or not

---

Extract from the **English Poor Law** *1834. Here less eligibility is recommended and the notion that the benefit to the individual has to be weighed against that of the 'country at large'.*

. . . in the administration of relief, the public is warranted in imposing such conditions on the individual relief, as are conducive to the benefit either of the individual himself, or of the country at large, at whose expense he is to be relieved. The first and most essential of all conditions, a principle which we find universally admitted . . . is that his situation on the whole shall not be made really or apparently so eligible as the situation of the independent labourer of the lowest class. . . . Every penny bestowed, that tends to render the condition of the pauper more eligible than that of the independent labourer, is a bounty on indolence and vice. . . . All relief whatever to able-bodied persons or to their families, otherwise than in well-regulated workhouses . . . shall be declared unlawful.

From the Report of the **Royal Commission on the Care and Control of the Feebleminded (The Radnor Commission)**, *HMSO, London, 1908. This made recommendations which informed the 1913 Mental Deficiency Act.*

The Royal Commission devoted much attention to the causation of mental defect, and arrived at the conclusion that feeblemindedness is largely inherited; that prevention of mentally defective persons from becoming parents would tend to diminish such persons in the population; and that consequently there are strong grounds for placing mental defectives from each sex in institutions where they will be retained and kept under effectual supervision as long as may be necessary.

From the **Report of the Wood Committee**, *HMSO, London, 1929. This shows the continuing eugenic influences even after the First World War to reinforce the control of the fertility of segregated groups.*

If we are to prevent the racial disaster of mental deficiency we must not deal merely with the mentally defective person but with the whole subnormal group.[. . .] Primary amentia may be, and often is, an end result – the last stage of the inheritance of degeneracy of this subnormal group. The relative fertility of this group is greater than that of normal persons.

---

*From the **National Assistance Act** 1948. Under this legislation, which is still in force, those threatening their own or others' health can be removed from the community. Section 47 of the Act allows for the removal to hospital or elsewhere of:*

persons who are (a) suffering from grave chronic disease or being aged, infirm or physically incapacitated are living in insanitary conditions and (b) are unable to devote to themselves and are not receiving from other persons proper care and attention.

50,000 Outside the Law, *National Council for Civil Liberties, London, 1951. This document, which describes the scandalous way in which 'mental defectives' were treated, exemplifies growing demands at the time to abandon a segregative social policy.*

This pamphlet tells a grave story! And this story belongs not to the England of the novels of Dickens, but to the England of 1951. Let us briefly summarise what it discloses:

1. Wrongful certification and detention takes place on a far from small scale. [. . .]
2. Breakdown of legal safeguards through failure of [the 1913 Mental Deficiency] Act to provide adequate machinery of appeal. [. . .]
3. Exploitation of defective labour. [. . .]
4. Growth in interests which may cause unconscious bias to be developed in favour of retaining high grade patients under certification.
5. Archaic conceptions of treatment in institutions and on license. [. . .]

Social welfare has been side-tracked from these people, who while certified remain a race apart. The community must accept responsibility for them – changing the concept of permanent segregation for that of integration within the community.

Some extracts from the 'anti-institutional' literature of the 1960s.

*From Russell Barton (1959), **Institutional Neurosis**, Bristol, John Wright and Sons, p. 13. In this book, Barton argues that institutions themselves can create mental disorder that is unrelated to the actual mental illness that brought the patient into hospital in the first place. He called this disorder 'institutional neurosis' and one of many causal factors he identified was staff brutality.*

Brutality is unsanctioned and usually goes undetected through the misplaced loyalty of other staff (only a traitorous deviant would turn in a fellow employee), and the intimidation of witnesses. It is usually unsuspected, usually denied and in many cases covered up by hospital authorities (since they themselves are held responsible) and thus it is condoned and perpetuated.

The usual brutality is slapping a patient's head or face, punching or assaulting with a stick or a wet towel.

Other forms of physical assault are beating patients in a boot room or bathroom with a rubber-soled slipper, punching in the abdomen with a wet towel round the fist, tossing in a blanket, twisting a wet towel round the neck, shaking and shoving so that the victim falls or hits his head against a wall. A ruthless attendant can encourage patients to beat up a patient who is causing trouble.

Rough handling of patients is a form of brutality in which physical coercion is used without actual hitting. Examples are: frog marching, dragging, gripping by the arms, shoving, pushing and forcing into chairs, into showers, on to a bed and so forth. Rough handling merges with brutality, on the one hand, and with that minimal and reluctantly applied physical force occasionally necessary for a few patients, on the other. In some institutions force is never necessary – they do not dispense with it by being more humane as their spokesmen sometimes pretend, but by refusing to admit difficult patients or giving them large doses of tranquillizers. Any psychiatric service providing care for the complete range of mentally disordered people will occasionally have to resort to some physical contact. However, there is a world of difference between a guiding hand, a forceful grip and clenched fist.

---

*From Peter Townsend (1962), **The Last Refuge**, London, Routledge and Kegan Paul, pp. 431–32. The evidence in this study came from visits to a random sample of 173 residential homes for older people.*

Let us review briefly and in broad outline the more critical evidence. First of all there are gross inequities as between different types of residential Homes. At one extreme there is the old workhouse with stone floors and unplastered interior walls and long dormitories with ten, twenty and sometimes even fifty beds, which have iron frames and upon which there are hair, flock or even, in isolated instances, straw mattresses. There are few articles of furniture in the dormitories – often only a wooden chair and a battered locker by each bed. Thirty, forty or more persons sit in the huge day-rooms, where standards of comfort are minimal. Coarse unpressed clothing with institutional laundry tags is issued. There is no real privacy and little to encourage self-respect. A man may have his trousers changed in full view of dozens of other people and may be obliged to get up at 6.0 or 6.30 in the morning, and sometimes sooner. The staff are too few in number and have rarely received any form of training. The turnover of staff is sometimes as much as 100 per cent in a year.

[. . .] At the other extreme from the old workhouse is the Home built recently as such by the local authority, or the small Home for ten or twenty people run by a voluntary association or a private individual. The quality of such Homes varies widely, as we have seen, but one of the best examples might be selected. A dozen people live in a fine house overlooking beautiful countryside. They are remote from their relatives and friends and the local community, but they each have their own bed-sitting rooms with fitted carpets, expensive rugs, handbasins, side-tables, not one but two or three wardrobes, chests of drawers, long mirrors, arm-chairs, pictures, rubber foam mattresses, quilts and three forms of heating – central heating, electric thermostat fires and electric blankets. All have their own radios and a few a television set. Some even have a small electric oven. When a nurse is required both a day nurse and a night nurse are secured through an agency to care for one person. Needless to add, breakfast is served in bed and many do not get up before 10 or 11 in the morning.

[. . .] this contrast [. . .] illustrates perfectly the different living standards enjoyed in our society by different people with similar needs.

---

*From Barbara Robb (1967) **Sans Everything: A Case to Answer**, London, Nelson. Following a letter to The Times about the plight of old people in hospital, published in November 1965, Barbara Robb, put together evidence from staff, patients and relatives who responded to this letter. Below is an extract from Lord Strabolgi's speech in the House of Lords in July 1966 in a debate on community care, which is in the Appendix to Barbara Robb's book.*

A great many old people are going into mental homes mainly for two reasons: first, there is a great shortage of old people's homes; and secondly, many of these old people's homes are not able to take old people who are incontinent and enfeebled. The result is that many of them have to go into mental hospitals, although they are not psychiatric cases at all.

Many of these mental hospitals are good, but some are really a disgrace to a civilised country. An example of the kind of hospital I have in mind is the one which was described by a psychiatric worker in this particular hospital in the issue of the *Guardian* of March 19th of this year. In hospitals of this kind, of which I believe there are six or seven in the country, old people, it would be no exaggeration to say, are treated worse than in the old-fashioned type of Victorian workhouses. They are treated worse because they are regarded as mentally deficient as well as merely poor. There is, for example, the practice of what is known as 'stripping'. This means that on entry all personal belongings are removed, including spectacles, deaf aids and dentures. There are no personal lockers. The food is appalling. In some cases the last meal is served at half-past three in the afternoon. Electro-convulsive treatment is given, I believe, to almost every old person, irrespective of whether it is needed or not. In certain cases it appears that this makes them worse.

But the worst thing of all, I think, is the fact that they are given nothing to do.

From Pauline Morris (1969) **Put Away: A sociological study of institutions for the mentally retarded,** *London, Routledge and Kegan Paul, p. 80.*

The old and overcrowded buildings were not the only ones with serious limitations; some of the most recently built villas failed to provide nursing staff with the facilities they needed. For example, in one hospital a children's ward had been built as recently as 1964 where the day room had also to serve as a dining room. As a consequence staff had to choose between returning the children to their dormitories after meals, or clearing away, stacking the furniture and wiping the floor while other staff 'potted' and cleaned up the children and attempted to keep them away from the debris of the meal. In other buildings of recent date, the staff often complained of sanitary annexes built too near the day rooms and with inadequate ventilation; alternatively they were built too far from the day rooms so that incontinent patients could not reach the lavatory in time, or had to be carried through a series of rooms, past many other patients and possibly upstairs in order to be cleaned up. Very few of the new villas were of the bungalow type and lifts were almost totally absent, although one would consider them an essential feature for the easy movement of patients with physical handicaps, or those confined to wheelchairs. Where lifts have been installed in old buildings, there are instances where the dimensions of the lift are such as to preclude their being used to transfer wheelchair patients. Due to overcrowding it was rarely possible to locate all such patients at ground floor level, a situation which resulted in a good deal of hardship for the nursing staff. Sometimes these arrangements meant that patients were confined to verandahs (or external covered corridors converted for the purpose) rather than being able to wheel themselves about in the grounds.

The Royal Commission on the Law Relating to Mental Illness and Mental Deficiency (The Percy Report), HMSO, London, 1957. This informed the 1959 Mental Health Act and stressed the need to move towards community rather than hospital-centred care, which required more financial resources.

There is increasing medical emphasis on forms of treatment and training and social services which can be given without bringing patients into hospital as in-patients, or which make it possible to discharge them from hospital sooner than was usual in the past. It is not now generally considered in the best interests of the patients who are fit to live in the community that they should be in large or remote institutions such as the present mental and mental deficiency hospitals. Nor is it a proper function of the hospital authority to provide residential accommodation for patients who do not require hospital or specialist services. [. . .] The local authorities should be responsible for preventative services and for all types of community care for patients who do not require in-patient hospital services or who have had a period of treatment of training in hospital and are ready to return to the community.

Social Workers: Their Role and Tasks (The Barclay Report) on the role of the social worker, produced for the Government by the National Institute for Social Work, Bedford Square Press, London, 1982, recognised the need to rely on informal carers.

The bulk of social care in England and Wales is provided not by the statutory or voluntary social services agencies, but by ordinary people who may be linked into informal caring networks in their communities. [. . .] Sharing social caring [with these networks] is a way both of promoting the better care and more care in the community, and of distributing the burden of caring for the disadvantaged more fairly. At present it often falls most heavily upon close relatives.

The 1983 Mental Health Act. These sections highlight the continuing dual role of the state in prescribing duties of care as well as powers to remove threatening people from the community.

After care. Section 117 (2). It shall be the duty of the District Health Authority and of the local social services authority to provide in cooperation with relevant voluntary agencies, after-care services for any person to whom this section applies until the District Health Authority and the local social services authority are satisfied that the person concerned is no longer in need of such service. [. . .]

Mentally disordered persons found in public places. Section 136. If a constable finds in a place to which the public have access a person who appears to him to be suffering from mental disorder and to be in immediate need of care and control, the constable may, if he thinks it necessary to do so in the interests of that person or for the protection of other persons, remove that person to a place of safety.

Residential Care: a Positive Approach (The Wagner Report) produced for the government. by an independent committee based at the National Institute for Social Work, 1988.

People who move into a residential establishment should do so by positive choice. A distinction should be made between need for accommodation and need for services. No one should be required to change their permanent accommodation in order to receive services which could be made available to them in their own homes. Living in a residential establishment should be a positive experience ensuring a better quality of life than the resident could enjoy in any other setting. [. . .] [They] should continue to have access to the full range of community support services [and] leisure, educational and other facilities offered by the local community. [. . .] Residential staff are the major resource and should be valued as such. The importance of their contribution needs to be recognised and enhanced.

Community Care – Which Way Forward? Confederation of Health Service, Employees, London, 1990, COHSE and other trade unions resisted many changes in the hospital-based services during the 1970s. However, during the 1980s they rapidly began to endorse a positive approach to community care, as shown here.

COHSE wishes to see a community care system which is fair, universal and under democratic control, which empowers the service users, values service workers and actively involves in promoting high standards, and which genuinely meets the needs of people. In particular we recommend:

1. Regular, uniform and nationwide assessment of need which involves consultation with service users.
2. Adequate funds, administered through the revenue support grant, specially reserved for community care. Redistribution of funds between rich and poor areas of the country. In addition, local authorities should not be prohibited from raising further funds through local taxes.
3. A framework of rights and entitlement aimed at enabling citizens to control the way their needs are defined and met.
4. Service users to have access to independent living advocates to help them put their views across.
5. Protection for staff moving between employers. The involvement of staff in consultation and decision making. Minimum staffing levels, determined nationally, for workers in residential homes and domiciliary and other community-based care.
6. Purchasing authorities to use contracts to specify adequate pay and conditions for service workers.
7. An independent inspectorate, whose job it is, firstly, to ensure high standards of care and, secondly, to ensure cost-effectiveness – in all forms of community care.
8. A concerted national strategy to ensure that people who are mentally ill are not kept in hospital unnecessarily, nor discharged into the community without proper care facilities and support being available for them.
9. To prevent the wholesale commercialisation of the independent sector and its 'swamping' by the values and tactics of profit-making business, a range of strategies should be considered e.g.:
   – the state to retain ownership of capital assets;
   – quality control mechanisms, imposed by contract, to insist that suppliers put quality of care before cost-control;
   – encouragement of not-for-profit suppliers;
   – encouragement of the advocacy and innovative work of the voluntary sector.
10. Positive policies to ensure that minority communities are properly consulted, and their special needs recognised and met, and that sufficient members of ethnic minorities are employed in community care.
11. The concept of asylum to be incorporated into locally based community mental health services.
12. Integration of housing policies with community care policies.

13. Special training for carers and other volunteers in community care, as well as for paid carers in the independent sector.
14. Improved arrangements for joint planning between health authorities and local authorities.

Waiting for Community Care, MIND, London, 1990. *Major charities such as MENCAP, MIND, Barnardos and the Spastics Society joined in the call during the 1980s for ordinary living for disabled children and adults. MIND's position is given here as an example.*

In MIND's view a policy framework is required which directs community care developments towards specified goals including:

- To transform the mental health service from one centred on unpopular institutions to one based on the actual wishes and needs of people who use the service.
- To move towards a comprehensive local mental health service in each area, offering nationally consistent standards. The service should address the diversity of people's needs, for instance, work, housing, emotional support and sanctuary.
- To create a climate which encourages people with mental distress to pursue ordinary, non-specialist options where possible: for instance, secure housing and work in the open market.
- To pursue change through a major resource transfer from institutional to community services, coupled with a gradually increased allocation to mental health.

Community Care: Agenda for Action (the *Griffiths Report*), 1988. *Here are key points of philosophy that were to be incorporated (in the main, barring the call for a minister for community care) by the government when constructing Caring for People (see below) and its consequent community care legislation.*

Central government should ensure that there is a Minister of State in DHSS, seen by the public as being clearly responsible for community care. [. . .] Local authorities should, within the resources available: assess the community care needs of their locality, set local priorities and service objectives and develop local plans in consultation with health authorities in particular (but also others including housing authorities, voluntary bodies and private providers of care) for delivering those objectives; identify and assess individual needs, taking full account of personal preferences (and those of informal carers), and design packages of care best suited to enabling the consumer to live as normal a life as possible; arrange the delivery of packages of care, building first on the available contribution of informal carers and neighbourhood support, then on the provision of domiciliary and day services or, if appropriate, residential care; act for these purposes as the designers, organisers and purchasers of non-health care services and not primarily as direct providers, making the best possible use of voluntary and private bodies to widen consumer choice, stimulate innovation and encourage efficiency.

Caring for People: Community Care in the Next Decade and Beyond, CM *849, Department of Health, HMSO, London, 1989. This was the White Paper, along with* Working for Patients, *which built on the Griffiths Report and prefigured the National Health Service and Community Care Act 1990.*

The Government believes that for most people community care offers the best form of care available – certainly with better quality and choice than they might have expected in the past. These changes [. . .] are intended to:

- enable people to live as normal a life as possible in their own homes or in a homely environment in the local community;
- provide the right amount of care and support to help people achieve maximum possible independence and, by acquiring or reacquiring basic living skills, help them achieve their full potential;
- give people a greater individual say in how they live their lives and the service they need to help them do so.

Promoting choice and independence underlies all the Government's proposals. [. . .] [T]he key components of community care should be: services that respond flexibly and sensitively to the needs of individuals and their carers; services that allow a range of options for consumers; services that intervene no more than is necessary to foster independence; services that concentrate on those with the greatest needs.

The Government's proposals have six key objectives for service delivery:

- to promote the development of domiciliary, day and respite services to enable people to live in their own homes wherever feasible and sensible [. . .]
- to ensure that services providers make practical support for carers a high priority [. . .]
- to make proper assessment of need and good case management the cornerstone of high quality care [. . .]

- to promote the development of a flourishing independent sector alongside good quality public services [. . .]
- to clarify the responsibilities of agencies and so make it easier to hold them to account for their performance [. . .]
- to secure better value for taxpayers' money by introducing a new funding structure for social care.

21

Human Need and the Moral Right to Optimal Community Care

LEN DOYAL

The report on community care by Griffiths in 1988 and the White Paper presented in 1989 both emphasised the importance of needs assessment and implicitly accepted the entitlement of individuals to needs satisfaction (Griffiths, 1988; Department of Health, 1989). In these documents and elsewhere it was argued that through participating in, rather than being excluded from, their local communities, individuals would optimise their self-sufficiency and their ability to contribute to the finance of their own care. In so doing they would realise or recover their self-respect as citizens.

Case work, it was suggested, should focus on 'empowerment' as its goal, with clients and community care workers becoming much clearer about their specific rights and duties (Meteyard, 1990, section 1). For similar reasons, a shift was recommended from care within large institutions to care within the community, which would also lead to increases in need satisfaction (Murphy, 1991, pp. 1064–5). Other proposed changes in social service administration and finance were justified in the same terms.

These proposals sound good but their practical feasibility has been questioned, with much of this criticism focused on under-capitalisation (Langan, 1990). However, more adequate funding would not resolve another problem that jeopardises the potential success of the new policies: the absence of a clear and detailed theory of human need on which accurate needs assessment can be based. Which needs must be satisfied in order to enable optimal social participation, and why do individuals have a right to those goods and services identified as necessary for this purpose? The answers to both of these questions are hotly disputed.

On the one hand, social service bureaucracies tend to perceive the identification of need as the province of experts versed in the generation of orthodox social and epidemiological statistics. Yet increasingly such orthodoxies are called into question. Both community activists and clients themselves demand more say in identifying local needs, but the insularity of bureaucratic perception can be more than matched by lack of clarity within communities about how to differentiate real needs from mere preferences.

On the other hand there is a tendency for carers and clients – like doctors and patients – simply to assume that the right to need satisfaction exists through justifications that amount to little more than the expression of emotional conviction. Such sentiments stand little chance of success against the articulate arguments of neo-liberals who deny the existence of welfare rights, who grudgingly tolerate a minimal welfare state and who constantly seek to reduce its size.

Unless these problems are adequately resolved, approaches to community care that attempt to combine elements of both decentralisation and centralisation stand little chance of real success. Without a coherent and properly operationalised theory of need, their results will be eclectic and difficult to assess. It is also more likely that the political argument for the expenditure necessary to finance more than just minimal levels of care will be lost.

This chapter briefly outlines a theory of human need developed by myself and Ian Gough to address the issue of how human needs should be conceptualised, and argues that individuals have a right to their optimal and not just minimal satisfaction (Doyal and Gough, 1991).[1] This theory, I will argue, can provide the moral foundation for what was best about the new proposals for community care while at the same time revealing the political and economic circumstances under which they will inevitably fail.

21.1   What are the basic human needs and why?

Let us begin by returning to the importance given to social participation in all the proposals for change in community care provision. There is no doubt about the correctness of this emphasis on the quantity and quality of interaction with others for the objective welfare of the individual. We discover who we are through learning from others what we can do. Others remind us – as we do them – of our individual narratives, of the goals we have tried to achieve in our everyday lives and the degree of success we have had in the process. They help us to remember what we have done and what we might reasonably try to do in the future.

Social participation thus empowers us by providing the space for practising old skills or acquiring new ones, which we and others identify as 'ours' . If we lack the capacity for such participation, we are seriously and objectively harmed as a result – disabled with respect to continuing to express ourselves through performing our present skills, learning new ones and reinforcing others in their attempt to do the same.

Identifying significant personal harm with seriously impaired social participation provides the key with which to identify universal and objective human needs. For these will be the necessary conditions that everyone must meet – wherever they may live and whatever their culture: to avoid such harm through being able to participate in society with as little serious impairment as their genetic or acquired state allows. These conditions are the personal attributes of physical survival/health and individual autonomy.

As regards the first basic need, without physical survival individuals can clearly do nothing whatever. Reduced physical health disables social participation by hindering an individual's scope of action and interaction. The specific ways in which this can occur are described by the physical consequences of diseases catalogued by the biomedical model. 'Illness' – the phenomenological experience of physical disease – can take a variety of forms, but provided that the associated disease is serious, so will be the illness to which it leads. The result will be disablement, and thus significant harm as defined above. Those who are suffering from the disease of, and are ill with, severe heart disease, for example, are objectively more impaired in their social participation than those who are not.

There are of course ways of identifying and treating disease other than those outlined by orthodox medicine. However all international organisations that aim to find ways of improving physical health on a global scale embrace both its diagnostic categories and therapeutic technologies. For this reason the weaknesses of biomedicine – which are many – should never be allowed to cloud its strengths. If you have a burst appendix then you need appropriate surgical and medical care, whoever and wherever you are. The same applies to the treatment of infectious diseases and to our complete understanding of how they are best prevented. We cannot treat cholera as successfully as we might, or understand why clean water is so important in its prevention, without the understanding provided by the biomedical model (Doyal, 1987).

Aside from physical health, the other basic human need is individual autonomy. In order successfully to participate in any form of life, actors require more than just physical health. They also require the capacity to formulate aims about what to try to achieve and beliefs about how to do this – the ability to reason and to act on the basis of reason. These attributes create the unique human potential to choose future goals and actions, to plan one's life. Autonomy is the exercise of such reasoned choice and individuals are thus able to participate in their form of life in proportion to their possession of autonomy.

So, like physical health, one's basic need for autonomy may be satisfied to a greater or lesser extent. The degree of satisfaction will depend on the value of the three component variables of autonomy: degree of understanding, emotional capacity and social opportunity. Let us examine each in turn.

Actors do not make up their own reasons for action – they are not intellectually self-sufficient. They must learn to use language to communicate and to act in ways that are normatively and vocationally appropriate to the rules of their social environment. Even though much of what we do and say may seem essentially private in character, the fact is that our actions and communication derive much of their meaning from such rules and their specific configurations in different social institutions. Clearly we must learn these rules from others, and once our correct understanding of them is confirmed we inevitably become teachers ourselves. Robinson Crusoe, that archetype of so-called self-sufficiency had had to learn from others the skills that enabled him to survive when he was shipwrecked alone.

Furthermore, autonomous individuals who have learned the manual and mental skills to participate within their form of life must have the emotional wherewithal so to do. This will depend on the absence of *serious* mental illness. As with physical disease, there is much we understand about the symptoms of such illness, even though its aetiology is much more contentious. Serious mental illness entails, for example, a sustained lack of capacity for intellectual understanding, for consistent reasoning, for confidence to try to interact with others, for the recognition of responsibility for action and for the empirical constraints that the physical and social environment place upon it.

Of course serious mental illness varies both in its severity and in the way in which associated disabilities are conceptualised in different cultures. What does not vary, however, is the universality of its symptoms or the objectivity of the personal harm to which they lead. For no matter how culturally valued the idiosyncratic expression of any of these symptoms, the fact remains that they describe the contours of personal experience that, if sustained, will seriously impair participation in any form of life. For example what is referred to in orthodox psychiatry as 'psychotic depression' entails severe harm in precisely these terms.

Finally, the autonomy of individuals can be measured in proportion to the *social opportunities* they have to exercise their cognitive and emotional capacities – their freedom to interact with their fellow citizens in pursuit of individual or common goals. Human freedom has negative and positive dimensions. Negatively, it is the ability to act without being prevented from doing so or physically and/or psychologically forced to do other than one chooses. Under such circumstances, the fact that you are physically healthy, educated and not suffering from severe mental illness will obviously not enable you to participate socially in ways that you choose.

Positive freedom is having access to the goods and services necessary to achieve the goals that we set for ourselves, always against the background of our social environment. Without such access our efforts will be limited, no matter how much we are left alone by others or how many opportunities exist for social participation. Political liberty, for example, will mean little to those whose daily labour is so focused on keeping body and soul together that they do not have the time or energy for active involvement in democratic decision making, even if the formal opportunity exists for them to do so!

If survival/physical health and autonomy are necessary conditions for all humans to participate in their form of life, what universal satisfiers or 'intermediate needs' must everyone have access to for these universal needs to be met satisfactorily? Generally speaking, the answer is clear.

Optimal physical health requires nutritional food and clean water, protective housing, a non-hazardous work environment, a non-hazardous physical environment and access to appropriate health care if physical disease develops through, among other things, lack of access to these intermediate needs.

Optimal autonomy *within* a culture demands security in childhood, significant primary relationships, physical security, economic security, basic education and, for women, safe birth control and child-bearing. Even greater levels of 'critical autonomy' will depend on the ability of the individual to make choices not only within cultures but between them. Here the extent of cross-cultural education and the opportunity for cross-cultural choice become crucial variables.

Again, each of the preceding intermediate needs are universal (for example nutrition), although the ways in which each is satisfied (for example different culinary traditions) are not. It follows that one can accept the universality of our theory of need without questioning the importance and viability of different cultural approaches to need satisfaction. It equally follows that its acceptance does not deflect emphasis from the needs of particular groups within a single culture.

For example specific types of permanent physical disability (such as paraplegia) demand particular, and often similar, types of satisfiers in order to optimise individual opportunities for social participation (such as relevant technologies for mobility and access) and to minimise the handicap they cause. Physical disabilities that are correctable (such as poor vision) or might be correctable (such as some forms of chronic disease) make similar demands for appropriate satisfiers. In the case of the former, the demand is for a known correcting technology that works in practice. As regards the latter, it is for research into technologies that might work in practice.

How much of each satisfier an individual requires – the degree to which the basic need for physical health and autonomy should be satisfied – is both an empirical and a normative question. Empirically, individuals need what is necessary for them to participate in their forms of life to specified levels. From this perspective, most individuals in underdeveloped nations or poor communities within developed nations might be argued to need less than those from more wealthy environments. Normatively, however, the issue is not whether or not such inequalities exist but whether it is possible to provide a convincing moral justification of them. It will now be argued that this cannot be done.

21.2   The right to optimal need satisfaction

To argue that an individual has a right to something is to make a very serious claim. It is to maintain that an entitlement exists that others have a strict duty to provide whether they want to or not. In other words, if we really believe that a person has a right, say, to good community care, then doing what we can to provide it is not simply a matter of altruism or charity. This is why there should be no social stigma attached to the receipt of such care.

Private property is a good example. To the extent that we believe that we have a right to use and dispense with our property as we see fit – provided we harm no one else in the process – then we impose a duty on others not to interfere with our exercise of it. We also impose a duty on ourselves to take seriously their rights to do the same with their property. Otherwise the social institution of private property would be called into doubt and there would be no reason why others should take seriously our beliefs about our own rights. Of course if others believe themselves to have identical rights as well, they in turn impose identical reciprocal duties. Empirically speaking, belief in the existence of rights corresponds to belief in the existence of corresponding duties.

As we have seen, all individuals mature in their self-awareness and social skills against the background of rules – a normative environment that explicitly or implicitly postulates a *vision of the moral good*. Such environments can differ even within the same society. The substance of the visions of the good that they embody can vary widely, some being quite similar and others dramatically in conflict.

Yet, logically speaking, different forms of social life implicitly or explicitly share a common theory of good citizenship, despite any moral conflict that might otherwise exist between them. The good citizen is the individual who does her or his duty, as prescribed by the values of the culture or subculture of which they are a part. This is as much the case in Manchester as it is in Mecca.

In Britain, for example, the good citizen is supposed to do and not to do a variety of things relating to home, employment, recreation and politics. Of course there are huge variations on the general theme, depending on things such as class, gender, race, region, religion and so on. But leaving aside subcultures that positively endorse criminality, there is still a consensus that everyone should do their best to work within the law to optimise their well-being and be as economically self-sufficient as possible. Certainly the Conservative government in Britain has a very pronounced moral vision of the good, which takes this model of self-sufficiency to its limit. In short, no one who takes morality seriously can question the reality of duties as such, although they might and do disagree about their content.

The imputation of duties of good citizenship entails at least two things on the part of those who impose them. First, they must believe that those on whom these duties are imposed have the right to basic need satisfaction – of access to culturally acceptable satisfiers of those intermediate needs that must be satisfied for physical health and autonomy to be sustained. In Britain this means, for example, the right of access to certain types of food and certain types of education. To be consistent, those who impute duties on others must also assume some responsibility for ensuring their access to basic need satisfaction, through, say, paying taxes for this purpose.

Otherwise potential good citizens will not necessarily be able to do what is expected of them. This inability will be due to the disablement they suffer as a result of physical, educational, emotional or social deprivation from which there is no escape. The imputation of duties of citizenship without the right to basic need satisfaction thus becomes meaningless. In other words, 'ought' implies 'can', and the belief that others should be good in our terms commits us to do what we can to help them to obtain the basic need satisfaction that is necessary for them to be so.

Second, if the imputation of strict moral duties on others entails their right to basic need satisfaction, the question remains of *how much satisfaction* is required for this right to be met. The simple answer is as much as is available for citizens to do their *best*. If a government expects less than the best of its citizens, through not providing them with the basic need satisfaction necessary for them to do their best, then this reflects badly on its own commitment to the vision of the good that it imposes on others. The professed good would not be that good after all! Another way of putting it is that to the extent that the state neglects the optimal objective welfare of its citizens, it potentially creates a group of moral outcasts who may well decide that since they cannot live up to the moral expectations of the state, they will ignore them (Harris, 1991).

So the belief in the duty of good citizenship entails a further belief in the right not just to minimal levels of need satisfaction but to optimal levels as well, recognising that optimal levels may differ in proportion to unavoidable practical constraints imposed by different levels of national scarcity. As far as community care is concerned, this means specific types of goods and services and as many of them as are necessary for individuals to achieve optimal levels of physical health and autonomy It is the achievement of this aim that must be at the heart of good community care and organisation, and provision of and training for it. Not surprisingly, it is an aim reflected in the detail of much contemporary literature in community care.

Therefore governments that impute visions of good citizenship cannot then consistently argue for a minimal welfare state. It is contradictory to claim that citizens who for whatever reason cannot do their best should still do so. The continuation of this contradiction through the perpetuation of political policies that embody it reveals either lack of awareness or, more likely, irrational self-interest.

This does not mean of course that citizens should not be responsible for as much of their own need satisfaction as they can be, and it may be difficult as a worker in community care to know where to draw the line. Yet decisions should always err in favour of the client. The worst thing that can happen if a mistake is made is that an already badly off client may get slightly more than they deserve, given their meagre personal resources. This is well worth the risk since, as we have seen, it will ensure that they are optimally able to accept their designated responsibilities in the future.

21.3   Putting principle into practice

We have seen that good community care necessitates access to those goods and services that are necessary for the satisfaction of the basic human need for health and autonomy. Unless these needs are optimally met, individuals will be unable to do their best to flourish as persons and as good citizens. In principle, many of the proposals in the Griffiths Report and the related White Paper were steps in this direction.

However none of these aims can or will be achieved in practice unless sufficient capital is made available to finance them. Thus far this has not been forthcoming and there is good reason to believe that it will not be forthcoming in the future. The problem of under-capitalisation is a major one in welfare provision in Britain, the National Health Service being the other obvious example. The advantage of linking basic need satisfaction to the rights that the duties of good citizenship entail is that this offers a cogent argument for their inclusion in a constitutional bill of rights. It is only then – when the state will allow itself to be taken to court for doing otherwise – that the human right to optimal community care will be seen to be taken seriously in Britain.

This said, problems still remain. So far we have outlined the substantive needs of citizens and linked them to their right to optimal community care. However we have not faced the dilemma of how to proceed when there is dispute about what constitutes the optimal level of related need satisfaction and how the detail of such satisfaction should be addressed in specific circumstances. In other words, for it to be a feasible moral foundation for the formulation of welfare policy, we must further link our substantive theory of needs and rights to a procedural theory of need. This must outline the necessary conditions for optimising the rationality of debate about community care on both the micro and the macro level.

The success of such debate will depend on its 'communicative competence' – the commitment of those involved to structure it in ways that optimise its rationality. Even when there is no absolutely 'right' answer, and when policies that are agreed are seen as compromises between competing interests, it is all the more important to arrive at solutions to problems concerning need satisfaction that can be supported in the local community by workers and clients alike. This means that those participating in policy formation must include representatives of all parties with a legitimate interest in the dispute. These will include, on the one hand, case workers, managers and researchers with codified expertise on the problem under consideration and, on the other hand, clients and community representatives with an experientially based understanding of what the problem entails in practice.

Only then will the best technical and experientially based information be available upon which rational decisions can be based. Furthermore, debates themselves must be monitored to ensure that their outcomes are not determined by the arbitrary power and vested interest of individuals or representatives in either group. And finally, when steps are taken to implement policies that have been established, they must be subject to regular review to ensure that what has been agreed in principle is followed through in practice. Many of the examples of how social planning in the past has had negative effects on community care have been due to the absence of one or more of these conditions.

There will always be a tension in the theory and practice of community care, as there is in politics generally, between those who opt for decision making from providers and those who do the same for recipients. The fact is that here, as in all other areas of public policy, we need the participation of both – a dual strategy for community care and for welfare provision in general. This will entail as much centralisation in administration, provision and expertise as is necessary for the efficient delivery of appropriate goods and services to those in need. Also required is as much decentralisation as is compatible with this aim, with the right of clients to participate in the processes of planning and execution also being guaranteed as a matter of legal right.

21.4   Conclusion

Thus through effective representation, participation and cooperation, all grounded in rational communication, providers and recipients of care can work together to ensure good community care through the optimisation of basic need satisfaction. If the procedures to ensure this possibility are not incorporated in the final shape of community care provision in Britain – along with the capitalisation sufficient for the right of the individual to optimal need satisfaction to be respected – then it will fail.

This will be a tragedy for those who are deprived in the process. For they will be unable to do their best when they demand it of themselves and it is demanded by others of them. Yet the tragedy also applies to all of those who remain aloof from such deprivation while having the wherewithal to help to bring it down to acceptable levels. For in not doing so they participate in undermining the moral foundation of the very values in which they purport to believe, with potentially destructive consequences both for themselves and the rest of society.

We know how to solve the major problems confronting community care. What is required is the political will.

Note

1. Much of this chapter is an outline of arguments developed in this book where further detail and extensive bibliographical references for all of the arguments are included.

References

Department of Health (1989) *Caring for People: Community Care in the Next Decade and Beyond*, Cm 849, HMSO, London.
Doyal, L. and Gough, I. (1991) *A Theory of Human Need*, Macmillan, London.
Doyal, L. (1987) 'Health, Underdevelopment and Traditional Medicine', *Holistic Medicine*, Vol. 2. .
Griffiths, R. (1988) *Community Care: Agenda for Action*, HMSO, London.

Harris, J. (1991) 'Equity in health care', talk given at the Royal Institute on Public Health and Hygiene, London.

Langan, M. (1990) 'Community care in the 1990s: the community care White Paper: "Caring for People"', *Critical Social Policy*, Vol. 29.

Meteyard, B. (1990) *Community Care Keyworker Manual*, Longman, Harlow.

Murphy, E. (1991) 'Community mental health services: a vision for the future', *British Medical Journal*, Vol. 302.

Community Care Policy: From Consensus to Conflict

ALAN WALKER

22.1 Introduction

The purpose of this chapter is to review some important contemporary developments in government community care policy. It focuses on policy changes since 1979 and looks at the impact of these changes on the provision of community care services in the 1990s. Towards the end of the chapter, the approach of the Conservative government of the 1980s and early 1990s to community care is contrasted with an alternative one based on user empowerment.

The main argument advanced in this chapter may be stated simply: community care policy underwent a significant transition during the 1980s, from a position in which there was an, albeit precarious, consensus about the central role of local authority social services departments (SSDs) in the provision of formal services, to one in which policy is directed towards residualising (or minimising) their role. Thus the main objective of community care policy during this period was the reduction of the role of local authorities as direct service providers while at the same time encouraging the growth of informal, voluntary and private welfare, often under the guise of promoting what is called a 'mixed economy of welfare'.

Before proceeding with the main analysis it is necessary to make two qualifications. First, the culmination of policy developments during the 1980s was the NHS and Community Care Act 1990. This legislation was phased in during the period 1991/92 to 1993/94, and in 1996 there were still major variations between local authorities in their interpretation and implementation of the 1990 Act (Lewis and Glennerster, 1996). This means that whether or not the *outcome* of stated policy objectives actually does represent a decisive break with the past must await a later assessment.

Secondly, while it is being argued that government policies during the 1980s represented a departure from the postwar consensus, the meaning of community care as it is experienced by the majority of older people, people with learning difficulties and others in need changed very little, if at all. Thus there is continuity in their *experience* of the formal sector of community care, as a casualty or last-resort service in which users have very little say in the organisation and delivery of services. This leaves the vast bulk of care needs to be met within the informal sector, largely by female kin (Walker, 1982, 1991; Finch and Groves, 1983; Qureshi and Walker, 1989). So this chapter is concerned with the shift from consensus to conflict in the policy arena. It is not intended to imply that there ever was consensus between policy makers, service providers and users. Indeed I have argued elsewhere that community care policy has always been underpinned by conflict between people in need of care and their carers, on the one hand, and the State on the other (Walker, 1983). Therefore this assessment of community care developments during the 1980s and early 1990s concentrates on their impact, or likely impact, on service users and potential users.

22.2   The end of the consensus on community care

The postwar party political consensus on community care policy was sustained, in part, by the symbolic nature of the term 'community care' and its wide appeal in the policy system. To paraphrase Edelman (1977): the words succeeded magnificently but the policy failed miserably. Not surprisingly the consensus was a precarious one, relying on ambiguity and uncertainty of purpose in policy and the absence of strategic planning; the maintenance of the family as the main provider of care, with SSDs occupying a very restricted and junior role; and the subordination of community care services to institutional interests in both the health and social services.

Nonetheless there was consensus among policy makers on both the secondary role of the formal sector to the informal sector and on the premise that, when services were provided *in* the community, the most appropriate location for the planning, organisation and delivery of these services was SSDs. It must be said, however, that beyond this general support on the part of policy makers for the value-laden and idealistic concept of community care, the primacy of the family and the leading role of SSDs in service provision, there was no deeper consensus even among policy makers (Titmuss, 1968; Walker, 1986a). For example, over the whole of the postwar period there was (and remains) a wide divergence between local authorities in both the levels of their service provision and the eligibility criteria for access to services (see, for example, Webb and Wistow, 1987, pp. 160–85; Audit Commission, 1996). Moreover the failure to extend social services provision in response to rising need (created largely by demographic change) has resulted in a growing 'care gap' between the need for care and the provision of domiciliary services (Walker, 1985).

So after 30 years of community care policy, by the late 1970s the burden of care in the informal sector was increasing and institutional budgets continued to dominate both health and social services (Gray, *et al.*, 1988). Then on to the stage came urgent economic pressures, stemming initially from the fiscal crisis of the mid 1970s, but given added impetus by the strong ideological commitment that followed the election of the Thatcher government in 1979. These produced severe budgetary and resource constraints and the *cost-effectiveness imperative* which, combined with a major expansion of need for care particularly among very elderly people, created the political will to overcome both the policy inertia and the power struggle between sectional interests that lay behind the precarious consensus on community care. But the policy itself departed significantly from the previous consensus. Thus the policy emphasis shifted away from care *in* the community by local authority personnel towards a confusing mixture of care *by* the community and private care, regardless of whether in domiciliary or institutional settings.

Signs that the postwar consensus on community care policy was about to be destroyed became apparent very soon after the election of the first Thatcher government. In contrast to its predecessors, it was characterised by an overt neo-liberal (or new right) ideology, and this remained the driving force behind policy throughout the 1980s and early 1990s. The government's first public expenditure White Paper (Treasury, 1979), combined with a speech by the secretary of state for social services (Jenkin, 1979), marked a radical break with the past – the ending of protected status for personal social services (PSS) spending, the abandonment of the coordination and monitoring of local service provision and increasing reliance on non-statutory forms of welfare (Webb and Wistow, 1982; Walker, 1986b) – a trend that was confirmed subsequently by a series of official reports and statements, culminating in the NHS and Community Care Act 1990. The rest of this section is devoted to outlining the three main dimensions of the new policy that unfolded during the 1980s.

22.2.1   Promoting the private sector

While the primary intention of community care policy during the 1980s and early 1990s appears to have been the negative one of reducing the role of health and social services authorities in the provision of care, the 1980s also witnessed, for the first time, active official encouragement of the private sector. This new policy direction was signalled early on in the life of the first Thatcher government, when the DHSS[1] encouraged a switch in the provision of residential care from the public sector to the private sector.

It did so, first of all, by reducing the resources available to local authorities, by 4.7 per cent in 1979/80 and 6.7 per cent in 1980/81 (Walker, 1986b, p. 17). Although cuts in PSS expenditure were carried out in the mid 1970s, these fell particularly on capital, with some limited protection (2 per cent real growth per annum) being offered to current spending. In fact, what happened in practice, in response to government policy in the early 1980s, was that many local authorities took steps to protect their PSS spending, that is until the introduction of the block grant system in 1981/82 and the subsequent imposition of rate-capping and poll-tax-capping, which considerably reduced room for manoeuvre (ibid., p. 27).

Secondly, while the public sector received the stick, the private sector was given the carrot. The DHSS agreed not only to meet the full cost of care in private residential and nursing homes for those on income support (then supplementary benefit), but also to allow local offices to set limits on such board and lodging payments as were deemed appropriate for their area. In effect the government had created a voucher system (Jackson and Haskins, 1992), whereby low-income older people and their families could choose a private home and have the fees paid by the Treasury. This not only extended choice in the field of residential care, but also created both an incentive for the private sector to expand and a disincentive for the health and social services to provide long term-care facilities.

As a result the number of places in private residential homes for older people and people with physical and learning disabilities nearly doubled (97 per cent) between 1979 and 1984, and by 1994 they had risen by more than five times their level in 1979. The parallel story of expenditure on both residential and nursing homes was that of a rapid increase from £6 million in 1978 to £460 million in 1988 and £2.5 billion in 1993. The proportion of people in private residential homes receiving help with their fees through income support payments increased from 14 per cent in 1979 to 35 per cent in 1984, and by 1988 had reached 56 per cent (Bradshaw and Gibbs, 1988, p. 4; NACAB, 1991, p. 6). By 1994 48 per cent of residents in private care homes were receiving fee payments from income support and a further 20 per cent from local authorities, with only 32 per cent being self-financed.

Since this growth in spending conflicted with the government's policy of reducing public expenditure, the DHSS acted to stem the flow of resources. In September 1984 it froze local limits, and then in April 1985 it imposed national limits for board and lodging payments (which still apply to those resident before the 1993 reforms – see below). These limited amounts, however, still represent a major source of income to the private sector. The picture sometimes painted of government ministers being taken by surprise by the 'unplanned' expansion of the private residential sector and 'subsidies spiralling out of control' sits rather uneasily with the purposeful encouragement given to these small businesses, the difficulty experienced in persuading Mrs Thatcher that curbs on such expenditure were necessary (Lewis and Glennerster, 1996) and the government's open antagonism towards local authority spending.

Some policy analysts (see for example Day and Klein, 1987) mistakenly viewed the growth of private-sector residential care as beneficial in terms of increasing choice in an expanding 'mixed economy of welfare'. Indeed the appeal to increased choice was an important source of popular legitimation for the rapid expansion of the private sector. However, while it is true that there has been a rapid multiplication of private homes, genuine choice requires a range of alternatives: public sector homes, day care, the chance to remain in an ordinary home with community support. But ironically this choice was restricted by the 'perverse incentive' to use residential care provided by social security payments (Audit Commission, 1986). Furthermore the need for residential care usually arises because of a crisis of care in the informal sector, leaving little time to exercise choice and 'shop around' for alternatives. Thus, as Bradshaw (1988) confirmed, the promise of choice held out by the supporters of the private sector was illusory.

A study of the private sector carried out by the Centre for Policy on Ageing, found that only a quarter of residents had exercised any choice about the home they were admitted to, while nearly a quarter said that their admission had resulted from unsolicited arrangements by a third party (Bradshaw, 1988, p. 18). Choice between private homes is severely restricted by factors such as geographical location, waiting lists and ability to pay. There is, for example, a clear north–south divide in the public/private mix of welfare. Private nursing home beds in the South-Western Region outnumber those in the Northern Region by five times. In two regions, South-East Thames and South-West Thames, the private sector was providing more than half the total unit health care for older people by the mid 1980s (Larder *et al.*, 1986). According to the Audit Commission (1986) a more equitable distribution of resources for health and social services, sought through NHS Resource Allocation Working

Party and Department of the Environment Grant-Related Expenditure Assessment (GREA) calculations, was being offset by board and lodging payments for private care.

Within local areas, choice can be restricted by the admission criteria applied by private homes, often excluding confused or demented people or those who are difficult to control. Thus a survey carried out by the Association of Directors of Social Services found a tendency for private homes to select the less severely disabled older people, leaving the more severely disabled for the public sector (ADSS, 1985). Also, private homes often levy charges above the income support limits, requiring top-up payments, or make supplementary charges for single rooms or items such as laundry. This problem worsened after the government imposed national limits on board and lodging payments in 1985 and then failed to raise the benefit ceilings in line with increases in residential and nursing home charges. As a consequence, and despite the high cost of these payments to the Exchequer, more and more older residents found their benefits inadequate to cover the fees charged. In 1988, 42 per cent of private residents on income support were paying fees above the national limits (Social Services Committee, 1990a). Now, under the new system of funding, no local authority will pay the maximum cost of residential or nursing home care in their area. Consequently those reliant on local authority funding have to make up the shortfall between what the local authority is prepared to fund and the fees charged by the home. It is estimated that only 10 per cent of pensioners are able to pay the full cost of long-term care entirely from their own resources.

The research evidence has also suggests that residents are not able to exercise much choice once they are inside private homes. For example, a study of homes in North Yorkshire found that 21 per cent had undergone a change of ownership in the previous 18 months (Bradshaw, 1988, p. 19). Residents had no say in such changes and were not always informed before they happened, nor did they have any choice about other changes in the character of their home:

> Residents entering small homely homes may find them enlarged. Residents have no control over the mix of residents or who shares their bedroom. As charges move ahead of (income support) limits, residents may find themselves shifted into double or treble rooms, required to commit their pocket money to supplement the (income support) allowance or being subsidised by relatives – often without their knowledge.
>
> (ibid., pp. 19–20)

The subsequent trend towards corporate ownership of residential and nursing homes and the increase in their size have removed the 'homely' character of many residences (one of the main advantages claimed by the private sector over the public sector) and further reduced their capacity to provide tailor-made services.

Questions have been raised not only about the distributional consequences of the government's policy of promoting the private sector, but also about the quality of the care provided. As the private residential sector mushroomed, evidence mounted of abuse, misuse of drugs, fraud, lack of hygiene and fire hazards in some homes (Harman and Lowe, 1986; Holmes and Johnson, 1988). Some of the worst cases of abuse have been documented by the media, such as Yorkshire Television's 1987 programme 'The Granny Business'. Evidence of abuse in the private sector inevitably invites comparison with the public sector and there are similar instances of ill-treatment to be found there (see for example Gibbs *et al.*, 1987). However, concentrating on this sort of comparison of rogues diverts attention from the key issues: the operation of power in a residential setting, regardless of whether it is publicly or privately run, and which of the two sectors can be sufficiently regulated to ensure that no abuse of power occurs, issues I return to later.

So far this discussion has concentrated on private care from the perspective of service users, partly in order to dispel the myth of choice that is usually associated with the private sector. But while the quality of care may be substandard in some private homes, there has also been plenty of evidence to show that the pay and conditions of staff working in some of them is well below those of their public counterparts. There have been documented examples too of untrained and low-paid staff having to bear high levels of responsibility for the care of vulnerable people and being threatened with dismissal if they join a trades union (Holmes and Johnson, 1988, pp. 82–105).

22.2.2   Care in the community

At the same time as imposing severe resource constraints on local authorities and encouraging the rapid growth of private residential and nursing homes, the government embarked on a radical programme of mental health hospital closure. The policy of hospital rundown, particularly of mental illness facilities, dates back to the Hospital Plan of 1962. However, prior to 1987 no major hospital had been closed (Social Services Committee, 1985, p. xix).

There has been a steady decline in the number of patients in both mental illness and mental handicap hospitals. For example in the 10 years to 1986 the average number of daily occupied beds in mental illness hospitals fell from 109 000 to 82 500 and in mental handicap hospitals from 59 000 to 42 500. But the decline accelerated during the 1980s as the government's discharge programme took effect.

The 1981 Care in the Community initiative (DHSS, 1981a, 1983) was specifically intended to promote the discharge of long-stay hospital patients by enabling district health authorities to transfer their funds (above and beyond joint finance) to local authorities and voluntary organisations in order to support ex-patients in the community. In addition, during the early 1980s the DHSS exerted considerable pressure on health authorities to close hospitals within specified time limits (Social Services Committee, 1985, p. xii). This contrasts with the earlier consensus period of community care policy as exemplified by the 1976 DHSS document on priorities in the health and social services:

> The closure of mental illness hospitals is *not* in itself an objective of Government policy, and the White Paper stresses that hospitals should not encourage patients to leave unless there are satisfactory arrangements for their support.
>
> (DHSS, 1976, p. 55)

Although the radical Conservative welfare policy succeeded where previous consensus policies had failed in overcoming institutional inertia and professional interests in the promotion of community care, the main motivation for so doing was cost-efficiency, with the effectiveness of care received in the community taking second place. This was the main thrust of the trenchant critique of the government's community care policy towards people with mental health problems and learning difficulties by the all-party House of Commons Social Services Committee (1985), one of the most authoritative of several similarly critical reports to be issued.

The Social Services Committee focused attention on the disaster course that had been set by forcing a closure programme without sufficient planning, preparation and consultation, and furthermore without any agreed understanding of what the intended community care would actually entail. It was especially mindful of the danger that community care would be perceived as a cheap option. In the Committee's own words:

> A decent community-based service for mentally ill or mentally handicapped people cannot be provided at the same overall cost as present services. The proposition that community care could be cost-neutral is untenable. . . . We are at the moment providing a mental disability service which is underfinanced and understaffed in its health and social aspects.
>
> (Social Services Committee, 1985, p. xiv)

The official rhetoric surrounding government policy may have been community care, but the reality was actually more like decanting and dehospitalisation, coupled with an increase in both public and private residential placements. For example between 1976 and 1985 there was an increase of 70 per cent of people with learning difficulties in local-authority-staffed homes and 154 per cent in private homes. The bulk of the increase (133 per cent) in the numbers in private homes occurred between 1981 and 1985, while most of the increase (47 per cent) among those in public sector homes took place between 1976 and 1981. So the result of hurried dehospitalisation in the face of the underfunding of community-based services was that many people with learning difficulties were merely shifted from one institution to a smaller one. People were ending up in residential homes when they did not need to because there was no realistic alternative, and private sector places were subsidised by DSS board and lodging payments.

The Social Services Committee summed up the irresponsible nature of the government's care in the community policy in its now famous sentence: 'Any fool can close a long-stay hospital: it takes more time and trouble to do it properly and compassionately' (ibid., p. xxii). In trying to bring some sense to bear, the Committee attempted to establish the basic principles of a community care policy and insisted that the statutory health and social services were central to the provision of community care. These attempts fell on deaf ears because they harked back to the pre-1980s consensus, though the government did act in response to the Committee's criticisms and ordered the slow-down of the discharge programme (DHSS, 1985). Moreover in the 1989 White Paper it was stated that 'Ministers will not approve the closure of any mental hospital unless it can be demonstrated that adequate alternatives have been developed' (DoH, 1989, p. 56). However the Social Services Committee (1990b, p. 31) subsequently questioned whether the government was monitoring adherence by health authorities to this modified policy and whether the government had an operational definition of 'adequate alternatives'. A series of subsequent reports criticised the level and quality of community mental health services, especially in London, and in early 1997 a long awaited consultation paper was issued by the government.

22.2.3   Residualising the social services

A series of what seemed as they occurred to be separate policy developments over the past 18 years may, with the benefit of hindsight, be seen as part of an evolving government strategy aimed at turning local authority social services from the main providers of formal care into something far more limited: the providers of those residual services that no-one else could or would take on.

In 1980, in a speech to directors of social services departments, the then Secretary of State Patrick Jenkin outlined a supportive and decidedly residual role for the social services: 'a long-stop for the very special needs going beyond the range of voluntary services' (Jenkin, 1980). In 1981 the White Paper on services for older people asserted, in a widely quoted phrase, 'care in the community must increasingly mean care *by* the community' (DHSS, 1981b, p. 3). The previous year, when giving evidence before the House of Commons Social Services Committee, Jenkin had justified the cuts in PSS expenditure and the closure of long-stay hospitals on the, unsubstantiated, assumption that the informal and voluntary sectors would expand:

> When one is comparing where one can make savings one protects the Health Service because there is no alternative, whereas in personal social services there is a substantial possibility and, indeed, probability of continuing growth in the amount of voluntary care, of neighbourhood care, of self help.
>
> (Social Services Committee, 1980, pp. 99–100)

This aim of placing greater reliance on quasi-formal voluntary help and informal support was reflected in the Care in the Community (DHSS, 1981a) and Helping the Community to Care (DHSS, 1984) initiatives.

But it was Jenkin's successor as secretary of state, Norman Fowler, in a speech to the 1984 Joint Social Services Conference in Buxton, who provided the clearest and most detailed outline of the new residual role proposed for social services. He argued that there were 'three paramount responsibilities' of SSDs: to take a comprehensive strategic view of all the sources of care available in the area; to recognise that the direct provision of services was only part of the local pattern and that in many cases other forms of provision were available; and to see a major part of their function as promoting and supporting the fullest possible participation of the other different sources of care. The fundamental role of the state, according to Fowler, was 'to back up and develop the assistance which is given by private and voluntary support' (Fowler, 1984, p. 13).

The Audit Commission's inquiry into community care came to the same conclusion as countless previous independent studies:

> Joint planning and community care policies are in some disarray. The result is poor value for money. Too many people are cared for in settings costing over £200 a week when they would receive a more appropriate care in the community at a total cost to public funds of £100–£130 a week. Conversely, people in the community may not be getting the support they need.
>
> (Audit Commission, 1986, p. 3)

Later the Griffiths Report was to echo exactly the same criticisms of government policy. The Audit Commission proposed various organisational changes aimed primarily at clarifying the overlapping responsibilities of health and social services authorities. For example, in the case of the physically and mentally disabled, local authorities were to be given 'lead' responsibility for their long-term care in the community, except for the most severely disabled who would remain the responsibility of the NHS. The long-term care of older people in the community would be financed from a single budget established by contributions from the NHS and local authorities. The budget would be under the control of a single manager, who would purchase services from the appropriate public or private agency. Health authorities were to be given lead responsibility for the care of the mentally ill in that community (ibid., 1986, p. 4).

The Audit Commission's critical report had much more influence on the government than any of the previous ones, including the authoritative analysis by the House of Commons Social Services Committee. The Secretary of State had been promising, for two years, the publication of a Green Paper on the personal social services. This did not materialise, and instead, in response to the debate following the Audit Commission report, Sir Roy Griffiths was appointed in March 1987 to examine problems in the arrangements for community care between the NHS and local authorities, and to explore the option of putting the entire service for older people 'under the control of a manager who will purchase from whichever public or private agency is appropriate'. (Sir Roy Griffiths conducted a similar inquiry into the management of the NHS in 1983, which led to the appointment of general managers at district level.) The report of the Griffiths inquiry was published in March 1988 (Griffiths, 1988), the White Paper, *Caring for People* followed in November 1989 (DoH, 1989) and within days the NHS and Community Care Bill was published.

These policy developments, together with those reviewed earlier, suggest a strategy aimed at residualising the social services. The issue of how far the Griffiths Report and the White Paper chimed with this strategy will be discussed in the next section. For the moment, the three main dimensions to the policy of residualisation may be summarised.

In the first place, the provision of community care was being deliberately *fragmented*. Though sometimes presented as promoting a more mixed economy of welfare, the main motivations were to curtail the monopoly role of local authorities in the delivery of formal care – an aim that, as we have seen, was already being achieved in several parts of the country with regard to the residential care of older people – and to encourage the growth of cheaper sources of informal and quasi-formal care. Sir Kenneth Stowe, the former permanent secretary of the DHSS, described this approach as 'letting a hundred flowers bloom'.

As mentioned earlier, Patrick Jenkin had hoped for the expansion of voluntary help, self-help and informal care, and to encourage the development of these alternative forms of provision, a series of special initiatives, including the Care in the Community and the Helping the Community to Care programmes, were introduced. Indeed, with the Department of the Environment so effectively controlling local authority expenditure by means of the block grant, the main influence exerted by the DHSS over community care was the promotion of these initiatives and the targeting of research resources on projects designed to extend informal and voluntary help, such as the Kent Community Care Scheme.

One result of this policy of fragmentation was the advent in the 1980s of a wide range of precarious, often short-lived projects relying on grant aid and government training schemes. For example, in September 1986 some 66 459 community programme workers were engaged in providing direct services to social welfare clients.

Secondly, there was *marketisation*. As we have seen, while finances for local authority services became tightly controlled the private sector was encouraged to expand by the open-ended provision of social security board and lodging subsidies. Contracting out, or the purchase of services, has a long history in the personal social services but it has been used primarily in relation to the voluntary sector (Webb and Wistow, 1987, p. 89). The Local Government Act 1988, however, gave the secretary of state for the environment powers to add to the list of services which must be contracted out, and there has been a rapid expansion in private domiciliary care provision as a result of the restriction placed on local authorities' ability to purchase public services by the implementation of the 1990 Act (see below).

As noted earlier, some policy analysts took the view that the expansion of the private sector, at the expense of the public sector, was simply an extension of welfare pluralism, leading to increased choice and efficiency; and, in any case, a reduced role in the provision of services could be balanced by an increased regulatory role (Day and Klein, 1987). The extent to which the private sector promotes choice has already been discussed. In addition, marketisation may be seen as one among many examples of the new right's antagonism towards the decommodifying aspects of the welfare state. It is intended to challenge the, albeit limited, extent to which the social services intrude on market values and threaten their reproduction by promoting citizenship rights and needs-based priorities. It is this ideological driving force behind the expansion of the market, and the simplistic assumptions it is derived from concerning the effectiveness of the market, that proponents of regulation tend to overlook. Regulation hinders the efficient operation of the market, and this might endanger the government's goal of expanding private provision.

Thirdly, the government pursued a twin-track policy of *decentralising* administration and operations while *centralising* control over resources. This was one manifestation of the general new right strategy of rolling back the frontiers of the state while centralising state control (Gamble, 1987). The process of centralising control over social services resources began early in the life of the first Thatcher administration, with the introduction of the block grant and, within it, detailed GREAs for the different elements of the personal social services (Walker, 1985, p. 27). This approach was translated into poll tax (or community charge) Standard Spending Assessments in 1990 (1989 in Scotland) and the Revenue Support Grant in 1992. But responsibility for the operation of social services, within centrally determined budgets, remains with local authorities. A similar policy has been implemented with regard to housing benefit and the health service. In theory the decentralisation of operations offers the prospect of greater user involvement. But this is unlikely to be realised unless resources and responsibility are also devolved.

The cumulative impact of these three sets of policy developments was a strategy aimed at further residualising the role of local authorities in the provision of community care. This was the process envisaged by the chief architects of the present community care policy, Patrick Jenkin and Norman Fowler, and echoed by senior DHSS officials in public statements. For example in 1980 the head of the social work service observed: 'I do not (therefore) have difficulty in accepting the role of the State as residual – the voluntary sector must to some extent return to providing and paying for services which we have come to expect from the State' (Utting, 1980).

Although some aspects of these policies were to be found under former governments (for example the 1977 Good Neighbour Scheme was the forerunner of the 1980s DHSS initiatives), a concerted strategy of this sort has not been identifiable previously. Of course, in relation to the totality of care, both formal and informal, the social services have never been anything other than residual. The essence of the Thatcher and Major governments' approach towards community care, however, was that they were trying, with some success, to reduce the role of local authorities as providers within the formal sector. Furthermore, it was intended to fill this artificially created care gap with a mixture of private, voluntary and informal care. The likely impact of this policy is considered in the next section.

The residualisation strategy outlined above, and especially its marketisation and devolution components, was responsible for introducing new management techniques into the social services that focused on cost efficiency, the reduction of labour costs, more flexible forms of organisation and a consumer orientation. A similarly economically orientated cost-effectiveness imperative has been imposed on other advanced welfare systems, and the preference for a mixed economy of care is becoming generalised. However very few countries have introduced the same radical reforms as those of the British government (Walker *et al.*, 1993).

22.2.4   National Health Service and Community Care Act 1990

The provisions of the NHS and Community Care Act represented the culmination of the previous decade of policy, as outlined above, and established a new framework for services. The Act was based on the White Paper *Caring for People* (DoH, 1989) which in turn was derived in large measure (80 per cent according to the Ministerial statement on 12 July 1989) from the recommendations of the Griffiths Report (1988). The Act received the Royal Assent on 29 June 1990 and was due to be implemented in full on 1 April 1991. However, on 18 July 1990 the secretary of state announced a delay in the implementation of the main financial provisions of the Act until April 1993. The government explained this delay in terms of its lack of confidence in local authorities to introduce the new system of community care within reasonable cost boundaries. But it would appear that, while the local authorities were prepared to implement the Act, the government itself had no idea what the cost would be, and therefore was rather nervous about the implications of the changes for poll-tax levels (Henwood *et al.*, 1991).

What are the main changes in policy that have begun to flow from the implementation of the Act? The White Paper defined four key components of community care, which together reflected the emphasis on promoting choice by policy developments over the previous decade, as well as being cast in the language of consumerism. They were services that respond flexibly and sensitively to the needs of individuals and their carers; services that intervene no more than is necessary to foster independence; services that allow a range of options for consumers; and services that concentrate on those with the greatest needs (DoH, 1989, p. 5). In the White Paper, 'choice' was defined as 'giving people a greater individual say in how they live their lives and the services they need to help them' (ibid., p. 4). This was to be achieved in two main ways: a comprehensive process of assessment and care management, which 'where possible should induce [the] active participation of the individual and his or her carer'; and a more diverse range of non-statutory providers among whose benefits is held to be 'a wider range of choice of services for the consumer' (ibid., pp. 19, 22).

The main policy changes were as follows. Local authorities became responsible, as lead agencies, for assessing individual needs, designing care arrangements and ensuring the delivery of services. Thus the *provision* of services was separated from their *purchase* (as under the quasi-market created by the reforms of the NHS) and it was expected that SSDs would make maximum use of private and voluntary services. Local authorities were charged with the task of producing and publishing plans for the development of community care services. A new funding structure was established for those with public support in non-statutory residential and nursing homes (though the changes did not apply to those in residence up to April 1993). Resources would come from a single unified budget, in the hands of local authorities, comprising existing social services resources *plus* the care element of social security board and lodging allowances deemed likely to be necessary by the government for new users. A new specific grant was created to promote the development of social care for people with mental health problems and, in this case only, health authorities were to act as the lead agencies.

The revised timetable for the implementation of the Act meant that the specific grant for the care of the mentally ill came into effect on 1 April 1991, together with the complaints procedures and 'arm's-length' local inspection units for residential care. From 1 April 1992 local authorities had to publish their first community care plans, and from 1 April 1993 the new funding arrangements started, with local authorities taking full responsibility for the funding of community care.

Some controversy surrounded the award of lead agency status to SSDs following the publication of the Griffiths Report. It was conjectured that the report's release on the day after the 1988 Budget, and the long-delayed response to it, signalled the government's displeasure with this central recommendation. On the face of it this proposal (now enacted) was completely at odds with the residualisation strategy set out earlier in this chapter. However Griffiths made a clear distinction between responsibility for ensuring that care is provided and actual provision: 'the role of the public sector is essentially to ensure that care is provided. How it is provided is an important but secondary consideration' (Griffiths, 1988, p. vii). This placed the Griffiths Report, the White Paper and the 1990 Act firmly in the mainstream of government community care policy stretching back to 1979. The role established for local authorities was the management of care, *not* its provision. As managing agents they were expected to oversee the further residualisation of public sector provision while encouraging the expansion of the private and voluntary sectors.

The only significant difference between the government's proposals and the Griffiths Report concerned the mechanism by which resources would be allocated to local authorities. Griffiths had recommended an ear-marked (or ring-fenced) grant, but the government rejected this in favour of maintaining the system whereby resources would be channelled through the general Revenue Support Grant to local authorities. Indeed so determined was the government that it overturned a House of Lords amendment to the NHS and Community Care Bill in order to prevent ring-fencing (though, under pressure from both the public and private sectors, it did allow ring-fencing for a short transitional period – see below).

22.3   Implications for users and carers

What have been the implications for users of these radical developments in the organisation and delivery of services? In making such an assessment it must be remembered that the Griffiths Report, from which the White Paper was derived, was designed from its inception as a top-down managerial appraisal intended to tackle the problems identified by the Audit Commission. Not surprisingly, therefore, the outcome has been management-orientated. In turn, the main justification for change provided in the White Paper was financial rather than, for example, the needs of disabled people or the quality of care. Thus it is impossible to imagine a document like the White Paper (or the Griffiths Report) being prepared by a group of service users and their carers. The official documents are management-orientated rather than user-orientated: their primary concern is with the cost and not the quality of care. It is for this reason that the promises of wider choice and the opportunity for service users and carers to exercise some significant influence over the care packages they receive have not been realised so far, and are unlikely to be in the future.

In the first place, despite the political rhetoric concerning choice and user involvement accompanying the White Paper, neither the Act nor the policy guidelines accompanying it contain any concrete proposals for user involvement or empowerment. In the absence of clear guidelines for such involvement, it is not surprising that professional opinions have continued to dominate. This is evident to some extent in the language employed: 'managers of care packages', 'case managers' and 'caring *for* people'. Thus rather than determining their own packages of care, service users are apparently still seen as passive receivers of care. Care (or case) management can be either administration centred or user centred, but in the context of the goals of value for money and efficiency it is likely to prove to be primarily an administrative tool for cost containment.

Secondly, also as a result of the ideological context of these changes, a premium is placed on non-state forms of provision. So local authorities are expected to employ competitive tendering, or other means of marketing the production of welfare. This gives a rather biased meaning to 'packages of care' or the 'mixed economy of care'. For example, the White Paper suggests that one of the ways in which social services departments can promote a mixed economy of care is by 'determining clear specifications of service requirements, and arrangements for tenders and contracts' (DoH, 1989, p. 23). But evidence from the US has indicated that competitive tendering may actually *reduce* the choice available by driving small producers out of the running (Demone and Gibelman, 1989). This is likely to affect specialist provision for some minority group needs, such as those for black people and particular groups representing disabled people (see below). It is too soon to assess the impact of compulsory competitive tendering on social services in the UK, but elsewhere in the public sector the primary source of savings from this is reduced labour costs. Care services are already dominated by low-paid, part-time women workers and compulsory competitive tendering is likely both to depress wages further and to reinforce the trend towards corporate takeovers.

There are two further important implications of the continued residualisation of SSDs as direct service providers. As the private sector 'creams-off' the less severely disabled and less costly users, leaving a rump of the most severely disabled in the public sector, staff morale problems arise. Griffiths had recommended that the government create a 'level playing field' between public, voluntary and private home funding, but this was rejected, and instead residents in non-public-sector homes receive an additional subsidy in the form of income support and housing benefit. This gives a financial incentive to local authorities to privatise their residential homes, and blows apart the idea that these changes were designed to increase choice. Some people with proven need are in effect prevented from choosing to enter a publicly owned home. The continued reduction in the service provision role of local authorities is likely to curtail the progress that some have been making towards equal opportunities policies and anti-oppressive practice. It will be difficult to sustain such policies under the new funding regime and in a world in which local authorities have very little influence over the terms and conditions of day-to-day service delivery in contracted agencies.

Thirdly, the government's professed aim of increasing choice and sensitivity to user requirements is being compromised by the process of assessment that is required to ration resources. Thus no-one can receive public funding for residential care unless they have been assessed and recommended by care managers. This process is bound to limit individual choice and user influence while, conversely, enhancing the power of bureau-professionals. Moreover users do not have a right to elect to be assessed, and there are no safeguards – such as an appeals procedure – for those who disagree with professional assessments.

Fourthly, despite the rhetoric concerning the needs of carers there are no proposals in the 1990 Act to ensure that their needs are taken into account. In the absence of such guarantees, of course, there is a danger that, under financial pressure, they will be ignored. Furthermore the fact that there might be a conflict of interest between carers and cared-for has not been recognised by the government. But this is a very real problem facing disabled people, their carers and service providers. The failure to address this dilemma stems from the assumption underlying both the White Paper and the Griffiths Report that the family should in all circumstances be the primary source of care. However research has shown that this confidence in familism is sometimes misplaced: family care can be both the best *and* the worst form of support (Qureshi and Walker, 1989). If policy makers continue to assume that it is always the soundest basis for care they will overlook inherent conflicts in the caring relationship and be guilty of imposing destructive relationships on both carers and cared-for. The introduction in April 1996 of the Carers (Recognition and Services) Act 1995 should begin to redress the imbalance in service provision between the needs of users and those of carers. But the long-standing neglect of carers' needs will take years to overcome.

Finally, as well as opportunities, the new system of organising community care heralds dangers for the voluntary sector. In a world of competitive tendering it has proved difficult for voluntary agencies to maintain their autonomy and act as independent representatives of the groups they serve. Financial pressures may limit the extent of user participation that voluntary agencies can sustain. Moreover, since contracts are between the local authority purchaser and the service provider, rather than with the individual service *receiver*, users are often excluded from care planning. Voluntary organisations that meet the neglected care needs of minority groups have a particularly difficult time in the new contract culture because they have to battle against racism as well as the cost-effectiveness imperative (Ahmad and Atkin, 1996).

Of course the precise impact of the changes rests on current and future resources, and as the Ministerial Statement on 12 July 1989 made clear, expanding the budget for community care in order to cope with rising needs was never intended. This means that, in line with the government's twin-track centralisation/decentralisation policy, local authorities have been given responsibility, but no guarantee that they will be provided with adequate funds to support the necessary growth in home care services. There is evidence of under-resourcing by the government in most local authorities, for example in the tighter rationing of home care services only to the most severely disabled, and in the pressure to privatise cleaning services or even, in the case of Kent, its entire home care provision. It is also clear now that service users themselves are having to contribute increasingly towards the financing of services and, as prefigured in the White Paper, a means-test has followed the assessment process in many local areas.

Prior to the implementation of the community care reforms in April 1993, there were two sources of pressure on the government to increase the resources to fund them. First, local authorities and groups representing older people were worried that the £2.5 billion being paid to support long-term care would not be transferred in full to the local authorities, or would disappear into other local spending priorities. Second, owners of private homes, a powerful and vociferous lobby created by the government's own policy, were worried that local authorities would not continue to spend the money on their sector. In response the government decided that the sum of money being transferred would be ring-fenced, to be spent only on community care services, for a transitional period. Thus over the three-year period 1993/4 to 1995/6 some

£1.5 billion was transferred from the Department of Social Security to the local authorities, with a significant saving accruing to the Treasury as existing recipients of support died off and the in-flow of new recipients was stopped. Furthermore 85 per cent of the social security transfer element of the total community care budget had to be spent on the 'independent' sector. In addition a sum of £140 million was paid to local authorities in 1993/4 to cover the setting-up of the infrastructure necessary to implement the changes. Unfortunately local authorities were not told exactly how much they would receive until late in February 1993, only a month before the implementation of the new funding arrangements. Needless to say it was not possible to do much advance planning.

With regard to charging users, recent research has shown that since the implementation of the 1990 Act most authorities have increased their domiciliary care charges and the main engine of change has been financial pressure (Baldwin and Lunt, 1996). This pressure includes a perceived inadequacy of the grants given to local authorities via the Revenue Support Grant; a perceived shortfall in resources to fund community care; and the rising demand for services and 'cost-shunting' by health authorities as they redefine community health services as 'social' care. Under the 1990 Act the government assumes that at least 9 per cent of the cost of non-residential services will be raised through charges, and that the level of central funding will be reduced accordingly.

The issue of the future funding of long-term care is being debated by politicians. The Conservative government published a consultation document on 7 May 1996 because of the political fall-out created by the mandatory means-test system for those permanently entering a residential or nursing home arranged by a local authority SSD (whereby those with capital between £10 000 and £16 000 pay some of the costs of their care and those with capital over £16 000 pay in full until it falls to this limit, and where the value of property is taken into account in some circumstances. The main aim of the proposals was to privatise the funding of long-term care by encouraging people at or close to retirement age to take out indemnity insurance, while those already receiving long-term care would have recourse to 'immediate needs' annuities, and people of working age would be expected to make additional private pension contributions to fund long-term care. The Labour Party's position in 1996, however, was that a Royal Commission should be appointed to investigate long-term care. Regardless of which Party is in power, how to ensure good quality care for frail and vulnerable people will be a major question for social policy well into the next century. The path chosen during the 1980s has not led, so far, to higher quality care.

22.4   From consumerism to empowerment?

Underlying the deficiencies of the new community care arrangements –
especially when viewed from the perspective of service users – are the
legacy of antagonism towards public welfare provision, discussed
earlier, and a very restricted conception of user involvement (Walker,
1991).

The Griffiths Report, the White Paper and the NHS and Community
Care Act all derive from the limited form of supermarket-style consumerism that assumes that, if there is a choice between 'products',
service users will automatically have the power to exit from a particular
product or market. Of course, even if this is true in markets for consumer
goods, in the field of social care many people are mentally disabled, frail
and vulnerable, so they are not in a position to 'shop around' and have
no realistic prospect of exiting.

Underlying the consumerist model of social care are two questionable
assumptions: that monopolies only operate in the public sector, and that
the private sector can adequately substitute for the public sector. But as
far as, for example, an older person currently resident in either a public
or a private home is concerned, her or his provider *is* the monopoly
power because she or he has no alternative. Having a range of theoretical
alternatives will not make the consumer sovereign if she or he cannot
exercise effective choice. Moreover a financial transaction does not necessarily mean that the purchaser is bestowed with influence or control over
the provider. Furthermore, unlike markets for consumer durables, in the
field of social care a private producer going out of business not only has
immense human consequences, but the public sector is expected to pick
up the pieces. In other words the power that the private sector exercises
over users is equivalent to that of public providers, but it does not necessarily bear the same responsibility.

The only way that frail and vulnerable service users can be assured of
influence and power over service provision is if they, or their advocates,
are guaranteed a 'voice' in the organisation and management of services.
This would ensure that services actually reflect their needs. In practice
the weak form of consumer consultation pursued under the 1990 Act
may consist of no more than an occasional survey among users, together
with minimal individual consultation at the point of assessment. Thus,
despite the rhetoric concerning 'packages of care' and making services
more responsive to users, in practice the government's proposals are
silent on how user involvement can be ensured, and in fact are characterised by old-style paternalism.

In contrast to the consumer-orientated model, the user-centred or
empowerment approach would aim to involve users in the development,
management and operation of services, as well as in the assessment of

need. The intention would be to provide users and potential users with a range of realisable opportunities to define their own needs and the sort of services they require to meet them. Both carers and cared-for would be regarded as potential service users. Where necessary the interests of older people with mental impairments would be represented by independent advocates. Services would be organised to respect the users' right to self-determination, normalisation and dignity. They would be distributed as a matter of right rather than discretion, with independent inspection and appeals procedures, and would be subject to democratic oversight and accountability.

What changes in policy will be necessary if community care services are to move beyond consultation to empowerment? In the first place it is necessary to recognise that, while the private and voluntary sector may extend choice in social care, they cannot substitute for the public sector. Only the public sector can guarantee the right to services. Moreover the motivations of a for-profit private producer are quite different from those of a public sector provider. Although both may provide opportunities to exploit vulnerable people, it is only in the public sector that a direct line of enforceable public accountability exists (Walker, 1988). It must be said too that, as far as Britain is concerned, the public sector of care is notably more successful at involving users than its private counterpart.

Secondly, change is necessary in the organisation and operation of formal services. The concept of social support networks is particularly helpful in emphasising the need for formal and informal helpers to cooperate, share tasks and decision-making, and 'interweave' (Whittaker and Garbarino, 1983). In addition, however, social service departments must develop an explicit strategy for the involvement of service users, carers and potential users (Walker and Warren, 1996). The essential ingredients of such a strategy are: first, to take positive action – to provide users and potential users (or their advocates) with support, skills training, advocacy and resources – so that they can make informed choices; and second, to create real access to decision making – the structures of the agency must afford opportunities for genuine involvement. According to Croft and Beresford (1990, p. 14):

> Unless both are present people may either lack the confidence, expectations or abilities to get involved, or be discouraged by the difficulties entailed. Without them, participatory initiatives are likely to reinforce rather than overcome existing race, class, gender and other inequalities.

Thus user involvement must be built into the structure and operations of SSDs and not bolted on.

Thirdly, change must be initiated in professional values and attitudes within the formal sector so that cooperation and partnership with service users is regarded as a normal activity. This does *not* mean that service provision must be deprofessionalised if user involvement is to flourish. Rather the role of professionals must change in order to share power with users. This means challenging, to some extent, the traditional basis of professional status and providing for the input of informed user knowledge and preferences. Ways have to be found for community members themselves to take part in the development of community care policy – in short, power sharing.

Fourthly, the previous two points suggest a major transformation in training and retraining for social services personnel. Thus the emphasis would shift away from autonomous expertise and individual diagnosis towards skills for working in partnership with service users and their carers, and encouraging community participation.

Finally, user involvement is not a cheap option; it is usually time-consuming and costly. Therefore there is a need for increased resources in the social services not only to improve the choice and quality of services but also to ensure that they provide sufficient space for the direct involvement of users.

Thus if significantly greater resources were made available, it would be possible for some of the reforms contained in the NHS and Community Care Act 1990 to be implemented in a progressive way. For example assessment could be operationalised as an open process designed to explore and create options rather than ration resources. It could be carried out by users and carers themselves, or in partnership with social services professionals. Contracts could be used to ensure that high standards are maintained, rather than low prices, and that agencies have equal-opportunities employment policies and anti-oppressive forms of practice. Quality could be guaranteed by granting users and carers *rights* in terms of both standards and levels of service. But arguably these sorts of development could alter the main thrust of current community care policy and therefore require a change in political direction.

22.5   Conclusion

Looking back over the postwar period it is clear that the precarious political consensus on community care held together because of the remarkable gulf between rhetoric and action and the interests of the most powerful groups involved in sustaining it. The consensus began to break down in the mid 1970s under economic and external pressures from the International Monetary Fund, but there was still a commitment to publicly provided domiciliary services. The serious challenge to the consensus came after 1979 when the government initiated a radical shift in policy, towards the increasing use of private and informal care and the residualisation of the social services. The debate following the publication of the Griffiths Report, culminating in the 1990 Act, could have marked a watershed in raising public consciousness about community care and provided a basis for the development of policies aimed at user involvement and empowerment. Unfortunately that opportunity was wasted, and the measures that have been implemented have been directed primarily at cost containment and the run-down of public social services.

Note

1. The DHSS was split into two departments: Health (DH) and Social Security (DSS) on 25 July 1988.

References

ADSS (1985) *Who Goes Where?*, Association of Directors of Social Services, London.

Ahmad, W. and Atkin, K. (1996) *'Race' and Community Care*, Open University Press, Buckingham.

Audit Commission (1986) *Making a Reality of Community Care*, Policy Studies Institute, London.

Audit Commission (1996) *Community Care Bulletin*, No. 3, HMSO, London.

Baldwin, S. and Lunt, N. (1996) *Charging Ahead: Local Authority Charging Policies for Community Care*, The Policy Press, Bristol.

Bradshaw, J. (1988) 'Financing Private Care for the Elderly', Department of Social Policy and Social Work, University of York.

Bradshaw, J. and Gibbs, I. (1988) *Public Support for Private Residential Care*, Avebury, Aldershot.

Croft, S. and Beresford, P. (1990) *From Paternalism to Participation*, Open Services Project, London.

Day, P. and Klein, R. (1987) 'The Business of Welfare', *New Society*, 19 June, pp. 11–13.

Demone, H. and Gibelman, M. (1989) *Services for Sale: Purchasing Health and Human Services*, Rutgers University Press, London.

DoH (Department of Health) (1989) *Caring for People: Community Care in the Next Decade and Beyond*, Cm 849, HMSO, London.

DHSS (Department of Health and Social Security) (1976) *Priorities for Health and Personal Social Services in England*, HMSO, London.

DHSS (Department of Health and Social Security) (1981a) *Care in the Community*, HMSO, London.

DHSS (Department of Health and Social Security) (1981b) *Growing Older*, Cmnd 8173, HMSO, London.

DHSS (Department of Health and Social Security) (1983) *Explanatory Notes on Care in the Community*, DHSS, London.

DHSS (Department of Health and Social Security) (1984) 'Helping the Community to Care', DHSS, London.

DHSS (Department of Health and Social Security) (1985) *Response to Second Report from the Social Services Committee*, Cmnd 9674, HMSO, London.

Edelman, M. (1977) *Political Language*, Academic Press, New York.

Finch, J. and Groves, D. (eds) (1983) *A Labour of Love*, Routledge and Kegan Paul, London.

Fowler, N. (1984) *Speech to Joint Social Services Annual Conference*, 27 September, DHSS, London.

Gamble, A. (1987) *The Free Economy and the Strong State*, Pluto, London.

Gibbs, J., Evans, M. and Rodway, S. (1987) *Report of the Inquiry into Nye Bevan Lodge*, Southwark Council, London.

Gray, A. M., Whelan, A. and Normand, C. (1988) *Care in the Community: A Study of Services and Costs in Six Districts*, University of York, Centre for Health Economics.

Griffiths, Sir R. (1988) *Community Care: Agenda for Action*, HMSO, London.

Harman, H. and Lowe, M. (1986) *No Place Like Home*, House of Commons, London.

Henwood, M., Jowell, T. and Wistow, G. (1991) *All Things Come (to Those Who Wait?)*, King's Fund Institute, London.

Holmes, B. and Johnson, A. (1988) *Cold Comfort*, Souvenir Press, London.

Jackson, P. and Haskins, D. (1992) 'Vouchers in the funding of residential care' in *Market-Type Mechanisms*, Series No. 4, OECD, Paris.

Jenkin, P. (1979) *Speech to Social Services Conference*, Bournemouth, 21 November.

Jenkin, P. (1980) *Speech to the Conference of the Association of Directors of Social Services*, 19 September.

Larder, D., Day, P. and Klein, R. (1986) *Institutional Care of the Elderly: The geographical distribution of the public/private mix in England*, University of Bath.

Lewis, J. and Glennerster, H. (1996) *Implementing the New Community Care*, Open University Press, Buckingham.

NACAB (1991) *Beyond the Limit*, London, National Association of Citizens Advice Bureaux.

Qureshi, H. and Walker, A. (1989) *The Caring Relationship*, Macmillan, London.

Social Services Committee (1980) *The Government's White Papers on Public Expenditure: The Social Services*, Vol. II, HC 702, HMSO, London.

Social Services Committee (1985) *Community Care*, HC 13–1, HMSO, London.

Social Services Committee (1990a) *Community Care: Future Funding of Private and Voluntary Residential Care*, HC 257, HMSO, London.

Social Services Committee (1990b) *Community Care: Services for People with A Mental Handicap and People with a Mental Illness*, HC 664, HMSO, London.

Titmuss, R. M. (1968) *Commitment to Welfare*, Allen and Unwin, London.

Treasury (1979) *The Government's Expenditure Plans 1980/81*, Cmnd 7746, HMSO, London.

Utting, B. (1980) 'Changing ways of caring', *Health and Social Services Journal*, 4 July, p. 882.

Walker, A. (ed.) (1982) *Community Care: The Family, the State and Social Policy*, Basil Blackwell and Martin Robertson, Oxford.

Walker, A. (1983) 'Care for elderly people: a conflict between women and the State', in Finch and Groves (1983) pp. 106–28.

Walker, A. (1985) *The Care Gap*, Local Government Information Service, London.

Walker, A. (1986a) 'Community care: fact and fiction', in Willmott, P. (ed.), *The Debate About Community*, Policy Studies Institute, London, pp. 4–15.

Walker, A. (1986b) 'More ebbs than flows', *Social Services Insight*, 29 March, pp. 16–17.

Walker, A. (1988) 'State of confusion', *Community Care*, 3 March, pp. 26–7.

Walker, A. (1991) 'Increasing user involvement in the social services', in Arie, T. (ed.), *Recent Advances in Psychogeriatrics 2*, Churchill Livingstone, London.

Walker, A. and Warren, L. (1996) *Changing Services for Older People*, Open University Press, Buckingham.

Walker, A., Guillemard, A. M. and Alber, J. (1993) *Older People in Europe – Social and Economic Policies*, Commission of the European Communities, Brussels.

Webb, A. and Wistow, G. (1982) 'The personal social services: incrementalism, expediency or systematic social planning?', in Walker, A. (ed.), *Public Expenditure and Social Policy: An Examination of Social Spending and Priorities*, Heinemann, London.

Webb, A. and Wistow, G. (1987) *Social Work, Social Care and Social Planning: The Personal Social Services Since Seebohm*, Longman, London.

Whittaker, J. K. and Garbarino, J. (eds) (1983) *Social Support Networks: Informal Helping in the Human Services*, Aldine, New York.

The Structured Dependency of the Elderly: A Creation of Social Policy in the Twentieth Century

PETER TOWNSEND

23.1   The effects of retirement in promoting increased dependency

[. . .] Retirement has become a social phenomenon of vast importance in the short span of the last fifty years. According to statistics published by the International Labour Office, between 40 per cent and 70 per cent of men 65 and over in all industrial countries were still economically active in the 1930s. But by the mid-1960s, with the exception of Japan, where the, percentage had declined only slightly, the proportion had shrunk dramatically to between 10 per cent and 40 per cent with the mean about 20 per cent. The reduction [. . .] continued during the 1970s, though not so rapidly. This change cannot be attributed to changes in the risk of ill-health or disability, or the masking of disability in periods before substitute pensions were available. It is attributable to changes in the organisation of work and in the kind of people wanted for work. Bigger work organisations, with more pronounced hierarchies, have become established and career promotion through the successive tiers of these hierar-

---

* The original complete version of this article referred to substantial empirical evidence to support the arguments summarised here. It was first published in *Ageing and Society*, Vol. 1, No. 1, March 1991, pp. 5-28.

chies is regarded as normal and to be expected. The objectives of economic growth, productivity and increasingly rapid replacement of skills have been adopted within these organisational settings and, as a direct consequence, more workers at older ages have found themselves misplaced. In the late 1970s another factor has become all-important. The development of multi-national corporations and improvements internationally in transport and communication have led to a deliberate shifting of manufacturing production to poor countries where the workforces can be paid very low wages. In 1975 the workforce of the overseas subsidiaries of German manufacturing industry represented 20 per cent of the manufacturing workforce in Germany itself.

Problems arise for companies and unions which can only be resolved by a kind of mass redundancy, which retirement has become. Retirement is in a real sense a euphemism for unemployment. The phenomenon has been enforced and is being enforced in a number of industrial countries at earlier ages and yet is, paradoxically, being represented as a social achievement in capitalist and state socialist societies alike. The spread of retirement is interpreted as reflecting the success of campaigns on behalf of the rights of workers when they have 'earned a rest', and is associated with the rights of old people to peace and dignity. But many older, especially active, people deplore the termination of economic activity. People reaching retirement age do not welcome it as warmly as they had thought they would. Many who have retired deeply regret their inactivity or loss of status. The satisfaction which is expressed by some retired people is more what they think is expected of them, and more an assertion of hope, than a true representation of what they feel. Closer historical examination of retirement as a social institution shows that its adoption has also been associated with pressures to shed moral if not contractual obligations to loyal workers and to exclude certain groups of workers from the bargaining process. The public are encouraged to accept the lessened value to the economy of workers past certain ages. Changing technology and the successive adoption of forms of training and educational qualifications have encouraged over-valuation of the productive capacity of older workers. This has affected other priorities. Less consideration tends to be given in sickness and disability at older than at younger ages and, indeed, retirement is cavalierly associated with failing health and capacity. Thus the combined effects of industrial, economic and educational reorganisation are leading to a more rigid stratification of the population by age. [. . .]

23.2   The effects of pensions in promoting dependency

While the institutionalisation of retirement as a major social phenomenon in the very recent history of society has played a big part in fostering the material and psychological dependence of older people, the institutionalisation of pensions and services has also played a major part. The propensity to poverty in old age could be said to be a function of low levels of resources, and restricted access to resources, relative to younger people. Secondly it is due to restricted access to the new styles and modes of living being promoted in the community. In Britain there is official evidence [. . .] of about 10 per cent being in poverty, as defined by the state, and another 30 per cent or 40 per cent being on the margins in the sense that they are living at the state's standard or within 40 per cent of that standard. [. . .] Independent measures suggest the first of these figures (10 per cent in poverty) is understimated because of methodological shortcomings. [. . .] Restriction of resources is determined by different causal factors. State pensions and other cash benefits administered centrally comprise the most important source of income for the elderly in most advanced industrial societies and the initial rate of state pensions after retirement, and the amount of substitute or supplementary benefits which are paid, after the pensionable age or upon retirement, tend to be low relative to the earnings of younger adults. In Britain, various studies put the net incomes of single or widowed retired people, allowing for dependents, at about a third, and of married couples less than half, of younger non-retired people. [. . .] State help is offered on condition that people retire from paid employment and this status is imposed upon elderly people at a fixed chronological age, or they are persuaded to accept it as a social norm. Pension levels are defined in relation to subsistence needs, and are usually pitched considerably below net earnings during the period of paid employment. The initial rates of private or occupational pensions, with some exceptions, are also low relative to the earnings of young adults. Provisions for widows under the terms of these schemes have generally been poor and this fact, together with the failure of many such pensions to keep pace with inflation, explains why so many people formerly associated with non-manual occupations, certainly in Britain, descend, along with their working-class counterparts, into poverty or near-poverty after retirement. Lacking access to many of the positions where sectional interests can be properly represented, the elderly find their position in a rapidly evolving economy getting worse. Their resources fail to keep pace in value with the resources of other groups in society; either certain forms of assets held, such as household goods and equipment and certain types of income from savings, and occupational pensions, depreciate in value absolutely or relatively to the rise in living standards, with increasing length of retirement, or many do not have, and have not in the past had, an opportunity of obtaining types of resources which are newly becoming available to younger people. What is more, greater exposure to certain forms of social desolation and isolation, brought about by the death of a spouse, the loss of close relatives or friends, and the decay of industries or city centres, as well as by retirement, tends to deprive the elderly of access to alternative or subsidiary resources and sometimes leads to additional costs. Liability to disablement restricts access to resources and, in the absence of compensating cash benefits and services, leads to additional costs for many which outweigh the savings consequent upon retirement.

There is a sharp contrast between the low status in which old people are held publicly and the regard in which they are held privately in their families. In the family age is of secondary importance. People are grandparents, parents, brothers or sisters and friends or neighbours first and foremost. Retirement from familial roles is a much more flexible contingency, dependent primarily upon health or disablement. In some respects the family also provides escape from the psychological and social bruises which can be inflicted externally, and up to a point provides meaningful activity and genuine respect. The positive contribution to the welfare of grandchildren and children of many elderly women is greatly underestimated just as their labour specifically on behalf of their husbands and in general on behalf of the economy throughout adult working life goes largely unrecognised. Capital and state separately or in combination, may have fostered the dependency of women within the family but, paradoxically, have created an independent system of interdependence, occupation, mutual respect and loyalty. The defensive and restorative mechanisms of the family temper the dependency created by the state.

23.3   The effects of residential care in creating dependency

Rich societies have still to come to terms with the engineering of retirement and mass poverty among the elderly in the twentieth century. These two are of course linked and they have been pre-eminent in creating the social dependency of the elderly. But their connection with the development of residential and community care is too frequently overlooked. When we turn to examine the part played by these two trends in fostering dependency it is important to understand how the assumptions of all the participants are already greatly affected by the facts of retirement and poverty. Not only do they materially restrict life chances. They govern the attitudes and not only the actions of professional staff, on the one hand, and elderly clients or residents, on the other.

A review of the history of residential developments and of the characteristics of the inmate populations shows that the institutions have been, and are, serving major functions other than those for which formally they were and are supposed to exist. In particular they have inhibited appeals in times of major stress for public help from the individual and the family, have operated as a cheap (because selective) substitute for public housing and community services, and have regulated public ideas of the lengths to which the family is expected to carry the burden of care. [. . .]

Socially, institutions are structured to serve purposes of controlling inmates. The type and level of staffing, amenities and resources have been developed not only in relation to the characteristics, including the perceived capacities, of inmates but also the roles staff expect inmates to play. Staff tend to resist any increase in the number or proportion of inmates requiring a great deal of attention. They become conscious of the value of inmates who perform large and small tasks in the organisation and tend to give excuses rather than rational grounds for the presence in the institution of these inmates. On the other hand, the roles are distinguished from those played by staff by their subordinate and even menial status and the derisory forms of payment which accompany them. Occupational roles are clearly distinguished partly to maintain the lower status and presumed dependency of inmates. The majority of residents in homes are placed in a category of enforced dependence. The routine of residential homes, made necessary by small staffs and economical administration, and committed to an ideology of 'care and attention' rather than the encouragement of self-help and self-management, seems to deprive many residents of the opportunity if not the incentive to occupy themselves and even of the means of communication. [. . .]

The maintenance and even increase of the share of resources going to hospitals and to residential institutions has been something of a paradox. Despite the powerful movements in favour of community care the emergence of that sector cannot be said to have properly materialised. This is not easy to explain. The failure to achieve a shift in priorities has to be explained partly in relation to the powerful vested interests of certain branches of the professions, unions of hospital staffs and certain sections of the administration. The brute fact is that the majority of medical staff and the vast majority of nursing staff work in residential homes. The failure to shift the balance of health and welfare policy towards community care also has to be explained in relation to the function of institutions to regulate and confirm inequality in society, and indeed to regulate deviation from the central social values of self-help, domestic independence, personal thrift, willingness to work, productive effort and family care. Institutions serve subtle functions in reflecting the positive structural and cultural changes taking place in society.

The numbers of bedfast, severely incapacitated and infirm old people living in the community dwarfs the number in institutions and there are real dangers in the present situation of committing available resources for the care of a few at the expense of the much larger number living in the community who require only modest forms of support to live independently with their families. [. . .] Our object must be a renewed attempt to replace institutional care by increased and new forms of support in the home. While the costs of care in residential institutions are not always easy to compare with the costs of providing alternative services when old people are living at home (depending on levels of disablement as well as the types of benefit or service included in the measurement) most of the studies that have been carried out have concluded that the costs of care at home are smaller.

However, so much energy has been invested by radical analysts in arguing for community care as an alternative mode of support for the elderly that some of the less happy practices incorporated within the conventional administration of community care services have attracted little scrutiny. Thus, day centres are sometimes organized on the same lines as residential Homes, but without residence at night. Meals and perhaps physiotherapy are laid on but little scope allowed for various forms of occupation and self-management. The duties of home helps and community nurses are also heavily circumscribed. The elderly are usually viewed as the grateful and passive recipients of services administered by an enlightened public authority. This can but reinforce their dependency both in their own eyes and that of the public. [. . .]

23.4   Summary

I have tried to argue that the concepts of retirement, pensionable status, institutional resident and other passive forms of community care have been developed in both capitalist and state socialist countries in ways which have created and reinforced the social dependency of the elderly. Such 'structured' dependency is a consequence of twentieth-century thought and action, and especially of the management of modern economies and the distribution of power and status in such economies. The severity and extent of that dependency cannot be justified by appeal to certain major types of evidence. Empirical studies of capacity and desire for productive occupation, reciprocation of services, and familial and social relationships, as well as self-care, challenge the assumptions which prevail. There is clearly room for an alternative interpretation of the roles to be played by the elderly whereby many more of them continue in paid employment, find alternative forms of substantial and productive occupation, have rights to much larger incomes, and have a much greater control over the place and type of accommodation where they live, and the kind of community services to which they contribute as well as have access.

When 'Ordinary' Isn't Enough: A Review of the Concept of Normalisation

HILARY BROWN and JAN WALMSLEY

24.1 Introduction

The idea of 'normalisation' has influenced the development of community-based services, especially for people with learning disabilities, for more than two decades. Essentially normalisation is about 'making available to all mentally retarded people patterns of life and conditions of everyday living which are as close as possible to the regular circumstances and ways of life of society' (Nirje, 1980, p. 33): in short, providing for 'an ordinary life' (King's Fund Centre, 1980). In the circumstances in which it was coined, when many people with learning disabilities were confined to large-scale specialist residential institutions, it made a good deal of sense to review service philosophies with 'normalisation' in mind. It gave impetus to the closing of large hospitals for people with learning disabilities in the UK in the 1970s and 1980s, and underpinned the growth of staffed and supported housing and independent living in a number of countries, including Scandinavia, North America, the UK and Australia.

However, like many apparently simple ideas, normalisation also creates its fair share of dilemmas and debates. In this chapter we describe two models of normalisation and then outline some of these tensions.

24.2   What is normalisation?

The term normalisation was first coined in Scandinavia to underpin reform of institutional services for people with learning disabilities. Building on the ideas of Erving Goffman (1961), whose powerful critique of institutions included the observation that inmates were forced to experience work, relationships and leisure under the same roof, the priorities of normalisation were to model life even in segregated services on the lives of ordinary citizens, so that the rhythm of the days, weeks, seasons and life-cycle would be made available to people in these settings and their rights upheld. These rights included the right to make choices, and were not conditional upon behaving 'normally' or learning new skills.

These ideas were then taken up and developed by Wolf Wolfensberger in the North American context. The normalisation strategy he outlined was based on reversing institutional models of congregation and segregation, and promoting integration with 'valued' individuals and institutions. Work undertaken by Wolfensberger and his colleagues, and exemplified by new services such as those in Nebraska, USA, established the principle that services should be evaluated against 'ordinary' and not abnormal (or subnormal) reference points:

> The implication of normalisation is that as much as possible any features of human services that can convey messages about clients at value risk should be positive. . . . Such features would include the physical setting in which the service is rendered (location, cleanliness, what is near etc.), the name of the service . . . the agency logo, . . . the appearance projected by the clients, what the clients are called, and what the service activities are called.
>
> (Wolfensberger and Tullman, 1989, p. 217)

Wolfensberger's work played an unparalleled part in mobilising people to achieve change on behalf of people with learning disabilities. However the vision was based on minimising difference and need. Wolfensberger wrote at a time when labelling theories were fashionable, and argued that people with learning disabilities were caught up in a self-fulfilling prophecy because of low, or distorted, public perceptions about them. The job of what he called 'human services' was therefore to do all that was possible to reverse the spiral, to promote positive images and the appearance of competence. The North American school of normalisation came to emphasise integration, as opposed to the Scandinavian reforms based on individual choices within segregated provision, partly as a goal in its own right and partly because it was believed that this would enable people to learn to behave in ways that did not mark them out as different. The importance of integration and of avoiding negative stereotyping for people with learning disabilities as a group tended to take precedence over considerations of personal choice and led to some quite extraordinary prescriptions, for example the 'conservatism corollary', which posited that:

> it is not enough for a human service to be merely neutral in either diminishing or enhancing the status of a devalued person in the eyes of others; it must seek to effect the most positive status possible for its clients. For example, on occasions where either a suit and tie or a sports jacket and sports shirt are equally appropriate attire the man at value risk in society would fare better wearing the suit and tie combination.

(ibid., p. 216)

This 'conservatism corollary' illustrates well how Wolfensberger's model of normalisation assumed that conformity would be a condition of acceptance into the mainstream. Valued roles came to be seen as the key to integration and acceptance, and in 1983 Wolfensberger advocated a change of terminology from 'normalisation' to 'social role valorisation'.

As we have seen, the early models of normalisation differed. Scandinavian countries adopted a rights model within the context of segregated services, whereas the North American model adopted an approach based on integration and assimilation. In this model, it is up to individuals, both people with learning disabilities and those in human services, to do the work of making people acceptable. There is no onus on others to change to facilitate the inclusion of devalued groups.

Both the Scandinavian and the North American model of normalisation have followers in Britain. For example segregated communities run by organisations such as L'Arche, Camphill and Rudolph Steiner pride themselves on offering their residents a valued place and normal patterns of life within protected communities. But it is the North American integrationist model that has been most influential, and it is to this model that the rest of the chapter refers.

24.3   Normalisation in practice

Normalisation has achieved a great deal as a guiding principle for services. Changes in provision for people with learning disabilities include homes in ordinary houses in ordinary streets rather than *extra*ordinary hostels or hospitals; programmes to provide paid employment, access to education, healthcare and community leisure facilities; a recognition that people with learning disabilities have a right to sexual relationships; and support rather than condemnation if they have children of their own.

However twenty or so years on it is evident that there are also problems. Because Wolfensberger's original analysis assumed that the discrimination experienced by people with learning disabilities was caused by negative labelling, normalisation-based provision stressed the need to disperse people who might be perceived as different and to help them to blend in. He advocated questionable practices such as the abandonment of aids (such as wheelchairs and hearing aids) in the interest of a positive image. The way deaf people are encouraged to communicate orally rather than use sign language could be seen as another example of this way of thinking.

The deceptively simple language of 'ordinariness' coined in the UK publication 'An ordinary life' (see King's Fund Centre, 1980; O'Brien and Tyne, 1981) has sometimes been used to deny the fact that some people with learning disabilities really do have 'special needs'. Lois Greenhalgh found this when researching the health information needs of a group of women with learning disabilities. She writes of the role of staff who worked with the women:

> it emerged that they were working to a model of 'normalisation' which pro-hibited them from taking any sort of pro-active role with clients. The philos-ophy was 'they are independent adults now. We can't interfere in what they do'. In other words they admitted that if a client had a very obvious problem they might suggest a doctor's appointment . . . but beyond that they felt they could not go.
>
> (Greenhalgh, 1994, p. 77)

Greenhalgh concludes that this was having the effect of making the clients 'less able and independent and therefore less normal than they could have been' (ibid., p. 77).

As this example shows, the model of 'ordinariness' has sometimes been interpreted as a minimalist approach to intervention, as a *laissez-faire*, hands-off model, on the grounds that, because another person would not require this degree of help, it should not be given to the person with learning disabilities who *does* need complex support. It may also be used to mask vulnerability, or to 'talk up' someone's skills and abilities to make choices for themselves. There is no shortcut to case-by-case judgements about structured intervention and the appropriateness of protection or proxy decision making, but sometimes the language of normalisation is wrongly used to imply that there is.

Within the normalisation model, integration is put forward as both an end in itself and a means towards that end. The assumption that it would be educative to live amongst non-disabled people rests on the belief that people will learn by imitation and that, if they have role models amongst non-disabled peers, they will learn appropriate skills and behaviours. In fact imitation has been shown to be a weak learning strategy, particu-larly for people with complex learning disabilities. More focused strategies are needed, but as Newnes (1994) points out, the absence of 'meaningful training' means that most workers are effectively 'forced to rely on common-sense'. Service evaluations suggest that there are serious gaps in common-sense that need to be addressed in services for people with learning disabilities. First, it is clear that, without conscious planning, staff engage very little with people with learning disabilities, especially those who are severely disabled and not able to reward their efforts with ordinary social interaction or feedback. Secondly, common-sense prescriptions tend to assume that all behaviour is 'attention-seeking' in motivation. Staff need training to consider alternative interpretations of challenging behaviour: for example that it might have biochemical causes, or may be a way of communicating physical or emotional pain or of avoiding or ending interactions or tasks that are too difficult. Without a more complex analysis, front-line staff are often left in a stressful position, usually characterised by a period of 'ignoring' followed by punishment of escalating demands. Thirdly, workers often lack the skill to communicate with individuals. They may use over-complicated language which appears to meet social goals at the expense of genuine communication. McGill and Emerson (1992) argue that, while normalisation provides the goals, it does not supply a sufficiently robust 'technology' to provide the means to normalisation's ends.

Where normalisation works well it is accompanied by sophisticated macro and micro organisation: by scrupulous implementation of behavioural techniques, by coherent planning, by robust mechanisms for ethical debate and decision making and by close interagency co-operation. However, too often it is interpreted wrongly by front-line staff and managers, and can be used as an excuse for not providing training or specialist techniques and resources when they are clearly a requirement.

24.4   An alternative model of change

A further fundamental set of criticisms is based upon the argument that normalisation is not an ideal model for change. Normalisation is about 'integrating the individual into society' (Williams, 1989, p. 258), a strategy that emphasises that individuals have the right to live like others, but, as has been pointed out, this puts the onus to change on individuals, and makes no demands on members of the wider society to change to fit the needs of individuals perceived as different.

An alternative strategy for change is that oppressed people, like people with learning disabilities, develop solidarity as a group, that they organise and demand change, and celebrate rather than hide difference. Movements such as Black Power, Gay Pride or the disability movement can be seen as embracing this challenging stance, and organisations of people with learning disabilities, such as People First, are also beginning to demand that the world changes to enable them to take part, by, for example, providing information on tape and in pictorial form as well as in print.

Normalisation, with its preference for integration and its insistence that relationships with non-handicapped people are more important than solidarity *between* people with learning disabilities, or other shared conditions, tends to work against collective action and pride in difference. As Jenny Morris explains:

> having given such a negative meaning to abnormality – the non-disabled world assumes that we wish to be normal, or to be treated as if we were. From this follows the view that it is progressive and liberating to ignore our differences because these differences have such negative meanings for non-disabled people. But we are different. We reject the meanings that the non-disabled world attaches to disability but we do not reject the differences which are such an important part of our identities.
>
> (Morris, 1991, p. 17)

At the heart of this conflict over strategy is the explicit challenging of dominant values, which has motivated disability activists, women, Black people, gay men and lesbians to resist rather than adapt to 'valued' social roles. Thus, instead of remedying devaluation by promoting 'normal' social roles and images, a more appropriate strategy for change may be for oppressed groups to re-assess themselves, disown the negative projections put upon them by others and demand that the world changes to accommodate them.

24.5   Normalisation and community care

Normalisation ideas fit well with both the explicit and the implicit principles of community care enshrined in the 1990 National Health Service and Community Care Act. The running down of institutional forms of care, for example, can be readily justified by reference to the importance of community integration. Furthermore Brown and Smith (1993) argue that the language of normalisation has played into deprofessionalisation and deregulation of the terms and conditions of service of people who work in services that are also on the community care agenda. The idea that people need opportunities for an 'ordinary life' more than they need highly trained professional input offers muted support to this aspect of the changes of the last decade because, unfortunately, people may need extraordinarily specialist input to achieve this ordinariness. Hence the North American version of normalisation has been readily adapted to, and adopted by, new models of service organisation and types of service agency.

The kind of dispersed service provision that supporters of normalisation advocate has not of itself led to more integration or greater openness. The practice of 'placing' individuals in one service for 24 hours a day, seven days a week persists and, given financial constraints, is unlikely to change. Smaller, staffed housing services still conform to Goffman's definition of an institution in that they 'provide everything under one roof' and fail to provide safeguards. As Crossmaker (1991) cautions, the move from institutions may not be an improvement of circumstances at all, as in the USA *deinstitutionalisation* has most often meant *trans*institutionalisation (that is, the movement from one institution to another). Crossmaker warns that:

> care must be taken as policies are implemented to ensure that larger, centralised institutions are not replaced by small less accountable residential facilities, with equal potential for abuse. People's isolation and feelings of inadequacy and differentness that can result when community services don't exist or aren't well planned, may increase victimisation.
>
> (Crossmaker, 1991, p. 207)

Meanwhile even those in smaller and more homely services may be isolated within, even if not from, the wider community. Many studies have revealed how fragile are the social networks of people with learning disabilities (see for example Flynn, 1987; Atkinson and Ward, 1987). leading Szivos to conclude that:

> many of the assumptions about community integration within normalisation may be potentially erroneous and damaging. Dispersal within the community does not guarantee that people will learn to behave in a way which will overcome intolerance towards them. Instead people may feel increasingly stigmatised and cut off by social distance from non-disabled people while being physically separated from others who share their difficulties.
>
> (Szivos, 1992, p. 125)

Isolation for service users may be mirrored for staff who now tend to work in small groups, or alone, and without supervision. This has implications both for their own support and for the standards of care, since they lack the opportunities that exist for the modelling of good practice from more experienced workers and the routine passing on of skills. Isolated working also presents opportunities for abuse and exploitation.

New arrangements such as direct payments, which have devolved rationing to service users or those nearest to them, might look as if they have the potential to make funding decisions more sensitive to individual need, and have been sold as such. But 'If government controls finance directly, the needs of different groups are much more likely to become politicised' (George *et al.*, 1995, p. 147). So making provision a matter of individual negotiation rather than collective bargaining is a way of defusing any disenchantment with inadequate resources, and of undermining shared action in response to service cuts. It also cuts across any collective 'voice' for workers.

There is also a clear political agenda in relation to the family and its responsibilities for caring that finds echoes within the normalisation philosophy. Implicit in normalisation is the idea that it is abnormal for individuals to rely on paid carers. But an exhortation for care to be given by people who are not paid inevitably means that the duty to care falls on the shoulders of women family members even though they are increasingly required to be part of the workforce. Again, the reference to ordinariness, when families often face extraordinary difficulties, can be used as an excuse for exploitation, an expectation that the family should take on increased responsibilities without paid help (ibid., p. 119).

24.6   Conclusion

There have always been contradictions in the way normalisation has been interpreted in relation to social inequalities. People have seemed to be able to advocate redressing the position of people with disabilities without embracing the global 'principle of equality'. While the Scandinavian model stressed adherence to a set of universal rights and standards of living, Wolfensberger's North American model of normalisation, with its emphasis on the 'most valued' option, assumes there is agreement on what is valued across lines of race, gender and class, and is clearly predicated on a hierarchical society, one in which conformity and status go hand in hand. But when normalisation is advocated in a diverse society that is becoming increasingly marked by inequality, it seems to have little in common with other movements for disadvantaged people. Normalisation only makes sense in societies that have either a threshold of decency or an egalitarian imperative.

So what of the future? Normalisation has provided a continuity of vision throughout a period of political change, and has helped people to maintain a valued and principled position in relation to service provision, which is much needed when the financial constraints associated with implementation of the 1990 Act are working against this. The language of rights and empowerment is now firmly established in the rubric of service and policy development, and is being made reality in a number of service settings. But it is not enough on its own: it is more helpfully seen as the yeast than as the dough.

There are real conflicts of interest that need to be addressed throughout the debate on how best to provide care to those who need it: between accountability and informality, between cost-effectiveness and sound employment practice, between empowerment and protection and between family carers and those they care for. The conflicts will not go away; they have to be addressed within a coherent commitment to all those concerned. As Rose Ackerman remarks:

> The normalisation movement faces the problem of all successful reforms – translating slogans into policy. Rallying cries are a useful way to get attention, but they are not very helpful when one must decide how to accommodate conflict.
>
> (Ackerman, 1982, p. 97)

Moreover as normalisation gives way to rhetoric that is more 'user friendly' and centred on notions of consultation and empowerment, it becomes easier to acknowledge differentness without glossing over people's difficulties, needs or limitations. Changing attitudes was always on the normalisation agenda even if it was to be achieved at the expense of individual diversity. Hence this new-found respect for differentness is not incompatible with the goal that normalisation set itself – integration – but requires a recognition that there are now multiple versions of 'mainstream' to be taken into account. The language of inclusiveness *is* one that has more universal application, and is used in relation to other groups and communities who are at risk of being marginalised because of poverty, ethnicity, culture or language. It is perhaps as one movement amongst many seeking to argue for a set of values beyond the market place that normalisation can come of age.

As has been shown here, whilst at one time normalisation was the undisputed value base for community-based services, there has since been a fundamental challenge to its theoretical stance on conformity and integration. The normalisation movement, which began with a focus on trying to make people with learning disabilities more 'normal' in order to counter the pressures that led to their being excluded, is now more likely to be arguing for making communities more responsive and inclusive. In short many advocates would now argue that it is the communities and not the people who need to change.

References

Ackerman, Rose (1982) 'Mental Retardation and Society: the ethics and politics of normalisation', *Ethics*, Vol. 93, pp. 81–101.

Atkinson, D. and Ward, L. (1987) 'A part of the community: social integration and neighbourhood networks', *Talking Points*, 3, CMH, London.

Brown, H. and Smith, H. (1993) 'Women Caring for People: the mismatch between rhetoric and reality for women?', *Policy and Politics*, Vol. 21, No. 3, July.

Crossmaker, M. (1991) 'Behind locked doors: institutional sexual abuse', *Sexuality and Disability*, Vol. 9, No. 3, pp. 201–19.

Flynn, M. (1987) 'Independent living arrangements for adults who are mentally handicapped', in Malin, N. (ed.), *Reassessing Community Care*, Routledge, London.

George, V., Taylor-Gooby, P. and Bonoli, M. (1995) *Squaring the Welfare Circle in Europe*, University of Kent, Canterbury.

Goffman, E. (1961) *Asylums*, Anchor Books, Doubleday, New York.

Greenhalgh, L. (1994) *Well Aware: Improving access to health information for people with learning difficulties*, Health Info Line, Milton Keynes.

King's Fund Centre (1980) *An Ordinary Life: Comprehensively locally based residential services for mentally handicapped people*, King's Fund Centre, London.

McGill, P. and Emerson, E. (1992) 'Normalisation and applied behaviour analysis: values and technology in human services', in Brown, H. and Smith, H. (eds), *Normalisation: A Reader*, Routledge, London, pp. 60–83.

Morris, J. (1991) *Pride Against Prejudice*, Women's Press, London.

Newnes, C. (1994) 'A commentary on "Obstacles in the professional human service culture to implementation of social role valorisation and community integration of clients"', *Care in Place*, Vol. 1, No. 1, pp. 57–64.

Nirje, B. (1980) 'The normalisation principle', in Flynn, R. J., and Nitsch, K. E. (eds), *Normalisation, Social Integration and Community Services*, University Park Press, Baltimore.

O'Brien, J. and Tyne, A. (1981) *The Principle of Normalisation: a Foundation for Effective Services*, The Campaign for Mentally Handicapped People, London.

Szivos, S. (1992) 'The limits to integration?', in Brown, H. and Smith, H. (eds), *Normalisation: A Reader*, Routledge, London, pp. 112–33.

Williams, F. (1989) 'Mental handicap and oppression' in Brechin, A. and Walmsley, J. (eds), *Making Connections*, Hodder and Stoughton, London.

Wolfensberger, W. and Tullman, S. (1989) 'A brief outline of the principle of normalisation', in Brechin, A. and Walmsley, J. (eds), *Making Connections*, Hodder and Stoughton, London.

25

Managing Madness: Changing Ideas and Practice*

JOAN BUSFIELD

The post-war policy shift towards community care has been explained in a number of different ways. A standard account, often favoured by psychiatrists, relates it to the therapeutic developments of the post-war 1950s, and, to a lesser extent, to the impact of the sustained and vocal critiques of institutional care that come from both within and outside psychiatry during the same decade.[1] The chemically synthesised drugs of the 1950s permitted, it is contended, a greater number of patients to be treated outside the hospital and facilitated the earlier discharge of those who did have to be admitted. This, together with an increasing recognition of the anti-therapeutic nature of institutional care led, it is argued, to general support for policies of shifting care away from the mental hospital towards the community.[2] Put simply we can characterise the policy change and the explanation that is offered of it in terms of the simple model set out in Figure 25.1.

There are, however, a number of problems with this explanation of the shift to community care, grounded as it is in the liberal-scientific view of medical work, as Scull in his book *Decarceration*, and others, have indicated.[3] First, it is defective on grounds of timing. The decline in the size of the resident population of psychiatric beds was apparent in national statistics for this country and in the US in the mid-1950s and in the statistics for particular hospitals from at least the beginning of the 1950s, yet the chemically synthesized drugs were only just beginning to be introduced in the mid 1950s.

---

* This is an abridged extract from Chapter 10, 'Community Care', of *Managing Madness: changing ideas and practice*, Unwin Hyman, 1986, pp. 326–43.

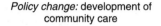

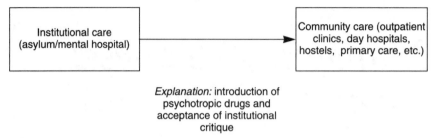

Figure 25.1

Scull presents a second objection to the thesis: that there is little evidence that the psychotropic drugs have been very effective in curing mental disorders. In his words there is 'a growing volume of evidence which suggests that claims about the therapeutic effectiveness of so-called "anti-psychotic" medication have been greatly exaggerated'.[4]

Scull has presented us with an alternative description of the policy transition and an alternative explanation that questions the benevolent assumptions of the liberal explanation. For Scull, the key policy change is a negative one: the rejection of the asylum; he uses the term decarceration as a 'shorthand for a state-sponsored policy of closing down asylums, prisons and reformatories', a policy more commonly described as deinstitutionalisation.[5] According to Scull this represents a movement away from what he calls 'an institutionally based system of segregative control'[6] He measures the adoption of this policy by the decline in the number of resident patients in state mental hospitals in the US and the UK since the mid-1950s, a decline more substantial in the US than in the UK and one that he recognizes is far from complete in either country. The results, he contends, are, however, clear enough. There has been a run down of facilities provided for the mentally ill and an indifference to their problems that has often been far from benign:

> Clearly a certain proportion of the released inmates are able to blend unobtrusively back into the communities from whence they came. After all, many of those subjected to processing by the official agencies of social control have all along been scarcely distinguishable from their neighbours who were left alone, and presumably they can be expelled from institutions without appreciable additional risk. But for many other ex-inmates and potential inmates, the alternative to the institution has been to be herded into newly emerging 'deviant ghettoes', sewers of human misery and what is conventionally defined as social pathology within which (largely hidden from outside inspection or even notice) society's refuse may be impressively tolerated. Many become lost in the interstices of social life, and turn into drifting inhabitants of those tradi-

tional resorts of the down and out, Salvation Army hostels, settlement houses, and so on. Others are grist for new, privately-run, profit-oriented mills for the disposal of the unwanted – old age homes, halfway houses, and the like. And yet more exist by preying on the less agile and wary, whether these be 'ordinary' people trapped by poverty and circumstance in the inner city, or their fellow decarcerated deviants'.[7]

Scull's description of the transition is not, therefore, of a move from mental hospital care to community care but from segregation in the asylum to neglect and misery within the community. This description of the nature of the transition generates its own explanation: that the main reasons for the adoption of the new policy were economic. Decarceration was introduced because 'segregative modes of social control became, in relative terms, far more costly and difficult to justify'.[8] For him the anti-institutional ideology of the 1950s may have facilitated decarceration but was not in itself sufficient to account for its adoption. As evidence he points to the critique of institutional care in the nineteenth century, which he asserts had little real impact. Portrayed graphically, Scull's interpretation of decarceration and its explanation is shown in Figure 25.2.

Like the liberal–scientific explanation he rejects, his own account is defective on grounds of timing. The fiscal crisis of the state[9] to which he refers is a phenomenon of the early 1970s and later, and not of the 1950s, when, although public expenditure was increasing, rapid economic growth and greater prosperity helped to ensure that there was comparatively little anxiety about the increase.[10] In addition his explanation ignores the changes that have occurred in the pattern of mental health service expenditure during this century. In particular it ignores the development and expansion of psychiatric services outside the mental hospital, especially in the field of primary care. While, therefore, Scull is right to draw attention to the dangers attendant on a policy of community care that can hide a failure to make provision for the mentally ill

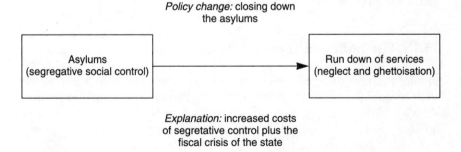

Figure 25.2

under a gloss of the apparent humanity of putting people back in the communities to which they belong; and while he is right to point out that during the last two decades or more there has been a mystification and distortion of a reality of neglect and lack of resources to those discharged from mental hospitals; nevertheless he cannot account for the introduction of the policy of running down mental hospitals in the 1950s and 1960s in simple economic terms.[11] Scull's argument fits events of the mid-1970s onwards much better than it does those of the 1950s and 1960s.

The move towards community care has been associated with a significant reorientation of services away from the chronic long-stay patients, towards those with less serious, shorter-term problems, who were formerly little catered for by public mental health services. It is not, therefore, that all mental health services have been run down under the guise of community care, rather that resources have largely gone into selected community services, those for acute, less serious mental disorders, and not into those dealing with chronic, more serious complaints. As a result aggregate expenditure on mental health services has increased, but this has largely been at the expense of those in need of some form of residential support, whether in a mental hospital or 'in the community'. Community services for the acute and milder forms of mental illness have by and large expanded over the post-war period. Community services for chronic, long-term mental illness, which have always been meagre, have not.[12] Hospital provision for them has been reduced, and little has been put in its place. The issue is not therefore of a reduced overall expenditure on the mentally ill to be accounted for by governmental reluctance to increase or maintain particular levels of public expenditure, though there is plenty of recent evidence of this in the last decade, but of the direction and form that expenditure has taken in the post-war period. Scull, in his concern to account for decarceration in economic terms failed to attend to the ideas, beliefs and objectives of those who formulate and implement policy, which have structured and mediated the economic concerns of the state.

15.1   The policy of community care

The first official use of the term community care apparently came in the 1930 Annual Report of the Board of Control when it was used to refer to a policy then being put forward, of making provision for the mentally handicapped to live outside hospitals wherever possible.[13] This policy paralleled that advocated by a number of nineteenth-century critics of asylums of making provision through the Poor Law system for chronic and incurable cases by boarding them out with friends or relatives under supervision. The National Association for the Promotion of Social Science had pointed to the advantages of such policies when discussing the treatment of pauper lunatics in 1869:

> Now . . . the question may properly be asked, whether . . . we cannot recur, in some degree, to the system of home care and home treatment; whether, in fact, the same care, interest, and money which are now employed upon the inmates of our lunatic asylums, might not produce even more successful and I benefi- cial results if made to support the efforts of parents and relations in their humble dwelling. . . . If only one-twentieth of inmates of our asylums could by any machinery whatever, be restored to their relations, we should have strengthened the bonds of family affection and enlarged the sphere of indi- vidual liberty. Moreover, such a mode of treatment would form a fitting exten- sion of the non-restraint system.[14]

Underlying these suggestions was the concern for the swelling numbers of asylum patients and the way in which chronic and incurable cases blocked up the asylums and stopped them from being real hospi- tals. However, in the second half of the nineteenth century the asylum was still the preferred locus of therapeutic intervention; care outside the hospital was to be a supplement to the asylum, freeing it for its proper role, not providing an alternative to it.

The policy of community care that developed in the twentieth century not only sought to free the hospital for its proper therapeutic purposes but no longer viewed the hospital as the ideal locus of treatment: the community was to be the place where treatment should take place wher- ever possible. The Report of the 1954–7 Royal Commission on the Law Relating to Mental Illness and Mental Deficiency (the Percy Report) marks the turning point in official policy concerning mental health ser- vices from a hospital to a community-based system of care and therapy. The Commission's report, published in 1957, extended and developed the arguments of the earlier commission that a mentally disordered person should be treated where possible like a person with a physical illness. Its starting point was not, however, an assertion of the close inter- connection of mental and physical illness, but the related claim that mental disorder was an illness and should be treated as such: 'Disorders of the mind are illnesses which need medical treatment.[15]

The recommendations concerning the use of legal procedures followed from this assertion of the proper identity of mental disorder as an illness. The 1930 Mental Treatment Act had moved in the direction of treating the mentally ill on comparable terms to the physically ill by introducing the possibility of voluntary admission. But the act still required that those with mental disorder should 'be well enough to sign an application form expressing a positive wish to receive treatment'.[16] Such a formality was not required of the physically ill. The Percy Report urged, therefore, that 'the law should be altered so that whenever possible suitable care may be provided for mentally disordered patients with no more restriction of liberty or legal formality than is applied to people who need care because of other types of illness, disability or social difficult'.[17] The Commission did not believe that compulsory powers could be entirely abandoned, but felt they should be used 'only when they are positively necessary to override the patient's own unwillingness or the unwillingness of his relatives, for the patient's own welfare or for the protection of others'.[18] They recommended, however, that the term 'certification' should no longer be used in connection with any legal procedures; instead the report spoke of 'formal' and 'informal' admission.[19]

The Commission's assertions about community care followed from the commitment to treating mental illness as an illness. Mental illness was seen as a broad category covering 'a much wider range of forms and degrees of mental disorder than the term of "unsound mind" (which it was to replace), and the appropriate form of treatment must be correspondingly diverse'.[20] As with sickness generally, in-patient treatment might not be necessary. 'The majority of mentally ill patients . . . do not need to be admitted to hospital as in-patients. Patients may receive medical treatment from general practitioners or as hospital out-patients and other care from community health and welfare services'.[21] Such treatment outside the hospital was embraced under the loose term community care, a term which was not given any precise definition in the report but was used to refer to services and benefits provided by the state for the mentally ill, whether specific to them or not, which did not involve in-patient admission.

The hospital was no longer the ideal locus of care, and if admission were necessary, the patient should be discharged as soon as possible. In part this was a reiteration of the old argument of ensuring that hospitals should be used for their proper therapeutic purposes and not end up merely providing a home for those with no suitable place to live: 'Patients should not be retained as hospital in-patients when they have reached the stage at which they could return home if they had reasonably good homes to go to.'[22] Local authorities should, therefore, take on the responsibility of providing residential accommodation for elderly mentally ill or infirm patients 'who need to be provided with a home and some help and advice but do not need psychiatric training or nursing care in hospital', as well as for others recovering from mental illness.[23] More importantly, however, the emphasis on community care involved a new model of therapeutic provision for the mentally ill in which the institution no longer had pre-eminence as the best place for the treatment. The new model of care aimed to provide services for every stage of the illness, and for prevention as well as cure: primary care facilities, acute hospital beds, hospital beds for chronic patients who still needed medical or psychiatric care, residential hostels, half-way houses, day hospitals, social work support as well as the health and welfare services more generally. This model of care contrasts very markedly with the model that underlay the establishment of the nineteenth-century asylums. It is not simply that the old asylum was now to be supplemented by a diverse range of public services that did not involve in-patient admission, but that the asylum was no longer considered the ideal therapeutic environment. Integration into the community rather than separation from it had become the new ideal.

In sum we can offer an alternative description of the policy change termed deinstitutionalisation, and an alternative explanation of it. It views the key policy change as the adoption of a new model of care for the mentally disordered, with services designed to cover all stages of the patient career and the full range of disorders, acute and chronic, severe and mild. This policy is in direct line of descent from the desire of medical reformers in the second half of the nineteenth century to encourage the early treatment of mental illness, and to transform the asylum into a mental hospital. A number of factors contributed to the adoption of this new model of care. First, the emergence of new medical ideas about the causes and treatment of mental illness undermined the support for and commitment to institutions as the desirable locus of care explicit in earlier environmentalist thinking about insanity. Second, the development of a broader range of state-funded services and benefits not only eliminated the institutional bias of the welfare system, but also increasingly made institutional care seem neither necessary nor appropriate. Third, the new model of care offered opportunities to psychiatrists for a fuller integration of their specialism with the rest of medicine

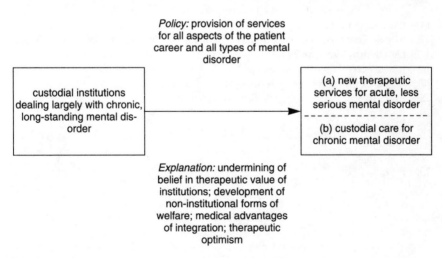

Figure 25.3

and a close approximation of their practice to that of the parent discipline. Fourth, the therapeutic optimism generated by the therapeutic innovations of the 1930s, 1940s and 1950s made shorter stays in hospital and adequate outpatient care seem a practical proposition. The alternative description and explanation is set out in Figure 25.3.

Notes

1. See, for instance, Jones, K. (1960) *Mental Health and Social Policy*, Routledge and Kegan Paul, London, p. 166. Also Scull, A. (1977) *Decarceration*, Prentice-Hall, Englewood Cliffs, NJ.
2. Barton, R. (1959) *Institutional Neurosis*, John Wright, Bristol; Wing, J. (1962) 'Institutionalism in mental hospitals', *British Journal of Social and Clinical Psychology*, Vol. 1, pp. 38–51.
3. Scull, *Decarceration*, op. cit., chapters 5 and 6.
4. Ibid., p. 82.
5. Ibid., p. 1.
6. Ibid., p. 64.
7. Ibid., pp. 152–3.
8. Ibid., p. 135.
9. O'Connor defines a fiscal crisis as the 'tendency for government expenditure to outrace revenues'; O'Connor, J. (1973) *The Fiscal Crisis of the State*, St James Press, London.
10. Ibid., p. 41.
11. A similar point is made by Sedgwick, P. (1982) *Psychopolitics*, Pluto Press, London, pp. 200–5.
12. Ibid., p. 213.
13. This claim is made by Hunter, R. and MacAlpine, I. (1974) *Three Hundred Years of Psychiatry*, Oxford University Press, p. 67.
14. Quoted in ibid., p. 66.
15. Royal Commission on the Law Relating to Mental Illness and Mental Deficiency (1957), p. 205.
16. Jones, *Mental Health.*, op. cit., p. 128.
17. Royal Commission, op. cit. pp. 3–4.
18. Ibid., p. 4.
19. Ibid., p. 133.
20. Ibid., p. 20.
21. Ibid., p. 5.
22. Ibid., p. 207.
23. Ibid., p. 211.

Mental Health Services in the Twenty-First Century: The User–Professional Divide?

DAVID PILGRIM

26.1 Introduction

By the turn of the twenty-first century, Western psychiatry will have endured forty years of sustained criticism. From internal professional dissenters and academics it will have been attacked for its crude and illogical illness model (Szasz, 1964; Boyle, 1990); its dehumanising practices (Laing, 1967); its social control role (Basaglia, 1980); and its brain-damaging treatments (Hill, 1985). Its preferred hospital base will have been condemned as inhuman, degrading and disabling in its large institutional form (Goffman, 1961; Martin, 1985) and in its transformed guise of the district general hospital (DGH) acute psychiatric unit (Baruch and Treacher, 1978). All of these criticisms influenced, and were incorporated into, the emergent new social movements of critical patients in alliance with sympathetic professionals in various countries during the 1970s and 1980s: the Netherlands (Haaflkens et al., 1986); the USA (Chamberlin, 1990); Canada (Burstow and Weitz, 1988); Italy (Ramon and Giannechedda, 1988); and eventually Britain (Rogers and Pilgrim, 1991).

In the light of the above summary, psychiatry's crisis may be its users,' opportunity. What the split or tension between professional tradition and patient resistance highlights is that mental health services can be organised broadly to serve one but not the other group's interests. In this short article, I want to rehearse two possible futures: one that is user-friendly and one that instead serves the interests of professional power, social order and drug company profits. So that this is not merely yet another critique of, or polemic against, psychiatry, I first want to base my arguments on some empirical data. For reasons of space the latter can only be given in summary and selected form – literally as a list of key relevant findings. The list is taken from the People First survey I and others conducted in collaboration with MIND in 1990. (A fuller version of the methodology and findings can be found in Rogers *et al.*, 1992. This provides numerous quotes from users that space does not permit here.)

The People First survey entailed a detailed (250-item) questionnaire being sent to 1000 users of psychiatric services. About one-third of the items were open-ended questions generating qualitative data to augment and clarify the type of frequencies listed below. All of the 516 respondents who completed and returned the questionnaire had had one or more inpatient stays, with 120 of them having seven or more admissions. In other words they were genuine users of the full range of services provided by psychiatry and its allied professions. For the purpose of this article the following findings are pertinent.

Hospital-centred practices. Hospital-based staff, supposedly helping the patients' return to the community, halved their contact following discharge. Even those staff specifically designated to work in the community (social workers and community psychiatric nurses) saw significantly less of their patients out of hospital than in. Of patients' last day-centre attendance, 57 per cent had been on the hospital site. And yet the further away from hospital the interventions were the better they were rated by patients.

Professionals damned by faint praise. Only 11.8 per cent thought that the most helpful aspect of day-patient attendance was contact with staff (compared with the 25.4 per cent who most valued contact with other patients). This trend was the same for attendance at occupational and industrial therapy. Inpatients found nurses the most helpful staff 30 per cent of the time and least helpful 10 per cent of the time. Psychiatrists were the least favoured, with respective figures of 11 per cent and 21 per cent.

Poor informed consent. Nearly half the sample had been detained compulsorily at some time, with 83.3 per cent never having been offered an alternative to hospital. At admission, 56.6 per cent had not been informed of their diagnosis and 63 per cent had never received a satisfactory explanation of why they had been admitted. Forty-three per cent had been given major tranquillisers against their wishes. Of those taking anti-depressants 71.5 per cent had never been asked for their consent.

The dominance of physical treatment. Ninety-eight per cent had been pre-scribed drugs, 80 per cent had been prescribed major tranquillisers and 75 per cent anti-depressants. Nearly half had had electroconvulsive therapy (ECT), of whom 98.5 per cent complained of side-effects. Eighty five per cent had never been offered an alternative to the treatment they were given.

Lack of information. Only 38 per cent of those given major tranquillisers had been told their purpose, and only 32 per cent had been told of their potential side-effects. Of those taking anti-depressants 70 per cent had been told nothing about their potential side-effects (which were experi-enced by half of this group).

Poverty. Of the sample 83.6 per cent were on one or more welfare bene-fits. Only 16.3 per cent were in full-time employment. Nearly half of the sample had been on statutory benefits for more than five years.

26.2   Transporting the medical model into the community

Now that some of the main findings of the People First survey have been presented, let us consider what their implications are for the two com-peting futures I outlined at the outset.

The data suggest that whether or not they are liked by their recipients, late-twentieth-century psychiatric interventions are centred on the hos-pital and are dominated by drugs and ECT. These are the very targets that professional and user critics of psychiatry have been shooting at since the Second World War. A related trend, which has also been the focus of criticism yet is clearly still strongly present in psychiatric prac-tice, is the enforcement of treatment. Let us now consider these three fea-tures (the hospital, physical treatments and lack of informed consent) in more detail.

26.2.1   The role of the hospital

The data highlight the fact that despite the gradual removal of the large Victorian psychiatric institutions, community care has not actually diverted psychiatry much from its traditional patterns. The shift of resources from the large old Victorian hospital to making the district general hospital the focus of medical activity is symptomatic of psychi-atry's inability to work without a territorial base. By moving to the DGH unit, psychiatrists have retained their power over clients by emphasising inpatient work. In many ways these units are more restrictive and repressive than the older hospitals. They typically have low ceilings and patients may be deterred from roaming into general medical wards by having to wear pyjamas. (This actually compares unfavourably with the spacious grounds of the older institutions.) Also note from the data how even other services, such as day-patient appointments, have been dominated by hospital sites. The extent of hospital-centred funding of mental health services is highlighted by the fact that in 1979 12 pence in the pound of state expenditure on mental health was spent on non-hospital services. This had only risen to 15 pence in the pound by 1989 (Sayce, 1990). As far as mental health was concerned, by 1990 community care still meant hospital-orientated services.

26.2.2   Physical treatment

Despite modern textbooks suggesting to their readers that psychiatry has become more eclectic (for example Clare, 1977), the data above demonstrate that drugs and ECT are still the dominant responses to emotional distress. Perhaps the most worrying aspect of this is the lack of information and alternatives offered on average. Also the amount of polypharmacy (taking more than one drug concurrently) evident from the respondents provides evidence that patients are vulnerable to the side-effects of not only one set of drugs but many in interaction with one another. These interactive effects are understood by the medical profession to be dangerous, yet in practice psychiatrists commonly impose polypharmacy on patients (Edwards and Kumar, 1984; Johnson and Wright, 1990). Although ECT understandably causes anxiety and anger in many of its recipients, and prospective recipients, major tranquillisers probably represent the largest iatrogenic scandal in modern psychiatry. They are effective only in a minority of cases (Bentall *et al.*, 1988) and yet they expose all their recipients to the dangers of irreversible movement disorders (tardive dyskinesia). The longer they are prescribed, the higher the chance of this iatrogenic effect occurring. For the many patients who are prescribed them on a long-term basis (as slow-release depot injections), the risk is very high.

26.2.3   Informed consent

The data describe two problems in relation to coercion. First, pressure from others is clearly widespread, even among those who are technically voluntary patients (in legal terms of 'informal status'). Second, the very fact that patients are so rarely given any alternative to hospital admission and physical treatment itself constitutes a form of coercion – one choice is no choice. The whole question of enforced treatment raised its head in 1988 when the Royal College of Psychiatrists sought, without success, to have the 1983 Mental Health Act modified to include the enforcement of 'community treatment orders'. The Act and its predecessors only permitted forced treatment in hospitals. The move to introduce the orders revealed the Royal College's attitude towards a respect for voluntary relationships with patients. The third dimension to this problem is shown in the data on satisfaction with information about treatment. Most patients were unhappy about the inadequate information given to them by psychiatrists. Generally medical practitioners rationalise the withholding of information on paternalistic grounds (that they want to avoid 'worrying the patient'). Were physical treatments effective and benign this paternalism would have its merits. However, as was discussed above, in psychiatry drugs are often ineffective and highly dangerous. In such circumstances, full information to patients is particularly warranted.

The prospect of services dominated by the above three characteristics looks, at the time of writing, to be a distinct possibility for the twenty-first century. Resources and professional practices are still bound up with hospitals (as the figures quoted earlier from Sayce indicate). The dominant discourse of 'mental illness' still pervades the way not only professionals but also lay people think about emotional difficulties. The drug companies are still profiting greatly from the medical profession's virtual exclusive reliance on their products for treatment. However, this dominant picture remains problematic. Anti-psychiatry (the critique of coercive biological psychiatry by internal dissenters) in one sense is a thing of the past. In another sense its mantle and concerns have been taken over by disaffected users. The latter now seem to represent a permanent opposition to medical theory and practice and thereby constitute a 'new social movement' (Rogers and Pilgrim, 1991).

26.3 A user-friendly future?

In a critical review of mental health policy in Britain Goodwin (1990) makes the point that government after government has made the mistake of believing that psychiatric practice is sound and effective. The rise of the users' movement and the survey data signal clearly that Goodwin's conclusion is well founded. The point here is that, as with other aspects of health policy, if governments rely for their opinion on the medical profession then they will inevitably endorse medically preferred policies.

One of the paradoxes of the conflict about the long Conservative administration's attitude towards the National Health Service (between

1979 and 1991) is that a user-led ideology was introduced for the first time by government. For its part, the Labour opposition focused, as it had done since 1948, on the resourcing and ownership of the health care system. What Labour had not done was challenge medical experts. Quite the reverse – their position was to see medical professionals as harbingers of progress. By contrast, as part of a wider restructuring of welfare provision, a political project of the Thatcher administrations was to challenge or undermine traditional power elites such as the mature professions of medicine and law. The Conservatives of the 1980s wanted to bring these groups to heel, by strengthening their accountability to state managers on the one hand and deregulating their services on the other. Some doctors were given more powers in the government reforms. However in general, as the British Medical Association's reaction showed, the Conservative government was recognised by doctors for what it was: an enemy of traditional medical authority in health care decision-making (Strong and Robinson, 1990).

One consequence of the 'consumerist' emphasis from the right was that a new discourse emerged, which even political opponents had to join. By 1990 the cross-party talk was of 'user-friendliness' and 'quality assurance' in welfare provision. Whilst the Conservatives still pinned their hopes for this on the 'mixed economy' and the discipline of business and market principles to serve the consumer, Labour (in opposition) favoured democratic accountability and efficient management in a better financed state system. In particular regard to mental health, the Labour Party, after intense lobbying from users' groups, began to acknowledge the problems of psychotropic drugs and advocated the greater availability of psychological intervention.

This new political ambivalence about professionally defined policies has created an opportunity for a more user-friendly service. Our data suggest that such a service would have the following characteristics, which can be seen to be virtually the inverse of the first scenario above.

26.3.1   Ordinary living

The data make it clear that the further recipients are away from hospital, the more they like their lives. Hospital interventions are not user-friendly. They are associated generally with an oppressive or distressing experience. If patients and prospective patients are to live as normally as possible in the community, the implications are that service *options* should be available in that setting. These would include crisis houses, outreach work and 24-hour, seven-days-a-week crisis intervention teams, counselling, drop-in centres and day centres housing a variety of activities. The availability of a range of affordable housing options about which service users can exercise genuine choice would be central to a non-hospital-based service. The data on welfare benefits show that mental health policy and employment and housing policy cannot be separated.

26. 3 . 2   Benign treatment

Basically, users are tired of physical treatments being the typical offer made to them when they have problems. Drugs cause unwanted side-effects and do not solve or address personal or social difficulties in the patient's life. They may be convenient for doctors, but they are not welcomed by their recipients most of the time. What service users would prefer, in the main, is a sympathetic ear. Sometimes this is expressed as a need for formal counselling or psychotherapy as an alternative to drugs; at other times it is only a plea for the patient to be listened to and respected. Respectfulness entails being taken seriously and having one's experience recognised as meaningful. The traditional psychiatric interview often violates both these principles The patient's account is only taken in order to make a diagnosis or to check whether or not prescribed drugs are working. By definition, the symptoms of mental illness are not recognised as meaningful because they represent pathology. For those distrustful even of psychological treatments, the service could provide the option of contact with other patients for fellowship as a worthy goal in itself. This could also involve facilities being used to house self-help groups.

26.3.3   Voluntary relationships

Psychiatric patients, being human, are no more welcoming of loss of liberty, or their bodies being interfered with without consent, than anybody else. A user-friendly service would minimise or eliminate coercion. It would also emphasise informed consent at every moment in a professional–patient relationship. Whenever professionals withhold information that is relevant to the patient's life, such as that concerning the dangers of prescribed drugs or psychological treatment, then the service is professionally led, not user-centred. Also, as was noted previously, voluntary relationships can only be encouraged in a context in which genuine choices are on offer to the patient. Where no choice exists, then the person is trapped by the sole offer being made by professionals.

Finally, there is the problem of predicting one or other of these two broad scenarios. Despite the fact that government social policy formation is now being sensitised to the 'view from below' of welfare clients, this is offset by other considerations. If medical–psychiatric dominance were to be subverted genuinely by government, then the advantages it has traditionally offered, particularly the role of policing the population and smoothing out infractions of rules in everyday life would be jeopardised. Under the hammer of the Conservative administrations of the 1980s, medical elites were shaken and angered, but not broken. Their culturally accepted authority at all levels in society remains evident. Politicians of all hues still defer to doctors to identify the 'clinical needs' of 'their' patients. This reinforces the tradition of paternalism in welfare provision in which professionals 'know best' and patients are not expected to speak for themselves. As yet, there is only a weak sign that the national or local state is prepared to ask people directly what their needs are. The users' movement has its work cut out at the turn of the century. In particular its success will hinge on allying itself successfully with that minority of professionals who themselves genuinely want to shift power to users.

References

Baruch, G. and Treacher, A. (1978) *Psychiatry Observed*, Routledge, London.

Basaglia, F. (1980) 'Breaking the circuit of control', in Ingleby, D. (ed.), *Critical Psychiatry*, Penguin, Harmondsworth.

Bentall, R. P., Jackson, H. and Pilgrim, D. (1988) 'Abandoning the concept of schizophrenia: some implications for validity arguments in studying psychotic phenomena', *British Journal of Clinical Psychology*, Vol. 27, pp. 303–24.

Boyle, M. (1990) *Schizophrenia: a Scientific Delusion?*, Routledge, London.

Burstow, B. and Weitz, D. (eds) (1988) *Shrink Resistant: the Struggle Against Psychiatry in Canada*, New Star Books, Vancouver.

Chamberlin, J. (1990) *On Our Own*, MIND, London.

Clare, A. (1977) *Psychiatry in dissent*, Tavistock, London.

Edwards, S. and Kumar, V. (1984) 'A survey of prescribing of psychotropic drugs in a Birmingham psychiatric hospital', *British Journal of Psychiatry*, Vol. 145, pp. 502–7.

Goffman, E. (1961) *Asylums: Essays on the Social Situation of Mental Patients and Other Inmates*, Penguin, London.

Goodwin, S. (1990) *Community Care and the Future of Mental Health Service Provision*, Avebury, Aldershot.

Haafkens, J., Nijhof, G. and van der Poel, E. (1986) 'Mental health care and the opposition movement in the Netherlands', *Social Science and Medicine*, Vol. 22, No. 2, pp. 185–92.

Hill, D. (1985) *The Politics of Schizophrenia: Psychiatric Oppression in the United States of America*, University Press of America, Lanham.

Johnson, D. and Wright, N. F. (1990) 'Drug prescribing for schizophrenic outpatients on depot injections: repeat surveys over 18 years', *British Journal of Psychiatry*, Vol. 156, pp. 827–34.

Laing, R. D. (1967) *The Politics of Experience and the Bird of Paradise*, Penguin, Harmondsworth.

Martin, J. P. (1985) *Hospitals in Trouble*, Blackwell, Oxford.

Ramon, S. and Giannechedda, M. (eds) (1988) *Psychiatry in Transition: the British and Italian Experiences*, Pluto Press, London.

Rogers, A. and Pilgrim, D. (1991) ' "Pulling down churches": accounting for the British mental health users' movement', *Sociology of Health and Illness*, Vol. 13, No. 2, pp. 129–48.

Rogers, A., Pilgrim, D. and Lacey, R. (1992) *Experiencing Psychiatry: Users' View of Services*, Macmillan, London.

Sayce, L. (1990) *Waiting for Community Care*, MIND, London.

Strong, P. and Robinson, J. (1990) *The NHS Under New Management*, Open University Press, Milton Keynes.

Szasz, T. S. (1964) *The Myth of Mental Illness*, Harper and Row, New York.

Housing Choices and Community Care*

JUDITH HUDSON, LYNN WATSON and GRAHAM ALLAN

27.1   Introduction

Independent living is promoted by the government for all community care groups, yet assisting people to move to appropriate housing is not seen by policy makers as central to the community care task. People looking for housing and support services face obstacles that arise from a shortage of appropriate provision, and most lack the resources to buy their way into the housing market and organise their own support. Our study set out to explore what factors influence the housing preferences of people with extra support needs, and the channels people use to obtain suitable accommodation and support.

The research involved in-depth interviews with 77 people in a range of living circumstances. The majority of participants were selected as having a current housing need. A smaller number who had recently changed their accommodation were also included.

The main sources for identifying study participants were social services professionals, social clubs/day centres, service user organisations and residential facilities. The support needed by the 77 people ranged from personal assistance with physical tasks to management of household finances, emotional support and help in establishing a daily routine. The age range was 17–66.

Sixty two people were interviewed once and a smaller group of 15 were interviewed twice, with a gap of 9–12 months. The study was carried out in four districts in Hampshire during 1994/95. What follows is a summary of our findings.

---

* This chapter is a summary of research carried out by the authors. The full report, *Moving Obstacles: housing choices and community care*, is published by the Policy Press, University of Bristol.

27.2 Impetus for moving

The reasons for wanting to move varied according to the current living situation. Those in the parental home wanted to gain independence or, in a small number of instances, to escape a situation of increasing family tension. Those in shared supported housing either felt they no longer needed the support provided or, again in a small number of cases, they did not get on with one or more of the other residents, or simply did not like shared living. For people living in residential homes, the main reasons given for moving were the need for more freedom, more space and more money to spend. Those in their own self-contained housing who wished to move usually wanted a more suitably designed or larger property, or disliked the area in which they were living.

Most of the study participants were in a position where they had to persuade others of their housing need before starting the process of negotiating for the right kind of accommodation and support. The exception to this was those living in shared supported housing, where moving on to other housing is often seen as part of a natural progression. Here too, however, there were examples of people becoming stuck in their accommodation because they were not awarded any priority for a tenancy in local council or housing association stock.

While most saw their own housing need as clear-cut, they recognised that in order to make progress they would have to argue their case or find someone else to act on their behalf. The great majority were in circumstances that gave them no statutory entitlement to housing and very few had had a formal assessment of their support needs under the system of care management.

27.3 Communication with 'the system'

The four main sources of practical help and advice were housing support workers, social workers, occupational therapists, and council officers concerned with applications for grants and adaptations. Social workers advising people wishing to leave residential care or the parental home often made referrals to specific services, such as a social services adult placement scheme, rather than offering broader information on housing and support options.

Individual housing preferences reflected ideas about desired lifestyle and level of responsibility. While some people wanted accommodation with integral support, those respondents seeking self-contained accommodation usually focused first on the housing. An offer of housing can give substantial leverage in ensuring the delivery of appropriate support. Some people found it very difficult to attract the interest of a professional to help them through the process of achieving a move. Making a housing application could also be quite a struggle, with housing officers in some cases putting forward obstacles or providing only partial information. Some were successful in obtaining accommodation, but only after much persistence on their part or through the active support of a particular officer.

John, who has a hearing impairment, was living with his parents. He had been wanting to move for more than a year. His social worker advised him to approach the council and he placed his name on the waiting list. A housing officer explained that he would not get an offer for a long time but did not offer any other options. John said he was relying on his father to find him accommodation.

Sophie was living in self-contained accommodation in a group of supported flats for people with mental health problems. The accommodation is not intended to be long term. When she approached the council for rehousing, she was asked if she was a 'one-parent family' but no mention was made of other reasons that might give her some housing priority. She planned to approach social services to check out her position before giving up the idea of council accommodation.

Martin was living with his father, who did not allow him to use most of the house. He applied for a one-bedroom flat but was told that without top medical priority he could only hope for a bedsit. He felt such accommodation would be too claustrophobic and isolating for him. After more than two years on the register, a new housing officer became involved and he was offered a suitable flat within six weeks of this officer's initial visit.

27.4   Expectations and housing options

People lack access to comprehensive written information on the housing options and support services in their area. Such information tends to be produced in a piecemeal fashion (for example lists of residential homes) and to exclude more imaginative combinations of accommodation and support (for example care packages for people with varying needs). Information on the financial aspects of living in different forms of accommodation is also lacking.

The respondents with learning disabilities tended to think in terms of a staged progression. Most of those wanting to leave the parental home said they wanted to live in shared housing or a residential home, while those in shared accommodation usually opted for self-contained housing. The desire for social contact within the home environment was particularly significant among younger people living with their parents.

The need for more formal support appeared to play a much smaller part in determining people's housing choices.

Among those with mental health problems there was a strong preference for self-contained housing. There was great concern among this group to avoid types of accommodation that were seen as having a 'special needs' tag. However those in shared housing generally made positive comments about their current accommodation and felt it had helped them to manage with less support. Many were anxious about how they would cope financially in their new accommodation and a smaller number worried about being lonely. They had expectations of continuing support in their own tenancies, although this was often vaguely described and the possible sources of such support were sometimes unclear.

Respondents with physical disabilities also strongly preferred self-contained housing for their next move. This included the majority of those in the parental home. Those living in residential homes tended to be more cautious, sometimes assuming that the level of support needed would preclude such an option.

Almost all of those intending to move on from shared housing or hostels in the near future were going to move to linked, move-on housing with support from the same organisation. While most were appreciative of this arrangement and some commented favourably on the quality and location of the move-on housing, others felt that the assumptions about a staged process had proved an obstacle to them obtaining the kind of accommodation they wanted.

> 'They didn't want to give me a flat until they knew I could look after myself on my own . . . but it has got nothing to do with them really. When you know you can do it, you can do it' . . . It just took a long time to convince them.' Simon moved from a hostel into a small shared house, where he lived for a year before moving on again into a housing association flat.

> 'It is K's choice [the keyworker in the hostel]. She thinks I should go to the bedsit first anyway. If I had a choice I would rather go to L . . . C . . . [a small block of flats].' Georgina has lived in the hostel for two and a half years and thinks she will be in the bedsit for about six months before getting a flat.

27.5 Negotiating a move

The particular obstacles people had to overcome centred on fears of (and subsequent adjustment to) a major change of environment and living circumstances, poor planning and communication, lack of suitable housing, inadequate support through the move, and financial constraints.

The fear of the change itself and of not coping in a new setting were recurrent themes. Some feared loneliness and others expressed concern about their ability to cope within the level of support services they anticipated receiving. While most people in shared housing felt they had been given the opportunity to develop skills and prepare for moving on, a number of those in larger residential homes felt the structures were lacking to facilitate such a move.

> Craig has been in a residential home for the past fifteen years. He was offered a council flat, which he initially accepted but later turned down after thinking through the implications of living on his own. He has decided now to focus on developing his self-confidence and skills such as learning to manage his money, and would like to move initially to shared housing.

Lack of communication and liaison between the various agencies involved was common experience and was often cited as a cause of delay. When a move required the participation of several different professionals, respondents frequently reported feeling confused and ill-informed. There was little evidence that formal care management was offering a more co-ordinated response, with only one person explicitly mentioning the involvement of a care manager in sorting out the complexities of the move.

The shortage of suitable housing was one of the main obstacles encountered. People felt they had little option but to accept the first offer of accommodation, for fear of losing the opportunity to move altogether. Allocation policies were regarded as too rigid and not accounting for the needs and circumstances of the individual. Several respondents were originally rehoused in inappropriate accommodation and then found it difficult, if not impossible, to obtain a transfer.

Financial anxieties were very much to the forefront. Assistance with household budgeting and dealing with the Department of Social Security benefits system were seen by many respondents as crucial to their success in establishing themselves in their new housing. Making the transition from a residential home into more independent housing was made more difficult both by the impossibility of saving up for the move and by the lack of opportunity to manage money while in residential care.

> Frank had his name on the council waiting list for ten years. During this period, the only contact he had from them was their annual request to update the list. Finally he received a letter offering him a one-bedroom flat. He only had a week to decide whether to accept this. 'Well, although I was a bit desperate to move, when it came to it, I just couldn't. I didn't have the finances to buy all of that.' He contacted social services to see if they could sort him out with items of furniture, but they were not able to respond. He rejected the offer.

27.6 Summary

- Many people want to move but are not in a crisis situation and do not have an immediate imperative to do so. Systems are not in place to encourage and assist such non-crisis moves, with the result that people can wait years to move out of the parental home or residential care.
- Those who make progress usually do so through making use of an informed and/or committed professional contact. Many of the professionals concerned have not had specific training on housing issues and may rely heavily on known or standard solutions (such as specialist accommodation facilities). Some individuals obtain peer support and advice from disabled people's organisations.
- Those wanting self-contained housing tend to see obtaining suitable accommodation as their first priority, to be followed by negotiations over support services. This runs counter to the assumption in community care policy that housing needs are assessed as part of an individual's community care assessment.
- People who live in sheltered settings have usually had little opportunity to develop the skills of money management and running a household. The lack of such skills holds people back from pushing for more independent housing, even when this is what they would like.
- The housing allocation process assumes people are poised to move and can make a rapid response to a given offer. This takes little account of the long-term applicant who requires extra support to establish and sustain a tenancy.

Part IV

PRACTICE

28

Introduction

This section of the Reader brings together a collection of articles and documents that relate to community care practice. You will find charters of rights, plans, checklists and declarations of rights as well as accounts from service users and paid workers alongside explorations and analyses of the implications for practice of policies and trends in community care provision. Some are personal accounts of problems solved and problems overcome. Some work through issues from a more detached stance, reviewing and discussing. What they all share is a focus on the dilemmas of resolving issues raised by the need for sensitive and acceptable provision of care and support for people living in the community.

'Good practice' sometimes raises the spectre of inadequacy and guilt feelings among workers and carers who feel that their actions are by implication less than perfect. None of the pieces included here has been selected for reasons of prescription or preference. We're aware that we could have chosen from a range of many experiences and perspectives. Our aim is to provide examples that can be drawn on as a basis for reflection as well as information. Bryan Glastonbury suggests that the introduction of information technology into social care provides no easy solutions to the issue of confidentiality and control in relations between care workers and service users. Christina Schwabenland, who is director of a small voluntary organisation, takes us along the rocky path to becoming a contracted provider for a local authority. The process resulted in changes for her organisatian, the users, the paid care staff and the local authority itself. Five years on, she looks back and considers what the experience suggests for longer-term trends for voluntary organisations involved in community care.

The anthology of charters includes demands for what sounds much like basic human rights: 'personal privacy' (Southwark Social Services residential and specialist day care); the right to 'an assessment which takes into account our language, culture, religion and general circumstances' (Black Carers' Charter); 'Opportunities to explore alternatives to family care' (Ten-point plan for carers); and 'Full and free access to all personal medical records' (Survivors Speak Out). That they require formulation at all is at once recognition of the rights of users, and at the same time recognition of the failure of many services to acknowledge issues of equity and choice in the delivery of care and support. Each raises issues for practice, for paid and unpaid carers as much as for other professionals and policy makers.

Most of the samples of practice selected have a wide reference and significance. For example Andrea Whittaker's approach to involving people with learning difficulties in meetings can be read from a number of points of view: from the user's perspective; from a chairperson's perspective; from an advocate's perspective; from the perspective of an older person or a carer; from the perspective of a potential service purchaser. Marilyn Taylor's argument for the continuing importance of a community development approach in community care practice and provision has relevance for community workers, care professionals, care planners and care users.

Ann Macfarlane in 'The right to make choices' takes over the role of broker. As a disabled person who feels that she has the right to manage her own affairs, she describes how she and her friend, Jane Campbell, hired their own personal assistance. Practical issues of representation, access to resources, personnel recruitment and budget management are all confronted in her account. Clare Evans, a service user herself, describes how the Wiltshire Users' Network has taken a more collective approach to user influence and control over services. Disabled people in Wiltshire have gained involvement in purchasing, the design of service specifications, policy proposals, care management and assessment, access to information and in reviews of services. As she explains: 'We work on the principle that it is a matter of riddling the system with as many user perspectives as possible' (p. 318).

Chapters that provide a framework for evaluating the impact of changes for provision at local authority and care management levels include Lesley Hoyes and Robin Means' 'The impact of quasi-markets on community care' and Malcolm Payne's 'Care management and social work'. Hoyes and Means review the prerequisites for 'successful quasi-markets' while asking if markets in community care are in themselves an unqualified success. Malcolm Payne takes a more historical approach, tracing the development of care management from earlier models tested in the USA to the government-funded research programme at the University of Kent which provided a testbed for policies that were later enshrined in the 1990 NHS and Community Care Act.

This 'Practice' section of the Reader highlights initiatives that, whether located in research, personal experience or problem solving at the level of day-to-day organisation and delivery of services, have in their different ways influenced the direction and nature of community care provision. There are no completely straightforward answers here. People, whatever their position, have found themselves struggling against barriers that are physical, social and above all resource determined. Constant appraisal and review of practice is perhaps one way of overcoming those barriers, as much as reading and reflecting on the strategies and struggles with which others have engaged.

29

Anthology: Charters

Compiled by JOANNA BORNAT

This anthology includes criteria for good practice, statements of needs, a Declaration of Rights and a Declaration of Intent as well as charters. These different descriptions reflect the varied perspectives of users, activists, workers and professionals. Reading through these documents reveals common themes, formats and language. Rights, communication, support, consultation are just a few. At the same time, each statement demarcates a defined population, and its particular needs and demands. Inevitably it raises difficult issues, for example the tension between plurality and collective responsibility, the possible contradiction between different sets of demands. This sharing of common forms and language, while at the same time fragmenting into a plurality of self-determining interest groups, mirrors the image of community care practice and policy in the 1990s.

---

*Survivors Speak Out is an organisation for people who use psychiatric services. The **Charter of Needs** was unanimously agreed at their 1987 national conference.*

The national conference of psychiatric system survivors, held on 18–20 September 1987, unanimously agreed the following list of needs and demands, which since then has been adopted by local Survivor's Groups as a blueprint for their own charters:

1. That mental health service providers recognise and use people's first- hand experience of emotional distress for the good of others.
2. Provision of refuge, planned and under the control of survivors of psychiatry.
3. Provision of free counselling for all.
4. Choice of services, including self-help alternatives.
5. A government review of services, with recipients sharing their views.
6. Provision of resources to implement self-advocacy for all users.
7. Adequate funding for non-medical community services, especially crisis intervention.

8. Facility for representation of users and ex-users of services on statutory bodies, including Community Health Councils, Mental Review Health Tribunals and the Mental Health Act Commission.
9. Full and free access to all personal medical records.
10. Legal protection and means of redress for all psychiatric patients.
11. Establishment of the democratic right of staff to refuse to administer any treatment, without risk of sanction or prejudice.
12. The phasing out of electro-convulsive therapy and psycho-surgery.
13. Independent monitoring of drug use and its consequences.
14. Provision for all patients for full written and verbal information on treatments, including adverse research findings.
15. An end to discrimination against people who receive, or have received, psychiatric services: with particular regard to housing, employment, insurance etc.

Southwark Social Services Residential and Specialist Day Care Charter of Rights. The London Borough of Southwark Social Services Department has drawn up its own Charter of Rights for residents and users of services.

1. Residents have the right to control their own financial affairs.
2. Residents have the right to the same access to facilities and service in their surrounding community as any other citizen.
3. Residents have the right to be given every opportunity of mixing with other people in the community.
4. Residents have the right to personal privacy.
5. Residents have the right to have their personal dignity respected.
6. Residents have the right to care for themselves.
7. Residents have the right to have their emotional, cultural, religious and sexual needs accepted and respected.
8. Residents have the right to look after their own medications.
9. Residents have the right to personal independence, choice and responsibility for their own actions.
10. Residents have the right to participate in a regular review of their needs at a period not exceeding 1 year.
11. Residents have the right to take a full part in any decisions about daily living arrangements within the home.
12. Residents have the right of access to and where necessary assistance to contact:
    – the locally elected councillor
    – the local member of parliament
    – Age Concern
    – Help the Aged
    – Pensioners' Forum

13. Residents have the right to have any comments thoroughly investigated and resolved to their satisfaction.
14. Residents have the right to request a move to another form of accommodation.

---

*A **Ten-point Plan for Carers** was drawn up by carers' organisations supporting the Kings's Fund Carers' Project.*

Carers are people who are looking after elderly, ill or disabled relatives or friends who cannot manage at home without help. They may be the parents of a child with a mental handicap, a husband whose wife has a physical disability or a daughter looking after her frail elderly mother.

Carers come from all racial, ethnic and religious backgrounds. Their circumstances vary enormously, with the severity of the condition of the person cared for, their economic circumstances and the overall help and support available. The majority of carers are women and many carry out the tasks of caring completely on their own.

Carers are deeply concerned about the needs of the people they care for; services need to be planned for and with them.

Carers need

1. **Recognition of their contribution** and of their own needs as individuals in their own right.
2. **Services tailored to their individual circumstances**, needs and views, through discussions at the time help is being planned.
3. **Services which reflect an awareness of differing racial, cultural and religious backgrounds and values**, equally accessible to carers of every race and ethnic origin.
4. **Opportunities for a break**, both for short spells (an afternoon) and for longer periods (a week or more), to relax and have time to themselves.
5. **Practical help** to lighten the tasks of caring, including domestic help, home adaptations, incontinence services and help with transport.
6. **Someone to talk to** about their own emotional needs, at the outset of caring, while they are caring and when the caring task is over.
7. **Information** about available benefits and services as well as how to cope with the particular condition of the person cared for.
8. **An income which covers the cost of caring** and which does not preclude carers taking employment or sharing care with other people.
9. **Opportunities to explore alternatives to family care**, both for the immediate and long-term future.

10. **Services designed through consultation** with carers, at-all levels of policy planning.

The UK Declaration of the Rights of people with HIV and AIDS.

Preface

This declaration is made by people with HIV and AIDS and by organisations dedicated to their welfare. The Declaration lists rights which all citizens of the United Kingdom, including people with HIV and AIDS, enjoy under international law; the Declaration then prescribes measures and recommends practices which the writers of the Declaration believe are the minimum necessary to ensure that these rights are respected and protected within the United Kingdom.

The Declaration

All citizens of the United Kingdom, including people with HIV and AIDS, are accorded the following rights under international law:

- the right to liberty and security of person
- the right to privacy
- the right to freedom of movement
- the right to work
- the right to housing, food, social security, medical assistance and welfare
- the right to freedom from inhumane or degrading treatment
- the right to equal protection of the law and protection from discrimination
- the right to marry
- the right to found a family
- the right to education.

These rights exist in international treaties which the United Kingdom Government has agreed to uphold. But these rights, as they apply to United Kingdom citizens with HIV and AIDS, have not been adequately respected or protected. We therefore make a public Declaration of the Rights of people with HIV and AIDS and of our commitment to ensuring that they are upheld.

---

*The **National Council for Voluntary Organisations' Rural Unit** was set up to support voluntary action in rural areas. The **Ten-Point Plan** forms a basis for voluntary work that is effective and sensitive to the needs of people living in rural areas.*

1. **Promotion** of the valuable role of rural voluntary organisations in all walks of life.
2. **Representation** of rural voluntary organisations' concerns to public, private and voluntary agencies.
3. **Resources**, including a 'Rural Premium' to compensate for the extra cost of working in rural areas.
4 **Partnerships** between statutory, private and voluntary agencies.
5. **Support** in practical ways to enable voluntary action, such as meeting places, systems for shared work and collaboration.
6. **Information**, advice and training for those involved with rural voluntary action to ensure their effective work.
7. **Assistance** from the private sector with cash, help in kind, and training for rural voluntary action.
8. **Recognition** of the value of local, mobile and outreach services to reach small numbers of people in rural areas.
9. **Understanding** of the special qualities of rural voluntary action and their relevance to all parts of the country.
10. **Targeting** of the work of rural voluntary organisations to alleviate disadvantage.

Values Into Action (VIA) is the national campaign with people who have learning difficulties. Previously called the Campaign for People with Mental Handicaps, it has worked since 1971 for an end to the injustice and misunderstanding that have impoverished the lives of people with learning difficulties.

What does VIA believe?

VIA believes that people with learning difficulties –
- Have the same rights as other people
- Should be treated with the same dignity and respect as other people
- Can live in the same ways and in the same places as other people
- Should have the same opportunities in school, college, work, and leisure as other people.

These beliefs apply to all people with learning difficulties, however severe their disabilities.

On 12–14 April 1989 representatives of disabled people from various European countries came together through support from the German Green Party via the **Strasbourg Independent Living Seminar** *at the European Parliament. They drew up the statement below. The seminar led to the establishment of the European Network of Independent Living (ENIL), which has since become recognised as the Disabled People's International (European Region) Independent Living Group. The Statement continues to be used in countries where the principles and practice of Independent Living are being negotiated.*

Preamble

We, disabled people from the Netherlands, UK, Denmark, Italy, Switzerland, Sweden, France, Austria, Finland, Belgium, USA, Hungary, Federal Republic of Germany and Norway have come together from April 12–14 1989 at the European Parliament, Strasbourg, France.

This conference has focused on Personal Assistant Services as an essential factor of Independent Living, which itself encompasses the whole area of human activities, e.g. housing, transport, access, education, employment, economic security and political influence.

We, disabled people, recognising our unique expertise, derived from our experience, must take the initiative in the planning of policies that directly affect us.

To this end we condemn segregation and institutionalisation, which are a direct violation of our human rights, and consider that governments must pass legislation that protects the human rights of disabled people, including equalisation of opportunities. We firmly uphold our basic human right to full and equal participation in society as enshrined in the UN Universal Declaration of Human Rights (extended to include disabled people in 1985) and consider that a key pre-requisite to this civil right is through Independent Living and the provision of support services such as personal assistant services for those who need them.

The recommendations of the UN World Programme of Action (S 115) specifically states that 'Member States should encourage the provision of support services to enable disabled people to live as independently as possible in the community and in so doing should ensure that persons with a disability have the opportunity to develop and manage these services for themselves'.

Resolution 1 of the 43rd UN General Assembly (1988) reaffirms the validity of the World Programme of Action, Resolution 2 stresses that 'special emphasis should be placed on equalisation of opportunities'.

Considering these and similar recommendations from both the European Community and the Council of Europe and to ensure that disabled people within Europe should have parity of equalisation of opportunities, we stress that these objectives must be achieved.

In support of the international movement of disabled people and of Disabled Peoples' International, which has a special commitment to setting up a network of initiatives for Independent Living as part of the implementation of equalisation of opportunities, we call on governments and policy makers to enforce the following principles:

Resolutions

1. Personal assistance services are a human and civil right which must be provided at no cost to the user. These services shall serve people with all types of disabilities, of all ages, on the basis of functional need, irrespective of personal wealth, income, marital and family status.
2. Personal assistance users shall be able to choose from a variety of personal assistance service models which together offer the choice of various degrees of user control. User control, in our view, can be exercised by all persons, regardless of their ability to give legally informed consent.
3. Services shall enable the user to participate in every aspect of life such as home, work, school, leisure, travel and political life etc. These services shall enable disabled people, if they so choose, to build up a personal and family life and fulfil all their responsibilities connected with this.
4. These services must be available long-term for anything up to 24 hours a day, seven days a week, and similarly on a short-term or emergency basis. These services shall include assistance with personal bodily functions, communicative, household, mobility, work and other related needs. In the assessment of need the consumer's view must be paramount.
5. The funding authority shall ensure that sufficient funds are available to the user for adequate support, counselling, training of the user and of the assistant, if deemed necessary by the user.
6. Funding must include assistants' competitive wages and employment benefits, all legal and union-required benefits, plus the administrative costs.
7. Funding shall be a legislative right and payment must be guaranteed regardless of funding source or local government arrangements. Funding shall not be treated as disposable/taxable income and shall not make the user ineligible for other statutory benefits or services.
8. The user should be free to appoint as personal assistants whoever s/he chooses, including family members.
9. No individual shall be placed in an institutionalised setting because of lack of resources, high costs, sub-standard or non-existent services.

10. There shall be a uniform judicial appeals procedure which is independent of funders, providers and assessors; is effected within a reasonable amount of time and enables the claimant to receive legal aid at the expense of the statutory authority.
11. In furtherance of all the above, disabled people and organisations controlled by them must be decisively involved at all levels of policy making including planning, implementation and development.

---

*A **checklist** drawn up for people working in mental health services. These ten points were arrived at following consultation with users from a wide range of backgrounds and in different settings. It is reproduced from Read, J. and Wallcraft, J. (1992) Guidelines for Empowering Users of Mental Health Services, COHSE and MIND, London, p. 15.*

Checklist on how workers can empower service users

Staff work within constraints imposed by their employers. But within these constraints there are choices. Depending on the choices you make, service users will feel you are on their side, indifferent, or against them. You can contribute towards our recovery or our hopelessness. Here we propose some dos and don'ts for staff wanting to relate to individual service users in ways which are empowering.

DO let us know what our rights are. Often we feel we have none, and are treated as if we have none. Let us know about our rights to refuse treatment, leave, make a complaint or be represented at a mental health tribunal. It helps to be told more than once, and to also be given the information in writing.

DON'T hide behind a mask for professionalism. Don't use words we don't understand. Don't pretend you know more than you do. Mental health work is full of uncertainty, confusion, controversy and contradictions. Honesty is empowering.

DO ask us what we want. You may not be able to provide it. You may disagree. But do ask us. Potentially at least, we are the experts on our own needs.

DON'T dismiss our complaints and worries as symptoms of our 'mental illness'. Too often people's physical illnesses have been disregarded, women sexually molested in hospitals and hostels have not been believed, and genuine grievances have not been taken seriously.

DO recognise our talents, capabilities and potential. Support us in trying new activities, taking on responsibilities and finding outlets for our creativity.

DON'T panic when we express feelings. Often it is useful to sob, shout, scream, shake or shiver. We appreciate being listened to and encouraged. We want space to do that without disturbing other people.

DO tell us as much as you can about the drugs we are on, the diagnosis we have and the options open to us.

DON'T write us off. We are fed up with being told 'You will have to take these pills for the rest of your life' or 'There's no cure for manic depression'. Throwaway negative or dismissive remarks may cause great hurt and be a source of pain to us for years. Many of us have overcome the most disabling distress, often despite the pessimistic predictions of co-called experts.

DO talk to us. Emotional distress is isolating. Help us break through it. Be friendly and treat us as equals. But don't try to force us to talk when we clearly don't want to.

DON'T forget we live in a multicultural society, in which people have different beliefs and values. Learn all you can about the people who use your service, not least by asking them.

---

*Sia is the National Development Agency for the black voluntary sector. It defines its role as 'to help build an infrastructure for the black voluntary sector and to help individuals, groups and communities manage in a changing environment'. At a meeting with representatives from black voluntary organisations and professionals in community care it agreed to set up a **National Black Community Care Network** which would, amongst other targets, seek to promote the '**Black Community Care Charter**' produced by the National Association of Race and Equality Advisers. This **Black Carers Charter** was produced by the National Black Community Care Network.*

Black Carers Charter

1. We have the right to have our role valued and acknowledged.
2. We have the right to be supported in fulfilling this role.
3. We have the right to training which meets our needs.
4. We have the right to be involved in any decisions which have an impact on our lifestyle as carers.

5. We have a right to an assessment which takes into account our language, culture, religion and general circumstances.
6. We have a right to challenge the assessment.
7. We have a right to be assessed in the language and format that is most familiar to us.
8. We believe that all assessments of Black communities should be carried out in a sensitive, respectful and objective manner and not based on any pre-conceived myths and ideas about Black communities.
9. We should approve all assessments and be given full information on the criteria used for such assessments.
10. We believe that information on the assessment process should be provided in plain, non-jargonistic language.
11. Where needs have been identified, information should be given as to when these needs will be met.

Freedom to Care (PO Box 125, West Molesey, Surrey, KT8 1YE) is an organisation set up to support individuals who seek to raise questions, complain or whistleblow in their place of work. The 'Ten Principles of Accountability' are written for employers and managers and in this form are a means of legitimising workers' right to complain or to identify bad practice without fear of reprisal or disciplinary action. They also serve as a possible plan of action for anyone who seeks to raise concern about questionable practice or behaviour at their place of work.

Ten principles of accountability

The following principles should ideally underlie any guidance which employers/managers issue to staff on raising concerns in the workplace:

1. TRANSPARENCY – A procedure for raising concerns which is recognised by all and accessible to all.
2. OPENNESS – a culture in which it is safe to raise concerns and discuss them with any relevant and appropriate person, and in which the presumption is in favour of openness rather than secrecy. Employers should not use 'confidentiality' as a means of gagging staff.
3. FAIRNESS – a procedure which is fair and is seen to be fair; which does not discriminate in terms of sex, race, conscience, status or position.
4. A HEARING – people who have concerns they wish to express should be heard, preferably in person, by those who have the power to change things for the better.

5. INDEPENDENCE – conscientious employees should be able to raise a concern with some person or body who/which is independent and impartial, i.e. has no interests to defend in the matter being complained of.

6. KNOWLEDGE – employers and managers should have working knowledge of ACAS rules on discipline, relevant codes of professional conduct, regulatory instruments, rights of staff under employment law and relevant anti-discrimination statutes on sex, race and disability, and civil rights.

7. PARTICIPATION – employers/managers should participate with employees/professionals in setting standards, and in drawing up and monitoring procedures for the raising of concerns.

8. PROMPTNESS – concerns should be dealt with as efficiently and quickly as possible.

9. SUPPORT – staff who raise concerns should be supported in doing so, e.g. being allowed to have the time and the resources to make their case, the appropriate access to evidence, and witnesses/observers/representatives at relevant hearings.

10. APPEAL – staff should have the opportunity to appeal and be given guidance on appropriate channels of pursuing their concern to the highest level.

30

Care Management and Social Work*

MALCOLM PAYNE

The practice of care management is central to the implementation of community care policy in the 1990s. Social work's relationship with care management is controversial. Care management, according to one view, is a form of social work, containing elements similar to conventional social work but emphasising assessment, liaison and planning, and the provision of services more strongly than therapeutic interventions. An alternative view sees care management as a form of service management, largely divorced from social work practice, although using some of the same skills. A third view is to see care management techniques as changing and reforming social work so that it deals more effectively with situations where co-ordinated service provision is required rather than interpersonal therapeutic help. This latter view may also, however, be construed as a degradation of social work's rich possibilities. It is within the context of these differing perspectives that I shall explore the application of care management in the community care reforms of the early 1990s.

Two main approaches to care management exist in Britain. First, 'social care entrepreneurship', which developed from American 'case management' and was adopted by the Department of Health in its guidance (DoH, 1990). Second, 'service brokerage', which developed from Canadian models and is used in the UK in more multidisciplinary, user-oriented projects. These projects focus on promoting cooperation between services and encouraging service users to plan and make their own demands. Pilling (1992) has developed a further distinction: between service brokerage and multidisciplinary care management. The latter focuses on organising a multidisciplinary team, particularly using a 'keyworker'.

*A summarised and updated version of Chapter 3 from the author's *Social Work and Community Care*, Macmillan Press Ltd, 1995.

30.1   American 'case management'

In the USA, case management accords with the first view outlined above: it is seen as a form of, or way of implementing, social work, rather than as something separate. American case management developed in the context of American social services where hospitals, community facilities and social work agencies are, typically, relatively uncoordinated, independent institutions, often in what in the UK would be the voluntary or private sectors.

Much early case management centred on the movement of people with mental health problems from hospitals to the community. It was 'viewed as a means of overcoming the complexity and fragmentation of our service system and of reaching the inadequately-served chronically and severely disabled population' (Miller, 1983). The techniques spread to other related services for children, older people and their families, people with learning difficulties, and disabled people, as well as people with mental health problems (Weil *et al.*, 1985). Weil and Karls (1985) define case management as 'a set of logical steps and a process of interaction within a service network which assure that a client receives needed services in a supportive, effective, efficient and cost-effective manner' (p. 2). This definition emphasises accountability, but it also focuses on personal relationship. As Moxley (1989) emphasises, even work between organisations and services concerns the client's personal needs, and should be worked on at that level, not as a managerial or bureaucratic task. Throughout, American case management, as it developed in the 1970s and 1980s, gave importance to personal relationships and direct work with clients.

Drawing upon evidence from the USA, Huxley (1991) concluded that there were three essential characteristics for making case management effective for people with mental health problems: being specific about objectives, the case management model used, and the target group of service users. Funding has also been highlighted as a crucial issue: 'in the United States, . . . failure of care management is epidemic in Departments of Human Services – for lack of adequate funding, to begin with, so that one never gets to the question of whether the concept is sound' (Schorr, 1992, p. 38).

30.2   Importing case management

The American concept of case management was imported into the UK by the University of Kent Personal Social Services Research Unit (PSSRU) in its work on the Kent Community Care scheme and, later, other schemes. The 'production of welfare' approach, which the PSSRU developed, provides a model for analysing community care: for assessing the cost and outcome consequences of substituting one service for another.

The Kent Community Care scheme involved a specialist team of workers in a typical generic social services area team (Davies and Challis, 1986). Its job was to provide additional or alternative care for older people who would otherwise be very likely to go into residential care. This was a clear and limited focus for its work. Clients came from the social services area team's caseload, the residential care waiting list and the home help caseload. A personal referral system by discussion (rather than form-based) produced more and more suitable referrals. The workers had small caseloads, relative to other workers in the team. Control of a budget was delegated, and everything – actual or notional – was charged against it, making workers aware of the relative costs of their decisions. The initial budget for each client was two thirds of the cost of a residential care home place (although more could be sought with management approval), so that expenditure was not concentrated on a few cases. Since the screening criteria and objectives of the project concerned people at serious risk of admission to residential care, this provision also reduced potential costs to the Department: if the community care scheme worked the number of people needing residential care would be reduced. New procedures were to be introduced, and from this new, more creative and flexible conventions in providing community care services would be developed, which would not be limited by regulations and procedures. Flexibility and resourcefulness would be enhanced by teamwork and debate within and between teams.

Accountability for cases managed by workers was important, and was enhanced by recording and case review systems that provided clear statements of clients' problems and needs and ensured that flexible budgets were used properly. Neighbours, relatives and other informal carers were recruited and paid small allowances or expenses to take up a role in providing services. Continuous *monitoring* was carried out by the workers through their regular contact with service providers, clients, carers and other helpers.

Significantly fewer older people in the project went into residential care; significantly fewer died; and their physical abilities declined less. They also made less use of other institutional facilities, such as the day hospital. They felt happier and thought that they had an improved quality of care. Informal carers experienced significantly less mental stress, and were not demotivated by the extra support given. Close, confiding relationships developed between older people, carers and workers on the project and this helped to improve the clients' personal relationships.

The community care scheme tended to allocate resources rationally according to the level of dependency, irrespective of how demanding the carers or clients were. Standard provision often perversely allocates more resources to those with less strong needs, because of demands made by carers or clients. In general, costs were lower for community care, and at no point did community care become more expensive. Community care was particularly cost-effective when it allowed extensive support to be given at an early stage to older people with considerable physical or mental infirmity; it avoided very expensive services at a crisis level later on.

Community care saved most money for the health service from services for very frail client groups. However it was cost-effective for virtually all client groups with lower levels of need since, if they received inappropriate residential care, there was a considerable gap between the cost of this and the fairly insignificant costs of the level of community care they needed. However it may not be possible to help very dependent people enough to make staying at home cost-effective. These findings suggest that community care needs to concentrate on identifying those with lower levels of need who would otherwise end up in residential care, since this would lead to an improvement in the quality and length of their lives, make the greatest cost savings and make available more residential care places for those with greater needs. Moreover the community care project workers showed that they could actually differentiate between levels of dependency and respond with appropriate services, without putting expensive services where they were not needed.

The Kent project was undertaken in a suburban retirement area, and the PSSRU applied similar techniques with largely similar results to urban areas, in Gateshead (Challis *et al.*, 1988; Challis *et al.*, 1990) and Darlington (Challis *et al.*, 1989). However the Care in the Community demonstration programme, which included the Darlington project, also contributed to developing case management concepts in the UK.

'Care in the Community' was launched by the government in 1983 to fund a number of pilot projects to help long-stay patients leave hospital, with the aim of demonstrating and encouraging the deinstitutionalisation of long-term hospital care (Renshaw *et al.*, 1989). Most projects were for people with mental health problems or learning difficulties, but some were for young people with multiple difficulties, for disabled people and for older people who were physically or mentally frail (Knapp *et al.*, 1992).

These projects were concerned with community care for people leaving an institution, rather than the preventive approach of the Kent project: they approached community care from the opposite end of the spectrum, and so they provide a useful comparison with the Kent project. They were also much more strongly concerned with the creation of new facilities for the patients, and in particular with their housing. A variety of case management models was used within what had become the standard PSSRU statement of the core tasks of case management (Challis *et al.*, 1990):

- case finding and referral
- assessment and selection
- care planning and service packaging
- monitoring and assessment, and
- case closure.

The PSSRU approach to case management was not the only one. The 'service brokerage' approach adopted from Canadian models was also used. This approach involves working with a service user as an advocate or broker to fill gaps in the services identified by the client. Brokers act as 'travel agents', working with users and their families to identify and share information and to help them implement their own vision of a good service (Brandon, 1989). This approach clearly places less emphasis on the coordination of services and more on the client's own action as part of the process of gaining services.

As mentioned at the beginning of this chapter, Pilling (1992) discusses programmes in which a *multidisciplinary team* is responsible for assessment and developing a care plan for an individual. She provides well-researched accounts of teams operating brokerage and multidisciplinary teamwork models; for example the Camden and Islington project for disabled people. This project worked on the premise that the user's needs and wishes should be the most important basis for deciding on services and should be separated from service-allocation decisions. There was an extensive assessment, followed by an agreement with the user, who was then given information about services that they could approach themself, or that the worker could negotiate on their behalf. Personal help and counselling was excluded from the case manager's role. A user group was formed, and there was advocacy for better services and involvement in decision-making. Eventually, a voluntary organisation with a service development role grew up. About 150 people were helped, and in spite of its advocacy role (which could have been seen as hostile) the organisation was accepted by local services (except by occupational therapists, who thought that it helped some clients 'jump the queue' for services). Clients were satisfied with the service and it did seem to improve the range of services offered. Advocacy and coordination seemed to support each other: the worker needed well-worked-out plans and full information in order to take an advocacy role. The main reason that tasks could not be completed was lack of resources in the services. The fact that the organisation was independent of mainstream services but seen as a resource, rather than in opposition to them, seemed to be an effective form of management.

Projects such as this and others in the 'Care in the Community' programme have a different emphasis from the Kent project. They offer
ways of promoting multidisciplinary work and of bringing advocacy
into practice. Such an emphasis seems to come from the organisational
base from which these projects arose. Several worked with disabled
people in the prime of life who sought and demanded greater independence by receiving a wide variety of services. Accounts of more recent
developments in community care have emphasised the empowerment of
other disadvantaged and oppressed groups (such as older people) by
facilitating user involvement in the planning and organisation of services
(Jack, 1995; Wilson, 1995). Care management can contribute to a 'new'
social work, one that is more responsive to clients' needs.

Another related concept, 'care programming', has developed within
services for people with mental health problems who need treatment in
hospital. The aims of care programming are similar to those of case management, in that they require a full assessment of needs, the appointment
of a keyworker who coordinates provision of services, and regular
review and monitoring of services (DoH, 1992). Research suggests that
most care programming work is carried out by community psychiatric
nurses, and does not involve extensive multidisciplinary work
(Schneider, 1993).

30.3   Applying case management to community care

As a result of the work of the PSSRU in the Kent project, 'social care
entrepreneurship' was well-established by the time Griffiths produced
his report on community care (1988). He recommended that: 'In cases
where a significant level of resources are involved a 'care manager'
should be nominated from within the social service authority's staff to
oversee the assessment and reassessment function and manage the
resulting action' (Para. 6.6).

The subsequent Policy Guidance (DoH, 1990) finally formalised *care
management* as a major part of its requirements of local authorities in
implementing the National Health Service and Community Care Act
1990. Its role would be to:

- Ensure that available resources would be used effectively.
- Restore and maintain independence by enabling people to live in the
  community.
- Minimise the effects of disability and illness.
- Treat service users respectfully and provide equal opportunities.
- Promote individual choice and self-determination, and build on
  existing strengths and care resources.

- Promote partnership between users, carers and service providers and the organisations representing them.

Care management comprises three distinct processes, emphasising user and carer participation:

- Assessment (which is given a separate section in the Guidance).
- Design of a 'care package'.
- Implementation and monitoring.

One consequence of this foreshortening of the American and PSSRU models of case management is the increasing emphasis given to assessment and design of the care package, perhaps leading to an assumption that implementation is a fairly routine consequence of the design process. This might have been brought about by the intended split between the provision and purchase of services. Since the care manager is seen as part of the purchasing machinery, with no responsibility for provision, involvement in interpersonal work with clients, as found in the Kent project, might well get lost. In this way we see the development of a model of care management that, unlike the American concept, is separate from the interpersonal work of social work. This is an example of the second view of the relationship of social work and care management discussed at the beginning of this chapter. This has led writers such as Sheppard (1995) to argue that, notwithstanding the advantages of responsiveness and empowerment offered by the 'new' social work arising from importing care management, community care policy risks making social work over-bureaucratic and inflexible.

The final stage of formalisation of care management as a part of post-Griffiths community care provision came about with the publication of two guides, for practitioners and managers respectively, to establishing care management and assessment services under the NHS and Community Care Act 1990 (SSI/SWSG, 1991a) (SSI/SWSG, 1991b). The increasing importance given to the assessment phase of care management is clearly evident in these documents. They set out their own formulation of care management in seven stages. The first two stages are outside the circular process of care management:

- *Publishing information* to inform potential users of the service 'about the needs for which care agencies accept the responsibility to offer assistance, and the range of services currently available' (SSI/SWSG, 1991a, p. 11).
- *Determining the level of assessment* so that simple matters do not result in unnecessarily complex early work.

After these two initial phases, care management is seen as a circular process that starts with Stage 3:

- Assessing need.
- Care planning.
- Implementing the care plan.
- Monitoring, which is concerned with checking how the plan is being delivered.
- Reviewing, which is a periodic review (and possible alterations) of the plan.

Reviewing then leads back to assessing need on the basis of the review. However the documents define *need* as 'the requirements of individuals to enable them to achieve, maintain or restore an acceptable level of social independence or quality of life, as defined by the particular care agency or authority' (SSI/SWSG, 1991b, p. 14). This definition of need places the responsibility for determining acceptable quality of life wholly with the agency, rather than with the individual user of the service. The following paragraph indicates that need varies with changes in national legislation and local policy, the availability of resources and the patterns of local demand. In reality the only acceptable needs, according to this policy, are those defined by legislation and the agency.

30.4   Introducing care management to community care: some conclusions

As the idea of case management has been converted from American concepts used in special projects, and particularly as official formulations have developed, the concept of care management has come to embody the central conflict in community care policy: between individualised, responsive care and the containment of costs. At the end of this process, need and the responsibilities of care management are defined always within the context of control of expenditure. Consequently care management has moved away from the American conceptualisation of case management as a form of social work. The possibility of seeing a 'new social work' as a more empowering and facilitating practice, as offered by brokerage approaches, has been imperilled. Instead UK care management for a 'new social work' focuses on cost control, assessment and restriction through bureaucratic and market mechanisms.

References

Brandon, D. (1989) 'The courage to look at the moon', *Social Work Today*, 50 (50), pp. 16–17.

Challis, D., Chessum, R., Chesterman, J., Luckett, R. and Woods, B. (1988) 'Community care for the frail elderly: an urban experiment', in Davies, B. and Knapp, M. (eds), *The Production of Welfare Approach: evidence and argument from the PSSRU*, Supplement to the *British Journal of Social Work*, vol. 18, pp. 13–42.

Challis, D., Chessum, R., Chesterman, J., Luckett, R. and Traske, K. (1990) *Case Management in Social and Health Care*, Personal Social Services Research Unit, Canterbury, Kent.

Challis, D., Darton, R., Johnson, L., Stone, M., Traske, K. and Wall, B. (1989) *The Darlington Community Care Project: supporting frail elderly people at home*, Personal Social Services Research Unit, Canterbury, Kent.

Davies, B. and Challis, D. (1986) *Matching Resources to Needs in Community Care: An evaluated demonstration of a long-term care model*, Gower, Aldershot.

DoH (Department of Health) (1990) *Community Care in the Next Decade and Beyond: Policy Guidance*, HMSO, London.

DoH (Department of Health) (1992) 'Care programming and mental health', *Caring for People*, 10, pp. 11–12.

Griffiths, Sir Roy (1988) *Community Care: Agenda for Action*, HMSO, London.

Huxley, P. (1991) 'Effective case management for mentally ill people: the relevance of recent evidence from the USA for case management services in the United Kingdom', *Social Work and Social Services Review*, Vol. 2, No. 3, pp. 192–203.

Jack, R. (ed.) (1995) *Empowerment in Community Care*, Chapman and Hall, London.

Knapp, M., Cambridge, P., Thomason, C., Beecham, J., Allen, C. and Darton, R. (1992) *Care in the Community: challenge and demonstration*, Ashgate, Aldershot.

Miller, G. (1983) 'Case management: the essential service', in Sanborn, C. J. (ed.), *Case Management in Mental Health Services*, Haworth Press, New York.

Moxley, D. P. (1989) *The Practice of Case Management*, Sage, Beverly Hills, CA.

Pilling D. (1992) *Approaches to Case Management for People with Disabilities*, Jessica Kingsley, London.

Renshaw, J., Hampson, R., Thomason, C., Darton, R., Judge, K. and Knapp, M. (1989) *Care in the Community: the first steps*, Gower, Aldershot.

Schneider, J. (1993) 'Care programming in mental health: assimilation and adaptation', *British Journal of Social Work*, Vol. 23, No. 4, pp. 383–403.

Schorr, A. L. (1992) *The Personal Social Services: an outside view*, Joseph Rowntree Foundation, York.

Sheppard, M. (1995) *Care Management and the New Social Work*, Whiting and Birch, London.

SSI/SWSG (1991a) *Care Management and Assessment: Practitioners' Guide*, Department of Health Social Services Inspectorate/Scottish Office Social Work Services Group, London.

SSI/SWSG (1991b) *Care Management and Assessment: Managers' Guide*, Department of Health Social Services Inspectorate/Scottish Office Social Work Services Group, London.

Weil, M. and Karls, J. M. (1985) 'Historical origins and recent developments', in Weil, Marie *et al.* (1985), *Case Management in Human Service Practice: A systematic approach to mobilising resources for clients*, Jossey-Bass, San Francisco.

Weil, M., Karls, J. M. and Associates (1985) *Case Management in Human Service Practice: a systematic approach to mobilising resources for clients*, Jossey-Bass, San Francisco.

Wilson, G. (ed.) (1995) *Community Care: asking the users*, Chapman and Hall, London.

31

The Implications of Information Technology in Social Care*

BRYAN GLASTONBURY

The phrase 'It must be true because the computer says so' has become a familiar one in modern societies, but so has the understanding that computers make mistakes and sometimes seem to behave stupidly. The largest area of information in the personal social services is about clients, and concerns about accuracy have a long history. Within Information Technology (IT) the much-used explanation of inaccuracy is GIGO – 'garbage in: garbage out' – the view that flawed information is caused by mistakes at the point of data entry, commonly made by clerical staff. An early indication that reality is more subtle and complex than GIGO, certainly for the social services, came from a Californian study (Dery, 1981) which suggested that not all inaccuracy stems from errors by data-entry clerks. In this research it was found that the intended uses of computerised client information, for example to enable calculations of the volume and location of workload in order to set levels and deployment of staff, influenced the quality of data submitted for entry. Fearful of seeing workloads increased, or perhaps some staff discarded, those who filled in the forms used for data entry to the computer seem to have given in to the temptation to categorise cases as more severe or demanding than they really were, to keep as 'live', clients who had passed elsewhere, and perhaps even to have embellished some files. What Dery's study did most effectively was to show that computer information can be rendered almost useless if those responsible for the mate-

*This is an abridged version of 'Risk, Information Technology and Social Care', *New Technology in the Human Services*, Vol. 8, No. 3, pp. 2–10. The author acknowledges the support of the Economic and Social Research Council's Risk and Human Behaviour Programme.

rial going into it, that is the front-line professional workers, do not have a vested interest in an accurate and up-to-date system.

Following this research, and comparable insights in many other locations, agency managers both realised and acted on the need to ensure that staff gained benefit from client information systems and did not have evidence of such systems being used to their detriment. Both measures helped all agency staff to feel a commitment to accuracy. It came as something of a shock, therefore, when another American study (Harrod, 1987) found error levels averaging nearly 20% in some of Michigan's Children's Protective Service files. These were not mistakes of interpretation but of fact, and were not in 'backwater' cases, but in high-profile current child abuse files.

The possibility that these were one-off maverick findings has been dispelled by UK research (Barnes, 1993) which sought to replicate Harrod's study. Taking 376 child care cases, all of which should have been given a computer file, Barnes first found that 25 (6.6%) had no computer file at all. For those with a computer file he checked on 11 factual indicators, as near as possible to those used by Harrod, and found an average error level of nearly 24%. There was wide variation – the child's name, for example, was right in all but one instance, while in two out of every three cases the name of the child's doctor was wrong.

To the level of inaccuracies in an individual file have to be added faults in the system as a whole, such as records of clients who have died, moved to another area, or ceased to need help. Overall the risk of inaccuracy is high, whether the system is being used for composite statistics (although there may be some 'swings and roundabouts' compensation here) or in relation to a specific individual. The onward risk stemming from such a scale of error is of incorrectly informed planning and resource deployment decisions, and mistaken awareness of the circumstances of individual clients. Inadequate information is a frequently identified causal factor of failures in work with clients, such as child tragedies.

Within agencies there is a growing tendency, particularly amongst professional staff, to treat computerised client details with some scepticism (while recognising that traditional paper files, often part-typed, part-handwritten, are just as flawed, and sometimes unreadable). However it is doubtful whether managers or professionals would conceive that *their* computer files have such levels of inaccuracy. There is also considerable political sensitivity about an agency admitting to a possible one in four level of mistakes. Overall the setting is in need of much more extensive research.

The threat of serious difficulties – in extreme instances tragedies, arising because of flawed computer information – is high because staff will not or do not want to acknowledge the possible level of error, and are increasingly obliged to make decisions based on this information, whatever its quality. Nevertheless there is growing sophistication in awareness of the likely causes of inaccuracy, and the solutions, as many managers have realised, cover a plethora of quality-enhancing activities, all of which can be expected to have some impact.

Here are some of the main perceived problems and potential solutions:

- The initial idea of poor clerical work at the point of data-entry is still pertinent, though not so dominant as first assumed. What is recognised is that a long chain of transmission risks errors entering at each stage. It is not uncommon, for example, for a social worker to take rough notes of an interview with a client, and later to use those scribbles as the basis to fill in a data-entry form for the computer. The handwritten form is then keyed in by a clerk and, after the harassed social worker has made a brief check, the new file or addition to a file becomes part of the information system. Shortening the chain, ideally to the situation where computer data is entered by the social worker or care manager at the point of interview with the client, offers a chance of more accurate entry.

- A client/worker interaction, whether for the purpose of something broadly-based like generating a social history or an assessment, or for some specific task, offers itself most conveniently to be written up as a descriptive and analytical document, seeking at all times to convey the nuances and uniqueness of the particular circumstances. In contrast a computer system is made up of standardised categories alongside factual data. Very often considerable manipulation is needed to fit the specifics of the interaction into the standard categories required by the computer, and the risk is high that such manipulation introduces error. The solution, still only a little achieved, has been to design information systems capable of holding both standardised and individualistic data (commonly in 'free text' sections). They thereby become longer and more complex, as well as a more accurate reflection of reality.

- Social services client information systems are dynamic because the circumstances of clients change all the time. Many errors arise from out-of-date material. Agencies have been forced to recognise that the only solution to this is substantial investment in system maintenance, to ensure that files are regularly updated and reviewed, and that past records are placed in an archive or destroyed. The build-up of system maintenance costs is nevertheless acting as a deterrent to developmental IT investment (Whitehead, 1995).

- While agency managers rely almost exclusively on computer data for composite information for planning or evaluative purposes, or for annual returns, front-line staff have retained paper files alongside the new computer records. This may be a transitional situation, perhaps stretched longer than necessary because social workers have not wanted to lose paper files which they possess in a personal sense through holding them in their own filing cabinets. Yet, as long as this situation exists, it is possible for front line staff to hold the view that it does not really matter if the computer files are full of mistakes – the paper files are always there instead.

None of these actions will, on their own, take away the risk of error, though they may contain it at more acceptable levels. This may be the best that can be obtained from dependence on computer-based information, just as in the past agencies have been reluctant to depend on their paper files alone. If so, then we are forced back to what has always been a delicate but vitally important balance in caring for people – between information and professional judgement.

If risks about accuracy have been kept a little under wraps, those about abuse have received international attention. Most industrial nations have data protection legislation in place, and most care organisations have their own in-house security measures. In the UK there is the additional right of clients to see what is held on file about them, unless it falls into a protected area (police sensitivity for the most part). The issue of security is important in the personal social services because systems made up of detailed information about people's lives, most often about times of stress, vulnerability and inability to cope, are so humiliating if they become public, and are valuable commodities in the information industry, for example to credit-rating companies.

There is a long-lasting concern in social work theory to establish that what a client tells a social worker in a one-to-one interview is private to the two of them. Details may have been set down in the client paper file in the worker's office, accessible to some other staff in the office, but a reasonable level of privacy could be ensured. This position was slightly weakened by a government decision that confidences given to social workers did not have the same protected status in law as those given to doctors, and it has been thoroughly challenged by computerisation and telecommunications. Within agencies there are now many more staff with authorised access to computer files than ever had access to paper files. At the same time the moves to network computers, and (increasingly) to take advantage of the 'information superhighway', create still greater risks.

The problem once again is of gaining a balance between taking care of people's right to privacy, and taking risks in the interests of better services. Politically and organisationally the pressures pull against giving highest priority to personal privacy. Better-quality and more cost-effective services are seen as depending on relevant information – for example, about an individual's level of eligibility for help in a policy framework dedicated to targeting services to where they are most needed. Cross-agency and intra-agency teamwork are valued, inevitably bringing up the issue of information exchanges between, for instance, health and social services. The political thrust to encourage and contract with an independent sector means that, for example, an elderly person's social history may be circulated around a number of private nursing homes in an attempt to make a suitable placement.

Much of this issue, as can be seen, is not directly related to IT, but IT is more and more the medium, the route which makes tasks like intra-agency sharing much easier to achieve. However, while sharing information to get better services is a justifiable objective, other uses of information are more questionable or seen as more threatening to agency staff. Work evaluation, staff supervision and appraisal, and quality monitoring can all now be informed by computer files in a way which was not feasible with paper files. A manager can log onto the computer and look at the state of a front-line worker's files, or work with particular clients, without the staff member being aware that this is happening. The traditional approach to the client/worker relationship offered privacy to the worker as well as the client, and this has been largely swept away by computerisation. The risk of exposure is greater for front-line staff, but so are the pressures placed on managers, who can no longer hide behind the statement that they did not know what their staff were doing.

In short, private personal client information is now part of the currency of agency management and quality control systems, thanks to the build-up of IT. Can it be long before that information becomes a commodity in the wider information industry? Will it always be morally and politically unacceptable for an impoverished welfare agency to sell the names and addresses of clients with bad money management records to a credit-rating company? Or for a law and order agency to sell lists of offenders in the interests of combating crime?

These are issues which people in the caring professions can influence, but not determine. Yet even to have influence the personal social services need to clarify where they stand in relation to the needs of the information age. Training is vital on a wide range of IT-linked matters if uncertainty, confusion, lack of confidence, suspicion and resentment are to be replaced by understanding, overall grasp and willingness to 'own' the social services part of a new technological era. Trust is also important, especially in the relationship between front-line workers and their managers, not only to avoid the sort of misbehaviours catalogued by David Dery (1981), but also to ensure that within social care there is a shared vision and action plan for the effective and ethical use of IT.

Of the specific risks discussed in this chapter, arguably the most important concerns working with poor-quality information sets. The limited amount of current research suggests a disturbing proportion of inaccuracy, which can be countered if the computer system is no more than a backup for more embedded manual information sources, but which becomes increasingly relevant as manual systems decline.

At a more general level the greatest risk for the personal social services is to be left behind, picking up the bits after all the important IT decisions have been taken elsewhere. Masuda, the intellectual leader of Japan's information age planning, makes a telling argument (Masuda, 1981) that, far from being a scientific matter, IT affects all of society and its cultural features, and impinges on society's whole ethical framework. IT is scientific, but it is also artistic, and part of the broad sweep of what he sees as the 'ethics industry'. A later Anglo-American effort sought to place the concept of an ethics industry in the context of a western industrialised society (Glastonbury and LaMendola, 1992), arguing that, while the artistic and cultural elements of society could not take a lead in scientific development, they could and should lead in the social integration and ethical positioning of IT. As people concerned with the welfare of society as a whole, and of the troubled and less privileged sections of it in particular, the staff of our social services, managerial and professional, have a key role in the ethics industry, and through that in influencing the use of IT.

References

Barnes, C. S. (1993) 'Collecting accurate information about child abuse, revisited', in Glastonbury, B. (ed.), *Human Welfare and Technology*, van Gorcum, Holland. A more detailed version is available as Colin Barnes MA thesis, University of Warwick.

Dery, D. (1981) *Computers in Welfare: the MIS-Match*, Sage, Beverly Hills and London.

Glastonbury, B. and LaMendola, W. (1992) *The Integrity of Intelligence: a Bill of Rights for the Information Age*, Macmillan, Basingstoke and St. Martin's Press, New York.

Harrod, J. K. (1987) *Collecting Accurate Data about Child Abuse*, University of Michigan Dissertation. A shortened version appeared in Schoech, D. (ed.), (1988) *Computer Use in Social Services Network*, University of Texas at Arlington.

Masuda, Y. (1981) *The Information Society as Post-Industrial Society*, World Future Society, Washington.

Whitehead, D. (1995) 'One gizmo too far', *Community Care Management and Planning*, Vol. 3, No. 2, Pitman, London.

32

The Impact of Quasi-Markets on Community Care

LESLEY HOYES and ROBIN MEANS

32.1 Introduction

A commitment to market mechanisms is embodied in the National Health Service and Community Care Act 1990, which incorporates the main recommendations of *Caring for People* (DoH, 1989), the White Paper on community care. This legislation represents a response to what is seen as the many years of failure to develop an adequate legislative and financial framework for community care services.

Local authority social services departments have the lead role in community care planning. However their role at the client level is increasingly being confined to the assessment of need, the designing of care arrangements to meet that need by appointed 'care managers', and the provision of funds to finance those arrangements. They are being discouraged from directly providing all care services themselves; instead services are to be provided increasingly by a 'mixed economy' based largely on the private and voluntary sectors. Local authorities act as 'enablers' through the allocation of funds, but they have a declining role in service provision.

This chapter discusses the main implications of introducing market mechanisms into community care provision. First, however, we look at the development of 'quasi-markets'.

32.2 The arrival of quasi-markets

Despite the 'new right' rhetoric of the post-1979 Conservative governments, much of the welfare state remained untouched in the late 1980s.

However, Le Grand (1990, p. 1) has argued that 1988–9 saw 'a major offensive against the basic structure of welfare provision'. Radical changes in the legislative basis of the provision of education, housing and the National Health Service have been enacted alongside those in community care, representing the most significant shift in British social policy since the 1940s.

These reforms are seen as having one common feature: the introduction of what might be termed 'quasi-markets' into the delivery of welfare services (Le Grand and Bartlett, 1993; Bartlett *et al.*, 1994). In each case the state ceases to be both the funder and provider of services. Instead it becomes primarily a funder, with services being provided by a variety of private, voluntary and public suppliers, all operating in competition with each other. The method of funding also changes. Instead of resources being allocated directly by bureaucrats to providers, a budget or 'voucher' is given directly to the consumer, or to someone acting on his or her behalf (such as a care manager), who then allocates the budget between competing suppliers.

Quasi-markets are 'markets' because they replace state provision with more competitive, independent services. They are 'quasi' because they differ from conventional markets in a number of important respects. The differences are on both the supply and demand sides. On the supply side, as with conventional markets, there is competition between service suppliers. However, in contrast to conventional markets, these organisations are not necessarily out to maximise their profits. Profit maximisation is clearly not the focus of an Age Concern group contracted by the local authority to provide day care for frail elderly people. But equally it may not be the main factor driving a small private residential home for people with severe learning disabilities. On the demand side, consumer purchasing power is not expressed in terms of cash, but in the form of a budget confined to the purchase of a specific service. Also, the immediate consumer may not be the one who exercises the choices concerning purchasing decisions; instead these may be delegated to a third party, such as a care manager.

32.3   Developing quasi-markets in social care

Most commentators have noted the pivotal role of social services authorities in market development – they need to create a market in social care and then to regulate that market through contracts and service agreements (Hoyes *et al.*, 1994; Wistow *et al.*, 1996; Means and Smith, 1994; Lewis and Glennerster, 1996). This has represented a major cultural shift for most local authorities and most independent-sector organisations. Not only this, but social services authorities took on their market-making role in a situation of great geographical unevenness in the availability of residential and nursing home care. Even more critically, independent sector provision of domiciliary services such as home care was much less developed, with few large suppliers and many small ones.

But what conditions are needed to help ensure a successful quasi-market in community care? Le Grand and Bartlett (1993, pp. 19–33) draw upon economic theories about conventional markets to identify the following pre-requisites for the development of 'successful' quasi-markets in welfare services:

- *Market structure* – for a conventional market to be efficient and offer genuine choice, there must be competition or the potential for competition. In other words, there should be numerous providers and many purchasers, or the opportunity for new providers to enter and existing providers to exit from the market relatively costlessly.
- *Information* – both sides of a market need access to accurate information about the costs and quality of the service provided. Monitoring of quality is an essential part of any quasi-market system.
- *Transactions costs* – those costs involved in the drafting and negotiation of contracts, and also the cost of monitoring compliance and resolving disputes after transactions are agreed, must be less than the costs of the administrative systems that contracts are replacing.
- *Motivation* – for markets to work appropriately, providers need to be motivated at least in part by profit-making, whilst purchasers must be motivated to maximise the welfare of service users.
- *Cream-skimming* – markets must restrict opportunities for discrimination (by either purchasers or providers) in favour of the cheaper or less troublesome users (the cream).

These prerequisites underline the fact that stimulating new and diversified markets is not easy, especially if their justification is their ability to respond to the needs of service users. Competition may be reduced by the existence of monopoly or near-monopoly purchasers and cosy relationships with dominant providers. Do users have the sanctions to upset these relationships and demand that the authority exit to another contractor? Quality in welfare is notoriously difficult to monitor; if it is defined by purchasers and providers, there is no guarantee it will fulfil user needs. Information flow is constrained by the fact that many choices are made under duress (mental health) or in crisis. Many welfare providers are not commercially motivated and may find it difficult to make the shift from considering the welfare of their users to the financial state of their provider units. Why should purchasers (indirect consumers) have the direct consumer's interest at heart? And how will they know what the consumer's interests are?

32.4   Managing contracts

The successful introduction of quasi-markets into community care services will depend partly on whether or not local authorities are able to specify, write, manage and monitor contracts that ensure a quality service. Each of these tasks presents difficulties, because of the nature of community care and the importance of high standards. These issues will need to be addressed, whether the main form of service provision is expected to be via internal markets based on splitting the purchasing branch of a department from its service delivery or provider arm, or through the award of external contracts to independent service providers.

32.4.1   Internal markets and the purchaser/provider split

The introduction of a 'contract culture' into community care services has had a profound effect upon the management structures of social services authorities. The most significant change has been separation of the purchaser and provider functions in many departments (DoH, 1989, p. 23; Lewis and Glennerster, 1996).

Such splits are seen as having two objectives; to ensure equality of treatment for alternative suppliers and the authorities' own services, so as to increase consumer choice; and identification of service provision costs, so that choices can be fair. However it is not at all clear that a structural split will always be the only or the best way of achieving the ultimate goal of enhanced choice (Means *et al.*, 1994). Where there are no alternative suppliers (for example, for respite care for highly dependent people), costs need to be identified, and this can be achieved by improved accounting. Where there are alternative suppliers, a split will only be necessary at the point of purchase, at care manager level, and will then be effective only if accompanied by real scope for care managers and users to exercise choice.

The formalisation of relations between purchasers and internal providers will profoundly affect relationships within the local authority. Research suggests many staff resent being redefined as providers, especially if this involves the loss of assessment roles (Hadley and Clough, 1996, p. 177). It can equally transform relations between purchasers and independent suppliers, especially where there is total separation of budget management from service delivery. This can make local authorities unwilling to tie up all their budget at the beginning of the year; this may in turn make the voluntary sector's income less predictable and its involvement more risky (Flynn, 1990).

32.4.2 Selecting external providers

When local authorities seek to contract out services to private and voluntary sector providers, they are faced with the problem of deciding with which organisation to enter into arrangements and on what contractual basis. Much will depend upon the ability of purchasers to select providers of good-quality services. This requires them to be able to observe and collect accurate information on all potential suppliers. If the characteristics of the supplier cannot be observed, 'adverse selection' may result; that is, the purchaser selects a poor-quality supplier because he or she cannot tell a good from a bad producer. It is likely that some authorities will attempt to avoid adverse selection by purchasing only from well-known, established suppliers. However, this strategy distorts the conditions for efficient market operation, namely that there should be many providers supplying services to many purchasers.

Policy guidance from the Department of Health lists options available to authorities for selecting service providers: these include open tendering, select list tendering, direct negotiation with one or more suppliers or setting up a new organisation, for example through management/worker buy-outs (DoH, 1991). The view of the Association of Metropolitan Authorities is that competitive tendering for social care services is impractical and not in the best interests of social care provision; there are not enough local agencies and the process would inevitably emphasise costs over quality (Association of Metropolitan Authorities, 1990). Moreover competitive tendering will bring contracts under the provision of the Local Government Act 1988, which prohibits contract conditions that are non-commercial, including terms and conditions of employment and composition of the workforce. This would not necessarily exclude considerations of genuine occupational qualifications and an organisation's ability to recruit and retain staff if these can be justified on commercial grounds. However it may well prove difficult for an authority, even when committed to non-exploitation of employees and equal opportunities, to build such factors into contracts. Early evidence from Common and Flynn (1992) on selecting external providers was that the imperative of making a deal or encouraging private and voluntary provision was a higher priority for purchasers than promoting user choice. More recent research suggests that local authorities are increasingly concerned with ensuring the reliability of supply, and that this might predispose them to concentrate upon block contract agreements with well-resourced, high-reputation providers (Forder *et al.*, 1996; Lewis and Glennerster, 1996).

32.4.3   Specifications and contracts

The main debate about contracts in community care services centres on how 'tight' or 'loose' they should be. A 'tight' formal contract might facilitate compliance, but it might still leave loopholes that the providers can exploit to their own advantage. On the other hand a service might be provided by a highly trusted supplier who is known to share the authorities' objectives, in which case there may be seen to be a need only for a very loose agreement. Between these two extremes will lie a whole range of situations that will influence the decision on the most appropriate arrangement.

In the field of community care services, the use of specifications and contracts as a means of ensuring services of a high standard is problematic. Specifications describe what is to be provided and contracts set out the terms under which the purchaser and provider agree to achieve compliance. Many social services departments would have difficulty in describing in detail the characteristics and costs of the services they provide directly now (Lewis and Glennerster, 1996). Such descriptions would need to reflect outcomes and processes as well as inputs. They may have even greater difficulty in describing the standards they are meeting. Services such as those involved in community care are difficult to describe and define, since it is often the less tangible and less easily quantified aspects that are of most importance to the consumers. Yet when the potential risks to those consumers of poor-quality services are serious, standards must be defined. If specifications are flexible to permit provider initiative, what happens when a decision is taken with which the purchaser disagrees? A good example of this is the need for local authorities to have clear procedures for the handling of the personal finances of elderly people with dementia who are in residential care (Means and Langan, 1996).

It is clearly important that authorities should think about and write down the standards of services that they will expect from providers (Barnes and Miller, 1988). Quality assurance is not just about inspection in the narrow sense of correcting a service that is badly provided, but should be a means of ensuring that services are high quality from the start. Specifications will need to include inputs, since it is on these that costings are based. Nevertheless contracts that are couched in general terms and emphasise the desired outcomes can have the details defined during negotiations between purchaser and provider in a collaborative effort.

32.5   Will markets in community care work?

The claims made in *Caring for People* (DoH, 1989) for markets and contracts are substantial and varied, and these claims need to be evaluated.
The major justification made for change is that markets generate competition and hence they are more efficient and effective than the bureaucratic systems they are replacing. But this is open to question. The
indeterminacy of the relevant organisations' objectives (profits, turnover,
social welfare) makes it difficult to predict how they will respond to
market incentives. Also, consumers of community care, even if aided by
a care manager, may find it difficult to shop around to find the best
'value for money'; and local authority purchasers may find it difficult to
exit from a contract with an inadequate provider if this involves, for
example, moving very frail elderly people to a new nursing home
(Forder *et al.*, 1996).

A second set of questions concerns choice. Another important justification for the introduction of quasi-market arrangements is that to do so
increases both the range and the quality of consumer choice. But again
this could be challenged. To what extent is the consumer able to choose
what he or she actually wants, and to what extent is service access
dependent upon the assessment and negotiation skills of a professional?
How much choice do the clients of a care manager have? Can they
choose their care manager? Will there be enough independent providers
to provide an adequate range of choice in all cases, especially where this
requires the stimulation of a market in independent domiciliary service
providers?

A third set of questions concerns equity. The White Paper is harshly
critical of the failure of the previous community care system to target
resources at those in greatest need, and this is backed by extensive
research evidence (Davies and Knapp, 1988). And yet an equally
common criticism of conventional markets (Foster, 1983) is that they
create inequalities and therefore inequities. Will quasi-markets have
similar effects? Will residential care providers compete for those with
straightforward needs, while ignoring those with the more challenging
behaviour? Will the poor – constrained by lack of resources – be particularly disadvantaged?

The importance of market-making and developing a clear contract
strategy has already been emphasised, and how this is tackled by individual authorities will have a major impact upon outcomes. An implementation problem faced by nearly all authorities will be the paucity of
their information and financial management systems. Technological
change opens up the prospect of tight–loose systems of public sector
management (Hoggett, 1991), but many social services departments are
woefully short of both the information technology hardware and the

officer expertise required to operate such systems. This could become a major stumbling block to the effective implementation of quasi-markets and contracts in the British social care system (Miller, 1991).

Finally, it is important not to lose sight of the question: success or failure for whom? The research of Smith and Cantley (1985) on psycho-geriatric day services underlines the fact that there are different interest groups (officers, managers, field-level staff, clients and carers) in any policy initiative, and that each stakeholder group will have different ideas about what will represent 'success' or 'failure' in any policy change. If the introduction of markets and contracts into community care services achieves efficiency in the narrow terms of cost minimalisation, this may represent 'success' for many hard-pressed senior managers faced with a growing gap between demand and available resources. However this might be achieved at the expense of a major deterioration in the employment conditions of many community care staff (residential staff, home helps, meals deliverers) since some elements of the private and even the voluntary sector may offer lower salaries than the public sector and be reluctant to recognise pension, holiday and trade union rights. Thus the changes could represent a disaster for some already low-paid community care staff. Equally, a central focus on costs may reduce choice for the individual consumer since expensive but preferred care options may be dismissed or ignored by the care manager; but it could equally be argued that such an approach will ensure the maximum number of clients are helped for any given amount of resources.

32.6   The impact of quasi-markets on community care

Some clear trends are now beginning to emerge within the 'new' community care. First, the anxiety of smaller voluntary and private sector providers about their capacity to meet the demands of bidding for and fulfilling contracts (Taylor *et al.*, 1995) seem to be justified in the light of evidence that local authorities find it easiest to contract with large, well-established providers (Common and Flynn, 1992). It is also becoming clear that new providers are most likely to be attracted into such markets as home care when the purchasing intentions of social services are clear and when there is an emphasis on trust and confidence (Wistow, 1995).

Second, campaigning and advocacy groups have often struggled for funding, or found themselves challenged in terms of the compatibility of campaigning and service provider roles. This has been particularly true of 'special' needs housing forums and specialist housing associations (NFHA, 1994; Means and Smith, 1996), while some coalitions of disabled people have had to form a separate provider organisation in order to develop the availability of user-controlled services while at the same time maintaining their campaigning role.

Third, Le Grand and Bartlett (1993) have argued that the development of care managers controlling their own budget represents a positive development of multiple purchasers. However, many care managers are still only operating notional rather than real budgets and they are obtaining services from what remains a fairly limited set list (Hoyes *et al.*, 1994; Lewis and Glennerster, 1996). In reality the social services department often remains the sole purchaser. Whilst this may make it easier for the authority to dictate terms, it may also deter potential suppliers from entering a market where they will be dependent upon a single source of funding.

Fourth, despite the above limitations, there is evidence that some service users in some local authorities are getting a more responsive and flexible package of services than would probably have been available under previous arrangements. Hoyes *et al.*, for example, cited that:

> a young woman with physical disabilities had been enabled take part in swimming, relaxation and T'ai Chi groups, using local facilities and volunteers where necessary. This reflected that authority's aim to move from a model of day provision dominated by more traditional statutory day centres.
>
> (Hoyes *et al.*, 1994, p. 19)

However it is equally clear that this kind of creative package may become available to declining numbers as social services concentrate on developing what might be called a 'Rolls-Royce' service for those deemed most at risk, and that this development will be at the cost of any response to the needs of others, with preventative services being especially at risk from cutbacks.

Finally, the emphasis on an intensive service for the few reflects the growing financial pressure upon local authority community care budgets. Wistow (1995) has stressed the link between this and changes in the National Health Service, such as reductions in long-term care beds and the more general speeding-up of discharge from acute hospitals. It may be that the development of quasi-markets is being heavily influenced, and possibly undermined, by policy developments outside of community care itself.

32.7 Conclusion

Community care remains in transition. The introduction of quasi-markets into community care represents a major challenge to local authorities at a time when they have been under severe financial pressure and subject to local government review. Research evidence is so far inconclusive in terms of the capacity of local authorities to operate a mixed economy of providers through the use of contracts in a way that delivers user-driven services. Our own view is that the changes will have failed if they do not lead to the provision of flexible care packages that are perceived as appropriate and high quality by consumers and their carers. A good test of this will be the experience of users from minority ethnic groups. Such individuals should receive services appropriate to their needs, not only when they happen to live in local authorities where a significant proportion of the population are from such groups, but also when they represent an isolated household in a largely all-white community.

References

Association of Metropolitan Authorities (1990) *Contracts for Social Care: the Local Authority View*, AMA, London.

Barnes, M. and Miller, N. (eds) (1988) 'Performance measurement in personal social services', *Research, Policy and Planning*, Vol. 6. No. 2, pp. 1–47.

Bartlett, W., Propper, C., Wilson, D. and Le Grand, J. (1994) (eds) *Quasi-Markets and Community Care*, School for Advanced Urban Studies, Bristol.

Common, R. and Flynn, N. (1992) *Contracting for Care*, Joseph Rowntree Foundation, York.

Davies, B. and Knapp, M. (1988) 'Costs and residential care', in Sinclair, I. (ed.), *Residential Care: the Research Reviewed*, HMSO, London.

DoH (Department of Health) (1989) *Community Care in the Next Decade and Beyond*, HMSO, London.

DoH (Department of Health) (1991) *Community Care in the Next Decade and Beyond: Policy Guidance*, HMSO, London.

Flynn, N. (1990) 'Seasonal business', *Insight*, 10 October.

Forder, J., Knapp, M. and Wistow, G. (1996) 'Competition in the mixed economy', *Journal of Social Policy*, Vol. 25 Part 2, pp. 201–22.

Foster, P. (1983) *Access to Welfare: an Introduction to Welfare Rationing*, Macmillan, London.

Hadley, R. and Clough, R. (1996) *Care in Chaos: Frustration and Challenge in Community Care*, Cassell, London.

Hoggett, P. (1991) 'The new public sector management', *Policy and Politics*, Vol. 19, No. 4, pp. 243–56.

Hoyes, L., Lart, R., Means, R. and Taylor, M. (1994) *Community Care in Transition*, Joseph Rowntree Foundation, York.

Le Grand, J. (1990) *Quasi-Markets and Social Policy*, School for Advanced Urban Studies, Bristol.

Le Grand, J. and Bartlett, W. (1993) (eds) *Quasi-Markets and Social Policy*, Macmillan, Basingstoke.

Lewis, J. and Glennerster, H. (1996) *Implementing the New Community Care*, Open University Press, Buckingham.

Means, R. and Langan, J. (1996) 'Charging and quasi-markets in community care: implications for elderly people with dementia', *Social Policy and Administration*, Vol. 30, No. 3, pp. 244–6.

Means, R. and Hoyes, L., Lart, R. and Taylor M. (1994) 'Quasi-markets and community care: towards user empowerment?', in Bartlett, W. *et al.* (eds), *Quasi-Markets in the Welfare State*, School for Advanced Urban Studies, Bristol, pp. 158–83.

Means, R. and Smith, R. (1994) *Community Care: Policy and Practice*, Macmillan, Basingstoke.

Means, R. and Smith, R. (1996) *Community Care, Housing and Homelessness: Issues, Obstacles and Innovative Practice*, Policy Press, Bristol.

Miller, C. (1991) 'Hungry for megabytes', *Social Work Today*, 4 April.

NFHA (National Federation of Housing Associations) (1994) *Housing Associations in the Community Care Marketplace*, NFHA, London.

Smith, G. and Cantley, C. (1985) *Assessing Health Care: A Study in Organisational Evaluation*, Open University Press, Milton Keynes.

Taylor, M., Langan, J. and Hoggett, P. (1995) *Encouraging Diversity: Voluntary and Private Organisations in Community Care*, Arena, Aldershot.

Wistow, G., Knapp, M., Hardy, B., Forder, J., Manning, R. and Kendall, J. (1996) *Social Care Markets: Progress and Prospects*, Open University Press, Buckingham.

Wistow, G. (1995) 'Aspirations and realities: Community Care at the crossroads', *Health and Social Care at the Crossroads*, Vol. 3, No. 4, pp. 227–40.

33

Elfrida Rathbone Islington: An Experience of Contracting

CHRISTINA SCHWABENLAND

In 1991 Elfrida Rathbone Islington took over from the local authority the running of a residential hostel for people with learning difficulties. Although such contractual arrangements quickly became commonplace, this was the first of its kind for the local authority and for Elfrida Rathbone Islington. Eighteen months after the negotiations we asked Christina Schwabenland to write an account of the experience from her perspective as Director of Elfrida Rathbone Islington. This account forms the first part of the chapter that follows. For the second edition of *Community Care: A Reader* we asked Christina Schwabenland to bring the story up to date with an overview of the whole five years' experience. The result is section 33.4: 'Overview from five years on'.

33.1 Background

Elfrida Rathbone Islington is a registered charity and limited company that for over 70 years has developed and run services for people in Islington with moderate learning difficulties. Prior to negotiating a new contract with the London Borough of Islington we ran three community education projects: an under fives' unit a literacy unit and a groupwork and activities unit (the latter for adults). We had three housing projects: a registered hostel for 12 residents and seven staff; and two houses with bedsits and flats and minimal support. We also run Elfrida's Cafe – a training scheme in catering and employment skills. We work with approximately 2000 users per year.

In June 1989 we were approached by the local authority and asked if we would be interested in taking over the social-services-run local hostel for 21 people with moderate learning difficulties. The impetus came from social services and there was never any question of competitive tendering. It was easy to see why Islington approached us. We were the largest voluntary organisation working with people with learning difficulties in the borough, we had an established track record and the work of our other hostel was well respected. We had an equal opportunities policy and trade union recognition – both important factors to the local authority, which had gone on record as saying that it would not contract out its existing services to the private sector or to voluntary organisations without good employment policies.

Islington's motives were primarily financial. The government had created a loophole whereby a resident who lived in a hostel run by the voluntary or private sector was entitled to claim a Department of Social Security (DSS) benefit called board-and-lodgings money. If they lived in a hostel run by the local authority or health authority, however, they were not entitled to this benefit and the authority had to pick up most of the costs. Therefore, simply by transferring ownership of the hostel from one sector to another, a large amount of central government money would be attracted into the borough.

The government had created this anomaly because it believed that the independent sector could run services better, because of smaller size, flexibility and closer proximity to service users. Islington never publicly said that they shared this belief or that it was a motivating factor. However it was occasionally hinted at privately and for us it had to be an important concern. We would not have wanted to take over the hostel if we did not think we could run it at least as well, and preferably better, than the local authority.

This was *our* main reason for agreeing to begin the process of negotiations. Our primary interest had to be that of providing the best possible service for people with learning difficulties. But we also had pragmatic reasons – the security of a contract that meant the local authority, our primary funder, needed us as much as we needed it, was very attractive.

33.2 The process of the negotiations

From the initial approach, it took over 18 months for us formally to take over the hostel. After we told the local authority that we were tentatively interested in proceeding we heard very little for about six months. Meetings were to be scheduled but somehow never happened. We used the time to find out as much as possible about any received wisdom about contracting in the great big world outside. The director (me!) took it on herself to do most of the leg work, especially in the early stages, and this took up a substantial amount of time. I went on courses on contracting and rang up everyone I knew who was involved in contracts. I made contact with the London Voluntary Service Council, the National Council of Voluntary Organisations and the Association of Residential Care. I discovered that a lot was being talked about the contracting out of existing services, but very little had, as yet, really happened, so there was little real experience upon which to draw.

However everyone I spoke to agreed that the most important element in negotiating a contract was to agree a statement of aims and objectives, because these would provide a firm base for negotiating the day-to-day bits and pieces. (The other important thing to do right at the beginning were the preliminary costings – but more of that later!)

For us this highlighted a major deficiency in our own organisation: we didn't have a clearly written statement of aims. So because we needed to have one in place by the time the negotiations began, we convened a small working party consisting of staff and management committee members, and drew up a statement of values, aims and objectives for the agency as a whole.

33.2.1 Negotiations begin

In January 1990 the first meetings with the leader of the council and ourselves took place and the negotiations were suddenly underway. We put our aims and objectives at the top of the agenda, but very little time was actually spent discussing them – about five minutes! The rest of the meeting concentrated on the practical issues that had to be resolved and a reasonable timetable was established.

All of a sudden there seemed to be vast numbers of meetings happening, nearly every week. Specific meetings were set up to deal with all the separate issues – the contract, the residents, staffing, finance, building works. I went to all of them. The local authority, of course, fielded different people for different meetings and no single officer was required to match the time commitment needed from us. Elfrida Rathbone established a sub-committee of management committee members who met regularly to talk through the issues that were coming up, and to give me support.

In March, nine months after the initial approach, we drafted a provisional working budget based on what was known about the current hostel budget and also on our experience of running our other hostel. Many costs were not known, as the local authority was not, at that stage, able completely to cost its services. We presented it to the leader of the council and a handful of other members and officers, and immediately sparks began to fly. Our initial budget gave the local authority only a very small saving on the current running costs of the hostel. The councillors were extremely unhappy and ordered us to go away and come back with something better. This was the first time that anyone had had a serious look at the finances.

The reasons why our budget seemed so high were various. First, we had allowed for management costs and various services that the local authority provided in-house and did not charge to individual projects. Second, our estimates for various unknown factors, such as building maintenance, were quite high because we wanted to minimise the risk factor: Third, our other hostel cared for a younger and more rumbustious group of people and our wear-and-tear costs were higher there.

So there was some scope for trimming costs. However what horrified us was the tone of the discussions at that and subsequent meetings. We felt that we had been harangued and browbeaten, and sent away to do better. Previous meetings had been conducted as if we were equals, each needing something from the other, and each prepared to negotiate and occasionally compromise. We had broad agreement on basic principles and a shared aim. But the finance meetings felt different. The underlying assumption suddenly seemed to be that our status was that of a rather junior department of the council that wasn't doing what it was supposed to do. Veiled and unclear threats were implied as to what might happen to our current grant aid if we did not produce a 'better' budget – one that would guarantee a higher level of savings for the council.

This was the most unpleasant and uncomfortable stage of the entire negotiations. We sat down with the officers of the finance department and eventually produced a compromise budget that we felt we could probably live with, and that produced a higher level of estimated savings to the council. We reduced our management costs a little, and lowered our assumptions about repairs and maintenance. The council increased their assumptions about staffing levels. In the end the negotiations continued.

33.2.2 Different understandings

But several significant things had emerged. One was about the difference in approach between the council and ourselves. We prepared budgets based on real assumptions about real costs. We were a smallish organisation with few resources, and our working budgets have to be as accurate as possible. The council used a lot of formulae, such as budgeting for a 10 per cent vacancy rate in staffing costs, which were just not appropriate for a small organisation. The council assumed a much lower rate of inflation than we did. Their approach seemed to be to underestimate costs and hope for the best, while ours was to get them as accurate as possible and build in a slight margin of error for unforeseen emergencies. Needless to say, we didn't entirely see eye to eye!

More importantly, there was no shared understanding of our status; this only emerged when we had a disagreement, and of course money was the issue over which that disagreement was most marked. We viewed ourselves as an autonomous organisation accountable to our management committee and our users. I think the local authority would have broadly agreed with that view, but they were our primary funders and expected us to satisfy certain criteria in order to receive funding from them. It felt to us as though beneath the finance negotiations the assumption of the councillors was that we were there to help them out of a fix, and that the finance officers felt we were obliged to manage the budget set for us. And indeed there seemed to be no objective clarity about these issues. We were constituted as an independent organisation. The council was our primary funder and could withdraw its funding if it wished the next day. We set our own budget for our hostels, but the local authority had to approve the level of the fee. The relationship was unclear and it seemed to me that it could only be managed if there was some degree of shared interpretation of these difficult areas. What emerged from this phase of the negotiations was that this consent and this understanding was partial. A negotiation like that involved so many disparate arms of the council; there may have been shared under-standing with a handful of officers in the social services department, but did that extend to the legal department, the buildings and maintenance?

Obviously in the end the negotiations continued and we papered over the cracks in our shared understanding. There were some negative sides to it – we did feel a little intimidated, and unsure of what would happen if we pulled out. We weren't sure the budget we ended up with would allow us to manage the hostel as we wanted. And we didn't quite know at what point the power balance had shifted, nor at what point we had become committed to the hostel takeover. Up till that time we had thought that we could simply pull out of the negotiations if they didn't go as we wanted, but that no longer felt possible.

However the other reasons for getting involved still remained; we met the residents and their families for the first time, and that provided more impetus to continue. A series of meetings was organised between ourselves, the residents and their carers to discuss the transfer. On the whole these went well, but it was rather distressing that many of the residents were deeply concerned about losing the current staff and worried about who the new staff would be, and there was no obvious way of allaying that concern before the new staff were appointed.

Meanwhile the draft contract was written, primarily by us. Initially there were joint meetings to discuss its content but we mainly took on the task of drafting it in order to save time. This proved very fortuitous as we were able to write it as we wanted and to ensure that it contained everything we wanted it to have.

In the early days of the negotiations various options about staffing were suggested, but we decided almost immediately that we ourselves would like to interview everyone who was to become an employee of Elfrida Rathbone, and that we didn't want to inherit staff whom we had had no part in selecting. The local authority unions NALGO and NUPE [now UNISON] were involved in negotiations with the council, and they asked for preferential interviews to be offered to anyone from the old staff team who was interested in applying to work for Elfrida Rathbone. The unions were interested in seeing a contract of employment and in comparing terms and conditions between the two agencies. There were some differences: salaries were on the same grades, but our sickness benefit was not as good as the local authority's. When the time to recruit the staff drew near, we asked the previous staff to let us know if they wanted preferential interviews. By 'preferential' we meant that we would interview them on their own ahead of any other applicants and offer them the jobs if they met the specification; we would only advertise externally if we still had vacancies. But none of them applied for the jobs. The local authority had a guaranteed redeployment policy, so the staff either took voluntary early retirement or were redeployed on their existing terms and conditions.

I have no idea whether or not any of the staff considered applying to work for us. I do know that they felt unhappy about the transfer and that the group had become a quite a powerful source of support for the individuals within it, and I speculate that it would have been hard indeed to break ranks! Also, of course, they had all applied for local authority jobs and had no commitment to or any real understanding of the voluntary sector. They kept referring to the transfer as a 'privatisation'. The unions did circulate a press release, fairly early on, hoping to mobilise support to stop the transfer, but only our local paper picked it up, and it didn't have any repercussions. After that the staff and unions cooperated in the negotiations, although they made it clear they did not think the idea was a good one.

One point they raised against the transfer, which I think was valid, was that the local authority would lose the ability to be flexible and innovative with their resources. The funding agreement was very tightly circumscribed – we could only take residents who could claim board-and-lodgings money, and so on – whereas had the local authority kept the hostel, in theory they could have changed its function and been more flexible about whom they took in. For example they could have turned it into a home for the elderly while our constitution allowed us to work only with people with learning difficulties. I think this is an interesting point. However we pressed to have the contract limited to five years and only to be renewed after a very thorough review.

33.2.3 Under new management

A steering committee was established by the local authority – chaired by the assistant director of social services and the principal assistant, with input from the finance, legal and architects' departments and the registration officer. We established a timetable for provisional takeover in mid to late autumn 1990.

33.2.4 Delays and stress

Several things happened to delay the handover. First, we discovered that although the hostel normally had 22 spaces, only 16 people were currently resident, and six of those were due to move out before we took over. We had done the budget on the basis of a minimum of 17 people and instead there were only likely to be 10! We sent three mailings to all the social workers in the department to drum up new referrals, but two months later we had received only two names. It became clear at that point that none of us had done long-term strategic thinking about what the need in Islington really was for this unit. No one really knew why the take-up of places was initially so poor and it seemed risky to make long-term plans without that information.

After much discussion we decided to go ahead on the basis of a smaller staff team and a smaller number of residents, and to retain the option of increasing the number at a later date if the need was there. But the overall lack of strategic planning was an issue for both agencies to address.

We negotiated a two-week handover between our new staff team and the outgoing team, who were being relocated in other jobs by the local authority. The handover went reasonably well, but it was clearly a stressful time for all concerned, as the residents were unsettled. The previous staff team was feeling a lot of antagonism towards us, and our new staff team felt somewhat overwhelmed by the amount of information they needed to learn quickly. We organised one day of team building for them with an outside facilitator, which helped give them a sense of identity. It proved very difficult for everyone to manage the boundaries between their obligations to the residents and loyalty to each other, and we discovered that some crucial pieces of information about residents had not been given to us because they involved disciplinary issues within the council. There were no clear guidelines about what we did and did not need to know, and of course there was no shared understanding of whether we were insiders or outsiders. This confusion was even reflected in such mundane issues as whether or not we should have access to the controls of the central heating system, normally restricted to only certain council employees. This was such a new situation with so little precedent that there was no blueprint for working through issues such as these.

33.2.5   The contract

The contract, however, did make the relationship between us fairly explicit, and it provided a very relevant and valuable basis for negotiations. The social services officers, councillors and ourselves were happy with the original draft and it was sent off to the council's legal department to be turned into a legally binding document. But here we ran into problems. The lawyers came up with the proposal that the basic agreement between us should be in the form of a lease, with an appendix containing the operating policy of the hostel. We said that, to us, an operational policy was a practice document about the day-to-day running of the hostel, and that it didn't need to be legally drawn up. What was needed was some sort of management agreement between us. The legal department didn't understand what we meant; we would be managing the hostel, so what might the agreement need to be about? It soon emerged that the legal department were blissfully (or not so blissfully!) unaware of all the recent discussions in the world at large about contracting. They didn't know what contracts, in the sense that the word was now being used, were all about.

This debate continued for several months until we finally gave them a book published by the NCVO entitled *12 Charity Contracts* which proved that it could be done! From that point on things progressed quickly. Our original document was unearthed, and nearly a year after it was written it came back barely changed, ready for official signatures.

33.2.6   Partnerships

On 11 February 1991 we finally took over the hostel. Eighteen months later building works were unfinished, the contract still needed some fine tuning and we were daily uncovering things that needed resolution – such as who would maintain the burglar alarm and the boiler, especially if the boiler belonged to a leasing company rather than to the council. But these problems were all manageable, if infuriating. The new staff had a great deal of enthusiasm and, generally speaking, the residents adjusted to the change remarkably well. We started regular residents' meetings so they would have a formal forum to plan with us how the hostel would be run in the future.

On the whole we felt quite optimistic about the future, but we had some reservations. The financial arrangements carried some risk: the local authority had not guaranteed to maintain a fixed number of spaces, and as the budget was worked out on the basis of a per capita fee, we needed to make sure we had enough residents to be financially viable. The question remained of the need for this kind of hostel in the long term. We established a review group, which would meet quarterly in the first year and six-monthly during the following four years. Its function was to monitor the work on the ground and also the terms of the partnership agreement, and it was hoped that it would provide a forum where these and many other questions could be raised.

33.3   The experience of negotiating the contract

When I looked back at the negotiations eighteen months later, I could see that they had had a very significant effect on our agency.

Time. The negotiations took up an incalculable amount of time and energy. The management committee regularly had extra meetings. The finance officer spent weeks drawing up new budgets, looking at the knock-on financial effects for the agency as a whole, cash flow projections, yet more budgets, inventories, new petty cash systems, DSS liaison. The social work coordinator was seconded to the hostel for two months to get it up and running. The administrator handled the staff recruitment side and our advertisements attracted over 400 enquiries about the jobs. For all those months I made this project my top priority and today couldn't begin to calculate the time spent on it.

Management system. The negotiations exposed all sorts of problems with our internal management system. I've already mentioned one – our previous lack of a defined statement of aims and objectives. Many other things were thrown up during those months: a lack of clarity about who our clients were; differentials in pay scales throughout the agency; and a lack of clarity about decision-making processes and who should or should not be consulted. I personally viewed this as a wholly positive side-effect, and found it incredibly useful to have so many issues exposed, but it may not be a process that smaller organisations would be prepared for, or able to respond to.

Growth. Elfrida Rathbone grew to be the single largest provider of residential services for people with learning difficulties in Islington, but this happened by default and we really didn't think through what this might mean in the future.

33.4   Overview from five years on

Five years on the contract is up for renewal. How have things progressed in the meantime?

33.4.1   The residents

Of the original group of 11 residents at the beginning of the contract, three have since died. Three others have moved into their own flats and now live independent of support from the hostel. Three residents who moved in after we took over have also moved into their own flats, and a further two have moved to smaller hostels.

Increased autonomy. For the residents living in the hostel there have been some significant changes. They are more involved in decision making. Early on we established a weekly residents' meeting. Agenda items include weekly menus, where to go on holiday, and how to deal with conflicting needs and desires such as loud music and sleep! Residents are also involved in staff recruitment and in regular presentations to the management committee.

The transition. Although the residents quickly felt at ease with the new staff team, for the first year they talked a lot about the 'old' staff team and were clearly disturbed by their abrupt disappearance. The day centre and a psychologist from the Community Team for People with Learning Difficulties set up a weekly group to give the residents the opportunity to talk about the changes and begin to come to terms with them. We discovered that there had been a number of institutionalised practices, such as a weekly 'weigh-in' after supper on Tuesday evenings, which we immediately stopped. Although the residents responded very positively to the new, more flexible 'regime', the changes were obviously unsettling. However it is clear, through direct feedback from the residents and from people who knew them well 'before' and 'after', that the quality of their lives has improved dramatically. There are, of course, all the myriad challenges that come with greater freedom, but no-one speaks nostalgically of the past.

Choice. The criticism has been made that 'giving' the hostel to a voluntary organisation to manage did not result in any increased choice for the residents. Although they were kept informed during the process of negotiation, they had no real say in the decision either of the local authority to contract out the hostel, or of the voluntary organisation as to whether or not to take it on. There was no increase in the amount or diversity of services available.

In one sense this is an absolutely valid point. However on a day-to-day basis we have worked very hard to ensure that the residents have as much autonomy as possible within the hostel and that their wishes are respected. And the advent of the community care legislative reforms has resulted in the development of new services which are having a direct impact on the hostel.

33.4.2   Developments

Homelink. One of these is Homelink, a new, supported-living scheme, that we set up using a small surplus to 'pump prime' the development costs. The impetus for the scheme came directly from the hostel, as a number of residents wanted to live more independently, in their own flats, but were unable to do so without support. The contract provides for three nominations a year for local authority housing stock, but we had been unable to take these up because there was no available scheme to provide tailored, individual packages of support to people with learning difficulties within their own homes. And without this support they could not move.

Three years ago a surplus of income over operating costs accumulated because the hostel ran at full occupancy for the whole year. This meant we were able, with the local authority's permission, to employ a development worker to set up the new scheme. Within six months three residents from the hostel had moved into their own flats, with support ranging from two to thirty-five hours per week. The following year two more residents moved out and another three are planning their moves now.

A research project conducted by psychologists attached to the Community Team for People with Learning Difficulties, found (not surprisingly!) that all those residents who had moved were very much happier with their new living arrangements.

Homelink is organised so that the service users can decide for themselves the times at which they receive support and with which areas of their lives they would like help (for example one service user has become a regular and highly valued volunteer at a local lunch club for Irish older people). The Homelink support workers all receive regular supervision and training, and a quality assurance system has been set up to monitor the scheme.

Registration requirements. In the last two years new, more stringent requirements have been introduced for hostels registered under the 1984 Registered Homes Act. The main implication for us is that all the bedrooms are too small to meet the new requirements, although there is a very generous amount of communal space. As the contract clearly specifies that it is the local authority's responsibility to make sure the building meets registration standards we are not expected to fund a major rebuilding programme, although we have carried out a host of smaller improvements within the basic budget.

33.4.3 The future

We had been offered the contract on an open-ended basis but decided to limit it to five years. This was not because we expected that we would no longer want to run the hostel, but to build in some capacity for taking stock and reviewing. We were concerned that implementation of the community care reforms would affect us in ways that at that stage were hard to predict. We also took on board the criticism that the hostel was too big and too institutional to satisfy current thinking about good practice.

We are now renegotiating the second contract. In the last two years the rate of referrals has slowed considerably. This is undoubtedly partly due to the development of a range of alternatives to residential care, Homelink for one. At least three of the direct referrals to Homelink were people who would probably have moved into the hostel, had there been no other option.

The other major development is the new registration requirements, and this effectively means that the hostel will soon be too expensive to run. To carry out the building works necessary to give each resident a bedroom large enough to meet the new standards would be horrendously expensive, and also very disruptive for the residents. It would also result in reduced occupancy, which would make the unit cost unrealistically high.

So I think that the writing is on the wall for the hostel. We are asking for a two to three-year contract, during which time the current residents should be resettled into smaller units, mostly one or two-bedroom flats. In the interim period, before the hostel closes, we will be able to offer a small respite service, which will make good use of the staff and the increasing number of empty beds.

33.5 Conclusions

I think the new plans are wholly positive. The original contract enabled us to provide a better service to the residents. Now we will be able to move all of them into smaller, community-based housing where most, if not all, will have their own tenancies. They will have individual packages of support that will give them much more control over how they live their lives. We have demonstrated that taking on a contract does not have to ring the death knell for creativity and innovation.

However when I talk to other colleagues in the field I wonder whether we are the exception that proves the rule. There are a number of factors that make our case unusual. One is that we were effectively allowed to write our own contract. Although there was some very hard bargaining on the budget, we were nonetheless able to design the service ourselves. Increasingly organisations are being given tight specifications against which they have to submit competitive tenders, and the scope to modify or redesign the service may be very limited indeed.

We have also been able to maintain an effective partnership with the local authority that is more akin to a collaboration than to a 'purchaser–provider' relationship. We see ourselves as working together to develop and deliver good services that are appropriate to the needs of people with learning difficulties in the borough. Without the support of the local authority we would not have been able to develop Homelink, and we would not now be jointly working on a reprovision scheme.

Another very worrying trend is the increased emphasis on regulation and control. This is an unintended consequence of the purchaser–provider split, which is effectively distancing the two sides. However all sorts of new mechanisms are being created to bridge the divide. Increased regulation is a means of giving some direct (although intended to be indirect) control over where the money goes and what is being paid for. But by defining so rigidly what the service is meant to do and how it is meant to do it, the possibility of creativity and flexibility is greatly reduced. This is a serious danger to the autonomy of the organisations providing the services. In place of the mutuality of collaboration there is an increasing atmosphere of distrust, which will benefit no-one.

34

Disability, Discrimination and Local Authority Social Services: The Users' Perspective*

CLARE EVANS

In discussing developments in Wiltshire social services, the particular focus that I can bring from Wiltshire Users' Network is the opportunity that the community care legislation has given us as service users to influence services for change and remove some of the barriers to participation. I think there is also a perspective from disabled people and from our role and our experience in the Users' Network about the role that social services departments can play in enabling that to happen.

Our organisation is a totally independent user-controlled organisation: 75 per cent of our management committee are service users. We are resourced by our service agreement – a legally binding service agreement with social services for the sum of £58 000 with the two aims of facilitating direct links between service users and the social services department and providing a network of support for service users countywide. Membership is free to all service users in Wiltshire, including potential users and ex-users. But the particular perspectives which prevail – and from where we get our energy – are the disability movement and the psychiatric survivor movement. We have 350 contacts on our mailing list. Some of these are individual users and others are

---

* This is an edited version of a chapter that was first published in Zarb, G. (ed.) (1995) *Removing Disabling Barriers*, Policy Studies Institute, London.

contacts in user groups of all kinds. We have also just received funding of £25 000 on our annual grant from the Wiltshire and Bath Health Commission.

It is important to us that our involvement is based on our terms and within a background of rights: the rights that we have as citizens like any others – the democratic right to participate in society and the right to have choice and control over our lives – which must mean that we have as much choice and control as we can over the services we receive. And certainly the one informs the other in the sense that that is what we are aiming at in all the user involvement. It is not to save social services money or make the services more efficient or anything like that (although that will be a spin-off for them). It is to make them more appropriate for all service users' needs. Obviously not everyone wants to join in collective user involvement. But hopefully, by enabling local authorities to learn from users' expertise directly, there is the opportunity for those who do chose to participate to change services for all service users. So user involvement has its place within the wider context of removing barriers to disabled people's participation.

We are very proactive in seeking opportunities for user involvement. We work on the principle that it is a matter of riddling the system with as many user perspectives as possible, and you win some and you lose some, but on the whole the more opportunities you develop for user involvement the more impact you can make. The aim is not participation for the sake of it and it is not to save ourselves having to sit at home watching television – which is what sometimes people think you would be doing otherwise. It is actually to bring about change. Users in the Network say, 'what's the point of me going and being involved with that, what effect will it have?' – and they will not go and participate unless they know that they are going to be able to have an effect by giving their perspectives as service users. So it is very much the emphasis of wanting to change the culture: from the dependency that we experience as people who use social services and health services and other agencies to meet our care needs; from the concept of us being dependent on them to the concept of having our right to independent living in the community and our right to help to achieve that. And it is partly just by participating; we have found that if you bring people who usually work with disabled people together with disabled people themselves, then the stereotypes begin to disappear and users' expertise is recognised. It is also partly that user expertise is being brought directly to bear on services, making it possible for professionals to learn how to change them, to be more empowering.

First, our involvement in purchasing. We have carried out research into need and developed a different model of research by groups of service users meeting together to identify gaps in information provision, for example, and then drawing on the research they did with other service users to make policy recommendations. We are also involved in designing service specifications, for example, in the specifications for domiciliary home care. One wonders how people, professionals, could have written service specifications without first learning from disabled people what the issues are. You want to be able to tell people what tasks *you* want done and not have the tasks listed for you.

Second, we also get involved with developing policy proposals, being involved right from the start. We do not put much store on consultation, because you cannot affect things when people have already half-way decided what is happening. But if you are involved right at the start then there is that opportunity. This was particularly the case perhaps with the Wiltshire Independent Living Fund, to which I refer again later.

Third, we have been involved in the development of care management and assessment. Care management was designed to be an empowering process, but most people find it is quite difficult to feel that. What is assessment, for example, and how does the process really support the individual? I think the development of care management in Wiltshire, and the way users have been involved with planning and developing the assessment form, has changed it from the sort of very structured questions about what you are not able to do, to the assessment form we have designed now, which is much more enabling and builds on what help *we* need. That has been important and that direct influence has hopefully improved the process for everyone. Training staff in care management has involved service users at all stages. The model in Wiltshire – because we quickly wanted to involve lots of services users – was about users as equal participants with welfare professionals. We have found that has certain spin-offs, although it is not the only model to be followed. We are not up there as tutors that everyone can criticise and reject. As equal participants, being paid to participate, we can share our expertise with other people in group discussions and so on and that has had quite an impression, particularly when a wide range of users' views are heard. Disabled people have found this kind of involvement particularly empowering because the effect of our involvement in changing professional attitudes is very noticeable.

Fourth, another area of activity has been the development of accessible information. User involvement in information provision is about enabling and working with local authorities to enable them to make the information they provide accessible to service users. If you are the officer in charge of information, the last thing you can know is what a service user needs to know about assessment; you are inevitably caught up in the system of jargon. So, to have a workshop which brings service users together to write that sort of information is hopefully an improvement on the system. I remember, for example, being involved in the training of staff who deliver home care services. In one session, it took a whole morning before one of the senior home carers said, 'So you mean it's not making assumptions about your need'. You know, I think we continually underestimate how difficult it is for people once they are in the system to start from where we are.

Fifth, we also have an involvement in service evaluation. When there are reviews of services, we expect to have users there as part of those working groups from the start in order to bring a users' perspective to bear. It is important to have service users defining the questions to ask when an evaluation is being carried out. For example, if the Inspection Unit are doing a survey about the home care service, then we have a meeting with them first and say what the key issues are in terms of what questions to ask; and, hopefully, that can inform the whole survey. Advising on appropriate methods of research is another issue. Does it always have to be able-bodied people interviewing disabled people, or can disabled people have a role to play in getting a more realistic view of people's views of services? People feel safer giving their real views to people they know will understand, who are seen as independent of services, and who do not have the power to penalise people for their views by taking services away.

In order to achieve effective user involvement and remove the barriers which prevent our participation, social services departments must recognise, value and resource user-controlled organisations. We have found in Wiltshire as disabled people that, through our own organisation, we have empowered each other to participate effectively and we are accountable to other users. I am employed by the Network and I am accountable to the management committee of users – and that for us is the essence of user involvement in Wiltshire. It is absolutely key. We get several enquiries a week about our work and I groan when people phone up and say 'I've been appointed to do user involvement' and you say, 'Well are you a service user?' – 'No'; 'Do you work for a user led organisation?' – 'No'. It is very difficult to know how to help such people to change the whole system round, to have the opportunity of building on the energy and the expertise of the disability movement, to inform the way services have developed, as we have been able to do in Wiltshire.

Three things follow from users having their own organisations and the recognition of the need for that by social services departments. One is that the agenda becomes a users' agenda and it is possible to start from identified need. It is not a matter of just fiddling about with the services at the edges; you can start at the point of what people need and repattern services accordingly. Second, we can get the good practice right; it is about paying for interpreters to come to meetings, for people to have their transport costs met and so on, and it enables local authorities to avoid tokenism because we can advise them on that too. We network with all the disability groups and individuals that are in touch with the Network in Wiltshire, so hopefully we get as good a cross-section of users' views as is possible. As a group of disempowered people, we feel a responsibility to reach out to marginalised groups. Older people, for example may find it much more difficult to participate for all sorts of reasons. People from ethnic minorities are also often marginalised. Third, progress in user involvement depends on trust being developed between users and allies. It has helped us that some of our allies are more senior members of the social services department, but at the same time it is actually quite important to recognise the ongoing imbalances of power and the ongoing tensions and we make sure things are not too cosy. Sometimes there are arguments and sometimes it is quite painful, but it is a matter of moving on once they have happened, learning as we go.

I want to turn now to the process of establishing the Wiltshire Independent Living Fund (WILF) and the role that users have played in that. In fact there have been five different roles.

First, once the Social Services Committee made the decision to place the cash into the community to set up an independent living fund, it was suggested that the network put the department in touch with service users who could develop the policy proposals and the financial criteria from their own experience of independent living. There were eight disabled people enabled by two staff from social services plus one or two voluntary organisation representatives to develop the policy proposals and criteria for the fund. Second, from this grew a proposal for the support service for applicants to the fund to be provided through our network, making use of the user expertise of people already living independently. The support service assists disabled people with the assessment process and with enabling them to employ their own staff directly and so on. Third, also out of the policy proposals grew the idea of the awards being made by a grants panel consisting of disabled people who will be making decisions about £1m worth of funding. Fourth, another way in which users' expertise will be used in connection with WILF is through monitoring the progress of the scheme. The policy group that set it up will be getting in touch with the users of the scheme to make sure that it is working according to their expectations. Finally, the by-product that I guess none of us imagined at the start was that we actually managed to change social services mainstream charging policy to get it in line with the criteria that users had set up. One of the things we recognised as important was that people should be financially assessed independently of their partners. We managed to persuade the Social Services Committee that this was a change for the better – which we felt was quite good.

The other area of work which it seems important for social services to enable us as disabled people to do is to run our own services if we choose. We do have opportunities for the Network to do that in the current year as we have got a budget of £250,000 this year to run our own services. Also, we made all the funding applications through the usual joint finance and departmental processes. I think sometimes people say disabled people's organisations should have a level playing field with other independent organisations in bidding for services. But, I am not sure we should not have it tilted in our favour because there is so much expertise in the disabled community that we know we can provide services very well – particularly if it is making use of things that we have real expertise in, such as provision of information, advocacy, and independent living.

There are five services we are running this year. The Patients' Council Project which is based at a local psychiatric hospital; the Information Federation, which has grown out of the knowledge that we have learned about schemes in other parts of the country; there is an Information Drop-in Centre in Salisbury which will be run by disabled people, employing disabled people and so on; the support service for WILF which I have mentioned; and, because of our concern about the lack of participation by people from ethnic minorities in the Network, and the feeling that we were excluding them as we seemed to gain more power, we developed a proposal with allies for a Living Options Partnership site. This is about reaching disabled people in Afro-Caribbean and Asian communities in Wiltshire and enabling them to access services.

I hope that this demonstrates something of the opportunities that we have had in Wiltshire and the support we should be able to expect from social services departments to enable us to participate in the services we receive.

35

*The Right to Make Choices**

ANN MACFARLANE

The personal assistant is someone every successful company director commands along with a Filofax. A personal assistant makes each day organised and more bearable, and adds those touches which humanise lifestyles. Until recently they have remained almost entirely within the province of the business community, but now the personal assistant is coming to change the lifestyles of disabled people.

In April 1988, Jane and I, both disabled people, sought a meeting with the Director of Social Services in Kingston-upon-Thames to enlist support for the development of our own personal assistance packages. It was crucial that we went together and supported each other as so often disabled people seek assistance in isolation and are marginalised and rejected or ignored.

Two disabled people who were able to identify and present similar requirements to the director resulted in recognition and, in April 1989, a pilot project was ready to go before members of the social services committee.

Meanwhile, in Strasbourg, disabled people were holding an independent living conference where it was resolved: 'Personal assistance services are a human and civil right which must be provided at no cost to the user'.

Following our initial meeting, the director of social services suggested that Jane and I should prepare a document setting out our requirements. Coincidentally our draft personal assistance package proposals were similar in principle and content to the Strasbourg recommendations so we felt we were on course.

It took Jane and me, who are both professional business women, five months to produce the document. Although we were clear about what

*This paper was first published in *Community Care*, 1 November 1990.

assistance we were seeking, it was, nevertheless, a painful process progressing our personal and financial self-assessments while 'laying bare' our private lives to establish what should be a basic human right. At the time of our applications, Jane requested 35 hours' assistance each week; I applied for 14.

We sat through the tensions of the Social Services committee. We have different experiences and backgrounds, mine mainly institutionalised, and the thought of committee members discussing our basic human needs, when probably none of them had ever experienced institutionalisation and never lacked control over their own lives, overwhelmed me.

Most of all I wanted flexible support which would enable me to work and socialise and it had already taken a great deal of confidence and organisation to return to the business world because of the difficulty in getting support when needed.

The pilot project was approved unanimously without further invasion of our privacy. The scheme was initially agreed for one year starting in April 1989 with a progress report presented to committee members in November.

The packages would allow each of us to arrange our own system of obtaining personal support, employing the personal assistants directly and controlling their conditions of service. In this way we would retain full control over our day-to-day living. It was to be a free service with the money paid directly into separate bank accounts which we would set up.

The job description requested that personal assistants be responsible for all or some of the following tasks: bathing, dressing, toileting, hair care, cooking, bedmaking, laundry, shopping, light gardening, sorting papers, books, files, maintaining electric wheelchairs, plus any other tasks which come within a personal or domestic situation.

The implementation of this unique initiative would include the appointment of a liaison officer between the two of us and the Department of Social Services, acceptance of the self-assessment procedure, as well as acknowledgement of our own understanding of our capabilities and need for assistance with the professional's role as that of adviser and listener.

Jane and I live within 200 yards of each other and planned to advertise the posts and interview applicants together. We had previously decided that it would be cost- and time-effective to share some of the personal assistants, perhaps employing one main assistant each as there are differences in our age and personalities.

We advertised in local newsagents as it was relatively inexpensive and hoped it would bring more responses from the area. We found a suitable number of applicants to set up the project by June.

Each employee was given a basic contract which included: 'You will be expected to respect each home and confidentiality, be a good timekeeper, and be responsible for your own insurance and tax.' It was important that Jane and I checked with our own insurance companies to ensure we were covered for people working on our premises. We were surprised that, in an area with low unemployment, it had been relatively easy to find people to cover early mornings and late evenings. We also selected people who had very few hours to give but who were willing to undertake just one of the tasks.

However, applicants were encouraged to undertake any task and it was decided to implement the project only partially for Jane and me to get used to being employers and to absorb a number of different personalities into our lives. I found this easier than I had anticipated and perhaps this was enhanced by the fact that I went from a state which 'imprisoned' to one which 'liberated'.

Between us Jane and I employ 10 personal assistants to undertake 49 hours each week. We keep our own records of when assistants work and we have retained all the assistants we initially engaged except one, who has now returned to her homeland.

The pilot project is now growing out of its embryonic state and the word has spread to other disabled people. Jane and I feel that the scheme's success lies in the coherent way in which it was established

There is a commitment to expand our pilot project to involve two or three other disabled people while developing new schemes for disabled people who are not yet ready or who do not want to take on the role and responsibility of employer. As we begin to empower disabled people they will demand flexible support services. With lifestyles in our control we will truly be contributors to the national economy, and not the 'burdens' we are so often accused of being.

Every disabled person has the right to make choices and decisions over their own lives and Jane and I are determined that we will be part of the momentum for demanding more personal assistant packages and other flexible support services from which disabled people can make informed choices.

Currently an information pack and short training video is being produced based on this project which will enable disabled people and service providers to develop their own individual and personal scheme.

36

Involving People With Learning Difficulties in Meetings*

ANDREA WHITTAKER

The meeting had been in progress for twenty minutes. There was a knock on the door and in came the last member of the committee. He was empty-handed. He glanced rather uncertainly around the room. He was greeted briefly and invited to take a seat. Discussion on the current agenda item continued. After a while, the latecomer began to join in: some comments were relevant to the topic – some were not. Now and then the latecomer would take up a point enthusiastically and talk at length in a way which appeared to the rest of the committee to bear little or no relation to the subject under discussion.

Nothing particularly unusual in that brief scenario you might say. We all know people who come to meetings late, have forgotten their meeting papers, and who waste everyone else's time by waffling on about their own particular hobby-horse! However, what made that scene different from dozens of similar occasions was that the latecomer happened to be a person with learning difficulties (former term: 'mental handicap').

It is now quite common for policy and planning documents about services for people with learning difficulties to include statements about the importance of service users participating directly in service planning and delivery. Unfortunately though, these are often no more than general statements of intent and nothing is said about how these intentions will be turned into action.

This chapter discusses one way in which service users can participate in the development of services, looking at how people with learning dif-

---

* This chapter was first published in Winn, L. (ed.) (1990) *Power to the People*, King's Fund Centre, London, pp. 41–8.

ficulties can play an effective part in meetings. It focuses on meetings specifically because, however much we may complain about their frequency or question their usefulness, they remain an important and often-used method of communication in service-providing agencies such as health authorities or social services departments.

This chapter focuses on people with learning difficulties, partly because of the author's experience (as advisor to the self-advocacy organisation People First) and partly because general progress towards participation by service users in Britain is more widely developed amongst people with learning difficulties than amongst other groups such as people with physical disabilities or mental health service users. Through membership of student or trainee committees in day centres and the activities of groups such as People First, many people with learning difficulties have become skilled at speaking up for themselves and identifying what they want from services.

To return to the scenario described at the beginning of this chapter. A keen observer of the scene might have noticed other ways in which people were behaving differently. Most contributions to the discussion would be acknowledged in some way by others present – by a nod of the head, murmurs of agreement (or disagreement), by eye contact; in these small ways, individual contributions would be woven into the general ebb and flow of the discussion. But comments from the person with learning difficulties seemed to be handled differently. Sometimes they were passed over – almost ignored. If the comment seemed irrelevant then silence descended and people seemed to be feeling rather uneasy. On the other hand, sometimes he was given the floor and allowed to talk at considerable length, unchecked by fellow committee members or by the chairperson. But when he stopped, discussion among the rest resumed as if he had not spoken at all.

This story illustrates several key issues which need to be considered when thinking about how to involve service users most appropriately in meetings.

36.1 Professionals with problems with participation

One of the most important points to emerge from the story is that it isn't only service users who may lack the necessary skills. Even when professionals are committed to the idea of participation, they may still find it difficult. The fact that someone may have worked with people with learning difficulties for many years may not mean that they find this sort of communication easy. For some people, moving up the career ladder may mean they end up spending little or no time in face-to-face contact with service users. But even when people do work on a daily basis with users they may still never really get to know the people they work along-side.

Genuine participation in situations like the one described above means involving service users as real partners. Services do not tend to foster that sort of equality of relationship. People with learning difficulties are used to a much more passive role, to being on the receiving end of services which have been planned and shaped by other people who have decided that they know what is best for them.

As a result of all this, people may feel uncertain about how to react or even how to talk to a service user in a group. They may feel impatient if the pace of the meeting seems to be slowing down; or frustrated by the need to explain or clarify more often than usual. Whatever the reason, it is not unusual for professionals to be anxious about the idea of working with a person with learning difficulties on the basis of participation and partnership.

36.2   People with learning difficulties as participants

People with learning difficulties have demonstrated time and again that they can make extremely effective contributions to all types of discussions – as conference speakers or in meetings or in small group discussions; the growth of self-advocacy has provided many more opportunities for people to express themselves. A person with learning difficulties will often say something which gives fresh insight to the discussion. Listening to someone speaking of their own direct experience can be a most effective way of keeping the real world in our minds. It can help prevent discussion drifting off into the realms of theory and help everyone present focus on people – rather than beds, buildings, service structures and systems.

Nevertheless, when it comes to being involved in meetings, it is unlikely that the service user will have the same level of skills as others in the group. Most members of the group will be used to attending meetings – usually as a regular part of their working life, but often as a part of their social and leisure activities too. They will have little difficulty in holding conversations on a one-to-one basis as well as taking part in group discussions. Most people with learning difficulties, however, have not had the opportunities to develop and practise these skills.

There are various reasons for this, most of which are the result of the way other people have acted towards them. For a start, people with learning difficulties have not been expected to have opinions or ideas of their own – or not ones which were worth discussing with other people. In many cases they will have spent most of their waking hours in an environment where other people told them what to do and where to go.

Responding to these sorts of 'orders' doesn't really require any verbal response at all. Even questions can usually be answered with a brief 'yes' or 'no'. A person's latent abilities may have remained hidden because of the low expectations of those around them.

It is not surprising, therefore, that the service user who joins a committee or working group may have some catching up to do in terms of learning new skills and may need special support in order to contribute effectively to the discussions. There are several ways in which the group as a whole can offer that support.

36.3 Commitment

Without the commitment of a majority of people in a group involving service users, their involvement is unlikely to be more than tokenistic, failing to develop into a real partnership and sharing of power.

Real commitment is about more than a written statement of intent (although that may be a useful starting-point). It means individual group members believing that service users have a right to be involved and that they have a valued contribution to make. At the start, it is unlikely that everyone will have the same degree of commitment or hold the same views on participation. Some may be for it, some against and others may be willing to give it a try. Sometimes user participation may have been 'imposed' on the group by more senior colleagues, causing possible resentment.

So, before service users become involved, the group needs to talk through how they feel about the idea, being as frank and honest as they can. A brief discussion at one meeting may be all that's needed – but it may take longer than that. Take your time – but take care that discussion doesn't become an excuse for inaction! '

The best way of breaking down barriers and prejudices is to get to know people as individuals. Think about where the potential service-user members of your committee or working group are likely to come from; it might be a local self-advocacy group or a student/trainee committee at a day centre. Invite a few people from that group to meet your group; this gives both sides the chance to explore whether they want to work together.

One way to arrange a meeting would be to write to the group, asking if they would be willing to meet members of your group. The letter should state clearly and simply why you would like a meeting, including perhaps one or two very practical examples of issues you would like to work on with service users. This meeting might form part of the agenda of one of your meetings, or the service users might like some of your group to attend one of their meetings.

When the Independent Development Council (IDC) decided it wanted to involve people with learning difficulties as members of the Council, it invited representative of People First to attend one of its meetings as observers. These observers then reported back to their colleagues in People First and the group was then able to decide whether they actually wanted to become more involved with the IDC.

Whatever you decide to do – keep it simple! Avoid lengthy letters and complicated enclosures. Avoid large gatherings of people. This is all about getting to know people as individuals – as potential working partners. As in other situations, a few people meeting together over a meal may do more to increase understanding and commitment to collaboration than any amount of formal education or training.

36.4   The importance of language

A chairperson was summing up at the end of a day's workshop. The day had begun with a contribution from two people with learning difficulties who had advocated passionately for the abolition of the term 'mental handicap'. This had obviously affected the majority of participants who made considerable efforts throughout the day to remember not to use that term. The chairperson commented on this, ending with 'We have learnt that we must watch our language – at least in the presence of people with handicaps'.

A joke? Or a sad reflection of how shallow our commitment and understanding can be? The way we speak about people with disabilities says a great deal about how we value – or devalue – people and how serious we are about working with them as partners in planning and developing services. A lifetime of being labelled has made labels a major issue and learning to use descriptive terms which are acceptable to people with learning difficulties is important.

But it is also important to think more generally about the language we use – particularly in meetings. We need to talk clearly and simply and avoid jargon. If a service user does not seem to be following the discussion in a meeting it is all too easy to assume that that is part of being handicapped. It may be that the discussion is not particularly meaningful or clear to others either. The onus is on everyone present to make the discussion comprehensible. This can be challenging at times but is likely to result in greater clarity and understanding not only for the person with learning difficulties but for all those present.

36.5 Listening

Listening is something we tend to do automatically, without thinking consciously about it, particularly when we are with people of similar interests and background who 'speak our language'; it rarely occurs to us that we might need to develop our listening skills; but if we did, some of us might become better listeners!

When we join a group such as a committee or working party, however, it can take time for the group to become comfortable in communicating with one another. So really listening to someone who is a newcomer to the group, and whose opportunities to develop conversational skills, think logically and get a message across clearly may have been severely limited, requires a deliberate effort on our part and even the development of new skills.

For example, the person with learning difficulties may say something which seems to be way off the point. But a good listener will often be able to detect a link. It might be the last word said by another person present. The person with learning difficulties has picked this up and related it to their own experience in some way. Other members of the group need to discover what this link might be – building on it to draw out something meaningful to the rest of the discussion – perhaps also helping to lead the service user 'back on to the track' and fostering their involvement in the group.

The baseline must always be 'Have we explained this carefully enough?' or 'Have we provided all the support that this person needs in order to participate in the discussions?' It should never be 'Oh, he can't be expected to understand that idea or that document'.

This type of listening needs time, patience and practice. But it is crucial if we are to enable service users to be effective participants.

34.6 Remember the usual pitfalls of meetings

It is useful to remember what happens ordinarily at meetings; there are people who talk too much while others may say virtually nothing; some people stick to the topic while others are inclined to wander off it. If the group is really committed to participation, they will want to do all they can to ensure that the service user feels involved with what is going on. But this does not mean making the service user into some sort of 'special' member of the group, entitled to 'special' treatment. As the story at the beginning illustrates, there is a danger that concessions may be made for the service user which are not applied to any other members of the group. On the other hand, the service-user member should not be expected to act as a 'super-participant' – never straying off the topic, never left alone, and expected to contribute to every single agenda item!

In short, although he or she may need extra help to become a real part of the group, the service user should be treated as far as possible like any other member of the group. There is a very important balance to be struck here – and it is not always easy – but a good chairperson should be able to ensure that this is achieved.

36.7   The fear of tokenism

Many people express concern about the dangers of tokenism, citing examples of people with learning difficulties being used as the token consumer. This can happen in a number of ways and for a variety of reasons. Service users may have words put into their mouths, or be asked questions in a way which allows only the answer the questioner wants to hear '(Don't you think we ought to . . .' or 'Wouldn't it be a good idea if . . .'). They may be 'paraded' in front of an audience like some sort of special exhibit, their presence, in some way, making professionals 'feel good' about themselves. Lastly, they may be asked leading questions which take advantage of the service user's inexperience at handling impromptu questioning.

These sort of concerns are valid, and these practices unacceptable and exploitative. But they can also become reasons – or excuses – for not doing anything about participation.

Although it is likely that someone joining a committee or working party as a service user representative will already have some of the skills needed to participate, there may well be times when that person appears not to be making any contribution. We need to consider carefully, though, whether that person makes a contribution simply by being there. The presence of a service user can say something positive about what we believe about that person's right to be involved. If we are committed to participation, then our awareness of that person's presence should have a positive effect on the outcome of discussions. If the issues discussed in this chapter have been understood and worked through, then tokenism should not be a real danger.

36.8   Providing additional support

It may be helpful if someone, is appointed to attend meetings as a supporter for the service user – either for an initial period, or perhaps on a more permanent basis (although that may not be necessary if the service-user representative becomes more skilled and comfortable in meetings).

It is important that the supporter is independent of other members of the group, to avoid any conflict of interest. For example, if the supporter is already a member of the committee or working group, then he or she will almost certainly find there are times when loyalty to the group will clash with loyalty to the service user.

In a meeting of residential care managers, it may seem logical and convenient for service-user members to be supported by one of the staff from their group home. But will that staff member always be able to put the wishes and needs of the service user first, or will they sometimes find they are supporting the wishes of their employers?

In the case of the IDC quoted above, it might have been thought practical for the People First group's advisor to be the supporter. However, the advisor also happens to be a member of the IDC so someone with no connection with IDC was appointed.

The supporter's job might include: helping the person get to the meeting on time, checking that they have the right papers, helping them read and digest papers before meetings, and reinforcing and developing the service user's group discussion skills.

During the meeting it is important that the supporter doesn't 'take over'. The supporter's role is to facilitate not to participate directly, to support and not supplant. It's very much a 'back-seat' role with as little intervention as possible.

However, although the supporter is there primarily to support the service user, he or she may also have a role in helping other members of the group – for example, asking for simpler language, asking for clarification on particular points. Gradually, though, the service user should be gaining the confidence to make those requests directly.

It is important for the supporter's role to be clearly understood by all members of the committee or working group. It might be helpful to write brief guidelines a very simple 'contract' – so that everyone knows the ground rules within which the supporter will work and their relationship with the service user.

36.9   In conclusion

In spite of all that has been written and said about 'consumer participation', when it comes to involving people with disabilities directly in the development of services, we are all beginners. Participation requires us to think about people in new ways. It challenges long-held beliefs and long-standing practices. This chapter has been concerned with how we deal with some of these issues, moment by moment, during the course of a meeting.

Perhaps the two most important words in the chapter are 'commitment' and 'listening'. Without commitment, participation is unlikely to get started. Without skilled listening, it is unlikely to develop in a way which will lead to the ultimate goal of participation – real changes for the better in the lives of people with disabilities.

37

Community Development: Changing Directions*

MARILYN TAYLOR

With the downturn in the economic cycle in the 1970s, new issues and resources emerged. Unemployment became a key issue in many of the already disadvantaged areas where community development was taking place, and welfare rights advice a major need. The availability of Manpower Services Commission funds through the government's special employment measures took community development in new directions, with the development of training and enterprise initiatives. This new money had an influence beyond employment, however. Its support of schemes which could be demonstrated to be 'of community benefit' meant that many community groups for the first time found themselves with workers and with premises to manage. Instead of community workers coming in from outside, more and more communities were employing local support and advice workers. Not all of these were community development workers, but there was a growing call from both the communities concerned and from existing community workers for the training and accreditation which would enable local people to acquire community development skills.

Meanwhile, although nothing as big as the Community Development Project [of the 1960s] was to emerge from a government that felt its fingers had been severely burnt, new small-scale initiatives were supported at neighbourhood level, through the Opportunities for Volunteering Programme, the Developing Local Voluntary Action Programme, the area resource centre experiment and a range of self-help support schemes. Many local authorities also employed community

---

* This chapter is taken from Marilyn Taylor's book *Signposts to Community Development*, chapter 2 'The Growth of Community Development', Community Development Foundation, 1992.

development workers or supported independent projects – by 1975 there were an estimated 276 full-time community workers in social services departments in England and Wales, largely in London and the North-West (Thomas, 1983). In Scotland, the predominance of public sector housing, the introduction of community councils in 1974, the boost given to community development by the Social Work (Scotland) Act 1968 and the Alexander Report, along with the lead given by Strathclyde, all contributed to an 'unprecedented growth' in community development during the 1970s (McConnell, 1983).

37.1   A new government

With the advent of a radical right-wing Conservative government in 1979 came a major challenge to the welfare state, under whose umbrella community development in its contemporary form had evolved. The welfare state was held to have eroded individual and community responsibility and to have allowed the interests of providers to dominate over those of consumers. Over three terms of this government, policies were introduced to reduce the State's responsibility for service provision and, so far as possible, for finance. Although the major policy changes did not take place until the third term, the directions were clear from an early stage.

Priority was given to *economic regeneration* in the belief that the wealth created would 'trickle down' through all levels of society. *Decision making and service delivery* were decentralised by encouraging public authorities to contract the delivery of services out to independent providers and introducing opportunities to take services out of local and health authority control. Where independent delivery was less likely, the purchasing and providing roles of the authority were separated to form an internal market. The intention was to develop a mixed economy of welfare with more choice and greater accountability to the consumer and community.

Although government still recognised a central role in finance, it was also seeking to *release new resources* for economic, environmental and social development and reduce the burden on the state. State responsibility for welfare was seen as 'nannying', and the emphasis was transferred to the individual and the family through, for example, benefit cuts, especially for young people, and the introduction of the Social Fund. Claimants to the latter were encouraged to see the State as a last-resort for financial support, with voluntary organisations reporting considerably increased demand. Under the slogan of 'active citizenship', government sought to encourage self-help, philanthropy and corporate responsibility, and to redress what they considered to be an overemphasis on rights.

The prospects for community development under this new regime were mixed. As an approach which had sought to persuade society to acknowledge its responsibilities, through government, for its weakest members, the withdrawal of the State posed serious problems. Although it clearly had a major contribution to make to policies which aimed to release new resources and energies, policies based on the market emphasised the individual and were critical of collective action, especially campaigning. The introduction of 'opting out' in housing and education during the government's third term, along with the devolution of power embodied in such measures as the local management of schools, represented a more collective approach to consumer empowerment. But consumerism generally meant individual consumer choice (where the consumer had the means to exercise this) and not political influence through the democratic system, especially as the role and powers of local government came under increasing scrutiny.

The battle between central and local government in the 1980s proved quite positive for investment in community development, as local authorities began to decentralise services and cultivated local support through funding local community initiatives. The Greater London Council was, during its latter years, a particularly prominent source of finance, especially to women and ethnic minority organisations. Many local authorities funded their critics at this time, but it could be argued that community organisations and local government were ultimately on the same side. Community organisations rarely sought to replace public services. Instead, they saw themselves as forcing public services to be more accountable and more sensitive to need, through providing advice and advocacy, through lobbying for improvements in services, and through demonstrating how services should be providing for their constituencies.

At the same time, community development itself was being forced to recognise the different interests within any given locality, particularly in inner-city communities. The conflicts and tensions within communities were becoming more apparent and it was no longer sufficient to regard communities as being uniform or assume that work with one part of the community would benefit the whole. Black and ethnic minority leaders challenged existing community development practice and their criticisms of institutionalised racism and the allocation of resources went to the heart of the empowerment principles of the community development approach.

37.2   Entering the 1990s

If the early 1980s were a productive time for community development, the latter part of the decade was a time of retrenchment and, if not despair, at least a crisis of identity. The funds which had contributed so much to the development of this new approach and to the growth of community control began to dry up. The metropolitan counties were abolished, and the rest of local government came under increasing financial restraint, culminating in the introduction of the community charge or poll-tax, first in Scotland and then in the rest of the UK. Many local organisations faced cuts as their authorities attempted to deal with, or avoid, capping – those in the advice and advocacy field were often the first to go. This not only meant less money to support community development. There was less money and flexibility to meet community demands, and the emphasis in many communities changed from seeking improvements to protecting existing services.

Meanwhile, the emphasis on economic regeneration saw a change in emphasis in inner-city policy and a move away from social projects. Employment and training policy was recast in 1988 with the transition from the Manpower Services Commission's Community Programme to Employment Training (which no longer recognised 'community benefit' as a criterion). As the recession began to bite, Employment Training was also cut.

Despite the cutbacks, a glance at the recruitment pages in the national press reveals a continuing demand for community workers. At the same time, the consumer has come to the fore on both sides of the political spectrum, with the production of citizen's charters from government and opposition and an emphasis on quality. New policies require consultation with consumers, and many public services are developing user-involvement strategies.

Meanwhile, with the advent of the Single European Market, the significance of the European Union is growing. As it has developed its social and political agendas, funds have become available to community development, through the employment and training programmes which are fostered by the European Social Fund and through the European Programme to Combat Poverty, introduced in 1971 and 1975 respectively. In 1989, the Council of Europe passed a resolution put to it by the Standing Conference of Local and Regional Authorities of Europe endorsing the importance of community development.

In recognition of these developments, links are being made between community groups in this country (especially those in Scotland, Northern Ireland and Wales) and others in the European Union, through the Poverty Programme, the European Women's Lobby, and many more emerging networks in the voluntary and community sectors (Baine *et al.*, 1992; McConnell, 1992; Harvey, 1992). There are also joint ventures between national community development agencies such as the Combined European Bureau for Social Development. The economic restructuring which the Single European Market entails will affect many of the communities with which community development is concerned, particularly peripheral localities and groups already marginal to the national economy. European social policy, including the Social Chapter, is based almost entirely on employment as yet, and there is little for those without access to the work force, with social issues regarded largely as being outside the competence of the EU. Ethnic minority groups are concerned about the prospect of Fortress Europe on anyone who is not, or does not look like, a European national. We can expect a number of new issues and new debates to emerge as the implications of the Single European Market become clearer.

37.3   Community development and current policy

Community development grew up in a period of relative expansion; it has now passed through a period of containment. It emerged against the background of the welfare state; it now operates in a much more open market. What are the prospects for the future?

In the 1990s, it is clear that the move towards the market is set to continue – indeed that it is part of an international trend. Whatever the government of the day, the general trend of recent policies will continue, even if the harder edges of 'Thatcherism' are softened. The resource situation may ease slightly, depending on the outcome of the recession, but there will be no return to the past.

37.4   New opportunities

Community development has a major contribution to make to national policies which seek to release new resources. It is equally relevant to policies at national and local government level which seek to devolve service provision. Community centres provide a base for decentralised services in a place which has the confidence of the community. Community development helps to create a pool of skilled and interested local people who can become involved in public life at all levels: managing a school or a housing estate; working with government agencies to plan more sensitive services; or providing information, advice and advocacy to help service users choose the provision they need.

The emphasis on a mixed market of welfare provides opportunities for community organisations to become providers of services, and there is growing interest from all parts of government in some kinds of partnership with the voluntary and community sector. The need to generate new providers along with the current emphasis on consumerism and consultation has led to a change of emphasis towards the 'enabling authority' which could result in local authorities putting resources into the community: to encourage new enterprises and cultivate community-based services, to inform and empower consumers, and to support consultation exercises. Opting out policies offer the opportunity for people to manage their own services and to get support and training in doing so. Rising crime will continue to force funds into community-based crime prevention activities. As short-term central government programmes to help the inner cities (for example, the Task Forces) come to an end, there is also considerable interest in the formation of community development trusts under community ownership continuing their work, drawing on the experience in the United States.

37.5   New partners

Many community organisations and community workers have learnt their trade working with and in local government; now they are learning to work with and in a great variety of institutions. New partners include the growing number of housing associations and the prospect of opted-out estates and housing action trusts; business, as it shows a new interest in corporate community responsibility (both independently and through the formation of such bodies as Business in the Community); local training and enterprise councils (TECs); privatised utilities; new governmental bodies at local level (like Task Forces and Urban Development Corporations); opted-out schools and NHS trusts; and new service providers entering the welfare field from the voluntary, not-for-profit and private sectors. The European Commission is also likely to increase in significance. Although funding from this source is still limited, community development organisations are becoming more aware of the significance of this body and of the need both to take European developments into account and to make links across Europe.

References

Baine, S., Benington, J. and Russell, J. (1992) *Changing Europe: Challenges Facing the Voluntary and Community Sectors in the 1990s*, National Council of Voluntary Organisations Publications/Community Development Foundation, London.

Harvey, B. (1992) *Networking in Europe: A Guide to European Voluntary Organisations*, National Council of Voluntary Organisations Publications/Community Development Foundation, London.

McConnell, C. (1983) 'The development of community work in Scotland', in Thomas, D. (ed.), *Community Work in the Eighties*, National Institute for Social Work, London.

McConnell, C. (1992) *Promoting Community Development in Europe*, Community Development Foundation, London.

Thomas, D. (1983) *The Making of Community Work*, George Allen and Unwin, London.

Index

343